PANIC AT THE PUMP

Panic at the Pump

The Energy Crisis and the Transformation of American Politics in the 1970s

Meg Jacobs

HILL AND WANG

A DIVISION OF FARRAR, STRAUS AND GIROUX   NEW YORK

Hill and Wang
A division of Farrar, Straus and Giroux
18 West 18th Street, New York 10011

Printed in the United States of America
First edition, 2016

Library of Congress Cataloging-in-Publication Data
Names: Jacobs, Meg, 1969–
Title: Panic at the pump : the energy crisis and the transformation of American
    politics in the 1970s / Meg Jacobs.
Description: 1st Edition. | New York : Hill and Wang, 2016. | Includes index.
Identifiers: LCCN 2015036518 | ISBN 9780809058471 (hardback) |
    ISBN 9780374714895 (e-book)
Subjects: LCSH: Energy policy—United States. | United States—Politics and
    government—1945–1989. | United States—Foreign relations. | BISAC: HISTORY /
    United States / 20th Century. | POLITICAL SCIENCE / Public Policy / General. |
    BUSINESS & ECONOMICS / Industries / Energy Industries.
Classification: LCC HD9502.U52 J33 2016 | DDC 320.97309/047—dc23
LC record available at http://lccn.loc.gov/201503651

Designed by Abby Kagan

Our books may be purchased in bulk for promotional, educational, or
business use. Please contact your local bookseller or the Macmillan Corporate
and Premium Sales Department at 1-800-221-7945, extension 5442,
or by e-mail at MacmillanSpecialMarkets@macmillan.com.

www.fsgbooks.com
www.twitter.com/fsgbooks • www.facebook.com/fsgbooks

10   9   8   7   6   5   4   3   2   1

WOODSON

TO JULIAN

Contents

PANIC AT THE PUMP

Introduction:
An Energy Pearl Harbor

FORTY YEARS AGO, Americans were suffering from what contemporaries called "the energy crisis," a crisis that in many ways defined the decade of the 1970s. During the twin oil shocks of 1973 and 1979, oil supplies dropped and prices soared, and the average citizen understood the energy crisis to mean a panic at the pump—the fear that we would not have enough oil to fill up our gas tanks, heat our homes, or run our factories. And whatever fuel we did have would go up and up in price. Ever since, gas lines, cardigan sweaters, dark Christmas trees, and even woodstoves have become part of the collective memory of that era. At the time, Americans worried that life as they had come to know it—big cars, big suburban homes, and boundless consumption—was over. John Updike's title character Rabbit Angstrom summed it up best when, surveying his car sales lot, he thought, "The great American ride is ending."[1]

Part of what made this a "crisis" was the sense that it happened all at once. The crisis began when the Arab producers of the Organization of Petroleum Exporting Countries (OPEC) put in place an embargo on oil exports to the United States in October 1973 and threatened to cut back overall production 25 percent. Led by Saudi Arabia, these Arab states sought to retaliate for President Richard Nixon's support of Israel against an attack from Egypt and Syria in the Yom Kippur War. The oil sheikhs wanted to change American foreign policy, making it less friendly to Israel, and they also hoped they could wield their so-called oil weapon to raise the price of this precious commodity. With less oil on the market, prices would jump. Indeed, by December, the OPEC oil ministers had quadrupled the selling price of each barrel of their oil, telling buyers to take it or leave it.

As soon as they announced an embargo, one of President Nixon's top advisers dubbed it "an Energy Pearl Harbor."[2] There were no bombs, no bloodshed, no loss of life. But the embargo stunned Americans, as if they had come under a surprise attack, if not an outright act of war, because of the serious implications for the economy and the country's security. By 1973, Americans relied on oil for almost half of all their energy needs, and each day imports made up an expanding portion of the country's supply. Americans were vulnerable to scarcity and shortages as well as to higher fuel prices, which rippled through the entire economy and plagued the pocketbooks of all consumers. Oil was both the lifeline of the economy and a vital resource for the country's national defense. American oil had played a decisive role in the Allies' World War II victory, and with the Cold War raging on, U.S. oil remained a top national security concern.

The news was also stunning because the public was generally not aware that the country imported any oil at all. The United States was still the greatest single producer of oil in the world, as it had been since 1901, when Spindletop, near Beaumont, Texas, became synonymous with a sometimes uncontrollable 150-foot-high gusher of black gold. But with the spread of cars, suburbs, and factories in post–World War II America, demand rose faster than supply. In 1970, U.S. oil fields reached their peak of production at 9.6 million barrels per day. Imports quickly filled the gap between what Americans produced and what they consumed, more than doubling in volume between 1970 and 1973, when the United States was importing 36 percent of its oil.

The embargo did not stop the oil tankers already en route from the Middle East from completing their journeys. But the Arab countries ordered the major oil companies operating in the Middle East, which included the American corporations of Exxon, Texaco, Standard Oil of California, Gulf, and Mobil, to halt any future shipments to the United States. These multinational corporations were powerful, but they were nothing without access to oil in the ground, which the OPEC members owned. No one knew for sure when the embargo would end; the White House was projecting a loss between 10 and 17 percent of the country's gasoline supply. It was hardly a total shutoff, but the use of the oil weapon sounded a clarion call, ushering in a future world very different from the recent past. The gas lines that curled their way across the American landscape seemed to embody a mentality that was a far cry from the 1950s motto "Fill 'er up."

In the winter of 1973–74, during the darkest days of the embargo, that sense of optimism, of unlimited bounty, was gone, replaced by doom and despair. *The New York Times* ran an article, one of a countless daily barrage, "For Gasoline, Little Is Certain but High Prices." It featured an eighteen-year-old nursing student from Westchester County, New York, who was searching for fuel at the height of the shortage. After visiting her sick mother, she got in her first gas line at 7:00 a.m., needing to get enough fuel to get back to college. By the afternoon, she still had not had any luck. "They closed down four lines on me this morning," the young student complained. When she finally landed in her last line, where she would have to wait for another hour, she "craned her neck toward the service station and gazed disconsolately at the 50 cars ahead of her, all waiting for a turn at the gas pump."[3]

Despair bled easily into anger, especially at the American oil companies. Feeling they had few choices but to comply with the Arab producers, these companies cut off shipments and cut back overall supply. But the public found it hard to believe that the oil sheikhs could tell these corporations—the biggest, most influential companies in the country ever since the days of John D. Rockefeller—what to do. Instead, the vast majority of Americans, something like three-quarters of the public, insisted that Big Oil, as the industry was disparagingly known, created an artificial shortage. Rumors spread that tankers were waiting offshore, hoping to jack up prices as pumps ran dry.

This sense of crisis, whether people believed it was real or manufactured, quickly triggered a panic, with drivers topping off at every chance, waiting in line so long they ran out of gas. These panic purchases magnified the shortage, because drivers chose to put gas in their car tanks rather than leave it in storage in the ground. A *New York Times* columnist captured the crisis mentality, writing, "'Chaos is come again,' to borrow a phrase from Othello, but our chaos arises from an 'energy crisis' about which no two people, even the best authorities, seem to agree, and this disagreement encompasses the legitimacy of the 'crisis,' its extent, and what to do, and how and when."[4]

If Americans were mad at the oil companies, they were even madder at the nation's politicians who seemed unprepared and unable to resolve this crisis. "We appeal to you for relief from the disastrous fuel situation in Central New Jersey," a group of housewives wrote to the president.[5] By now, Nixon was already suffering politically because of his troubles from the Watergate break-in and the White House cover-up. The panic at the pump threatened greater political trouble for the weakened president. A resident of Fair Lawn, New Jersey, complained, "What is worse than 'Watergate' and all the various charges against the President? Answer—the gas crisis in Bergen County."[6]

Americans sent letters to the White House because they expected the president to do something. That mind-set reflected the persistence of a New Deal mentality, one born in the depths of the Great Depression, that not only saw markets as malleable and businessmen as manipulative but also regarded the president and his policy makers as both responsible and capable of providing relief. "Government has final responsibility for the well-being of its citizenship," said Franklin Roosevelt. In this view, dominant for much of the early postwar era, politics and the market did not exist in separate spheres but were one; wages, prices, profits, production— all resulted as much from negotiations in congressional hearing rooms and in the halls of Washington's regulatory agencies as from the wheels of commerce.

Politics and policy making were also central to recessions, unemployment, and inflation, according to this view. In 1952, in *American Capitalism*, the liberal economist John Kenneth Galbraith described what he saw as the secret to the country's success. The nation had a political economy that worked to generate robust levels of steady economic growth. He stressed the importance of countervailing powers—the trade unions and consumer groups, which bargained with the nation's businessmen—all under the watchful eye of Washington politicians who stood ready to provide a stabilizing force in the marketplace. Without this system, he wrote, "private decisions could and presumably would lead to the unhampered exploitation of the public."[7]

The energy crisis ultimately helped shift American politics to the right in the 1970s and bring an end to Galbraith's conception of the American system. This seismic shift in national politics, however, was anything but inevitable. When the crisis began in 1973, the strong arm of the New Deal seemed intact for much of the country. That outlook—one that saw government as the solution to national crises—resulted in a dramatic expansion of government intervention, especially as liberals in Congress advanced policies to place price controls on oil and create the Department of Energy (DOE) as a massive new government agency. The problem of shortages caused by international events was new, but the political solutions—from price controls to rationing to antitrust initiatives to break up Big Oil— were old. Washington was stuck in the past.

Richard Nixon himself was not a New Dealer, but he lived and governed in this world. Three weeks into the Arab embargo, on November 7, 1973, he delivered a nationally televised address from the White House to confront the energy crisis head-on. The centerpiece of the speech was what Nixon called "Project Independence." The goal, Nixon declared, was for the country to achieve energy self-sufficiency by 1980. For the rest of the decade, the object of American energy policy was to become independent. Only by freeing itself from reliance on unstable sources of foreign oil, according to this view, could the country reclaim and maintain its global hegemony, economic vitality, and national security.

By naming the solution, the president was also implying the problem: dependence. Not only was our economy threatened, but so too was our status as the global leader of the free world. The Arab embargo heightened Americans' sense of vulnerability. The day before the embargo began, the Nobel Peace committee awarded Henry Kissinger the prize for his successful cease-fire negotiations in the Vietnam War. The peace accord was not an American triumph but rather a sign of substantial defeat, and the Arab embargo solidified the idea that America was indeed in decline. When OPEC announced the embargo, few thought that a military solution was on the table. After a decade of failed policies in Vietnam, the country was war weary, and the United States had no regional military presence in the Middle East and feared triggering hostilities with the Soviets, whose military stood in closer striking distance. Still, the idea that the leaders of what Americans regarded as small and powerless countries could attempt to blackmail the United States seemed hard to fathom. In a single act, the Arab oil producers were bringing this superpower to its knees.

Even worse, the nation's political leaders appeared unable to devise any effective domestic policy. Project Independence was a grand vision. But there was little consensus on how to achieve self-sufficiency. The result was a pitched political battle, an epic conflict that got to the very heart of how much government was good for the economy and forever changed American politics. Some, like Nixon, called for greater production of domestic energy and the scaling back of environmental and economic regulations, many of which he had put in place himself, under pressure from a Democratically controlled Congress. An ambitious generation of young conservative insiders, all working within the administration of Nixon and then in that of his successor, Gerald Ford, said that government restrictions made it more difficult, and more expensive, to discover and refine oil, burn coal, and build nuclear power plants. Arriving in Washington for the first time, these young conservatives, free from New Deal influences, argued that it was these very regulations that thwarted American production of energy and made the country vulnerable. Without them, said their champion Milton Friedman, there would be no crisis. "Big brother is the problem, not the cure," he wrote in the pages of *Newsweek*.[8]

Others called on the nation to use less oil. The Democratic senator Henry Jackson, who was both a committed environmentalist and a foreign policy hawk, as well as a longtime New Dealer, supported federally funded development of alternative energies. "Oil supplies are limited," he warned. "By failing to act now to develop alternative sources of energy we are prolonging the period during which the supply and price of imported oil can be dictated by whoever might happen to control a handful of Persian Gulf nations."[9] In addition, Jackson promoted a policy of conservation, even government-enforced rationing if necessary. He found it appalling that Americans could not fight back against the oil weapon by curbing their seemingly unbounded appetite for petroleum. "We need to ask whether we must put ourselves in hock to Middle Eastern sheikdoms to keep roads clogged with gas-hungry automobiles," Jackson said.[10]

But neither approach—greater production or greater conservation—gave Americans the immediate satisfaction they wanted. The motorists, the country's truckers, the factory workers, the housewives—all wanted Washington to stare down the big oil companies and, if necessary, the Arab sheikhs, and demand more oil, and fast.

For nearly the next two decades, the nation's leaders devoted enormous political capital to make the United States more independent, but they failed. While conservatives advanced their free-market agenda, their ideological opponents in the Democratic Party divided among themselves. Old New Deal liberals wanted the government to guarantee fair and equitable access to affordable energy; it was up to Washington to give American consumers the oil they wanted and, as many saw it, deserved. At the same time, environmentalists called on Americans to scale back and use less. Jimmy Carter, when he came into office, declaring the energy crisis the moral equivalent of war, said that it was his job, as chief executive, to make sure Americans changed their wastrel ways to save not only the environment but ultimately their souls.

From within their perches of power, conservative Republicans challenged all kinds of governmental activism. While they drew support from conservative grassroots activists, intellectuals, and think tanks, these Washington insiders knew better than anyone how hard it was to transform American politics, especially when shortages and high prices made Americans demand help from government, confounding conservatives' hopes for a frontal assault on liberalism. To them, there would be no energy crisis if the government got out of the way and let the market work. Democrats from oil-producing states agreed. These political battles led to a stalemated Washington where the result was greater imports and a public that grew frustrated with the lack of effective leadership on this fundamental issue.

As the pages that follow show, the failure of the nation's politicians to address the energy crisis contributed to the erosion of faith that Americans had in their government to solve their problems. There were many causes of that erosion, but the energy crisis, with its long gas lines, soaring prices, and sense of vulnerability, was an important object lesson in the limitations of governmental power.

If the Vietnam War and the Watergate scandal taught Americans that their presidents lied, the energy crisis showed them that their government didn't work. Even worse, according to conservatives, by the very act of trying to help, Washington policy makers made things worse. When Ronald Reagan was governor of California during the Arab embargo, he said the federal government created the energy crisis. When the gas lines returned in 1979, in the wake of the Iranian Revolution, the country was ready to listen.

As Washington proved unable to design an effective national energy policy, the inability to develop resources and conserve made Americans more dependent on oil from abroad. The story of the 1970s energy crisis truly culminated in February 1991, when George H. W. Bush sent ground troops into war to repel Saddam Hussein and his Iraqi army's invasion of Kuwait, which Bush believed threatened a cutoff of Middle Eastern oil. This short war is now seldom discussed, but it proved a decisive marker and transformed the political and military content of the energy crisis. Washington would now solve the problem of energy dependence not by reforming American energy production and use but instead by sending troops abroad to protect what President Bush called the "security and stability of the Persian Gulf." With the United States importing more than half its oil supply, Project Independence had clearly failed. The solution to failed domestic policy at home was, as it turned out, military intervention abroad. As a *New York Times* reporter concluded, "Mr. Bush has replaced energy policy with foreign policy."[11]

Today, and for the time being, America seems awash in oil and gas. It is perhaps no coincidence that the current skepticism about our military commitments in the Middle East coincides with the very increase in domestic production that many in the 1970s hoped but failed to spur. In 2016, it seems at last that the market, with production nearly at record levels, has promised to bring security, if not independence.

But all that lies ahead. We begin our story in an earlier moment of optimism with a young George Bush, right after World War II, arriving in the oil fields in West Texas at a time when the future looked bright.

Part I

Stuck in the Past

1

In Search of Oil

IN 1948, a handsome, athletic twenty-four-year-old George H. W. Bush moved his young family to West Texas in search of oil and the American Dream. Bush was not the typical wildcatter. A graduate of Yale and son of a successful Wall Street investment banker and future senator, George could have had his pick of careers. But Poppy, as he was known, traded in his Ivy League comforts for the dust and sandstorms of the Permian Basin. It was there that Bush, albeit with his family's connections, would seek his own fortune. "I am convinced that there is a real opportunity here," Bush wrote when he turned down a job offer from his father's prestigious New York banking firm.[1]

Risky Business

In the summer of 1948, Bush set up home in the small, no-frills town of Odessa, Texas, with his wife, Barbara, and their two-year-old son George. The young Ivy Leaguer sent away for L.L.Bean catalogs, regularly attended the Yale-Princeton game, and went frequently to socialize in the booming cities of Dallas and Houston. But the former U.S. Navy pilot also worked hard to learn the oil business from the bottom up and enmesh himself in Texas living. Sitting in a storefront, he sold drilling equipment made by Dresser Industries for the oil and gas industries. He also acquired on-the-job knowledge in the oil fields and on a Dresser shop floor in California, where he joined the local union. Back in Midland, Texas, Bush decided to go out on his own, forming a company to trade in oil leases and develop new wells.

Bush was in the oil business at the right time and place, given the discovery of large oil reserves in the fabled Spraberry Trend, near Midland. Bush's family was growing—three more sons and two daughters (one of whom died from cancer)—and so was Midland. Along with neighboring Odessa, this town, which sprouted up from nine thousand to sixty-two thousand residents in just a few years, became home to one out of every fourteen oil rigs in the country, and thousands of prospectors and speculators flooded in.[2] Soon the state was responsible for more than a third of all drilling in the country. After seeing the marquee for the 1952 Marlon Brando movie, ¡Viva Zapata!, which chronicled the story of the Mexican revolutionary, Bush named his new company Zapata Petroleum to suggest a swashbuckling spirit.

Demand for oil was skyrocketing. If you could find oil, you could sell it. Oil had started as a source of illumination, but it quickly joined its fellow fossil fuel—coal—to generate power for factories and homes; it was the engine of a mass-consumption revolution based on middle-class consumer industries, with cars leading the way. In 1908, the Ford Motor Company had introduced its first gasoline-powered, mass-produced Model T, and in 1925 this huge corporation was turning out a new Tin Lizzie every ten seconds. By 1950, Americans owned forty million cars, nearly one for every family. With gasoline at twenty-five cents a gallon, Americans took to the roads.

On the surface, these were the boom times of Texas oil. In 1948, *Life* and *Fortune* magazines both profiled the new rich oil barons, forever cementing their image as fabulously nouveau riche jet-setting businessmen. Yet underneath the wealth and glamour, the reality was different. Risk, as well as a sense of adventure, was an ever-present part of the business. Each time he bored down into the earth's surface, a wildcatter was placing a bet. On the frontiers of free enterprise, these independent oilmen did much of the exploratory drilling in unproven areas, hoping to find fossil fuels buried deep below. In Texas, as profitable as drilling was, the industry believed that eight out of every nine holes came up dry.[3] Soon after

Bush formed Zapata, he explained to his college friend Thomas "Lud" Ashley, a future Democratic congressman from Ohio who had entrusted him with $500 to invest, that any investment was "risky, very risky." "If you elect to ride a wildcat," Bush warned, "I hope you will be prepared for the 100% loss which might occur."[4]

Beyond the inherent risk in searching for oil, there were already indications of bigger problems that were starting to bear down on the industry. Well before the 1973 Arab embargo, even amid the boom years, it was clear that the oil patch could one day have a difficult time supplying sufficient fuel at affordable prices, or at least at prices that Americans wanted to pay. Between 1945 and 1959, production grew by more than 50 percent, but in that same period consumption rose by 80 percent.[5] Since early in the twentieth century, the United States had assumed its steady place as the world's leading producer of oil, first with the Rockefeller discoveries in Pennsylvania and later with the Texas discoveries, starting at Spindletop in 1901, where the first six wells outproduced all existing wells in the East, then in East Texas in 1930, and now in West Texas. The major oil companies that formed after an antitrust suit broke up Rockefeller's trust—Standard Oil of California, Texaco, and Gulf along with what became Exxon and Mobil—were vertically integrated, highly successful corporations, extending their reach over much of the industry, from the wellhead to the gas pump. They were the ones who bought the black sludge when the wildcatters released it from the ground. But 1948, the year Bush arrived, marked the last time that the United States would export more oil than it imported.

As demand was soaring—with new suburbs, new highways, new shiny automobiles—the costs of exploring for new sources of domestic oil were rising. Independents, who continued to do much of the exploration, were searching deeper beneath the ground and farther afield for more and more oil. After a few successful years prospecting in Texas, Bush founded the Zapata Off-Shore Company. The company developed some of the earliest mobile deepwater rigs to drill below the ocean's surface and explore off the coasts of Louisiana, Texas, and California, all of which required enormous capital investments.

As the expense of domestic drilling was mounting, independents were facing increasing competition from the major oil companies' exploration and production of cheaper oil in the Middle East that cost substantially less than domestic oil. In these newly developing oil fields, all under authoritarian regimes, labor costs were dirt cheap with no unions to raise the cost of everything from drilling to producing the steel for pipeline casings. In the desert fields of Saudi Arabia, deposits were closer to the surface and more concentrated, which made them easier and less costly to extract. Indeed, Bush sought to capitalize on this foreign boom, deciding to concentrate his offshore business overseas, and he moved his family to Houston, which was emerging as an international capital of global oil. The Connecticut oilman could do this only with the substantial help of his family bank connections back east.

A couple of years before Bush decided to shift his investments abroad, a Supreme Court decision had struck fear into the hearts of oilmen in Texas and throughout the Southwest and made it clear that the world of Washington policy makers could pose as many risks as a dry hole in an oil patch. In 1954, the Supreme Court heard *Phillips Petroleum Company v. Wisconsin*, a case brought by the state against Phillips, an independent producer, claiming that natural gas prices were rising and the federal government ought to regulate them. When wildcatters discovered oil, they usually found natural gas too, which, after the construction of a national system of pipelines, supplied electricity and heat to homes and factories in the Mid-Atlantic and the Midwest. Urban residents, especially those who had recently converted from coal to natural gas when their cities hooked up to interstate pipelines, protested loudly, believing rising costs violated what they had understood since the New Deal as their right to cheap electricity and fuel. On the campaign trail in 1932, the Democratic hopeful Franklin Roosevelt had said, "Electricity is no longer a luxury. It is a definite necessity."

The Supreme Court ruled that the Federal Power Commission (FPC), which under the Natural Gas Act of 1938 set the rates for transportation and sale of natural gas through the interstate pipelines to local utilities, also had authority over prices at the wellhead where gas came out of the ground. From here on, the country's several thousand producers would have to sell their product at rates fixed by federal bureaucrats in Washington.

The judgment caused an instant uproar in the Southwest, where oilmen immediately understood the implications of this Supreme Court ruling. A cap on natural gas prices would also keep oil prices down as the two increasingly competed as a source of residential and industrial fuel. They were competitive fuels, often found together in the same wells, and the decision, the oilmen feared, would set a precedent for the government to regulate prices of any commodity. During World War II, Roosevelt's planners, with the famed New Dealer Harold Ickes at the helm, had regulated everything in the oil industry from the fields to the pumps, a job Ickes as head of the wartime Petroleum Administration did with zeal. (In 1943, he published a book chronicling his experiences, which he called *Fightin' Oil*.) Now it looked as if the bureaucrats were back in business. "If the one can be regulated, where will such regulation stop?" asked lawyers representing the industry. "We should stop this trend to Federal control in our country."[6]

According to George Bush, the Yankee transplant living in Texas, there was one way to stop this trend: vote for the GOP. Only the Republican Party, which had for years fought the regulatory reach of the New Deal, could defend against this federal onslaught. If the independents needed more capital and the ability to raise prices, then the Republicans—the party of free enterprise—could help.

The problem, though, was that since the Civil War Texas, like the rest of the South, had been a one-party, Democratic town. The oil industry had done well by the Democrats, who had provided and protected favorable tax breaks. Nothing was more prized than the depletion allowance, which permitted oil drillers to deduct roughly one-quarter of the value of their revenues from their taxable income. The idea was that a well would dry up over time—literally become depleted—and the tax break offered an incentive to replace what had been used up. After World War I, when it became clear that the modern army and navy ran on oil, the American Petroleum Institute, one of the early trade associations and lobbying organizations, found a sympathetic hearing in Congress, where southern Democrats, with their seniority, controlled the tax-writing committees. But as much as these southerners protected the oil producers, their northern Democratic brethren were committed to defending the interests of their oil-consuming constituents.

Could the GOP save the oil patch? As he was developing his oil business, Bush was also rounding up campaign contributions for Dwight Eisenhower in Midland, Texas. In 1952, Eisenhower was the first Republican to win Texas, in part on the promise of sympathy from Washington toward the oil industry. Ike lent his support to the legislative undoing of natural gas price controls and other pet issues. As Midland County chairman for the 1956 Eisenhower campaign, Bush told local business-men, "If we hope to see the oil industry's position maintained, and if we expect to get any favorable legislation passed in the next session of Congress, Texas must do its part in supporting the Republican part[y]."[7]

The young Bush understood that the industry could face real opposition from liberal Democrats and even moderate Republicans who, sensitive to consumer interests, fought against rising prices and defended price controls. It was an era of relatively low inflation, but Americans still expected their politicians to protect their pocketbooks. That included Bush's father, Prescott Bush, who as senator, first elected in 1952, came out against legislation to eliminate the FPC's price-fixing authority. He might have been a Republican—indeed, in many ways, he was the archetype eastern establishment Republican, but he represented Connecticut, where consumers cared deeply about the prices they paid for fuel and demanded that their politicians defend them.

The independents had more success in pressing their case in Washington for protection against cheaper Middle Eastern oil. Along with the rising costs of domestic drilling that they feared they could not pass on, this low-priced foreign competition was the big threat. On this front, they received help from President Eisenhower, when they persuaded him to impose import restrictions. Here national security arguments prevailed. In October 1956, before there were supertankers that could carry oil around the coast of Africa, the Suez Canal crisis temporarily shut down shipping from the Middle East. The independents argued that reliance on foreign oil made the United States vulnerable, and in 1959, to their loud applause, Eisenhower established the Mandatory Oil Import Program, setting quotas on foreign oil at roughly 12 percent of domestic production. "There Is No Security in Foreign Oil for the Defense of Our Own Borders," read the letterhead of the Independent Petroleum Association of America, an organization in which George Bush assumed a leadership role.

The major oil companies, who were the ones responsible for developing the Middle Eastern oil fields and shipping their products around the globe, accepted this protectionist policy. They were focused on extending their reach beyond American shores to new markets in Europe and Japan. And they already had their own deal with the U.S. government. Aware of the Middle East's strategic importance in the unfolding Cold War, the government encouraged the development of a close relationship with Saudi

Arabia and the formation of the Arabian American Oil Company (Aramco), made up of four of the five major American oil companies. Thus began the concessionary era in which the majors would share 50 percent of the profits with Saudi Arabia, where there had been discoveries of vast reserves, and other oil-rich governments in exchange for the right to produce and distribute oil. The U.S. Treasury Department allowed these corporations to credit these concession payments to foreign governments against their taxable income, which meant they often paid virtually no income taxes at all.

This so-called Golden Gimmick, agreed to by Harry Truman and King Ibn Saud of Saudi Arabia, served their countries' mutual interests. Although it represented a substantial loss of income to the U.S. government, this arrangement facilitated American Cold War aims of containing Soviet influence in this oil-rich region, developing new reserves of oil, conserving Western Hemisphere resources, and facilitating European recovery, where the coal mines and railroad infrastructure had been damaged in wartime and countries were desperate for new sources of fuel. In addition, the channeling of substantial funds into the hands of the Saudi government to pay for this country's modernization helped to offset hostility over American recognition of the new state of Israel in 1948. In 1950, Aramco completed the laying of the Trans-Arabian Pipeline, which facilitated the flow of oil from the region.

American commitment to the free flow of oil from the Middle East became clear in its relationship with Iran. In 1953, the United States helped to orchestrate the overthrow of Mohammad Mossadegh by the CIA and the installation of Mohammad Reza Shah Pahlavi as the absolute monarch. Mossadegh, as the popularly elected prime minister, had fought for the nationalization of the Iranian oil industry and the expulsion of the British oil companies. Fearing Soviet influence in the country and the blocking of Western access to oil, the Eisenhower administration made a commitment to the shah in exchange for his support of ongoing concessions to the multinational oil companies. After the Suez crisis, in what became known as the Eisenhower Doctrine, the United States assumed the role of guarantor of Western-friendly conservative regimes in the region through military and economic assistance in exchange for favorable treatment of the majors.

Big Oil, as it was now coming to be known, was solidifying its reach as a global empire. In 1963, Bush traveled to the Middle East to arrange contracts between the oil governments, including Kuwait, and the majors. The business was still risky: in 1965, Zapata lost an offshore rig to Hurricane Betsy. But the market for oil, including among oil-thirsty American allies in Europe and Japan, was growing. These were massive companies at the top of the corporate hierarchy. In 1957, Exxon, Gulf, and Mobil all had assets greater than General Motors, with several others, including Standard Oil and Texaco, also worth over $1 billion.[8] The Seven Sisters (the five American firms along with Royal Dutch Shell and British Petroleum) controlled a substantial majority of all non-Communist production. Their operations extended from the oil fields through the tankers and refineries down to the local gas stations.

If Eisenhower had been friendly to the interests of the oil patch, then oilmen were hopeful that after the election of 1960 Lyndon Johnson, the larger-than-life Texas Democrat, as vice president and, after John F. Kennedy's assassination in 1963, as president, would continue to serve them well. As a senator, Johnson had been a stalwart ally, fighting for more sympathetic treatment from the FPC and defending tax breaks. But after his 1964 presidential victory over the deeply conservative Barry Goldwater, with huge liberal Democratic majorities on Capitol Hill, Johnson pushed hard for civil rights, Medicare, the War on Poverty, and other landmark pieces of his Great Society agenda. In Washington, the solution to any problem—from race to education to consumer protection—would be more government intervention. With Johnson as the leader of a liberal Democratic Party, it looked as if the GOP were their only realistic solution if they wanted to reform the regulatory status quo.

One small source of optimism came straight from the Lone Star State. In 1966, the oil industry gained a new ally in Washington when, at forty-two, George Bush ran a successful race for Congress. His victory came after winning a redistricting battle, which he pursued up through the Supreme Court. This New Englander argued that Houston, like many other rapidly expanding suburbs, deserved an additional seat in the House of Representatives. Bush had worked hard to build up the GOP in Texas. Proof positive was James Baker, whose family had established the law firm of Baker Botts, which represented many oilmen, and had been mainstay Democrats. With Bush as a tennis partner, close family friend, and confidant, Baker joined the GOP. Lyndon Johnson's Texas adviser Jack Valenti wrote to Bush, "I clang the alarm bell to rally all us fat, lazy, languid Democrats."[9] With his good looks and a substantial television campaign, Bush launched an impressive political career. After Prescott Bush had returned to private life, his son the Texan oilman moved into GOP politics. Perhaps now the oil patch would see its problems solved.

When Bush came to Washington, the Texan cast his lot with younger Republicans who were charting a new path for the GOP from inside Washington and through an agenda that revolved around reforming economic policy. While there were Republicans who stoked the flames of racial hatred in the 1966 midterm campaign in order to win the support of southern whites and northern white working-class urban voters who were unhappy with Johnson's civil rights agenda, others, including Bush, realized that racism and ultraright extremism would not be a winning formula. In the year he won, Barbara Jordan, an African-American Democrat from Houston who ran successfully for the state senate, became the first black person elected to the Texas legislature since Reconstruction. At a moment when there was a vibrant world of grassroots activism seeking to build a conservative movement from the bottom up, such as the John Birch Society or the Christian Anti-Communist Crusade that propelled Ronald Reagan to the California governorship, Bush believed that the best path forward for his party was to work within Washington to push for deregulation.

Bush instantly became part of a group of Republicans whose principal concern was shifting economic policy to the right. He developed a close friendship with the Wisconsin representative William Steiger, another freshman, who, along with his intern Richard Cheney, called for budget austerity and fiscal conservatism amid the growing deficits resulting from Vietnam. They joined Donald Rumsfeld, a young congressman from Illinois first elected in 1962, who had helped stage a coup, after the 1964 electoral disaster, to depose the House minority leader, Charles Halleck, and replace him with Michigan's congressman Gerald Ford in 1965. For them, race relations, social policy, and red-baiting were not the main concerns. Economic deregulation was at the heart of their conservatism. Limiting the imprint of the federal government on economic relations was the key, Bush and his allies thought, to a robust American economy. While Bush fought hard to defend subsidies for the oil patch, he opposed Washington's efforts to dictate managerial decisions about production. The Texan wanted to deregulate the economy in order to free oil and other types of markets.

With the help of his father's influence, Bush won a seat on the powerful Ways and Means Committee, where the young southern Republican was an unswerving supporter of the oil depletion allowance. Even as the oil business was booming—indeed, before entering Congress, Bush sold his shares in Zapata for $1.1 million—the argument was always that future discoveries, which required drilling in less proven grounds, depended on maintaining these tax breaks. "We need less control, more incentive to drill, more realistic pricing policies," said the congressman. "I pledge to hang in there and keep fighting for more government understanding of what makes this risky business work."[10]

By this time, Bush believed a dangerous threat to both the industry and the country was coming from overseas. With his eyes set on higher office, he could capitalize on his knowledge of global oil markets to position himself as a statesman and foreign policy leader. Even as war raged in Vietnam, Bush worried about the instability in the Middle East and the growing dissatisfaction with the concessionary system. In 1960, Iran, Iraq, Kuwait, Saudi Arabia, and Venezuela had formed the Organization of Petroleum Exporting Countries to try to counteract the power of the major oil companies, who unilaterally set a posted, nonnegotiable price on the oil they were pumping out of the ground and selling around the world. The OPEC oil ministers wanted a say over this price, seeking to assert their influence and recoup bigger profits.

The 1967 Arab-Israeli War, in which Israel scored a decisive victory over its Arab neighbors and which disrupted oil shipments, saw a failed attempt by OPEC to impose an embargo on the West for its support of Israel. These efforts by the oil kingdoms to flex their muscles, even if they fell short, suggested a growing ferment in the region, which became clear when the Arab members of OPEC formed their own organization. OPEC, as a whole, possessed 67 percent of the world's known oil reserves and was responsible for 38 percent of production and 90 percent of international trade.[11] To Bush, the 1967 war and the rumblings by oil sheikhs "brought home . . . the fact that the free world could not risk a dependence on Middle East oil."[12] "The next struggle will be in the Middle East," he wrote in April 1968.[13]

The United States became more dependent and therefore more vulnerable to overseas supply interruptions because of a basic geological fact: American production was thought to be peaking and slowing. In 1967, drillers discovered massive oil reserves in Prudhoe Bay, Alaska, but it would be years until that oil could be brought to market. Even with this discovery, it appeared that, as predicted by the Shell geologist M. King Hubbert, the U.S. oil industry was reaching its geological peak of oil production. In 1970, American oilmen had one-third the number of drilling rigs in operation compared with when Bush set up his business in the mid-1950s.[14] By 1970, OPEC would produce twice as much oil as the United States. Even more significant was the decline in U.S. spare capacity—its ability to increase production and bring additional oil to market within a month. Spare capacity gave producers leverage to influence the supply and therefore the price of global oil.

The peaking of American production sparked heated debate about overseas imports. Bush emerged as the key defender of import restrictions even as his political opponents, such as his father's replacement, Senator Abraham Ribicoff, a liberal Democrat from Connecticut, pushed hard for their removal. Importing oil would satisfy growing consumer demand, but according to Bush and domestic producers cheap Arab oil would depress the American market and would further slow domestic discovery and production.

The problem for oil producers was that George Bush was not at the heart of the GOP; Richard Nixon was. Bush supported Nixon, and there was even some speculation that Nixon would pick Bush as a vice presidential running mate. Certainly his group of young Washington Republicans preferred Nixon to Ronald Reagan, who seemed too far to the right and an improbable victor, as the 1968 GOP presidential nominee. They also strongly preferred Nixon over Nelson Rockefeller. Rocky had accommodated himself to the world of big government as the first undersecretary of health, education, and welfare and then as New York governor, whereas Nixon had made a career of opposing heavy-handed government regulation.

But Nixon understood that for a Republican to survive in the 1960s, he had to work within the world of the New Deal and the Great Society, not around it. In 1968, even as he had burnished his reputation as an anti–New Deal Republican, which he was, he knew better than most that he would be under pressure to continue with and even expand the regulatory apparatus of Washington. Oilmen wanted less; Nixon, it seemed, would grudgingly accept more. In November 1968, Nixon won the election, narrowly defeating Vice President Hubert Humphrey, the liberal Democrat. Surely Nixon was better than Humphrey. But the problems in the oil patch were about to get worse.

The Era of Cheap Power Is Over

A week after Richard Nixon's inauguration, the new president's first order of business was to attend to a massive oil spill off the coast of Santa Barbara. On January 28, 1969, 200,000 gallons of crude oil spewed out over an eight-hundred-square-mile radius six miles off the California coastline after a natural gas blowout thirty-five hundred feet beneath the ocean's surface. Local citizens formed an organization, Get Oil Out (GOO), which instantly generated national publicity. The local news editor Thomas Storke remarked, "Never in my long lifetime have I ever seen such an aroused populace at the grassroots level. This oil pollution has done something I have never seen before in Santa Barbara—it has united citizens of all political persuasions in a truly nonpartisan cause." The nature writer John McKinney recalled the outpouring of support to rescue oil-covered birds: "Energetic college students, shopkeepers, surfers, parents with their kids, all joined the beach clean-up. I saw a Montecito society matron transporting oily birds in her Mercedes." Fred L. Hartley, president of Union Oil Company, which was responsible for the spill, could not fathom the reaction; after all no one had died. "I am amazed at the publicity for the loss of a few birds," he said. But Hartley was sorely out of step.[15]

The environmental movement, which appeared to come out of nowhere, had huge implications for the oil industry. In their never-ending search for oil, drillers had to move to more remote locations, with more fragile ecologies, and the extraction and distribution of ever more oil posed an environmental threat. So too did the mining of coal and the development of nuclear plants. The demand for more energy, with greater risks to the environment, gave momentum to a broad social movement for environmental protection, which fomented popular resistance to coal strip-mining, new power plants, offshore drilling, and the newly proposed Trans-Alaska Pipeline. Barry Commoner, a founder of the field of ecology, captured a new environmentalist mind-set in his idea that "everything is connected to everything else."

The Santa Barbara oil spill pushed environmental issues to the fore of public debate and put politicians on notice that a clean environment was something that many voters supported. Citizens in New England, New York, New Jersey, Florida, Michigan, Wisconsin, Minnesota, and three Pacific coast states—Washington, Oregon, and California—expressed deep interest in quality-of-life issues.[16] Under pressure to respond to the spill, Nixon traveled to his home state and reflected, "The Santa Barbara incident has frankly touched the conscience of the American people." The *New York Times* editor Robert Bendiner confirmed that the interest in ecology was more than a fad: "Call it conservation, the environment, ecological balance, or what you will, it is a cause more permanent, more far-reaching, than any issue of the day—Vietnam and Black Power included."[17] Another *Times* editorial headline summed up what was at stake: "Fight for Survival." "Sacrifice will be required and so will large-scale expenditure of governmental funds," wrote the editors. "But the price of evasion will be self-annihilation."[18]

There was enough support among liberals and moderates in both parties for Congress to pass, in late 1969, the National Environmental Policy Act, a sweeping piece of legislation that signaled a fundamental challenge to private property, markets, and states' rights. The act's aims were bold: "To declare a national policy which will encourage productive and enjoyable harmony between man and his environment; to promote efforts which will prevent or eliminate damage to the environment and biosphere and stimulate the health and welfare of man; to enrich the understanding of the ecological systems and natural resources important to the Nation; and to establish a Council on Environmental Quality."[19] Under Section 102(C), the Council on Environmental Quality was charged with reviewing environmental impact statements, which were now required for any project receiving federal funding and represented a substantial victory for the inscription of environmentalism into public policy.

The rapid, if not sudden, success of the environmental movement suggested a need to discover and rely on cleaner, less polluting energy sources, which would mean higher costs to energy companies and consumers. In 1970, coal provided nearly half of the power used for generating electricity. Natural gas accounted for nearly one-quarter of electrical energy and oil for just over 10 percent. Water power accounted for another 16 percent and nuclear 1.4 percent. Coal producers, believing that coal would soon be displaced by nuclear power (General Electric built the first commercial reactor for a public utility in 1959), were reluctant to invest in cleaner mining. Under public pressure, power plants began the conversion to natural gas and oil as cleaner sources of energy. Oil was already supplying almost half of total energy use, and the cost of new exploration deeper underground, farther offshore, and in harsher locales like the Arctic was expensive. To prevent damage, all those new explorations now had to comply with strict environmental regulations, which further raised costs.[20]

The oil and natural gas industry, chafing under prices fixed by the Federal Power Commission and the rising costs of environmental protection, warned about an impending energy "crunch." According to F. Ritter Shumway, president of the U.S. Chamber of Commerce, government policy was bringing Americans to the brink of disaster. The FPC was interfering with the natural forces of supply and demand. Price controls not only shrank supply but also distorted markets and led companies to sell more natural gas intrastate where prices were uncontrolled and where demand was growing as the Sunbelt population rose. Shumway explained, "Because of some very bad government planning, some ill-considered moves to protect the environment, and some unforeseen difficulties in the development of atomic power, we are experiencing a serious energy shortage."[21] Producers had little cause for hope that Nixon would help; with so much bad publicity, the new president acquiesced to a slight reduction in the industry's coveted depletion allowance.

The oil and natural gas industry threw down the gauntlet: without proper incentives, namely higher prices, there would be no domestic additions to the nation's power supply. Its solution was what the FPC chairman, John Nassikas, a Nixon appointee and friend of the industry, called "just and reasonable rates." "The free enterprise system itself holds the best hope for resolving the crunch looming ahead between supply and demand for natural gas—not some expanded federal bureaucracy," he explained.[22] The idea was to unloose prices from federal control to stimulate additional exploration and necessary capital development. Proponents of deregulation hoped that their warnings that "without energy, the lights, quite literally, will go out" would provide political momentum for reform.[23]

By the end of the 1960s, Americans were confronting the disparity between their ever-increasing demands for more energy and a decreasing domestic supply. American cars were as big as ever, consumers wanted more and more oil and natural gas, and they did not want to pay higher prices. But there was growing pressure on supply. It was more expensive to drill in more remote locations with greater environmental costs. Oil flowed from OPEC powers, and the amount Americans imported was inching up, even with quotas in place. If it remained uncertain how this clash between booming demand and shrinking domestic supply would play out, one thing was becoming increasingly clear: as the *Fortune* journalist Lawrence Mayer eulogized, "The era of cheap power in the U.S. is over."[24]

When Richard Nixon signed the National Environmental Policy Act on January 1, 1970, he revealed his true colors as a political pragmatist. With its strong bipartisan support, Nixon sought to co-opt this new political force as he was thinking about the 1970 midterm elections and his own reelection campaign. He had won the 1968 election with only a slim electoral majority—just over half a million votes separated Nixon from his Democratic rival—and he was looking to improve on those returns. The president hoped that a demonstrated concern for the environment would offset some of the tumult over the Vietnam War and make him more appealing as a moderate candidate. In his 1970 State of the Union address, Nixon asserted his commitment: "Clean air, clean water, open spaces— these should once again be the birthright of every American. If we act now, they can be."

Activists kept constant pressure on Washington to make the sweeping language in the environmental bill have real impact. With the help of Senator Gaylord Nelson, twenty-five-year-old Denis Hayes spearheaded an effort to plan a national earth day. He created Environmental Action as a coordinating committee for demonstrations across the country. Teach-ins started in January, the first at Northwestern University, where eight to ten thousand students and faculty members participated. Barry Commoner addressed the audience as "fellow survivors," and he, along with other critics, described Nixon's environmental budget requests in his State of the Union address as laughable.[25] Speakers dismissed Nixon's efforts as nothing more than a way to outmaneuver them. "President Nixon seems to think that the environment issue is a good thing to quiet down the campuses and patch up the country," said Andy Garling, one of the student leaders.[26]

On April 22, 1970, nearly 20 million people participated in the first Earth Day. The event, spread out in communities across the country, suggested both the culmination of grassroots organizing efforts and the beginnings of a newly institutionalized movement. Newspapers established regular environmental beats, universities and colleges set up new ecology centers, and organizers transformed their groups into permanent fixtures of local and national politics.

Political support in Congress led to a whole new regulatory regime dedicated to implementing and enforcing environmental strictures. In July 1970, Nixon created the Environmental Protection Agency (EPA) to oversee existing and future regulations. The new agency had broad powers to police businesses across the economy, impose compliance costs, and establish mandates for the states. Nixon was hopeful that by centralizing responsibility in a single executive agency, he could exert influence. But he also understood the issue was gaining steam.

At times, Nixon balanced this lurch to the left with a pro-business agenda. In 1969, he had assembled a cabinet task force on oil import control under the direction of his labor secretary, George Shultz. Given the growing energy demand, Shultz thought the time had come to scrap quotas and allow for greater imports, even if that meant increasing reliance on cheaper overseas fuel. But Nixon did not endorse that finding. In 1970, he asked George Bush to give up his safe seat in the House to make a run for the Senate. This was part of a larger strategy of attempting to increase GOP numbers in that body. While Bush was running, Nixon did not want to alienate these Sunbelt businessmen by abandoning protectionist policy. When word leaked of Shultz's recommendation to free imports, more than a hundred congressmen wrote to Nixon in opposition.[27] The president overruled the task force and kept quotas in place.

As it turned out, Bush lost to the conservative Democrat Lloyd Bentsen. Elsewhere Democrats also fared better than Republicans, maintaining their majority status in both houses. These results reinforced Nixon's belief that pushing for more environmental protection was the best path toward his reelection. The Clean Air Act, which Nixon signed on December 31, 1970, set national air-quality standards as well as statutory deadlines for compliance. The act took aim not only at factories and power plants but also at automobiles, which were the biggest source of pollution.

In this political climate, Nixon decided not to push for the oil industry's demand to deregulate natural gas prices. He courted the Sunbelt oil-men and protected import quotas, but he could not appear too close to this constituency. And thus the industry continued to feel under pressure from higher costs, price ceilings, and growing demand. In the fall of 1970, Paul McCracken, Nixon's chief economic adviser, recognized the dim prospect for deregulatory reform: "The most helpful solution . . . at the moment would be to pray for a benign weatherman."[28] That would help keep demand within the confines of existing supply as the cold months approached. Hollis M. Dole, assistant secretary of the interior, echoed these hopes: "We're praying for a warm winter."[29]

In 1971, the president was worrying about the threat of Senator Edmund Muskie, who seemed as if he would be a front-runner for the 1972 Democratic nomination and was one of Capitol Hill's most vociferous environmental advocates. Activist groups that had organized Earth Day were turning to campaign politics. Environmental Action launched its "Dirty Dozen" list, naming the twelve legislators in the House and the Senate with the worst voting records on the environment.[30] Nixon requested fourteen pieces of new legislation, including bills to regulate water pollution, strip-mining, ocean dumping, toxic waste, and noise. He asked for legislation to tax sulfur in fossil fuels and lead in gasoline, which would add two or three cents at the pump and encourage the switch to unleaded fuel.

The United States was heading toward the perfect storm. Since 1967, energy consumption had been increasing at a faster rate than economic growth. While Americans made up only 6 percent of the world population, they consumed one-third of its energy. They used more energy than the people of the Soviet Union, Britain, West Germany, and Japan combined. The biggest single gas-guzzler was the American automobile. Since World War II, the number of cars had risen from 34 million to 118 million. In a single year, auto manufacturers put more than 10 million new cars on the road. Manufacturers installed air conditioners in 73 percent of all new cars, a luxury that ate up roughly 2.5 miles per gallon. At four thousand pounds, the average full-size American car weighed over half a ton more than its European and Japanese equivalents and was 22 percent bigger than it was in 1965. At that weight, these behemoths got half the gas mileage of a subcompact. With the rise of suburban living, more than three-quarters of Americans drove to work, and most drove alone. In certain cities, especially in California, almost 90 percent commuted by car.[31]

Aware of the gathering storm clouds, in June 1971, Nixon sent the first-ever presidential message on energy policy to Congress. The days of cheap and abundant fuel were coming to an abrupt end, said the president. Producers were running up against geological limitations, and new environmental regulations, many that he had put in place himself, were leading to further reductions of domestic output. By the early 1970s, the nation had experienced brownouts, power shortages, and rising fuel costs. As the president explained to a national audience, "We cannot take our energy supply for granted any longer." The president put forward a range of proposals from government support of alternative energies to nuclear power to conservation. In reality, he was not willing to push hard for these, more interested in lip service than in real change or additional budget outlays. But even as he limited his commitment, Nixon had already done more than most previous presidents to regulate the American energy industry.

And he was just getting started. In August 1971, Nixon announced a landmark decision: he would impose wage and price controls across the economy. To tackle inflation before the 1972 election, he was pushing for yet another expansion of the regulatory power of government. As much as Americans were aroused by environmental causes, their leading concern, in 1971, was the inflation that started to take hold. As a result of Vietnam War spending, a slowdown in productivity, an increase in the money supply, and worldwide food shortages, the economy was experiencing inflation, which was up on Nixon's watch from where it had hovered in the postwar period between 1 and 2 percent to more than 5 percent.

A year earlier, amid mounting inflationary fears, a Democratic Congress had passed the Economic Stabilization Act of 1970, giving the president authority to establish price controls. The Democrats did not believe that a Republican would use them, and certainly not Richard Nixon. Nixon had spent much of his first years in the Oval Office resisting controls, denouncing them as a retrograde and ineffective policy tool. In a 1969 radio address about the rising cost of living, he said, "Wage and price controls are bad for business, bad for the workingman, and bad for the consumer. Rationing, black markets, regimentation—that is the wrong road for America, and I will not take the Nation down that road." "What worries me," he explained, "is putting the economy in a straitjacket under the control of a bunch of damn bureaucrats for any length of time."[32]

Nixon believed he knew what he was talking about. His first job in

Washington had been working for the Office of Price Administration (OPA) in World War II, which he looked back on as both a testament to his early commitment to public service and the incubator for his antiregulatory views. The son of a Southern California grocer, he had inherited the perspective of the small-business owner and would later attribute his own success to hard work and long hours. When he took the job at the OPA in 1943, everything about it smacked of heavy-handed socialistic interference in the daily operations of the small-business man. The OPA employed tens of thousands of people to ration scarce goods and enforce an economy-wide system of price controls. Within several months, he left his post and enlisted in the navy. While Nixon served in the Pacific, his wife, Pat, took a job in the San Francisco OPA. Pat shared her husband's sensibilities. When they had first met in Whittier, California, Pat was teaching business courses at the local high school. She must have had the same reaction to the OPA as her husband, especially because the San Francisco office was known as a hotbed of radicalism with popular-front OPA field-workers such as the well-known Communist Jessica Mitford, who eagerly confiscated the books of small-business men she suspected of wrongdoing.

After the war, when Richard Nixon launched his political career, he ran for Congress on a fierce anti-Communist platform. The nation's leaders had to fight against Soviet expansion abroad and Communist encroachment at home, said this conservative Republican. Beneath his bluster was a serious message: the New Deal regulatory state had destroyed the autonomy and entrepreneurial spirit of Americans. In his 1946 campaign, with World War II price controls still in place, his central pledge was to get government off citizens' backs. Over two decades later, Nixon was still fighting against what he perceived as the smug certainty of liberal policy makers and politicians who professed to know better than businessmen and average citizens how to run their lives. The price system, not price controls, would guarantee economic prosperity. As president, Nixon was not eager to support this kind of intervention in the economy, which he called "total Federal bureaucratic domination."

But it was one thing to believe that price controls were counterproductive, another to be sitting in the White House trying to figure out how to win reelection in an era still steeped in the New Deal. Ever a shrewd politician, Nixon understood that ideological conviction would not always work to win him votes. He recognized that the New Deal held its place as the essential paradigm of American politics and price controls remained popular as a cure for inflation. He was well aware that he and many of his congressional colleagues were all products of the Roosevelt years of governmental growth, and so, too, were millions of Americans, who saw federal regulation, with elaborate state mechanisms and far-reaching interventions in industry, as the proper response to the nation's problems, including inflation, unemployment, the environment, and energy. This belief in big government, born for some from personal admiration of Franklin Roosevelt as a savior during the Great Depression and crystallized for others in World War II, the Cold War, and the Great Society, characterized the entrenched liberal mind-set that favored the expansion of government regulation as the legitimate solution to any national crisis.

Monetarists like Milton Friedman argued for a different approach, whereby the Federal Reserve would tighten the money supply as a way to restrain inflation. In this view, inflation was a monetary phenomenon, not the result of exogenous shocks to the system, nor the outcome of political bargains among countervailing powers, but strictly a matter of the money supply. Nixon, inveterate critic of New Deal–style controls, was gathering around him a cohort of market-oriented advisers. "Would not [the country] be better off with less government intervention rather than more?" suggested Hendrik Houthakker, an outspoken member of Nixon's Council of Economic Advisers (CEA), just as Nixon was deciding in favor of the price freeze. "As an instrument of economic policy the free market is hard to beat."[33]

But the poor showing by the GOP in the 1970 elections made the White House hesitant to go in that direction, and as inflation continued upward, the voices of market approaches were drowned out by the still dominant New Deal worldview that even its opponents like Nixon recognized as a political reality. Moreover, Nixon feared that at some point inflation would cool and would end in recession just when he was up for reelection. The first time Nixon had run for president, in 1960, he had lost to John Kennedy, not because Kennedy looked better in their famous television debates, but because of the downturn that occurred in 1958, when Nixon was vice president. Nixon was determined not to let a recession beat him again.

The president believed that putting on price controls in the summer of 1971 would enable him to recommend tax cuts and levy a 10 percent import surcharge on all dutiable imports, two measures intended to prevent a slowdown before the election. Controls would also allow him to undertake an equally radical act by devaluing the dollar and ending the convertibility of dollars to gold that had been the hallmark of the postwar Bretton Woods system of international exchange. Instituting controls and freeing the dollar would spark the economy and restrain balance-of-payments deficits. This would give Nixon more room to engineer an election-year recovery without worrying about escalating prices.

Thus, without any prior warning, Nixon took to the airwaves on August 15, 1971, to announce that he was instituting a ninety-day wage and price freeze to be administered by the newly created Cost of Living Council. No single act of Nixon's first term was as popular as the adoption of price controls. The president's standing in public opinion polls got a boost; the vast majority of Americans approved of his action. The day after Nixon's speech, the Dow Jones Industrial Average posted the largest single-day gain in its history. The president had worried that the public might see him, in light of his earlier opposition to controls, as a waffler. Instead, they saw him as a courageous leader, in the mold of Franklin Roosevelt, who did what needed to be done. This was exactly what he had intended. Using his executive authority, Nixon was fighting against price gougers who were charging too much for their goods. For the time being, Nixon was ruling as a New Dealer and reaping the benefits.

Once established, controls were hard to get rid of, given the fear of a price spurt after they were removed and given that the underlying causes of inflation remained. Nixon's market-oriented advisers had warned him about this. After Phase I expired in November 1971, Nixon extended controls under Phase II, which lasted until January 1973. It fell to Donald Rumsfeld, who as a congressman had voted against the authorizing of controls, to oversee them after Nixon asked him to head the new Cost of Living Council.

There could be no doubt that Nixon had outflanked his liberal opponents. To Nixon, this move made political sense. He was the first president to take office with Congress under the control of the opposition party since Zachary Taylor in 1849. After his narrow victory in 1968, Nixon had sought to broaden and deepen his electoral support, and he had fastened on economic liberalism as one strategy to convert Democratic voters, particularly white working-class men, into his backers. To be sure, Nixon moved to exploit what was coming to be known as the Social Issue as a way to recruit voters. He hoped to appeal to what he called the silent majority of Americans by stressing patriotism, morality, and law and order. He was reaching out to Middle Americans who supported his efforts in Vietnam and abhorred the unrest of the antiwar protesters on college campuses. Nixon also made clear his opposition to programs like forced busing that the Supreme Court ruled in April 1971 in *Swann v. Charlotte-Mecklenburg Board of Education* was a legitimate solution to the problem of segregation. But he believed it was the gut economic issues, and politicians' commitment to guarding them, that mattered most to voters.

In this political environment, decontrol of natural gas was off the table. The oil industry would have to wait. A large percentage of Americans resisted a free-market approach, especially with regard to energy. Nixon's adviser Peter Flanigan, an antigovernment, anti-regulation Wall Street investment banker, understood this: "A deregulation initiative would no doubt be viewed as another massive give-away to big business at the expense of the American consumer."[34] Decontrol would also lead to pressure to end price controls on oil. That policy would raise the specter of Big Oil, with its monopolistic tendencies since the days of Rockefeller's Standard Oil trust, once again behaving badly. Ralph Nader, who was spearheading a consumer movement, calling for government to regulate America's corporations, had the energy industry in his sights. The twenty largest oil companies, which in 1955 turned out 55.7 percent of domestic crude oil, produced 69 percent in 1970. Of the approximately 180,000 service stations, the largest oil companies accounted for more than half.[35] These facts confirmed for many Americans their mistrust of business and markets and their comfort with New Deal–style conceptions of government's role in setting prices fairly.

The turn to economy-wide price controls came at the worst time for the domestic oil industry. Keeping prices low was politically popular, and that was what had guided Nixon. However, as far as the industry was concerned, this decision was the kiss of death. Together the FPC and the Cost of Living Council were holding down prices just as supply was shrinking. In choosing to use his authority to impose controls, Nixon relied on the advice of John Connally, the former Democratic Texas governor who was now the Treasury secretary and was known for supporting grand gestures. Connally, a longtime friend to the oil patch, had given little regard to how this policy would affect the industry. While oilmen were hoping in vain for regulatory relief from Washington, it looked as if Nixon were accelerating the chances of stormy weather ahead.

In 1972, George McGovern, the Democratic presidential candidate, delivered only a single energy speech. It was enough, though, to confirm what Nixon's rivals thought of the oil industry and its close ties to the current administration. Nixon's FPC, in the absence of any prospect of legislative reform, had begun to use its administrative rate-making authority to allow increases in natural gas prices. McGovern charged that, once again, "Big Oil won out over the people." He criticized Nixon's FPC appointments for being puppets of the oil industry, for "ma[king] a mockery of the FPC mission: to protect consumers from exploitations at the hands of the natural gas companies."[36] Nixon, of course, wanted to avoid the accusation of being in the pocket of Big Oil, and thus he placed any deregulation on hold until after the election.

Nixon's victory over McGovern was a landslide, as decisive as Lyndon Johnson's election had been in 1964 and Franklin Roosevelt's reelection in 1936. This time it was the Republican candidate who captured more than 60 percent of the popular vote, winning every state except Massachusetts. Nixon was a president caught in a moment of transition for the Republican Party. The traditionally important northeastern moderate wing, sympathetic to programs like environmental regulation, social insurance, and even price controls, maintained its place, while business-oriented conservative Republicans and an increasingly right-wing faction rooted in the South and the Southwest expressed much stronger hostility toward government. Those on the right hoped this 1972 victory would set the stage for a more conservative approach to governance, including on energy and the environment.

A New Regulatory Sandbox

On January 20, 1973, in his second inaugural address, Richard Nixon made the case for limited government. "We have lived too long with the consequences of attempting to gather all power and responsibility in Washington," he told the nation. "Today I offer no promise of a purely governmental solution for every problem . . . In trusting too much in government, we have asked of it more than it can deliver. This leads only to inflated expectations, to reduced individual effort, and to a disappointment and frustration that erode confidence both in what government can do and in what people can do . . . Let us ask not just what will government do for me, but what can I do for myself?" asked Nixon, who hoped to turn the clock back on big government.

The rhetoric was grand, but Nixon's landslide victory did nothing to change the political calculus on the Hill, where Democrats still outnumbered their GOP rivals. Nor did it make Nixon any less of a pragmatist. In January, he extended wage and price controls, replacing Phase II with Phase III, which, even as it relaxed the freeze, would last until August 1973. Charles DiBona, the main White House energy adviser tasked with developing a plan for deregulation, complained to John Ehrlichman that his staff was "working out of briefcases."[37]

At this moment, the energy crunch that the oil industry was warning about finally arrived. The Northeast and the Midwest were reporting tightening inventories of heating oil and natural gas. Bringing more energy onto the market and encouraging greater discovery, production, and refining required deregulation, said Tom Medders, president of the Independent Petroleum Association of America. He claimed, "Almost 20 years of unrealistic regulation has been one of the primary factors that has led us into the present fuel crisis."[38] Executives from Texaco, Exxon, Mobil, and Shell agreed.[39]

The White House got to work building its case that only deregulation would boost supply. Peter Flanigan argued that "government interference with the free market system should be as limited as possible." Kenneth Lay, undersecretary of the Department of the Interior, helped to draft legislation to end natural gas price controls. Lay reflected the ideological conservatism of a new breed of young Washington bureaucrats. From 1965 to 1968, he worked for Humble Oil in Houston and then earned a Ph.D. in economics on the detrimental impact of Vietnam deficits while working as a Pentagon economist. In 1971, at twenty-nine, he became an aide to the federal power commissioner Pinkney Walker, his former economics professor. In 1972, Lay moved to the Interior Department, where he would remain until 1974, when he left Washington to become vice president of the Florida Gas Company. In 1985, he would found Enron and build it into the world's largest energy trader. In April 1973, Lay urged Nixon to explain to the public that "our problem . . . has resulted from outmoded

Government policies—from excessive tinkering with the time-tested mechanisms of the free market."[40]

The White House was up against a formidable foe. Senator Henry "Scoop" Jackson, one of the powerhouses on Capitol Hill, said what the country needed was more regulation, not less. Since 1963, Jackson had chaired the Senate Interior Committee and was the leading congressional authority on energy. Jackson was an old-fashioned New Deal liberal Democrat, first elected from the state of Washington to the House of Representatives in 1940 and then to the Senate in 1952. He was also a committed cold warrior, and on foreign policy he was to the right of the administration. Jackson warned Nixon about the danger of depending on Arab oil, fearing that either another Middle East war or an Arab alliance with the Soviets could disrupt American supply. Aware of the great instability that plagued that region, Jackson was very much concerned about the need to conserve domestic resources and, as a New Dealer, distribute them equitably.

In 1973, in part with his eye on the next presidential Democratic nomination and in part out of genuine security concerns, Jackson was eager to formulate a national energy policy. The senator was broadly sympathetic to the idea of allowing higher natural gas prices to boost supply. That would ease the pressure on oil, which looked as if it would run in short supply in the upcoming summer. But as a New Deal liberal, he was not about to do away with the FPC. In a radical move, Jackson pushed to extend the commission's jurisdiction to the intrastate market, where, in the absence of any government regulation, natural gas prices and thus supply were much higher. The idea was to create one national market with prices set by the government. The senior White House staff member John Schaefer characterized the Jackson proposal as "ridiculous," simply prolonging the introduction of the price mechanism. "At best, this proposal will allow for higher prices," he said, "but provides a new sandbox for the regulatory lawyers to play in."[41]

Jackson was just warming up. In the spring of 1973, as demand for fuel was outpacing supply, the major oil companies began cutting off their gasoline distribution to independent refiners and independent station owners. Historically, these independent retailers attracted customers by selling at a discounted price. As these dealers were forced to shutter their doors, the concern was that the majors would have no competition and prices would rise. Jackson said the government had to make sure these independent dealers stayed in business and that customers could get the fuel they needed at the prices they wanted.

In a bold gesture, Jackson called for an amendment to the Economic Stabilization Act to give the president the authority to allocate all petroleum products. This was World War II all over again, when Washington extended its reach into every nook and cranny of the industry. Jackson had delivered his first radio address in support of the OPA and saw this wartime agency as a useful precedent. He calculated that a nationwide system whereby the government decided how much gasoline each state, each refiner, each retailer, and possibly each consumer would receive would have widespread popular support, especially if Americans saw running out as the alternative. To a generation that still had their wartime ration booklets in their scrapbooks, saved as souvenirs of patriotic sacrifice, new ration coupons would provide assurance that each citizen would get his due. Jackson believed that the energy issue could rejuvenate the Democratic Party around core economic issues and paper over the divisive social issues that were roiling American politics. If homeowners and drivers were running short, then it was up to government to guarantee their supply.

Nixon and his administration fought tooth and nail to beat back allocations. They argued that government should not have the power to decide to whom companies should sell their products or the quantities of various petroleum products they should manufacture. Allocation involved a series of key and at times fateful decisions when the industry switched its refineries from producing home heating oil to producing gasoline, both made from the same petroleum. This required risky gambles about how Americans would use their resources, based in part on unknowns such as how cold the winter would be or how much summer driving tourists would do. Such distribution and production questions were complex, involving hundreds of refineries and tens of thousands of storage facilities and wholesale distributors, and the administration didn't want to touch them. Nixon's advisers knew making allocations would be a political nightmare for government, and they truly believed that government interference would only make shortages worse. Yet leaving these decisions in the hands of oil executives did not have broad support in a Democratic Congress, where politicians in both parties represented oil-consuming states.

On April 18, 1973, Nixon delivered a major energy address. The speech had only one major newsworthy item: the president would end import restrictions to ease short-term shortages. With Democrats calling for more government to regulate domestic oil, Nixon called for more oil to come from abroad. Nixon hoped that this politically expedient action taken by executive authority would derail the move toward allocations. He also pushed for decontrol of natural gas prices, postponement of clean air standards, and construction of the Trans-Alaska Pipeline. But the key thing was the ending of Eisenhower's import quotas. With oil so central to every aspect of the economy, and the search for domestic oil ever more in doubt, imports would provide a safety valve, greasing the wheels of America's commerce. Like the fabled western frontier in the nineteenth century or the elusive China market for American exports in the early twentieth, now oil imports appeared to political leaders as the way to defuse social tensions and avoid ugly conflicts. They just might delay momentum for more government regulation, too.

The speech fell flat. Imports were good, said the liberals, but the government should still regulate prices of this scarce commodity and decide who should get what. Representative Donald Fraser, a Democrat from Minnesota, typified the skepticism on the Hill. We cannot "rely on the philosophy that what is good for big oil companies is good for the country." Counter to Nixon's approach, Fraser insisted that "reliance on the free market will not solve the oil distribution problem . . . Government regulation is really the only way we can minimize inconvenience and hardships to the consumer."[42]

In addition to this liberal attack, environmental critics faulted Nixon for not pushing for energy conservation. Governor Francis Sargent of Massachusetts, a liberal Republican, came down hard on the president. "This country is like an addict," said Sargent. "The more energy we get, the more we demand. And the more we demand, the more we eventually obtain, which leads to still further demand."[43] The solution would be to go on an "energy diet," with tougher fuel-efficiency standards, mass transit, better building codes to promote energy savings, and other public policies to support conservation.

By the early 1970s, left-leaning environmentalists remained dubious of any agenda other than conservation to reduce what they saw as Americans' overbloated consumption. Many argued that the only sustainable future was one of reduced dependence on oil. In 1972, the Club of Rome released its influential study *The Limits to Growth*, advancing the idea that finite supplies of natural resources, especially oil, required a fundamental rethinking of continued expansion. A year later, the British economist E. F. Schumacher published an instantly successful book, *Small Is Beautiful*, which captured the increasingly popular challenge to economic growth as a social good. Amory Lovins, who would emerge as a leading critic of the energy industry, put it starkly: "Utopian visions encourage us to think that energy is unlimited and free; they do not teach us thrift or moral responsibility."[44]

David Freeman, director of the Ford Foundation's Energy Policy Project, warned of "the danger of a breakdown if we continue our thoughtless habits of energy gluttony in the face of tighter supplies, pollution problems, rising prices and foreign policy concerns." Freeman had worked in the Nixon White House as an energy adviser but had quit in disgust. In *A Time to Choose*, the report from his $4 million investigation into American energy, which the foundation would publish a year later, Freeman wrote, "We are free to choose slower growth," and by making this choice, Americans could reduce their consumption of fossil fuels.[45] Nixon of course rejected that approach. Imports would be his solution.

Would this safety valve work? Just as Nixon made his announcement, Saudi Arabia's minister of petroleum, Sheikh Zaki Yamani, told Secretary of State William Rogers that his country would not be willing to increase production unless the United States put pressure on Israel to relinquish territories won in the 1967 Six-Day War. The Saudi minister might have been motivated by his stated diplomatic considerations, or he might simply have wanted to claim a right to greater control over his country's oil.

By this time, OPEC was becoming more effective at asserting its collective strength. These oil countries understood that the market was tightening as demand was growing faster than supply. Western Europe depended on oil from the Middle East for 47 percent of its energy consumption, while Japan drew on this supply for 57 percent of its total consumption.[46] Though the proportion was much smaller for the United States, the aggregate amount of U.S. imports was substantial. Given the heavy reliance on the automobile, gasoline was an integral part of the economy. With the end of quotas, imports rose to 6.2 million barrels per day compared with 4.5 a year earlier and 3.2 in 1970.[47]

The OPEC ministers wanted to set the price of their oil. In 1971, the major oil companies had signed the Tehran agreement with OPEC in which the companies agreed to OPEC's demand for a price increase. OPEC sought to offset a global rise in food prices, which had recently started to spike upward. In addition, its income, which the majors paid in U.S. currency, was worth less in the wake of President Nixon's decision to devalue the dollar. OPEC rulers were eager to raise greater funds for additional modernization and arms purchases. And finally, they pressed their claims as part of an insurgent movement by Third World countries against international corporations. The Tehran agreement, along with a corresponding Tripoli agreement that raised prices in Libya, started a process whereby OPEC insisted not only on higher prices but on greater participation in ownership of its oil. "The economic terms of world trade in oil have been radically altered," concluded the international oil expert Walter Levy. "The winds of change for the oil industry . . . have now risen to hurricane proportions."[48]

Under these circumstances, foreign prices of crude now surpassed American domestic prices for the first time. The major oil companies were complicit in these higher prices. For one thing, of course, higher crude prices benefited them, especially if they could pass these costs on to customers. But more than that, they felt they had no other option. They worried that the oil countries would either try to nationalize the industry or make deals with smaller, but growing, independent firms that were looking to gain access to new supply. The State Department, too, accepted higher prices, which would funnel additional funds to Saudi Arabia and Iran, America's two major regional allies. That diplomatic goal became even more important when Britain announced that after 1971 the country would pull its military presence from Iran. At the same time, the Soviet Union, which was reaching nuclear parity with the United States, was starting to exert its influence in the region, deploying naval forces to the Indian Ocean.[49]

Alert to the changing world oil market, OPEC leaders were champing at the bit. In early 1973, Colonel Muammar al-Qaddafi of Libya, who was a radical Arab leader intent on limiting the power of Western oil companies, told the U.S. ambassador, "We have the oil weapon and the financial weapon and we intend to use them both." Just as the United States was negotiating a cease-fire in Vietnam, the Middle East oil situation raised the specter of what one commentator called "imperialism-in-reverse." Through its control of oil, Arab leaders could disrupt Western economies and dictate demands, or at least that is what these regional leaders hoped.[50]

No one in Washington was taking this threat seriously, with one exception. Just before Nixon's decision to free imports and the Saudi announcement, the State Department's Middle East analyst James Akins was warning of disaster. In the pages of *Foreign Affairs*, Akins published an article, "The Oil Crisis: This Time the Wolf Is Here," expressing the view that it was just a matter of time until OPEC used its collective market power against the United States. "The threat to use oil as a political weapon must be taken seriously," insisted Akins. "The vulnerability of the advanced countries is too great and too plainly evident—and is about to extend to the United States."[51]

As the director of the State Department's Office of Fuels and Energy, Akins had a deep knowledge of the Middle East and the region's oil politics. A Quaker by background, he served in the navy and then volunteered for relief work in Europe in 1946. Later, he joined the Foreign Service and held posts in various European and Arab countries, including Syria, Lebanon, Kuwait, and Iraq, before his post in the State Department in 1967. According to Akins, the specific threat from OPEC was to limit the supply of oil, which would drive up prices and possibly disrupt economic growth. The producer countries were taking in American dollars faster than they could spend them. If they could boost prices by cutting production, they believed that oil in the ground, which they hoped to sell later at higher prices, would be worth more than money in the bank. Before Congress, Akins testified about the growing threat. "We believe that the foreign policy pitfalls of an excessive reliance on imported energy are too serious to risk," he said.[52]

The correct policy to reduce U.S. vulnerability, according to Akins, was to grant concessions to Middle Eastern allies—primarily to give them more power over the price and production levels of their oil. "Whether an Arab is a Harvard Business School graduate or an illiterate Bedouin, he strongly dislikes being cheated," wrote Akins, who was sympathetic to the idea that the Arab producers were indeed not getting their fair share. Simultaneously, he also advocated conservation at home. Akins himself walked three and a half miles to work, set his thermostat to sixty-eight degrees during the day, and shut off the heat completely at night.[53]

The White House was not too worried. Having recruited Akins to help with the president's April energy message, Nixon's advisers soon marginalized and dismissed him. When Akins told John Ehrlichman that the speech had to emphasize reduced consumption, Ehrlichman replied, "Conservation is not a Republican ethic."[54] Eager to get him out of the White House, Nixon appointed him ambassador to Saudi Arabia.

Letting more oil into the country might ease the situation, but Nixon was facing mounting pressure, especially on the question of prices. As independent refiners and retailers found their access to domestic fuel cut off by the majors, they turned to higher-priced imports, and prices at the pump were rising. In March, after Phase III relaxed controls, the rate of inflation had soared, with meat prices alone increasing at 75 percent annually. Nixon, in what seemed like only a thinly veiled act of desperation, imposed an immediate freeze on the retail price of beef, pork, and lamb. He also slapped controls on the price of gasoline at service stations.

George Bush understood how much Nixon was hurting from these rising prices. After he lost his Senate race, Nixon had appointed Bush the U.S. ambassador to the United Nations. Now Nixon named this New England–southern hybrid Republican National Committee (RNC) chairman to try to translate the 1972 landslide win into a permanent new GOP majority. As Bush traveled the country, many local politicians expressed fear that the high cost of living would punish them at the polls.

Bush was so concerned that he placed the problem of prices ahead of the Watergate scandal, which by the spring of 1973 was gaining momentum. The last two defendants in the trial of the break-in at the Watergate Democratic National Committee headquarters had been convicted on January 30, 1973. The trail followed by journalists and congressional investigators was leading to the White House; three top Nixon aides accused of obstruction of justice, including H. R. Haldeman and John Ehrlichman, resigned on April 30. Yet, according to polls, Watergate was not yet Nixon's biggest problem. Inflation was. In one poll, 86 percent of those surveyed chose rising prices over Watergate as a bigger personal concern.

That was both good and bad news for the White House. It was good in the sense that Watergate did not necessarily mean the president would have to leave office. Bush dismissed the charges against the White House and wrote off the entire break-in as a "grubby" affair. He saw the fund-raising dollars drying up, but if the president remained above the fray, Bush believed the scandal would blow over. What he worried about was how the bread-and-butter issues would play. If the public cared more about rising prices than Watergate, the White House needed a solution to the nation's unfolding economic problems.

As summer arrived, the early signs of a gasoline shortage appeared. The major oil companies rationed sales to their customers for the first time since World War II. Exxon, which operated all the stations on the New Jersey Turnpike, limited purchases to ten gallons per car. Amoco did the same thing on the New York thruways. The majors also cut back supplies to independent retailers. Soon, the majority of the nation's service stations did not have enough fuel to fill customers' tanks completely. Many stations closed early. Things got steadily worse for consumers, with at least half the stations reporting shortages. Corner gas stations displayed SORRY NO GASOLINE signs. Some drivers, worried they would not get enough gasoline, started filling up daily, and this meant there was less gasoline for other drivers.[55]

The long-standing skepticism about the oil industry made Americans mistrust that energy shortages were real. Many on the Hill, and not just those from oil-consuming states, believed that the majors were deliberately holding supplies off the market as a way to manipulate prices, a view that, according to public opinion polls, the majority of Americans held. While Scoop Jackson had a sophisticated understanding of the global market for oil and the declining excess capacity of domestic producers and refiners, he was not above tapping into these conspiracy theories. The idea was that if the majors reduced the amount of fuel available, claiming the need for higher prices, they could force a policy change on Capitol Hill to end price controls and scale back environmental regulations.[56]

Senator James Abourezk, a liberal from South Dakota, wrote an open letter to President Nixon denouncing what he saw as monopolistic efforts by the majors to obtain higher prices, drive independents out of business, win tax breaks, and ease environmental regulations. "Our energy 'crisis,' I believe, is deliberately contrived by the major oil companies," he insisted. Les Aspin, a liberal congressman from Wisconsin, echoed the charges. "There is little doubt," said Aspin, "that the so-called gasoline shortage in the Midwest is just a big, lousy gimmick foisted on consumers to bilk them for billions in increased gasoline prices."[57]

Senators Jackson and Hubert Humphrey requested the Federal Trade Commission investigate the "contrived effort" to hold gasoline off the market. Humphrey said on the Senate floor, in response to a letter from a concerned housewife from Minnesota, "The major oil firms have irresponsibly abused their market power." The agency's report a month later charged that the eight largest oil companies, which accounted for half of the refining and sales of all gasoline, deliberately held down supply to jack up prices. Many independent station owners added their voices to the chorus of accusations against Big Oil. As one put it, the majors manufactured shortages to get "the Alaskan oil line, get the offshore pipeline, get a price increase, and to drive the small independents out of business."[58]

The popular belief that oil companies cooked up the summer shortage accelerated demands for government intervention. If ever there was a powerful industry that Americans loved to hate, it was the oil industry. While the image of the independent adventurous oilman fit with a stereotype of American individualism and swagger, the portrait of Big Oil tycoons, starting with Rockefeller, gave rise to a negative view of corporate malfeasance, strong-arm tactics, and misdealing. Beginning with the muckraking journalist Ida Tarbell's exposés of Rockefeller in the pages of *McClure's*, Americans had harbored suspicion about the industry and its monopolistic anticompetitive nature. Upton Sinclair's 1927 novel, *Oil!*, perpetuated the image of bloodsucking oil magnates growing wealthy off the needs of everyone else. The 1969 Santa Barbara oil spill furthered the view of oil companies as selfish corporate agents with little regard for workers, consumers, or the environment.

Politicians and industry opponents both fed and reacted to the popular belief that oil companies were contriving a shortage. Robert Moretti, California state assembly Speaker and Democratic gubernatorial candidate, charged that the gas shortage might be "the greatest pure hustle in American business." The state attorneys general of Massachusetts, New York, Connecticut, North Carolina, Florida, and Michigan all filed suits against the major oil companies for artificially raising prices.[59] The majors, according to this view, had overplayed their hand. "A little shortage to scare people but not enough to get Congress mad. But now, Congress is mad," said David Freeman. Freeman warned that if the administration decontrolled prices, like the producers wanted, industry profits would soar with little guarantee that companies would use their gains for additional exploration. "The 'energy crisis' could well serve as a smoke-screen for a massive exercise in picking the pocket of the American consumer to the tune of billions of dollars a year," Freeman cautioned.[60]

On June 29, 1973, Nixon appointed Colorado's governor, John Love, as energy chief of the new Energy Policy Office in the White House. Announced with much fanfare, this appointment was meant to signal a presidential commitment to the energy problem, if for no other reason than to stall Jackson's mandatory allocations bill. The Senate had already passed it, and now it was before the House. Nixon proposed the creation of a new department of energy and natural resources to direct a five-year, $10 billion commitment to research and development, the majority of it on nuclear energy. (Jackson was sponsoring a measure for a ten-year, $20 billion program.) The chief executive also insisted that the federal government reduce its energy consumption by 7 percent. In response, the interior secretary replaced his Cadillac limousine with a Plymouth Fury, while chauffeurs waiting outside the Department of Defense were ordered to turn off their engines. At the General Services Administration headquarters, officials unscrewed bulbs in one-third of all thirty thousand light fixtures.[61]

Both the administration and the oil industry correctly understood that immediate conservation was essential to prevent shortages from becoming a crisis that would escalate demands for a dramatic government response. If a few months earlier Ehrlichman dismissed the need for conservation, now the White House embraced it. In a grand appeal, Nixon called on all Americans to cut back their individual energy use. Under Virginia Knauer, the Office of Consumer Affairs launched a nationwide conservation program. It was seemingly innocuous, with lots of helpful tips. But at the same time it was very intrusive in people's daily activities. It was fine to be asked to turn off lights or, if you had the money and time, to insulate homes. Beyond that, Knauer's office offered lots of little recommendations that seemed pesky or even petty: Don't open the oven door or you'll lose 20 percent of your heat. Run the dishwasher only with a full load in nonpeak hours. Take a vacation closer to home. In the summer of 1973, Knauer's Dear Consumer columns appeared in more than five thousand small newspapers.[62]

Even the oil companies got behind this new "conservation ethic." All the major companies pulled their gasoline advertisements and replaced them with appeals to conserve. "The American public must develop a new national ethic with respect to the use of energy . . . because the energy shortage will be with us for a long time," said Mobil's chairman, Rawleigh Warner Jr.[63] Amoco's spokesman Johnny Cash delivered its message, "Drive slow and save gas," replacing its spots of the country singer praising the open road. And the industry echoed environmentalist demands for production of smaller cars, or as Fred Hartley, Union Oil's president, put it, "the elimination of the Gargantuan models which so often are dedicated to a driver's ego."[64]

All of Nixon's economic advisers urged him to resist any kind of mandatory program. The Treasury secretary, George Shultz, argued that allocations would not eliminate the shortage and would distort the market. Once in place, controls would be impossible to shed and would only encourage complaints directed at the administration, rather than at the oil companies. As the presidential adviser Ken Cole told Nixon, "By December, hundreds of schools, hospitals, municipalities and even private citizens could be contacting the White House for relief of their specific problems. There is no way we could handle this and even if we could we ought not to want to." The situation did not look good. "You'll wind up taking the heat no matter what," warned Cole.[65]

For Nixon, this was a tough issue with no good outcome. The speechwriter David Gergen expressed concern to the chief of staff, Alexander Haig, that the "public is baffled. Why should [the] most prosperous people in the world face [the] prospect of freezing homes and empty gas pumps?" Why indeed. The president, according to Gergen, "is not out in front on this issue."[66] By midsummer, the White House was under immense pressure to institute a mandatory fuel allocation program.

Politics and ideology dictated opposite courses of action. The administration talked out of both sides of its mouth, one day pushing for deregulation and the next announcing the latest round of controls. Plans to declare a national energy conservation month in September symbolized the tension between grand gesture and a reluctance to act. The administration kicked off a high-profile national campaign with a Charles Schulz *Peanuts* cartoon. Under the caption "I believe in conserving energy," Snoopy lay asleep on his doghouse; the solution to an energy shortage, apparently, was taking a nap.[67]

The White House announced another round of price freezes to keep the lid on oil prices. Phase IV, to run from August 13, 1973, through April 30, 1974, relied on voluntary compliance. The oil industry was the notable exception. The Cost of Living Council devised a system by which all domestic crude oil was slotted into two artificial categories, "old," which was any oil produced from existing wells up to the production levels of 1972, and "new," which was everything else, including oil from stripper wells that produced fewer than ten barrels a day. Phase IV fixed the price of "old" oil, which accounted for approximately 60 percent of production, at $4.25 a barrel, the price on May 15, 1973, plus thirty-five cents; "new" oil was uncontrolled. This elaborate system, according to its designers, would encourage additional production, while keeping price controls in place on much of this commodity.

All the major oil companies and independent producers shared in the opposition to these price controls, predicting that they would only hinder production and worsen the shortage. To their great horror, amid this unfolding crisis, it looked as if the New Deal mind-set was alive and well. Businessmen wasted no time in protesting to the White House. An independent Texas oilman complained that Phase IV would "create confusion, calumny and possibly make liars and cheats out of those oil men not already afflicted with some weakness."[68] A Colorado energy executive told the Energy Policy Office's John Love, "The Living council's guidelines were put together by a very naïve group unknowing of the oil business, and I have to be very blunt in saying it is a nightmare . . . and will never work. It encourages cheating, dishonesty and is full of bureaucratic red tape."[69] George Bush, the GOP Texas congressman, had warned against this specter of government control, and now it was a reality.

By the fall of 1973, even before the Arab embargo, the administration was deep in the regulatory sandbox. As much as Nixon and his advisers had hoped to push hard to the right after his landslide victory in 1972, the worsening energy situation and the expectations of a broad majority of the country were preventing him from doing so. From the point of view of Texas oilmen, Washington was making the oil business very risky indeed.

2

Coming Up Dry

IN THE FALL of 1973, Americans were worried. Everyone seemed to know that demand for energy was running up against supply. But no one seemed to know what to do. Democrats on Capitol Hill were saying that the nation's politicians had no choice but to ration and allocate the fuel that existed. That way millions of families, factory owners, and farmers could count on getting enough to heat their homes, power their plants, and harvest their crops. Drivers across the country would also need to be sure they could fill up. Price controls, too, would have to stay in place. The year was 1973, the problems were new, but the policy solutions came right from the era of Franklin Roosevelt. Nixon seemed unable to stop this momentum. On October 6, when Egypt and Syria invaded Israel, all bets were off. John Love told Henry Kissinger, "It may be necessary to implement rationing."[1]

The End of Independence

Tensions had been on a low simmer in the Middle East since the Israeli victory in 1967. The Six-Day War had left Israel in possession of lands in the Sinai Desert and the Golan Heights, as well as the West Bank and East Jerusalem. The United Nations Resolution 242 provided for Israeli withdrawal in exchange for diplomatic recognition from its Arab neighbors. But in the years since, the possibilities for a permanent peace had stalled. In August 1973, Saudi Arabia's king, Faisal, secretly promised the Egyptian president, Anwar Sadat, to cut oil production if Egypt initiated a war. Feeling pressure from radicals within his own country to demonstrate his commitment to the Arab cause, the Saudi king publicly declared his willingness to use the oil weapon to support his Arab brethren in the pages of *Newsweek* magazine.[2]

President Nixon, in a September press conference, downplayed the threat. He did not think a war in the Middle East was likely. The conventional wisdom held that Egypt and Syria would act to reclaim lost territories only when they could score a decisive victory. Few thought that was the case. Moreover, the president and his advisers believed the Saudis would not risk their relationship with the United States, on which they depended for their security to repel Soviet influence. Without the Saudis, the other members of OPEC would have a hard time forming a united front. None, the thinking went, would be willing to risk cutting off their economic lifeline, which came from the sale of their oil. In early September, Colonel Qaddafi of Libya took the radical step of nationalizing control of the oil companies in his country, insisting that his government, not the oil executives, owned the oil and could set the price it sold for. But Nixon seemed unfazed. "If they continue to up the price," remarked the president, "they will lose their markets." "Oil without a market as Mr. Mossadegh learned many, many years ago," intoned Nixon, "doesn't do a country much good."[3]

The October attack by Egypt and Syria on the day of Yom Kippur, the holiest of Jewish holidays, took the White House by surprise. When Egypt and Syria sent troops into the Sinai Desert and the Golan Heights, they were counting on catching the Israelis off guard. Given that this was a day of prayer, Israeli forces were slow to mobilize, and the Arab powers scored initial battlefield victories. The Israeli army had more modern equipment and greater tactical strength, but Sadat hoped to force all sides to the bargaining table and end the stalemate.

The Arab advance startled and worried the White House, especially Henry Kissinger. Kissinger had assumed the position of secretary of state just two weeks earlier, while retaining his role as national security adviser. For Kissinger, the Arab-Israeli conflict was part of the larger Cold War struggle between the United States and the Soviet Union, with each supplying weapons to their regional allies. Throughout the Nixon administration, he had not ranked Middle East affairs at the top of his list of priorities, focused instead on Asia. At the National Security Council (NSC), Kissinger had centralized all foreign policy matters under his control, but the Middle East stayed in the hands of the secretary of state, William Rogers.

The goal in the region was stability so as to avoid giving the Soviet Union an opportunity to take advantage of unrest and increase its presence. Rogers had carried out a policy of aid to Saudi Arabia and Iran as the "twin pillars" of American-backed regional stability. This reliance on regional powers rather than American military forces emerged in the wake of domestic discontent over Vietnam. Announced in 1969 as part of the de-escalation in Vietnam, the so-called Nixon Doctrine committed the United States to a policy of economic and military aid to indigenous governments rather than direct intervention.

In 1973, American foreign policy was at a delicate point. The war in Vietnam had led many at home and abroad to question the military strength of the United States, as well as its overall strategy. In the run-up to the 1972 election, in an attempt to soften his image, Nixon supported a new policy of détente, intended to thaw Cold War hostilities, which included an arms treaty with the Soviets and Nixon's dramatic visit to China. As much as détente appeased Nixon's critics on the left and won his administration praise, it made the president vulnerable to attack from foreign policy hawks on the right. Any instability not only threatened to undo the progress made through détente but also gave its opponents a platform to push for a return to a more aggressive diplomatic stance. With the outbreak of fighting in the Middle East, it remained unclear how this conflict would challenge U.S.-Soviet relations.

In evaluating the situation, Kissinger did not focus on the internal dynamics between nations in the region, or on oil, so much as how everything affected the basic balance of power between the Soviets and the United States. Above all, Kissinger hoped the fighting would lead to a resolution of the tensions since 1967 and would neutralize this region as a source of ongoing instability. To achieve that goal, neither the Arabs nor the Israelis could be perceived as scoring a unilateral win. Kissinger did not want the Israelis to obliterate their opponents, nor did he believe that

Israel would be able to retain possession of the occupied territories, but he would not tolerate a loss. That would not only give the Arabs the upper hand in negotiations but also increase the Soviets' standing in those dealings.

According to Kissinger, the only solution was a U.S.-brokered peace, a position that grew organically out of his life experiences and his vision of foreign policy.[4] Born in Bavaria in 1923, Kissinger grew up as a German Jew who fled the Nazis in 1938 and moved with his family to New York City. Drafted into the U.S. Army five years later, Kissinger became a naturalized citizen through his military service as a counterintelligence officer stationed in Germany. Upon his return, Kissinger attended Harvard University, embarking on a long and distinguished career as a grand theorist of international relations. A believer in realism, as someone who harbored reservations about the intrinsic virtues of human nature and the democratic process, Kissinger argued at once for the greater use of diplomacy and a greater display of force, including the consideration of limited nuclear warfare. This perspective promised the possibility of moving the superpowers past the Cold War stalemate while also affording greater national security, a vision that won him support from Nelson Rockefeller and then Richard Nixon, who recruited him to the White House in 1969. For Kissinger, the first task was to get the Soviets to put pressure on their Arab clients to accept a cease-fire.

If the outbreak of hostilities caught American policy makers by surprise, they were even more unprepared for the use of oil as a weapon in this regional conflict. In September, the OPEC oil ministers had announced a meeting with the oil companies to take place in Vienna on October 8. Saudi Arabia's oil minister, Sheikh Zaki Yamani, made it clear that the oil corporations would have to allow a price increase. Yamani, who was born in Mecca in 1930, had spent time in the United States. Just as George Bush was traveling overseas to secure oil contracts for Zapata's offshore exploration, Yamani was receiving advanced degrees from New York University and Harvard Law School. Upon his return to Saudi Arabia, Yamani started his own law practice and soon rose in prominence, becoming the oil minister in 1962 as the country was reaping substantial revenues from its Aramco concessions. When Crown Prince Faisal became king in 1964, the two worked together to assure increasing revenue to finance the modernization and security of their country.

In 1973, the time was ripe for OPEC to strike. As the oil market was becoming tight and oil prices were rising, the majors were selling their oil on the market above their posted prices. But the OPEC countries still collected only 50 percent of the posted price. In Vienna, the majors offered an increase of forty-five cents a barrel. The OPEC ministers insisted on a price increase of 100 percent, seeking to raise the price from $3 to $6. Although no one discussed the outbreak of hostilities two days earlier, the conflict would likely drive prices up as buyers worried that the fighting might interfere with supply. When the major oil companies balked, the OPEC leaders decamped for Kuwait, where they would meet by themselves.

As the situation was unfolding, Nixon's attention was elsewhere. Day by day, he was becoming a weakened president. On October 10, days after the Arabs launched their surprise attack, Vice President Spiro Agnew resigned to avoid prosecution for income tax evasion and bribery. On October 12, Nixon announced that he had selected Representative Gerald Ford as a replacement. George Bush was among the names floated for the number two spot. But with the selection of Ford, who was the minority leader in the House, the hope was a quick confirmation from Congress, where Nixon's standing was in decline because of Watergate. On the same day that Nixon selected Ford, the House passed the War Powers Act, requiring congressional notification and authorization for the use of force, which the Senate approved.

With the Israelis facing the possibility of a battlefield defeat, Kissinger urged the president to authorize a resupply effort against Soviet-backed Egypt and Syria. On October 14, American flights stocked with arms and ammunition began arriving every hour in Israel. The flights were meant to fly under the cover of darkness, but when weather delayed the mission, the American planes landed in full view. There was no denying that the United States had entered the fray. For three weeks, with war matériel supplied by the United States and the Soviet Union, these Middle East countries engaged in the largest tank battles since World War II.[5]

On October 16, the OPEC ministers of the five Arab Gulf states along with Iran met in Kuwait and made a unilateral decision to increase prices from $3 per barrel to just over $5. This was the single largest price increase in the history of the industry. From 1945 through this moment, oil prices had stabilized between $2 and $3 a barrel. No longer did the oil companies set the price of the oil they pumped from the ground and distributed throughout the non-Communist world. From here on out, the oil ministers themselves would determine what price the companies would charge. The majors could accept this new arrangement or leave.

The next day, October 17, the Arab members of OPEC made an equally consequential decision: each producer would cut back its production by at least 5 percent a month for each month that Israeli forces remained in the occupied territories. Saudi Arabia, the largest oil producer—the only power with enough spare capacity to affect global oil supply through its unilateral actions—announced a 20 percent cut, with the threat of more cuts until Israel withdrew. At the time, the Saudis were producing eight million barrels per day, with the expectation that within a decade that number would go as high as twenty million to meet the growing demands of the West and Japan. A cutback seriously confounded those projections. Most of the other Arab producers opted for a 10 percent cut. The economic loss and security risks to Western Europe, where millions had recently switched from coal to oil for home heating, and Japan, which was entirely dependent on imports for its oil, were cause for great concern. After Nixon's public announcement of a $2.2 billion aid package to Israel, the Arab producers announced a total embargo on all shipments to the United States and the Netherlands.[6]

In a single blow, these Arab acts against the United States and its allies signaled a substantial shift in international geopolitical power to the Third World. The psychological shock was devastating. But it was the production cuts and the price increases that were most consequential, with each of those actions having a spiraling effect on global oil markets. "What the producing countries appear to have done is to have raised the price of running a factory, heating a home and powering a car around the world by an unprecedented degree," said the oil expert John Lichtblau.[7] These announcements brought the end of the concessionary era and the start of OPEC's assertion of its collective power.

Most stunning of all was the ability of the Arab producers to launch this assault without resort to conventional weapons of war. Rather than deploying warships, these leaders fought their battles by issuing a ban on the movement of oil tankers to embargoed countries and scaling back their production. Scaring other importing countries with possible cutoffs, the Arab producers relied on a divide-and-conquer strategy, attempting to isolate the United States from its allies. The Saudis also threatened to penalize the Aramco oil companies if they did not comply with the embargo. Already, the Saudi government owned 25 percent of the company. Under threat of total nationalization, the executives of Exxon, Mobil, Texaco, and Standard Oil of California, the four Aramco partners, agreed to cease future shipments to embargoed countries. "If we want to continue to do business . . . we must obey," explained an oil spokesman. As a publisher for *Petroleum Intelligence Weekly* put it, "The oil companies are policing the embargo for the Arabs."[8]

American policy makers now faced a difficult decision: What was the right response? The new secretary of state believed that he could broker peace between the belligerent nations. In Kissinger's view, oil was secondary. He was a political theorist, not an economist, and he believed that resource issues could be managed through American-led diplomacy in the region, trading security guarantees to regional rulers, especially to Saudi Arabia, which deeply feared Soviet interference, for continued access to oil. To that end, he sought to downplay the effect of the embargo so as not to give the Saudis and other Arab leaders the leverage they so desperately sought. He received help in delivering that message to the American public from the former secretary of defense Melvin Laird. "Buy a sweater," advised Laird, who was now the president's domestic policy adviser. "It might get a little cold."[9]

The new ambassador to Saudi Arabia, James Akins, had a different point of view on American interests. If Kissinger thought the key was to negotiate the terms of a peace settlement, Akins thought it was to capitulate to oil minister demands, or that is how his critics on both the left and the right saw it. On October 11, before he departed for Saudi Arabia, Akins appeared before the Senate Foreign Relations Subcommittee on Multinational Corporations chaired by Senator Frank Church, a liberal Democrat. Church took Akins to task for doing the bidding of the large multinational oil corporations, whom Church accused of benefiting unfairly from price increases. While Kissinger was seeking to sideline resource questions, Akins was warning publicly that the embargo would bring the United States to its knees. "We're not talking about one cold winter but many cold winters to come," said Akins. Upon his arrival in Saudi Arabia, the American ambassador received a tongue-lashing from King Faisal, who said, "I am an old man . . . Before I die, I want to pray in the Mosque of Omar" in Jerusalem.[10] Akins appealed to Aramco executives to put pressure on

American policy makers. "Urge that industry leaders in USA use their contacts at highest levels of USG to hammer home point that oil restrictions are not going to be lifted until political conditions are settled," he cabled.[11]

Secretary of Defense James Schlesinger thought that approach was disastrous. Schlesinger was an economist who, unlike Kissinger, made resource issues a priority. The armed forces were the single biggest consumer of oil. From his post in the Pentagon, he worried vitally about keeping American forces fully supplied. Rather than give in to Arab demands or rely on negotiations, the United States had to consider the possibility of sending its own troops to guarantee the continuing flow of oil. Kissinger disagreed. "He is insane," Kissinger told Alexander Haig, Nixon's chief of staff.[12]

Schlesinger was not insane, as his colleague knew, but he did operate from a different perspective from Kissinger. The two looked remarkably similar on paper: both were children of European Jews, both graduated from Harvard University in 1950 summa cum laude, both pursued graduate degrees from the same institution, and both were two of the most important, influential thinkers of post-Vietnam Cold War policy. But Schlesinger was deeply mistrustful of détente, disagreed that weapons systems should be bargaining chips in negotiations with the Soviet Union, and advocated strongly for building up American defenses.

Born in 1929, just before the onset of the Great Depression, Schlesinger grew up in New York as the son of middle-class German Jewish immigrants. Six years younger than Kissinger, he was not old enough to serve in World War II. After graduating from college, Schlesinger traveled the world and upon his return converted to Christianity and became a practicing Lutheran. After receiving his Ph.D. in economics, he quickly established himself as a national security and nuclear weapons expert. From his post at the RAND Corporation in Southern California, Schlesinger became a foremost authority on Cold War spending strategy. The Nixon White House recruited this young whiz to the Bureau of the Budget, where he developed a reputation as a committed cold warrior whose job was to repel attacks on defense spending from opponents of the Vietnam War. Schlesinger then chaired the Atomic Energy Commission. A serious birdwatcher and supporter of environmentalism, Schlesinger was also a strong nuclear advocate. He took his wife and two of his eight children to watch a nuclear test on the Aleutian Islands. In 1973, Nixon appointed him to head the Central Intelligence Agency. After several months, Schlesinger moved to the Pentagon. Few knew the ins and outs of defense spending and the nation's military capabilities better than he did, and the Middle East situation deeply unnerved him.

In all his political battles, Schlesinger had a key ally in Senator Jackson, who had recommended Schlesinger for his first Washington appointment. As Nixon and Kissinger were crafting a policy of détente, Jackson, whose advisers included Dorothy Fosdick, Richard Perle, Richard Pipes, and Ben Wattenberg, became a critic. As the son of Norwegian immigrants, he attributed his fears of the Soviets, who shared a heavily militarized border with Norway, partly to his "ethnic" inheritance. Jackson had entered electoral politics in the crucial year of 1940, when for Roosevelt partisans an interventionist foreign policy came to redefine the meaning of their liberalism. These feelings ran very deep, reinforced in no small measure by Jackson's visit to the Nazi death camp at Buchenwald two days after its liberation. He was an anti-Communist liberal in the late 1940s, battle scarred from confrontations with Seattle waterfront Communists, whose ideology and organization were more formidable than the Popular Front liberalism that Nixon swept aside in his 1950 California Senate campaign against the former Hollywood actress Helen Gahagan Douglas, "the Pink Lady." One senior Democrat explained in confidence, "Nixon was an opportunist capable of change, but Jackson is a true believer, a zealot, whose rigidity could land us in real trouble."[13]

The October Arab-Israeli War hardened Jackson's anti-Soviet views. "Without Soviet support and material encouragement, without Soviet training and equipment, without Soviet diplomatic and political backing, this war would not have been started," declared Jackson in a public speech. "And yet Dr. Kissinger, the Secretary of State, comes before the American people to say that Soviet behavior has been moderate and not irresponsible. I cannot agree."[14] Jackson routinely told audiences that the Soviets encouraged the Arab embargo and therefore bore responsibility for higher energy prices.[15] According to Jackson, the outbreak of war in the Middle East was only the most recent demonstration of the decline of American prestige and power. "The nation has lost its vision," said Jackson. "The problem began in Korea, which was a war without victory, and then was reinforced by the traumatic experience of Vietnam. Perhaps all this led to the social revolution—the mass drug problem and blatant sexualism."[16] And now the oil crisis threatened further national decline.

Even as Nixon came under pressure from his right for a greater demonstration of American force, he did not have that kind of maneuverability. A strong foreign policy response to the embargo was not, in 1973, a viable option. The White House was committed to détente, the public was reluctant to deploy troops in the wake of Vietnam, and few in the policy-making establishment or among the public thought the situation in the Middle East ranked as a national security threat that justified military action. On the day that OPEC announced the embargo, Senator Mike Mansfield, the Democratic majority leader, said, "I do not believe that we should become involved with American forces anywhere except as our national interest and security are at stake. One Vietnam is one Vietnam too many."[17]

If a show of force was out of the question, then that left domestic solutions to deal with the energy shortage. On October 18, just before OPEC announced the total embargo, Henry Jackson introduced the National Emergency Energy bill, a sweeping measure that called for standby rationing authority for the president and other major conservation measures to compel cuts in energy consumption by as much as 25 percent. At the same time, Congress took up Jackson's Petroleum Allocation bill, which required implementation of allocation rules for crude oil within fifteen days of passage. The embargo announcement gave these measures added momentum.

Nixon's rapidly declining political stature made a serious White House counteroffensive unlikely. On October 20, Nixon fired the special prosecutor Archibald Cox rather than comply with the demand to turn over taped recordings of Oval Office conversations that might reveal Nixon's role in the Watergate burglary cover-up. The press quickly dubbed this assertion of executive authority the "Saturday Night Massacre," and while Nixon might have temporarily headed off the investigation, his approval rating in the polls plummeted to 27 percent. On October 30, the House Judiciary Committee voted to open impeachment hearings against the president.

Nixon's political standing was at a low. As Patrick Buchanan told him, "The immediate need is to stop the hemorrhaging, to prevent the falling rocks from cascading into a landslide of defections." The RNC chairman, Bush, was traveling the country to defend the president and rally the troops.

When Georgia's governor, Jimmy Carter, questioned Nixon's fitness for office after he fired Cox, Bush flew to Atlanta to attack Carter before four hundred local Republicans at a $100-a-plate fund-raiser. It was one thing, though, to preach to the choir; it was another for Nixon to come back from an approval rating below 30 percent.[18]

The energy shortage made Nixon's return to popularity nearly impossible. The public was unhappy and even outraged over Nixon's handling of the Watergate break-in and subsequent cover-up. But the fuel situation hit them where it counted: in the pocketbook. In late October, John Love, the president's energy adviser, warned Nixon, "Considerable public fear and indignation, cries of industry conspiracy and government ineptitude, and possibly real hardships, appear imminent."[19] Nearly two weeks had gone by since the announcement of the embargo, and the president seemed frozen in his tracks. The pollster Daniel Yankelovich told Nixon's top advisers that this issue would "either make him or break him." "If people get the impression that no one is in charge, or that there is no advance planning, or that they are being asked to make sacrifices while the oil industry raises big profits," counseled the pollster, "they are going to get very angry and this issue will destroy Nixon."[20]

The start of the Arab embargo made a full-blown energy crisis—with gas lines, rising fuel prices, slowed employment, public panic, social chaos, and the president focused on this issue as his highest priority—a real possibility. Yankelovich laid out the political stakes for the White House: "No issue has such a potential for producing social instability of the magnitude of the depression as does the energy crisis. This crisis entails a radical change . . . Their lives will be disrupted and altered at the gut level." Residents of a small rural village in eastern North Carolina wrote to inform the president, "People are spending every waking hour worrying over the gasoline situation."[21]

Nixon understood these gut-level issues and had campaigned on them successfully in his 1972 electoral appeal to the silent majority, those who stood for so-called traditional values, did not protest in the streets or on college campuses, and yet had legitimate concerns about their economic well-being. But the energy shortages, rising prices, and now the embargo exposed the fragility of Nixon's electoral advantage. Faced with a major economic shock, millions of Americans, and their representatives in Congress, wanted not less government but more.

The president had to do something about energy, but, as David Gergen understood, "we face possible charges of ineptitude or even the cry that [the president] has cooked up another diverting dish." As George Shultz put it, "Crisis is upon us and time is short." Given his low standing, Nixon was operating from a substantial deficit. "Our margin for error has disappeared; our reservoir of credibility with the American people is dried up," reported Patrick Buchanan in what was beginning to seem like a statement of the obvious.[22]

One year after his landslide victory, Nixon's political stock was in shambles. At its annual convention, the AFL-CIO's president, George Meany, who in the 1972 election had refused to endorse George McGovern, a step that everyone understood as sympathetic to the president, called on Nixon to resign. On November 5, Senator Edward Brooke from Massachusetts was the first Republican senator to echo that sentiment. The *New York Times* columnist James Reston said this was "the greatest fall since Lucifer." Scoop Jackson was publicly putting pressure on Nixon to appear before the House impeachment committee. And Watergate was hurting the Republican Party. The 1973 off-year election results, for all of George Bush's efforts, were disastrous. In New Jersey, Democrats ousted the GOP, with Brendan Byrne winning the governorship in a two-to-one landslide, and captured the state government for only the third time in the century.

For Nixon, the paramount issue was how to lift the embargo. He believed that if he could announce this news, and prevent the shortages from becoming worse, he could survive Watergate. He feared, however, that failing on the energy situation would likely seal his fate and make a political comeback impossible. Nixon was a master politician who had a long, practiced history in orchestrating his political survival. Few were as astute as he was at understanding the kinds of pocketbook politics that made and broke politicians. And few were as opportunistic. Yet this was a difficult situation where there was no easy fix.

Within weeks, Kissinger successfully brokered a cease-fire between the warring parties, but the embargo remained in place, as did the production cuts and price hikes. After the cease-fire, Kissinger began his shuttle diplomacy in the region, meeting first with Anwar Sadat. Egypt had historically held the place as the key leader of Arab nationalism. That regional role had shifted to Saudi Arabia in the wake of the 1967 war losses. But it was

impossible to bring an end to the embargo without restoring relations between Israel and Egypt. As much as Kissinger attempted to persuade the
Arab countries that ending the embargo would facilitate the peace process, their leaders thought otherwise, believing that the oil weapon would
ensure a more favorable resolution.

In addition to their own internal politics, Arab leaders were further
emboldened by the defection of American allies and the apparent impotence of Nixon on diplomatic affairs. On November 6, the countries of the
European Community issued a joint statement, widely interpreted as pro-
Arab, supporting the withdrawal of Israel from the occupied territories.
That diplomatic decision reflected tense relations with these American
allies who were substantially dependent on oil from the Middle East. The
French diplomats pursued their own bilateral negotiations, and others were
wavering. "Europe, which gets 80 percent of its oil from the Mideast, would
have frozen to death this winter unless there had been a settlement,"
snapped an indignant Nixon.[23]

Richard Nixon was used to fighting from behind, and now he sought
to quell the nation's anxieties about the embargo's impact and assert his
leadership. On November 7, from the White House, he delivered a nationally televised address. "We have an energy crisis," acknowledged the president. The Arab embargo would result in the worst gasoline shortage since
World War II. "Some of you may wonder whether we are turning back the
clock to another age. Gas rationing, oil shortages, reduced speed limits—
they all sound like a way of life we left behind with Glenn Miller and the
war of the forties." But, he reassured, "there is no crisis of the American
spirit." "We are running out of energy today because our economy has
grown enormously and because in prosperity what were once considered
luxuries are now considered necessities," Nixon explained.

The solution, he said, was for Congress to support his Project Independence. Citizens might have to cut back a little, become more efficient,
but above all, liberation would come from producing more energy at
home, especially coal and nuclear. If Congress passed his deregulatory
agenda, Americans could continue to be the most prosperous people in
the world, with the highest standard of living, and they could free themselves from dependence on foreign oil. "Let us pledge that by 1980," said
Nixon, "we shall be able to meet America's energy needs from America's
own energy resources." The key to achieving independence, according to

the president, was for Congress to get rid of government regulations and make it easier and more profitable for oil companies to discover, refine, and distribute new domestic sources of energy. "We can't fight the economics of the market place," said Nixon to state and local officials.[24]

Earlier in his presidency, Nixon had adopted the liberal policies of his opponents in response to the country's problems. But he had to balance that impulse against the pressing political reality that he was now fighting to keep his job. The politics of the moment helped to push Nixon to the right as he sought to shore up support. Facing impeachment proceedings at the hands of a Democratic-controlled Congress, Nixon needed to win loyalty from congressional conservatives. Indeed, he closed his Project Independence speech with a strident announcement that he would not resign. "I have no intention whatever of walking away from the job I was elected to do," he said, looking into the television camera, before bidding the national audience good night.

The Country Gets an Energy Czar

While Nixon floundered, Scoop Jackson rushed to take the lead. As defiant as Nixon was, the situation was not looking good for the oil patch. Jackson's Petroleum Allocation bill already had substantial backing as the response to the summer shortages, and now it quickly became the solution to an international crisis. Allocation would not increase the supply or make any more energy available, but it did reflect the ongoing New Deal–World War II mind-set that in the face of crisis the government should shoulder the burden of distributing resources equitably. That was especially true when the public perceived Big Oil behaving badly. The new law, which Congress passed with large majorities in mid-November, required mandatory allocations on crude oil and its refined products to go into effect December 1.

An amendment to require mandatory rationing at the retail level—with consumers getting their own ration books—fell only eight votes short in the Senate. Jackson would not stop. He pushed forward with his broader emergency energy bill, which would require rationing, extend Phase IV price controls to all oil, and order a full public audit of oil companies to make sure they were not holding back on supply or profiting at the consumer's expense.

President Nixon tried to stop the momentum. From Disney World, Florida, with no apparent irony, he urged Americans to step up their voluntary conservation efforts. He demonstrated his own personal commitment, and deflected charges that he traveled too much to his home in Key Biscayne, by announcing that he was dispensing with the customary presidential backup jet that always accompanied the chief executive. Injecting some wry humor, he added that if Air Force One "goes down, it goes down—and they don't have to impeach." Citizens could avoid the nightmarish possibility of government rationing, he said, if they followed his example and cut back. Rationing would be a bureaucratic disaster. Nixon knew, he said, from his OPA days. Even so, he could not rule out the possibility. Indeed the front-page headline read "President Is Open on Gas Rationing."[25]

In the White House, George Shultz took the lead in rejecting a "rationing army" along with the CEA chairman, Herbert Stein. Both were rightfully quite worried. Despite "the President's clear aversion to rationing," Stein wrote to Shultz, "there seems to be a growing feeling around here that rationing is inevitable. I fear that this attitude will in fact make rationing inevitable." They objected on ideological grounds, and they were also certain that such a program would not only be ineffective but make matters worse.

Early on, they sought to derail a system of World War II–style rationing. The wartime OPA had distributed ration coupons, which entitled each driver to a set weekly amount of gasoline and no more. Shultz and Stein preferred a program in which citizens would be allowed to sell their government-issued coupons on a "white market" to other drivers for cash. That would in effect raise the cost of gasoline and would also eliminate the need for a massive bureaucracy to administer, enforce, and grant exemptions. They preferred, however, to scrap controls altogether. As these economists saw it, if the market were free to operate, prices would rise, which would reduce demand and match it to existing supply.[26]

Nixon was desperate to end the embargo and to demonstrate that he was in charge. To that end, he contemplated inviting King Faisal to the White House, where he could sit down and negotiate directly with the Saudi Arabian ruler. Kissinger quickly killed this idea. As he explained in a telegram to his deputy Brent Scowcroft, "An attempt to set up meeting with Faisal in Washington is total insanity . . . Only repeat only course that can work is course we are now on. Invitation to Faisal would be interpreted throughout Arab world as collapse. It would magnify, not reduce, Arab incentives to keep pressure on US via oil weapon."[27] At his first news conference after returning from his round of diplomatic talks, Kissinger said that the United States would not be intimidated by the embargo. Assuming an aggressive stance, Kissinger said, "It is clear that if pressures continue unreasonably and indefinitely, that then the United States will have to consider what countermeasures it may have to take."[28]

Americans began to feel the real impact of the embargo as the last of the tankers from the Middle East arrived and the first shortages appeared. The "Gas Scramble Is On," announced the *Washington Star-News*.[29] No one could know the exact severity of the decline in petroleum supply. The president himself suggested a possible shortfall of 17 percent. For the time being, the major oil companies were able to redirect resources from non-Arab sources to the United States. But additional production cuts, which the Saudis were threatening, would make this sharing more difficult and further strain America's relations with its allies. Moreover, suspicions ran high that without any official data on inventories the companies were holding oil off the market to drive prices up further.

To forestall an immediate crisis that winter, Nixon ordered the reduction in gasoline refining by 15 percent. That would allow for a necessary supply of home heating oil for the cold months. Nixon was trying to head off an acute situation in New England, where fuel companies were cutting back power. The Boston Housing Authority announced that it did not have enough oil to heat three major public housing projects and was running short for ten others. Many New England colleges extended winter break to avoid having to heat dorms.[30] The president also requested the closing of gasoline stations on Sundays to discourage weekend road trips and a lower, more fuel-efficient speed limit of fifty miles per hour.

Schoolchildren sent thousands of letters to President Nixon, which captured a new ethos of sacrifice. Teachers from around the country clearly prescribed this assignment. But that was the point; these letters reflected a new prescription that counseled personal restraint. Young students pledged support in saving energy. They would turn off lights, use less hot water, watch less television, and urge their parents to drive slower.[31] Nixon expressed gratitude for the children's willingness "to work, and give of yourselves, so that our country can be a better place to live."[32]

The mood could also turn ugly. If the president asked for sacrifice, then the public expected no less from him. "What right have you to abuse the position given you by riding around in a gas-guzzling limousine?" asked one resentful citizen. In the atmosphere of Watergate, the public was even more mistrustful. "We are angry and ashamed of the lack of credibility in the Nixon Administration," wrote this upset housewife. "When will Mr. Nixon relinquish his trips to Florida and California and behave in a manner of cooperation he asked of the people?"[33]

It became harder for Nixon to confront the energy crisis as the Watergate investigation came to focus squarely on him. Yankelovich distilled the problem: "how to secure public cooperation and avoid panic in the current climate of public mistrust and suspicion." Americans did not believe that there was a crisis as much as they believed it was a diversion. To the extent that a shortage existed, the public thought industry contrived it to extract higher prices. Confidence in business to serve the public interest had declined precipitously from 70 percent in the mid-1960s to 34 percent. Recent revelations of the oil industry's $5 million campaign contribution to Nixon raised further suspicions.[34]

A worsening situation, one with no clear end in sight, stoked social antagonisms. When asked to sacrifice, many Americans responded by defending their right to maintain their lifestyle while questioning the right of others to do so. The political direction in which the energy crisis was moving the country was hard to pin down. Even as many Americans railed against the business world and expressed frustration with the Nixon White House, liberal reforms that had generated controversy before the energy crisis now came under attack as luxuries the nation could no longer afford and should not have to. High on the list was federally backed school integration by busing, which in the early 1970s reached a peak of controversy. "Why must I avoid visiting a friend or running an errand when buses all over the country are driving children back and forth across cities?" one Tennessee housewife asked a sympathetic Nixon.[35] Another Tennessee woman protested against "this sinful practice of hauling defenseless children for miles upon miles through city streets," a practice she blamed as a "major reason for the present gasoline shortage."[36]

This solution to the energy crisis gained political backing in Congress. As the House took up Jackson's emergency energy bill, members voted 221 to 192 in favor of an amendment to ban busing. Representative John

Dingell, one of the leading liberal voices on the Hill and a drafter of energy legislation, claimed the measure could save millions of gallons of gas. Dingell represented part of Detroit and its suburbs, and although he supported civil rights legislation and even bused his own children, he opposed mandatory busing from the inner city to the surrounding communities. The energy crisis offered an opportunity to challenge this means of achieving racial balance in schools that he and his Catholic and working-class constituents thought violated their rights. Though this amendment was removed in conference, it inspired similar local actions. In Pasadena, California, the school board fought to eliminate busing.[37] In the South, mayors also proposed ending court-ordered busing as a way to save fuel. "The President is asking all of us to make a sacrifice," explained Ronnie Thompson, mayor of Macon, Georgia. "Maybe some of our liberal judges could make a sacrifice."[38]

Environmental reform also came under attack. The White House's John Love recommended junking air pollution emission standards, licensing nuclear reactors without public hearings, and revoking many other legislative restrictions on the energy industry. In an important and symbolic reversal, the administration allowed drilling to resume off Santa Barbara, the site of the 1969 spill. The Environmental Protection Agency permitted utilities to burn high-sulfur coal once again. And even congressmen sympathetic to environmental issues recognized the need for flexibility. To free up oil and gas, Senator Jackson introduced a bill to require power plants to switch back to their use of coal. And he also pushed the Trans-Alaska Pipeline through Congress, which the president gladly signed.[39]

The automobile industry seized on the energy crisis to fight back against emissions standards. Edward N. Cole, president of General Motors, declared that removing emission controls would save five billion gallons of gasoline a year, arguing that controls greatly reduced auto efficiency. That began a lobbying campaign in which auto dealers across the country, as well as individual car owners, protested to the administration.[40] As one Chicago resident put it, "Get rid of the damn emissions controls! What a waste of the precious energy." The House barely defeated a proposal to remove them.[41]

The Left believed that the energy crisis posed a real threat to liberal reform and to the economically disadvantaged. Grassroots activists mobilized to defend the rights of the poor. The Eau Claire County Welfare Rights Organization made it clear that Nixon's calls to turn down the thermostat did not simply require goodwill and a sense of patriotic sacrifice. "People with upper and middle class incomes will be able to provide their children with a sweater to wear at home and school and an extra blanket for their beds," these activists argued, while "mothers of A.F.D.C. and low income elderly people will be unable to supply these needs out of the monthly income that they receive."[42]

The Reverend Jesse Jackson, director of Operation PUSH, called for legislation to declare a moratorium on paying utility bills for those laid off as a result of the energy shortage. Jackson led a protest in downtown Chicago outside the Standard Oil headquarters with picketers carrying placards that read THE HOAX IS ON and OIL COMPANIES' PROFITS SOAR WHILE WE FREEZE. Vernon Jordan, executive director of the National Urban League, feared that "ruthless landlords" would use the crisis to turn thermostats down well below the recommended sixty-eight degrees. "The government shouldn't foster flu epidemics in the ghettos," he said. Representative Charles Rangel of Harlem was also concerned. As the journalist Eliot Marshall of *The New Republic* pointed out, "His constituents are happy when they're that warm in the winter. The congressman worries that patriotic landlords will dial down to 50 degrees and say the President told them to."[43]

Jordan and other black leaders feared that the energy crisis would serve as "the all-purpose alibi to justify further erosion of black rights." The antibusing amendment was a clear example. And Jordan felt certain that blacks would bear a "disproportionate burden" when it came to jobs. Walter Heller, Kennedy's CEA chairman, agreed that the crisis was likely to hit blacks hardest. "They take the worst drubbing," he warned. If the national unemployment rate advanced from 6.5 percent to 8.5 percent as projected, then black Americans could be looking at a rate as high as 20 percent, predicted Carlton Goodlett, president of the black press's National Newspaper Publishers Association. "The black masses faced with this bleak hopelessness will surely be propelled toward frenzied, sustained violence, the ultimate weapon of the oppressed," cautioned Goodlett.[44]

The energy crisis also became freighted with continuing dissent over Vietnam. Representative Elizabeth Holtzman, a Brooklyn Democrat, introduced an amendment to ban the use of oil for military purposes in South-east Asia, a measure that the House passed 201 to 172 and the Senate passed 60 to 33. For many, support of this ban flowed naturally from existing antiwar sentiment. For others, the energy crisis, along with the rapidly deteriorating economic conditions, made the cost of American interests in Vietnam seem too high. "My job is in jeopardy. Why should my tax dollars be used to subsidize foreign economies when my work is being taken from me?" a North Carolina man who supported the ban wrote to the White House.[45] Wasn't it unfair to ask Americans to sacrifice while, as one California woman put it, "you are sending millions of barrels of oil to Cambodia and So. Vietnam? We should come first!"[46]

As future prospects grew worse, the public became angry at government officials in Washington. If business contrived the shortage to make a profit, as many believed, the government failed to take effective action, either because of incompetence or because of some general notion of "politics." A Harris poll revealed increasing blame for business and government, with 83 percent of the public attributing fault to oil companies and 75 percent also pointing the finger at politicians. As the shortages continued, it appeared that Washington was lacking solutions. As one young mother from Toledo put it, "Is there anyone who cares, will listen, and Do Something?"[47]

The White House would have to take aggressive steps in handling the crisis. That was the conclusion of Roy Ash, director of the Office of Management and Budget (OMB), who told Alexander Haig, "Whether we like it or not, we must temporarily inject the government into the private sector in ways reserved only for emergencies." What he had in mind was astounding: "We've got to do so by starting with a state of mind *a la* the War Production Board . . . In effect, we've got to keep the American economy from failing, not just distribute the marginal discomfort." The time for action was now: "We need to get and keep in front of the problem, not just in speeches but in real world action, deep into the American economy." He argued that the Energy Policy Office was too ineffectual and policy making too diffuse. The White House needed to replace this office, which was largely window dressing, with a new agency, one at the cabinet level that had sole responsibility for allocation, pricing, and development of energy resources.

Ash's idea of a World War II–style War Production Board was alarming because it conjured up memories of total government regulation. The key factor, though, was that it was a wartime agency dominated by dollar-a-year businessmen. The head had been Donald Nelson, a former Sears, Roebuck executive. This new agency, too, had to have the right business leader at its helm, someone Ash called a "'doer'—an executive fully knowledgeable in managing workings of the real world economy and how to get things done in it."[48] If there had to be a new agency, then at least the White House and someone with the right credentials and conservative ideology could control it.

On December 4, 1973, Nixon announced that William Simon would become the head of the newly created Federal Energy Office (FEO). Simon was the country's most unlikely energy czar. Before coming to Washington, he was a partner at Salomon Brothers on Wall Street. Born in 1927, Simon grew up in Paterson, New Jersey, in a middle-class household, with a father who was an insurance agent. After serving in the army and graduating from college, Simon worked his way up as a successful municipal bond trader, where he was reportedly earning $3 million a year when he resigned to take up his post as deputy secretary of the Treasury in early 1973 with an annual salary of $42,500. He was fiercely committed to market solutions and had little faith in Washington bureaucrats. As he commented to Alexander Haig, "It is really quite an experience to work in a place that has more horses' asses than horses."[49]

Simon's appointment as energy czar came from the support of his key allies, his boss at Treasury, George Shultz, and CEA's Herbert Stein. William Safire called them the "free-market Mohicans."[50] It was widely reported that Love got pushed aside because he had supported rationing. Simon, like Nixon, saw rationing as "an administrative nightmare—an absolute last resort." Along with Shultz and Stein, Simon shared the belief that only the unfettered marketplace would end the energy crisis, in both the short and the long terms.[51]

But it was too late. Here was Simon, a proponent of the free market, sitting atop a new government agency. Soon Garry Trudeau would make the energy czar the central character of his *Doonesbury* cartoon strip, portraying Simon as having the great powers of a king. In one sequence, his secretary, who addressed him as "sire," asked, "Have you given any thought to speaking in the first person plural?" "Hmm," he replied, "we like that idea." The reality was that, whether he liked it or not, Simon presided over a massive governmental program of mandatory allocations and price controls that cut wide and deep into the economy.

From the moment he stepped into his office, Simon understood the pressure the White House was under. Gerald Parsky, Simon's legislative adviser, explained what was more than apparent to his new boss: "Congress wants action on energy policy and they are tired of getting blamed for inaction—they now want the lead."[52] With his years of experience, Henry Jackson was rolling over other members of his committee, especially the minority members. As a White House aide told the president, "Our troops on the Interior Committee . . . have a major inferiority complex when it comes to Jackson, because, frankly, he Scoops the hell out of them."[53]

The administration, its Republican allies, and oil-state congressmen were working hard to block additional energy legislation. For that, they had a new ally in Gerald Ford, who was confirmed as vice president on December 6. Ford was the choice of the inveterate Republican Party operator Melvin Laird. After enlisting in the navy during World War II, Laird served in the Wisconsin state senate, taking over his father's seat, and in 1952 he ran successfully for the House, where he served until Nixon recruited him as his first secretary of defense, a post he held until January 1973. Later in the year Laird returned to the White House to assist the White House as it was coming under attack. He strongly pushed for Ford as the nominee to orchestrate a smooth confirmation process and to forge closer relations between the White House and congressional Republicans.

Ford also had appeal as a conservative who knew his way around Washington. Ford was what Nixon was not: a Republican insider. Of course Nixon had as long a life in Republican politics as Ford had, and for the moment it was Nixon who occupied the Oval Office. But Ford, unlike Nixon, had built his career as a congressional Republican, committed above all to advancing the interests of the party. In 1972, Nixon did not campaign for the party or for other Republicans on the ticket, hoping instead to build a new conservative majority that transcended party labels. Now Nixon would need these GOP lawmakers as his allies if he were to survive the challenge to his presidency. With Ford's help, he could fight against Congress, engage in stalling tactics, and try to derail the liberals' agenda.

But Nixon could no longer deny what was a basic political reality. The White House was now officially in the energy business. With each bill and executive order, the government was becoming ever more enmeshed in the inner workings of this complex industry and, with each regulation, ever more implicated in the shortages that were developing. Incredibly interventionist, the newly enacted allocations, which Simon was tasked with overseeing, controlled to what industries, dealers, and regions the oil companies sent their products. They also required the major oil companies to sell a portion of their product of domestically produced oil, which was under price controls, to independent refiners who bought most of their crude overseas and were being priced out of the market. This "entitlement program" reflected the power of independent refiners and distributors, scattered across the country, to lobby effectively for their cause.

The regulations also mandated what the oil companies refined and when. For instance, it was up to the FEO to apportion the refinery mix between home heating oil and gasoline and dictate when the industry should switch from one product to another. Gerald Parsky, who was in charge of allocations at the FEO, put it bluntly: it was his job, he said, to decide how long drivers in each state should wait in line.

As soon as the new energy czar took office, William Simon announced the plans for mandatory fuel allocations at the wholesale level. At first, he said the cutback in gasoline dispensed at the pump would be 25 percent. The next day, in response to great outrage, he announced that the correct amount was actually 5 percent. But still Simon asked that drivers limit their purchases to ten gallons per week. Drivers would comply only if they felt such sacrifices were truly necessary. And therefore Simon was constantly telling the public that the energy crisis was real and that it would mean a serious change in lifestyle for Americans. Under the sign on the Federal Energy Office, someone penciled in, "Chicken Little was right!"[54]

Simon deliberately propagated a new conservation ethos hoping that voluntary restraint could help forestall more mandatory measures. Short of rationing or four-day workweeks—policies that were adopted in other countries—it was up to each citizen to change his personal consumption practices. Under Simon's leadership, the Office of Energy Conservation launched its "Don't be fuelish" campaign, sending out millions of decals for homeowners to put on light switches as a reminder to turn them off before leaving a room. The FEO urged Americans to carpool and was considering other recommendations like designating one day a week as a no-driving day.[55] Simon was fond of saying, "We are going to have to reduce our wastrel ways."[56] The nation's first priority, he announced at a press conference, was to "establish a new energy ethic."[57]

As much as Simon pushed for Americans to cut back voluntarily, as the nation's energy czar he had to make top-down decisions over seemingly trivial, though very symbolic, matters. When the Federal Energy Office issued a ban on holiday lights, it cut the Christmas season short. Kansas City's Country Club Plaza, the nation's oldest outdoor shopping mall, was traditionally the site for a spectacular holiday display. But now the government's order rendered the city's annual celebration unpatriotic. Immediately, the town center went dark. Senator Bob Dole, one of Nixon's chief congressional supporters, made a direct appeal for a presidential dispensation. Christmas lights "would lift the spirit of all" in this otherwise dreary holiday season, explained Dole. Nixon agreed and thus, rather than forgoing all decorations, the White House was lit with about 20 percent of the usual amount. Immediately, the Country Club Plaza executives figured out a comparably scaled-back display, and they turned the lights back on.[58]

The problem was that all restrictions seemed to have consequences greater than what Americans felt they could live with. Now, with their rules and regulations, Washington officials became the apparent gatekeepers to jobs, commuting, recreation, and many other facets of daily life. Given his disdain for governmental intervention, Simon regarded these decisions as distasteful. And it was unclear how to make them. Should there be high school football games at night or only during daylight hours? Should the Indianapolis 500 car race take place or be suspended? It was, after all, an enormously popular sporting event that drew 350,000 spectators and contributed to the regional economy. When the Federal Energy Office gave its directors permission to proceed, Representative William Hudnut III expressed gratitude for the administration's decision not to begin a "national retreat from auto racing." But why not? As one journalist put it to Simon, "How can you expect the general public to conserve, or truckers to hold the speed to 55 miles an hour, when this Government allows fuel to be allocated for this driving around in circles at 190 miles an hour?"

Simon's response that "it is part of Americana" was precisely the problem. What wasn't a part of American culture? If an energy-wasteful event still took place, it became tinged with a lack of patriotism or at least subject to scrutiny. Perhaps the crowd at the Indy 500 would still have fun. But racers had half as many days to qualify, and fans got to watch one week less of practice. Striking a compromise, the National Association for Stock

Car Auto Racing announced its decision to cut the Daytona 500 to 450 miles.[59]

The government, too, came under scrutiny. Alexander Haig personally monitored the progress made on White House conservation. Simon sent Caspar Weinberger, secretary of health, education, and welfare, a list of temperatures recorded in his department building, all of which were well above sixty-eight degrees.[60] The FEO greatly restricted the use of federal limousines by January 1, 1974. This led to much wrangling over who would still be able to justify their use. "You can bet that there will be camera crews in front filming White House cars going in and out of the compound" on New Year's Day, one top aide told Alexander Haig.[61] In the spirit of these symbolic politics, Governor Russell Peterson of Delaware, who now served as Nixon's chairman of the Council on Environmental Quality, switched from a chauffeur-driven limousine to a chauffeur-driven Ford Pinto.[62]

Wall Street had hailed Simon's appointment as signaling the defeat of rationing, but the energy czar was coming under pressure for greater governmental action. With the prospect of larger shortages, a majority of citizens supported the implementation of a federal system of distribution. "Equitable rationing is a MUST," wrote the employees of a small company in Illinois who advocated a World War II–type program. The FEO reported that it received more than two thousand letters and telegrams daily with the overwhelming majority in favor.[63] Governor Jimmy Carter of Georgia accused the administration of "gross mismanagement" and insisted that rationing was the only fair solution.[64]

As shortages worsened and the public's nerves frayed, Scoop Jackson and other Democratic leaders pushed forward with plans to subject the oil industry to even greater regulations. They called for measures ranging from the federal chartering of oil companies to a major public works program for those put out of work by energy shortages to freezing mass transit rates. As Jackson's energy bill worked its way through both chambers of Congress, it became more liberal, including the addition of a windfall profits tax to recoup the large gains the oil companies were making.

At William Simon's request, Gerald Parsky, his legislative aide, set up camp in Vice President Ford's new Senate office. Parsky made it his mission to defeat the windfall profits tax, warning of a presidential veto. While Parsky, Simon, and Roy Ash worked behind the scenes, oil-state senators led by Russell Long, Democrat from Louisiana, threatened a filibuster. Parsky also tried to eliminate the provision for congressional collection of company data from the oil industry, advanced by Representative John Dingell, who was fuming about what he believed was the gross deception by the oil companies. When Congress recessed in late December, its failure to pass an energy bill fanned liberal flames. "You're going to see the most punitive legislation in 1974 ever adopted by the Congress against any one industry," threatened Scoop Jackson.[65]

Nixon's Not-So-Silent Majority

On December 4, the ink had barely dried on the executive order naming Simon as the nation's new energy czar when he faced an immediate crisis. On the same day as his appointment, the simmering social unrest from the energy situation boiled over when one hundred long-haul truckers came to a halt on Interstate 80 in eastern Pennsylvania. These big rigs brought morning traffic to a standstill for fifteen miles near the Delaware Water Gap. Across five states, hundreds of truckers staged similar demonstrations on the nation's highways. The truckers were angry. They were mad about their search for fuel, mad that when they found it, it cost fifty-four cents a gallon, and mad that they got barely enough to make it to the next truck stop. As independent contractors who got paid per haul, they saw rising fuel costs, nearly doubled since the summer, come out of their bottom line. The person most responsible, the one they thought should do something, was Richard Nixon. "We want Nixon and his people, when they turn on their television sets, to hear us," said one driver who had parked his rig at the Delaware Memorial Bridge.[66]

The trucker blockades captured national attention because they were disruptive and also because they tapped into the frustration millions of other Americans were experiencing at the pump. "These men are the first victims of the energy crisis," said Ohio's governor, John Gilligan. The truckers were also exactly the kinds of voters Nixon had imagined as a prime part of his 1972 silent majority, and their protests made for good political drama. The truckers who led the strike had supported the Vietnam War, owned their own trucks, did not belong to the Teamsters, worked hard, and hated government bureaucratic red tape, such as weight and length limitations on their trucks, which cut into their earnings. Now these truckers took to the streets, adopting the collective action tactics of the Left. These "normally strong law-and-order men," reported a *Time* magazine journalist, had become the "new highway guerillas."[67]

What made the truckers' revolt so powerful was the way in which their grievances resonated with American politics at that moment. Even as Nixon had won in a landslide, the energy crisis revealed that there was no permanent new conservative majority, let alone a Republican one. These truckers were fiercely independent, yet they were also having a hard time making it on their own. William Hill, a steel hauler who had tried for years to organize them, captured the truckers' mind-set. "All these guys have that American dream, man, that they're gonna work hard and they're gonna be millionaires. And they'll own their own trucking company some day. Bullshit . . . Pretty soon they phase out of that and say 'Fuck it, if I can just keep *this* truck goin' I'll be O.K.'"[68]

Throughout the early 1970s, these long-haul truckers pointed to too much government regulation as the one thing that blocked their path to greater prosperity. Unlike the majority of the 400,000 truckers in the Teamsters, the 100,000 independents owned their own rigs and hired them out along with their services. They moved about one-third of the intercity goods. But the Interstate Commerce Commission (ICC) strictly regulated what truckers could haul and favored the large companies rather than independents in awarding licenses to carry goods across state lines. With restrictions on what they could carry, the independents saw the government as unfairly protecting the big companies from competition.[69]

The government also required all truckers to keep a log of their hours so they could document compliance with a mandatory ten-hour-per-day driving limit. It was common practice to keep two logs, one phony and the other off the record. "You can't drive 70 hours a week and make a living," reported Al Trafford. Trafford was a fifty-two-year-old owner-operator who leased his tractor to one of the larger interstate moving companies and had been driving trucks for over three decades. "I'm not a college graduate, and I know it. The D.O.T. knows it. Bekins [Van Lines] knows it. The rules ought to be changed." Another trucker put it more directly: "No bureaucrat's going to tell me when I'm tired."[70]

The truckers wanted to get government off their backs, and in that way their political ideology resonated with Richard Nixon's. Nixon's Project

Independence, which amounted to the deregulation of the oil industry, aimed its free-market rhetoric at them. Amid the great reforms of the civil rights era, which expanded government assistance for minority and impoverished Americans, the independent truckers felt as if their political status were slipping. Many of these social conservatives abhorred student protesters and civil rights demonstrators and were focused on their own entrepreneurial success. What they objected to most was a sense of entitlement among protesters from student activists to organized labor, including the Teamsters. These conservatives voted against welfare and busing, two programs that they felt doled out benefits from their hard-earned tax dollars to those who did not deserve them. Al Trafford, who was married, had four children, and owned a home in Westchester, New York, believed he could easily distinguish the difference between "niggers" and "colored." The former were on welfare and did not have good jobs; the latter owned their own homes, earned a decent income, and educated their children. "When they live on my block, they're colored," he said. "The colored on my block are my friends. They're so nice that after a while you don't know they're colored."[71]

The energy crisis was more than they could take. They needed relief, and for that they turned to the government to hold down prices at the pump, give them more fuel, and get the oil companies to comply. As the journalist Harry Maurer explained, the crisis "dealt a stunning shock to the truckers' philosophical and political framework. They believed passionately in free enterprise but they were going broke. They had voted eagerly for Richard Nixon but he was ignoring them. They called themselves independent but their livelihoods clearly hinged on the Arabs, the government, the oil companies—and one another. It was time for a change in their thinking."[72]

Pushed beyond their breaking point, the independent truckers took action. On December 4, soon after the first shutdown in Pennsylvania, eighteen hundred independent truckers blocked the Delaware Memorial Bridge in New Jersey, leading to a twelve-mile backup on Interstate 95 that lasted for seven hours. These owner-operators belonged to no national union and did not have any organizational structure, but the shutdown spread quickly because it tapped into building resentment. As Paul Dietsch, another driver, explained, "They're trying to win back recognition as good guys, as important people." Truckers also staged protests on the Indiana

Toll Road outside Chicago, and a thousand parked rigs closed down 112 miles of the Ohio Turnpike. In the South, twenty trucks tied up Interstate 40 between Little Rock, Arkansas, and Memphis, Tennessee. "We figured if trucks could do without fuel, the country could damn well do without trucks," fumed one angry protester.[73]

The political implications of the truckers' revolt were not lost on the White House. Nixon was the law-and-order president. But he was in a bind. The economic impact of dwindling energy resources was now causing problems with a segment of the constituency on which he counted, working-class Americans whose political support Nixon had solicited. The political threat to Nixon was clear. It was one thing to crack down on crime and even student protesters. But Nixon imagined these truckers as part of his base. Indeed, the blockades were meant to get his attention.

The White House held the first cabinet meeting in a month. The truckers' unrest was politically explosive. But with no good solutions, Nixon's advisers sought to keep the handling of this situation out of the Oval Office.[74] For the time being, all the White House offered was a tough stance against price gouging by dealers who sold diesel above price ceilings. The FEO said it would look into increasing diesel allocations, which were made from the same crude supply as home heating oil.[75]

The truckers wanted more than vague promises. Unless Washington guaranteed more fuel at affordable prices, the independents promised they would stage a national shutdown that would make these December stoppages seem like child's play. River Rat Edwards, one of the self-appointed leaders, told the news media the "public thinks you can wipe your feet on a trucker." The country "knows now we can shut it down." The truck blockades of early December were merely a taste of what was to come. Another driver threatened, "There ain't enough tow trucks on the whole East Coast to move us."[76]

The energy crisis reinforced a group consciousness. The recent proliferation of citizens band (CB) radios enabled truckers to communicate on the road to break a sense of isolation, warn each other of speed traps, and now coordinate mass action. Nothing bred camaraderie as much as a collective sense of victimization. When truckers stopped for fuel or passed each other on the highway, they could bond instantly over the hard times they were facing. Amid sky-high prices and scarce supply, routine discussions about fueling up took on a political cast.

In the midst of this chaos on the nation's highways, Congress passed a national fifty-five-mile-per-hour speed limit law to make this suggested speed compulsory. This measure had broad bipartisan support because it was a Band-Aid that seemed better than hotly contested alternatives to reduce consumption like a steep gasoline tax. The administration believed that no other politically feasible conservation measure would save as much gasoline as a national speed limit, which would require Americans to drive at more fuel-efficient speeds. The White House made it clear that individuals would have to sacrifice their driving before industry cut back on its use of energy, which might lead to a loss of jobs. Truckers drove for their job, and the faster, the better. The passage of the speed limit law, combined with the continuing scarcity of fuel and increases in price, guaranteed more truckers' strikes.

The energy crisis displayed and intensified the rank and file's capacity for radicalism. The independent truckers were becoming more self-conscious of their power. They had no fixed political identity, and they captured the plastic and politically ambiguous character of working-class consciousness at this time. These social conservatives had clearly rejected McGovern's brand of Democratic Party liberalism. But the extent to which they had become a solid part of the Republican electoral base remained open to question. The path from New Deal Democrat to the Reagan Democrat of the 1980s was not straight, and in the 1970s the economic crisis was creating a period when many politicians found it hard to discern which way voters were moving. A self-identified Nixon supporter wrote to the president, "Why must every crisis be dumped on the working man?"[77]

In the early 1970s, political elites on both the left and the right, from George McGovern to Richard Nixon to George Wallace, rediscovered and tried to capture the white working class.[78] Across the political spectrum, leaders expressed sympathy for their discontent. Senator Joseph Biden, a newly elected young liberal Democrat from Delaware, rushed to embrace the truckers. Biden gained some attention when he rode 536 miles from Delaware to Ohio on a big rig and experienced firsthand the economic squeeze that resulted from restrictive freight rates, reduced speeds, and rising fuel prices. He reported that hundreds of truckers he spoke with at stops along the way were "angry and frustrated." They felt "left out" without any political recourse, said Biden, who saw these truckers as only the latest oppressed group in need of government aid.[79] As one Missouri driver put it, "My Lord . . . I kinda understand why the younger generation puts on all these demonstrations and shit—'cause they can't get nobody to hear 'em."[80]

A *Boston Globe* journalist quipped, "Now let's hear it from all the apologists and lyricists of terror bombing, the scholarly sponsors of community action and participatory democracy and the theorists of political violence as constitutionally protected free speech. Hurrah for the truckers!" In a culture of "glamorized dissent," "who is to say that their convictions of unjust treatment by their government are less meritorious or less firmly held than a war resister's?"[81] *New Times*, a left-leaning weekly, ran a cover story by Studs Terkel, "The New New Left—A Trucker Speaks Out." The cover featured a close-up picture of a paunchy middle-aged owner-operator, one foot perched on the bumper of his big rig and a fist raised in the air.[82] There was something romantic and terrifying about this not-so-silent majority. Even if the truckers did not quite match the New Left's ideal image of the working class, theirs was indeed a democratic voice.

And they were not alone. Over the Christmas recess, congressmen returned to their districts to find angry voters. The driving public was experiencing a full-scale panic at the pump. William Simon sought to downplay the gas lines that were forming as nothing more than a "localized problem" brought on by holiday travel.[83] But to the public, lines that stretched for hours and snaked their way through local communities symbolized a national breakdown. In suburban Suffolk County, New York, 76 percent of the residents identified the energy crisis as the most serious problem facing the country, far outdistancing concern with Watergate at only 15 percent. Another poll of urban residents in the Midwest, the East, and the South found similar results. White House polling data confirmed, as one aide put it, the "overwhelming preoccupation with the energy issue, and a decided fall-off of concern about Watergate."[84] George Bush reported that voters cared deeply about energy, with one Louisiana state poll, for example, putting it above inflation, high prices, and Watergate.[85]

What created the panic at the pump? To be sure, public panic, once it set in, developed a momentum of its own. After the lines began, they did not end until the embargo was over. Uncertainty, as much as the actual shortage, triggered panic buying, which fed itself and even extended to other commodities. In late December, the *Tonight Show* host, Johnny Carson, made a joke about a shortage of toilet paper. The next day thousands of consumers made a mad rush to the markets, clearing the shelves of this bathroom necessity. Though this episode gave comedians fodder for more jokes, it also captured the sense of pandemonium generated by the energy crisis. In Japan, the oil shortages were causing such a serious slowdown that toilet paper and other basic commodities did run in short supply. That reality underscored the destabilizing effects of this global crisis and contributed to greater fears in the United States.[86]

Panic buying led motorists to line up even when their tanks were half-full. The situation was most severe in places more dependent on imported oil like the Northeast. Other states, too, experienced shortages for various reasons: some did not have good distribution facilities, others had a large number of independent retailers who were now hard-pressed to secure a supply, and others had a greater number of less profitable stations that the major oil companies simply shut down. States like California, New Jersey, and Georgia, which were all growing rapidly in the early 1970s, experienced serious shortages. The FEO used the 1972 consumption levels of each state to set current allocations; whatever each state had used two years earlier, they would receive 5 percent less. But for regions like metropolitan Atlanta or Los Angeles that were experiencing large population influxes, these levels were off, and the allocations exacerbated the shortages.

The absence of a systematic rationing government program, with clear rules, accelerated public panic. Instead, Americans got "rationing by inconvenience." Service stations closed on Sundays and reduced the rest of their weekly hours. Many stations limited the number of gallons for each purchase and sold only to their regular customers. Often motorists waited on long lines, with no guarantee of service. The journalist Judith Viorst got to her local station hours before it opened at 7:00 a.m., only to find fifty-one other cars in front of her. Although she tried to conserve, she complained, "I still spend a lot of my life buying gasoline."[87]

When they were able to find gas, Americans had to pay much more for it. In December, OPEC, led by Tehran, raised prices from $5.12 per barrel to $11.65. While Iran was not directly engaged in the Arab-Israeli conflict, its leadership was desperate to raise additional money for modernization and defense spending. That was the second doubling of prices in two months. In early January, prices at the pump went up 20 percent with FEO approval and were projected to rise even higher. Those increases translated into roughly $8 a month more for the average driver. Stations started pricing by the half gallon because the price on many pumps went only as high as 49.9 cents.[88]

By now, the public had little faith in Big Oil. The Arab embargo led to a sharp decline of available fuel, but Americans continued to blame the oil companies, not the Arab producers. Indeed, before the embargo, few Americans knew that the country had imported any oil at all. The animosity toward oil industry executives was extraordinarily strong. The consumer advocate Ralph Nader made regular news appearances to stoke the fires of suspicion. Instead of an international fuel shortage, Nader insisted the world was "drowning in oil." He declared this was "the most phony crisis ever inflicted upon a modern society."[89] Nader told the public that the shortage was all a big conspiracy to raise gas prices to seventy or eighty cents a gallon.

National news routinely reported the belief that the crisis was somehow the result of corporate manipulation. As Jules Bergman, ABC editor, put it to Simon, "There's widespread bitterness in the American people. Are the people being victimized by the oil companies so they can get higher prices?" Simon replied no, of course. He tried to dispel this "misconception" by reminding the viewers that OPEC had banned the shipping of oil to the United States. But he was less than effective as the public still searched for answers.[90]

On January 21, Congress's first day back in session, Scoop Jackson went on the warpath. In a gesture designed for maximum publicity, Jackson subpoenaed the executives from the seven largest American oil companies. Interrogating them at the same table where the Watergate defendants sat, Jackson demanded that these corporate leaders explain what he disparagingly denounced as their companies' "obscene profits." Exxon, Gulf, Shell, Texaco, Amoco, Mobil, and Standard Oil of California represented half of all sales of the American petroleum industry, and collectively their profits were up 45 percent from the previous year. Jackson played to public fears that oil executives were manipulating prices and supply to their advantage. How was it that, in the midst of an embargo, their profits had risen so substantially? The only explanation seemed to be that they were bilking the public, charging extortionist prices. Jackson suggested that the companies held back their inventory to make the shortage worse and thereby raise prices even more. With moral indignation in his voice, he announced, "The facts are—we do not have the facts."

Behind closed doors, Jackson was working with the administration to pass an energy bill, but publicly he was leading a well-orchestrated attack on Big Oil. He grabbed at national headlines, championing the independent station owners and consumers, calling for Big Oil to roll back the prices it was charging for gasoline. He aimed his performance as much at the television cameras, which broadcast the hearings live, as he did at these seven men sitting side by side behind one long table. Jackson was a master at using the media to his advantage. "The American people want to know why the prices of home heating oil and gasoline have doubled when the companies report record high inventories and stocks," he declared.

Jackson's questions appeared to confirm the public perception that the crisis was manufactured—that, in fact, the companies were holding back. He went on, "The American people want to know if this so-called energy crisis is only a pretext, a cover to eliminate the major source of price competition—the independents—to raise prices, to repeal environmental laws and to force adoption of new tax subsidies." Jackson led what the press called the "cheat probe," and he was not alone. His colleagues jumped at the chance to tar and feather these men. In a typical accusation, Abraham Ribicoff, the Democratic senator from Connecticut, charged the executives with "cheating the American public."[91]

The major oil companies took a lot of heat. Their officers could not deny that price hikes benefited their interests. In defending their record profits, these businessmen pointed to the need for capital to explore for new sources of fuel and expand refining capacity, an explanation defended by William Simon but ridiculed by Jackson. If the industry was so pressed for capital, why did Gulf, just weeks before, purchase Ringling Bros. and Barnum & Bailey circus? Ribicoff accused them of "reaping the greatest profits in their history" while paying the lowest tax rates of all manufacturers. This assault made national headlines for a week. As William Johnson, Simon's right-hand man, put it, "The majors have been remarkably oblivious to the need for a good public image. They have operated on a business-as-usual basis at a time when extraordinary statesmanship and self-sacrifice is needed."[92]

In their defense, the oil executives explained the situation as they saw it. They were doing their best under difficult circumstances not of their making. They were working hard to offset the impact of the embargo by diverting non-Arab oil to embargoed countries. They explained that government policies in the United States amplified the shortage. As a result of the recent reduction in the oil depletion allowance, they claimed they had inadequate tax incentives to discover new oil. They also insisted that they would need even bigger profits in the future to finance additional supplies of energy, which would be harder to extract. In response to the specific charges of price gouging, they claimed that the advance in profits from the previous year resulted from a poor performance in 1972.

The oil executives did understand that the political landscape was changing. Some had made campaign contributions to Jackson, and now they felt betrayed and even vulnerable. Shell's Harry Bridges explained, "For us to stand on our soapbox and talk about going back to the free market would be political suicide . . . the surest way to be nationalized." That was an unlikely outcome. But liberal Democrats were calling for the breakup of the majors, sponsoring measures for divestiture to separate the exploration, refining, and retailing parts of the industry, while Ralph Nader and George Meany repeatedly proposed that oil be turned into a public utility. The oil executives were running scared. On *NBC Nightly News*, Jackson promised to go after the executives until "they are in their birthday suits." After the hearings, Gulf's president, Z. D. Bonner, said, "They made me feel I was at a criminal trial."[93]

Perhaps the leading symbol of the oil industry's declining political status was the attack on the oil depletion allowance. This had been a prized policy for the oil industry, one the House Ways and Means Committee had protected for decades. Throughout the 1950s and 1960s, liberal reformers waged unsuccessful campaigns to get rid of this most hated tax concession, and now the death of this special provision seemed likely. The world the oil industry had known seemed forever changed. As another oil executive explained, "Whenever we got into trouble, we always went to Sam [Rayburn] and LBJ to get us out. We never prepared for the day when liberals would be in charge in Congress. That day has come."[94]

The White House accused Jackson of demagoguery, and *The Wall Street Journal* chimed in: "With blood in its eye, Congress seems bent on smashing [the oil industry]. And if there are not sufficient numbers of clear heads in Washington to resist this wrecking crew, there will soon be a lot more retribution and a lot less energy." In his desire to win a national reputation, Jackson was threatening vital American interests. The *Journal* noted that in spite of record profits, oil stock prices had plummeted because of the fear of congressional retribution.[95] *Human Events*, a leading conservative journal, denounced Jackson's witch hunt against the oil executives, accusing him of "mercilessly berating" them. "The senatorial lynch mob was searching for a victim," and the executives "had been targeted for the honor." This was all quite perilous, though, and could spell disaster if their attacks gained traction. Senator James Buckley, a member of New York state's Conservative Party, warned that the "danger in this mad stampede to punish the producers" is that "it'll wind up making a temporary shortage a chronic one."[96]

In late January, with the profit scandal as backdrop, leading liberals amended Jackson's energy bill to include a rollback of crude oil prices, a measure with wide support among the Democratic membership. Far more radical than a windfall profits tax, this would mean the extension of price controls to all domestic crude. Senator Walter Mondale of Minnesota introduced rollback legislation along with Senators Ribicoff, Edward Kennedy, Edmund Muskie, Thomas McIntyre, John Pastore, and Lee Metcalf. This measure, they explained, was justified by the "unconscionable rises" in domestic oil prices.

The only fair thing to do was to push back the price to November 1, 1973, a date that preceded OPEC's drastic price hike to $11.65 a barrel in December. If enacted, this rollback would entail a significant price cut. Jackson, who quickly scrambled to attach his name to this proposal, promised that the rollback could mean slashing prices at the pump as much as five cents a gallon. Tapping into a long tradition of antimonopoly sentiment, Jackson said this was the only responsible course of action. The idea was simple: Big Oil controlled too much of the market, and it used that power unfairly against American consumers. Lower prices, mandated by the government, would not bring forth more oil. If anything, this remedy would make the problem in the oil patch worse. But for now this was the politically popular solution. If the United States wanted OPEC to roll back prices, asked Jackson, then "why don't we roll back our own Arab cartel prices?"[97]

While Nixon came into office talking about law and order, the panic at the pump threatened to bring chaos to the streets. From the angry truckers on the nation's highways to Americans waiting on long gas lines to the restless legislators in Congress who were demanding that the government intervene, President Nixon was under immense pressure to do something.

The oil crisis was wreaking havoc on politics, on the economy, and on daily life. In this context, the public, even its more conservative elements, could become radicalized. "We need price rollback at the gasoline pump," wrote Ruth King, a Nevada housewife, to the president, signing her letter from "one of the silent majority."[98] Just as the president was trying to survive an unfolding scandal that threatened his demise, he was facing an economic crisis that appeared to be spinning out of control.

Part II

Washington Conservatives

3

Turning Right

WILLIAM SIMON'S WIFE, Carol, stopped filling up her car at the local gas station. With angry drivers everywhere, Mrs. Simon feared being recognized as the wife of the energy czar. She had done her part to save energy during the embargo. "Casseroles, candlelight, and fewer baths," this forty-one-year-old mother of seven replied when asked how she managed to conserve fuel. She encouraged her children to pitch in too: their six-year-old daughter, Katie, had given up her night-light. After months of daily inconveniences, however, the "czarina" had had enough. As William Simon recounted, "That normally cheerful, loving, upbeat woman sprang at me like a cobra." "Do you know how long I waited in line?" his wife shrieked. "You have to do something." His response: "Et tu, Brute?"[1]

Crackdown

On January 30, 1974, when President Nixon delivered his State of the Union address, he was desperate. Scoop Jackson was pushing forward on rolling back the price of crude oil. The gas lines were longer than ever. And the nation's truckers were threatening to go on a countrywide strike the next day. The House Judiciary Committee was also moving forward with its Watergate investigation. With these concerns in mind, Nixon told Americans the embargo would soon be over. "I can announce tonight," said Nixon, "that I have been assured, through my personal contacts with friendly leaders in the Middle Eastern area, that an urgent meeting will be called in the immediate future to discuss the lifting of the oil embargo. This is an encouraging sign."

Nixon was bluffing. Henry Kissinger was making progress in the negotiations with warring countries. But there was no deal on the table. In the days leading up to the speech, under White House pressure, James Akins, the American ambassador in Saudi Arabia, pleaded with King Faisal to allow Nixon to say something. But Faisal made it clear that any public pronouncement would likely backfire, with his then needing to prove the Saudis' allegiance to the more radical Arab states. While Faisal required secrecy and discretion, Nixon's desire to save his career had pushed him to go public. Kissinger was upset. If anything, Nixon's comments would prolong the boycott until the Saudi king could restore his credibility among his Arab allies.[2]

And the speech didn't work. The next day, January 31, 1974, the truckers made good on their threat and shut down the nation's highways. These workers were in no mood for Nixon's promises. Their number one demand was a rollback of oil prices, and they wanted to force Nixon's support of them. The December stoppages had spawned a crop of newly formed truckers' associations, gave the truckers a taste of their power, and mobilized them. They were organized, ready to go, and prepared to take any action necessary.

Parking their rigs on the highway provided an immediate sense of strength and gave leaders a platform to demand price rollbacks. Across the country, long-haul truckers turned their ignitions off and refused to move. "We've definitely been mistreated by Washington," said River Rat Edwards, one of the leaders from the December stoppages. "I think we are a long way from ending this mess."[3] Members of the United Truckers of America, a group that had recently emerged, blockaded many of the nation's thousand diesel fuel stations to prevent nonstriking truckers from refueling. Ginger Bays of the Texas chapter explained, "Our keys are out of our trucks. We're not going any farther." Billie Gentry, a co-organizer of the Texas strike, explained, "We don't want any violence. We want to talk to some government officials about our problems."[4]

But the strike was violent. To shut down all commerce and halt all truck drivers, the strikers slashed tires, cut brake lines, and littered the highways with nails. Arsonists set aflame fuel tanks and big rigs, and gunmen opened fire on noncomplying trucks. Younger drivers who had served in Vietnam compared the highways to a combat zone. On the first day, more than one hundred truckers were arrested in Ohio, and in Pennsylvania a striker dropped a rock from an overpass, smashing a passing truck's windshield. The driver, thirty-three-year-old Ronald Hengst, died when he lost control of his truck and crashed. Pennsylvania, Ohio, and West Virginia were struck the hardest, but by the end of the day the strike affected forty-two states. CBS interviewed an Arizona female truck driver who claimed she was dragged out of her truck and beaten until two other nonstriking drivers came to her defense with a shotgun.[5]

William Simon tried to reassure the nation's governors that the shutdowns were nothing but "the irresponsible actions of a militant few."[6] But the situation on the ground and the broadcasts on the nightly news suggested otherwise. There were hundreds of thousands of drivers off the road; the independents, who led the strike, numbered more than 100,000, and many of the Teamster long haulers turned off their engines, partly out of sympathy and partly out of dread of attack from the strikers. With the prospect of all interstate highways shut down, the strike generated fears of anarchy and chaos, and the White House had no plan. Nixon was not prepared to give the truckers what they wanted. If the strike lasted more than a week, it would cripple the economy. What was the outlook, according to the Labor Department's Richard Schubert? "In brief, not good."[7]

With the White House offering no public comment, Governor Milton Shapp of Pennsylvania stepped in to fill the breach. Shapp faced a complete breakdown of commerce and traffic in his state, and he also harbored presidential ambitions. A Kennedy Democrat with strong support from the AFL-CIO, liberals, and minority voters, Shapp had once driven a truck delivering coal, and now he expressed sympathy for the truckers. Two days into the strike, with Nixon silent, Shapp appointed himself chief negotiator. He invited truckers, congressmen, other governors, and the president to a meeting at the Statler Hilton hotel in Washington on February 3. Facing the prospect of bare supermarket shelves and idle factories, Shapp put it to Nixon bluntly: "Either we find [a] way for independent truckers to continue operation profitably or we face [the] possibility of continued unrest and national economic collapse."[8] But the president ignored him.

The truckers demanded a rollback in fuel prices to May 1973, which meant cutting diesel prices from as high as sixty cents to thirty-three cents a gallon. More than twenty truckers' groups sent representatives from across the country to meet with Shapp. They appeared like a motley crew, some wearing suits, others sporting cowboy hats and big belt buckles, but they stood united behind this key demand. They also insisted on a price freeze for ninety days, a 5 percent freight rate increase, and a greater diesel allocation. Their rigs held two or three hundred gallons, but many drivers could get only twenty-five gallons each time they fueled up. Les Salsgiver of the Council of Independent Truckers explained, "I've been lucky to make it from one truck stop to the next." On average, the trucks got five miles per gallon. That meant they had to stop every few hours for gas, a delay that slowed them down considerably, and for truckers time was money. They also sought an end to the fifty-five-mile-per-hour speed limit plus a relaxation of load limitations.[9]

Shapp asked the strikers for a forty-five-day moratorium while he worked on these demands. But the truckers rejected his plea, skeptical that in the absence of a strike more talk would yield anything. It also seemed unlikely that Shapp, whose calls were not accepted at the White House, was in a position to deal. Michael Parkhurst, who had emerged in December as one of the truckers' spokesmen, boycotted the meeting, dismissing it as nothing more than a "publicity gimmick."[10]

The White House was worried. Behind the scenes, the Office of Management and Budget set up an interdepartmental crisis management group. The two point people for the White House were Michael Raoul-Duval, a member of President Nixon's Domestic Council, and Frank Zarb, who worked for Roy Ash as associate director at the OMB. In the Ford administration, Raoul-Duval and Zarb would assume responsibility for energy policy, having learned firsthand how explosive the energy crisis was. Raoul-Duval took the lead and told members to act in a "confidential and low key manner to avoid creating a crisis atmosphere." That was precisely because they knew how combustible the situation was. "Parkhurst wants to bring the USA to its knees," wrote Raoul-Duval in his personal notes.[11]

To the meeting at the Statler, Raoul-Duval dispatched Willie Usery. Usery had many virtues. As director of the Federal Mediation and Conciliation Service, he was outside the Labor Department. This was not a regular contract dispute with clearly elected union officials, and thus, to avoid giving the strikers legitimacy, the White House ordered Labor to stay out. Usery was also a strong Nixon supporter, one of the few laborite people in the administration. He came from the machinists, and though he had considered leaving government service to return to the AFL-CIO, he decided to stay on to distance himself from George Meany's call for Nixon's impeachment in early January. For his loyalty, Ford would appoint him secretary of labor. Not the least of his virtues was his skill and reputation as a tough negotiator. "He can sit there all night," remarked George Shultz. To which Nixon replied, "Yes . . . he has got as much stamina as Kissinger." Sending him into the line of fire with little to offer, Raoul-Duval remarked, "Usery must have enough guts."[12]

When Governor Shapp convened his February 3 meeting, Scoop Jackson was there. The state of Washington had experienced little violence, but the truckers' demand for a diesel price rollback fit his agenda, and therefore he rallied to their cause. "We're going to roll back those terrible increases in domestic crude prices," he told them.[13] The truckers were the vanguard of what could become a groundswell of support for the rollback legislation in Congress. The White House understood this. Under pressure, William Simon froze diesel fuel prices at the pump for thirty days.

That was not enough to get the wheels rolling. Over the next week, there were 228 highway shootings spread across twenty-nine states. Outside Pittsburgh, a bomb exploded under the Pennsylvania Turnpike. An eighteen-mile stretch of Maryland highway became known as the "corridor of fear." An Iowa trucker was beaten and stabbed in Chicago. In Delaware, a car pulled up alongside a truck, and its passenger shot Claude Nix, a trucker from St. Stephen, South Carolina, with a 12-gauge shotgun.[14]

What was the cause of the violence? In part it stemmed from the logistical challenges in staging a successful long-haul trucking strike. The independents did not belong to a union; the associations that had sprung up lacked cohesion; and the strikers lived and worked literally all over the country. Without a factory, an office, or a mill, it was hard to pull off a united, well-coordinated effort. To compensate, many independents sought to choke off traffic at strategic locations like state border crossings, and they also staged park-ins at truck stops. The strikers made wide use of CB radios to intimidate nonstriking trucks and force them off the road. Twelve strikers descended on a truck terminal in Woodville, Ohio, announcing, "It will not be safe to operate tonight, all overpasses will be covered with men with bricks and clubs from Ohio to the Michigan border."[15]

Truckers on both sides, striking and nonstriking, were heavily armed. Many came from a rural background where guns were a part of life. John Elliott, a truck driver for seventeen years who partnered with his wife, refused to be intimidated: "They're taking away my right to earn a living." Both he and his wife carried guns. After one encounter in which he was shot at and held his fire, he set out again: "This time, I'll do the shooting if anything gets in my way."[16]

The government also contributed to turning the highways into zones of armed combat. Governors called out the National Guards in Pennsylvania, Ohio, Illinois, Indiana, West Virginia, Kentucky, Maryland, and Michigan to patrol for snipers and rock throwers. Five counties in West Virginia declared martial law. In several states, local leaders ordered police convoys. In Iowa, a fleet of a hundred trucks carrying over $1 million in processed meat received an escort from the highway patrol, the National Guard, and police helicopters. The group traveled with its own private fuel tankers because all of the region's truck stops were closed.

These state officials were not only concerned about injury; they feared even more the impact on their states' economies, which was very real. Truck traffic declined by more than half in states across the country. In some regions, the drop-off was considerably greater. Southern citrus growers halted all shipments north, midwestern meatpackers shut down, and the auto and steel industries were watching carefully. In Ohio, Republic Steel laid off thousands of workers. After a few days, the shutdown put at least 100,000 people out of work, and the numbers were rising.

Consumers, too, were feeling the impact. Meat supply was down 40 percent in New York, and Massachusetts shoppers faced shortages of milk, poultry, and eggs. In Boston, the Stop & Shop supermarkets rationed beef and flour to their customers. In Nelson County, Kentucky, three thousand gallons of milk cascaded out of a truck when a sniper shot three bullets into its tank. The Great Atlantic & Pacific Tea Company launched "foodlifts" by United Airlines to get beef to its East Coast stores.

McDonald's, too, hired commercial planes to distribute its hamburger patties to retailers.[17]

Worst of all, the strike magnified the shortages of gasoline. The shutdown resulted in the driest days since the embargo had begun. At the end of each month, gas stations were low on fuel, having used up their monthly allocations, and the blockades prevented restocking. The *Chicago Tribune* headline read "The Week That Was—Panic at the Pumps." "No Trucks, No Gas, Angry Motorists," proclaimed the New York *Daily News*. The situation was particularly acute in New England, where shortfalls ranged from 20 to 40 percent. One in four New York City gas stations closed its doors. Lines in New Jersey were over a mile long, and Senator Clifford Case telegraphed Simon to warn him that "the situation is rapidly becoming explosive" with fistfights breaking out at gas stations.[18] Tampa and Pittsburgh had barely any fuel, and in New York, Maryland, and West Virginia schools closed down when buses could not get gas.

Time magazine announced that "gasoline fever" was plaguing the nation. Motorists everywhere were desperate to tank up whenever possible. Like the truckers, frustrated motorists could turn violent. "If you can't sell them gas, they'll threaten to beat you up, wreck your station, run you over with a car," reported one Miami Amoco station owner. In Lexington, Massachusetts, a local Texaco dealer confirmed the chaos: "They've broken my pump handles and smashed the glass on the pumps, and tried to start fights when we close. We are all so busy at the pumps that somebody walked in and stole my adding machine and the leukemia-fund can."[19] What would one factory worker who was waiting in line do if the gas station ran out before he got to the front? "Probably bomb the place," he told a reporter.[20]

Even if drivers could get gas, the truckers' strike could still cause great inconveniences. At 7:00 a.m. on February 6, Gene Lopez, a twenty-five-year-old truck driver from Metuchen, New Jersey, jackknifed and unhitched his trailer in the Holland Tunnel between New York City and New Jersey. This one-man protest caused thousands of cars to be backed up for miles during the morning rush hour.[21]

The psychological impact of truckers raising hell on the highways also took its toll. Two hundred trucks staging a park-in in Breezewood, Pennsylvania, instilled both awe and fear. Truckers engaged in demonstrations as far apart as Concord, New Hampshire, and Phoenix, Arizona, where in both cities hundreds circled around the capitol buildings in protest. The scope of the shutdown was impressive and scary, with incidents occurring in nearly every state. The public hardly took comfort from the attorney general's remarks at a press conference. When asked why the government failed to halt the violence, William Saxbe responded defensively that it was indeed hard to stop "a person off in the woods at the side of the highway, 200 yards, with a high-powered rifle shooting at anything that moves."[22]

Much of the media celebrated, or at least gave airtime to, the image of the truckers as authentic, hardworking Americans who had been wronged—wronged by the oil companies and now by Washington policy makers who were not coming to their defense. Jimmy Hoffa, the former head of the Teamsters, said on CBS, "They're entitled to make a profit and a decent wage."[23] On the *Today* show, Wilbur Moore, truck driver of the year, said the strikers suffered from the same plight as all other drivers; they too were the victims of price gouging and scarce supply.[24]

With federal policy makers unwilling to act, the nation's governors stepped in, with many implementing their own "odd even" rationing programs. Owners of cars with license plates ending in even numbers could buy gas on even calendar days, and vice versa for odd-numbered plates. Oregon put in place the first program, followed soon by Hawaii. When "inconvenience . . . disintegrated into chaos," Governor Francis Sargent of Massachusetts did the same; gas was available to each driver only half of the week, and not at all on Sundays, when all stations were closed. Fifteen states, including New York and New Jersey, and the District of Columbia adopted alternating fuel purchase days, and nine others drew up plans.[25]

At a press conference, a White House reporter suggested to William Simon that the truckers' strike was "simply the tip of the iceberg of vast popular discontent with the fuel situation." Simon conceded the point: "The American people are confused about the energy situation and in many instances angry. I don't suggest that anybody likes to wait in line an hour . . . or two . . . for a ration of gasoline." For him to respond otherwise would have strained credulity.[26] But beyond the thirty-day freeze of diesel prices, Simon offered nothing else. When asked about rationing, he heralded the local initiatives as a great success. "The states can do it better than a Washington bureaucrat can."[27] Milton Shapp denounced Simon's comments as an "abdication of federal leadership." "To pass the buck on rationing to the states . . . cannot resolve the problem," said the governor.[28]

The public agreed. To them, the energy crisis stemmed not from a shortage of gas but from a shortage of effective government leadership. Less than 20 percent of the public believed the crisis was real; instead, they thought the companies orchestrated a conspiracy, with the help of their political allies, to force prices up. In Miami, where 75 percent of stations were shut down, an angry motorist barked, "There's no shortage at all—they're full of baloney." One New Jersey driver told an NBC reporter, "The government ought to be shot—it's a hoax."[29]

The White House was taking a hard line. It looked as if Jackson's energy legislation would easily pass both houses and would include a price rollback provision. Ken Clawson, the White House communications director, told Alexander Haig, "Let me remind you that every poll shows energy to be the number one concern of Americans."[30] But the administration would not budge on rollbacks. They sound good, said Secretary Shultz before the House Ways and Means Committee, but they would destroy the domestic oil industry. Investment would dry up if the industry came to be "governed primarily by the laws of politics rather than the laws of economics."[31] In his annual economic message to Congress, the president said, "These experiences [with controls] have confirmed the view that the free market is, in general, our most efficient system of economic organization." Delivering the speech during the strike, Nixon made it clear that the White House was not caving to any popular demands.

The Watergate investigation was pushing Nixon further to the right. As the investigation drew closer to the president, it weakened his capacity to take independent action. Conservatives worried that this weakness would make Nixon less able to resist liberal measures. But the political calculus within the White House, which was becoming more bleak by the day, was that the threat of impeachment made the president more dependent on conservative allies. As Alexander Haig put it, "the need to hold in line our traditional support" was essential.[32] This group, of course, despised the idea of a rollback. Senator Paul Fannin of Arizona, the administration's main Republican ally in opposition to Jackson's energy bill, told NBC that rollbacks would not look nearly as attractive to the consumer who "may lose his job if [this] half-baked scheme is enacted."[33]

Governor Meldrim Thomson Jr. of New Hampshire, a prominent conservative, captured this right-leaning perspective in a direct appeal to Nixon. He saw the current situation as only the latest battle in a grand historical struggle between New Dealers and their opponents. Thomson condemned Simon's freezing of diesel prices as a misguided response forced on the White House by political expediency. "Freezing fuel prices at the nozzle . . . is no more the answer to the truckers' problems than a pail of water would be for a raging fire," he told the president. The truckers' problems stemmed from "archaic" Interstate Commerce Commission regulations that restricted rates and market entry and that only regulatory reform would fix. That was the conservatives' cure—less government. "Live free or die," the New Hampshire state motto, symbolized this antigovernment spirit.

Instead of freezes and rollbacks, Thomson urged Nixon to stand up for the "free enterprise system that challenged every man to do his best for the highest possible reward . . . We need your positive leadership to see that that great system is promptly relieved of the stifling web of bureaucratic restrictions." The problem was that Nixon was responding with more bureaucracy. "Rationing, striking and price controls must never be America's ultimate answer to economic woes," said Thomson, who saw America's future on the line. He continued, "We must lay aside old ways and old habits or we shall quickly become an old, tired and declining nation like Britain."[34] Thomson's was no abstract lament. The conservative prime minister Edward Heath was forced to step down from office; his country was suffering under an economic slowdown induced by rising energy prices, and Harold Wilson, the leader of the Labour Party and former prime minister, returned to office.

Within the White House, the most ideologically committed policy makers had the greatest influence. As the Watergate investigations gained momentum, Nixon adopted a bunker mentality, surrounding himself with and soliciting advice from only the most loyal supporters. Someone like Roy Ash was one of Nixon's chief allies, loyal to him even at a personal level. His wife wrote "Support RN" on all her Christmas cards, bills, and letters, while George Shultz's wife and thirty other top-level wives sold "Get Off His Back" stickers. Carol Simon displayed one on her Mercedes.[35]

Nixon was keeping his distance from the truckers. He would not meet with Shapp or take his calls. William Safire praised Nixon's unwillingness to employ the "Lyndon Johnson method, with all-night bargaining sessions in the White House showing the President's personal concern . . . It has taken five years to wean disputants away from Oval Office maternal care."[36] Safire had an important point. Since the New Deal, the Democrats sought to link political and economic decision making. In 1937, after his landslide reelection, won with the overwhelming support of labor, Franklin Roosevelt lent a supportive hand to striking autoworkers in their successful struggle against General Motors for union recognition, and every Democratic president since had been personally involved in negotiating labor disputes. But Nixon was not about to send an emissary to the truck stops of America to resolve this shutdown.

At the Statler, as meetings continued, Usery worked hard to get an agreement. On February 8, he announced that Nixon would sign a congressional resolution to order a 6 percent freight rate surcharge. That rate increase, Usery explained, would cover increased fuel costs.[37] He also announced an increase in diesel fuel allocations. He was careful not to call it a settlement because this was not a formal labor negotiation. He made it clear that this was all the administration would be offering. No rollback. No repeal of the fifty-five-mile-per-hour speed limit. And no more freezes.

The truckers wanted more. Frustrations ran deep, and simply passing on costs seemed inadequate. A trucker who drove two thousand miles a week had to pay out $100 more for fuel. Only a rollback would assure that that money did not leave his pocket. "We're grown men with families . . . We want a rollback and we want it now," said Edward Cheroski, a Pennsylvania truck driver.[38] A New Jersey trucker told an NBC reporter that "even if the President came up" and told him to put his truck back on the road, he would not budge.[39]

The White House was taking a wait-and-see approach. If the strike continued into a second week, everyone knew the economy would be in trouble. The president of the Illinois Chamber of Commerce predicted at least half a million people would lose their jobs. Grocery stores would have bare shelves, schools would close down, hospitals would run short of blood, and municipal water treatment plants would not get essential chemicals.[40] The president of Grand Union supermarkets, with 3.5 million customers on the East Coast, appealed directly to the White House to intervene, warning of "serious shortages."[41] L. J. Moules, president of a Pennsylvania electrical company, told Nixon, "There is tyranny, anarchy and lawlessness in Western Pennsylvania . . . The full impact of our armed services and National Guard may be the only reasonable answer."[42]

Representative John Heinz III of Pennsylvania agreed and called on

Nixon to intervene. "Your personal leadership and involvement are absolutely necessary," he cabled the president.[43] From Pennsylvania's Ninth
District, Bud Shuster implored the White House to act: "This is a national
emergency. Repeat. This is a national emergency. Urge all necessary action
immediately."[44] After the South Carolina driver was murdered, Senator
Strom Thurmond asked the White House to send out troops. It was too
soon and "too heavy," thought the White House aide William Timmons.
Alexander Haig agreed. "Let's watch a bit," he said.[45] But the situation was
deteriorating.

Nixon's leadership came in the form of a crackdown. Unwilling to
accede to demands for a price rollback, the administration depicted the
truckers as greedy traitors. On the *Today* show, Secretary of Labor Peter
Brennan called their actions "ridiculous . . . I find disruption inexcus-
able."[46] Brennan, the former president of the Building and Construction
Trades Council in New York, had been a key labor supporter of Nixon's
in the 1972 election. Having led the so-called hard-hat riots in 1970, when
construction workers clashed with antiwar supporters in the wake of the
Kent State shootings, Brennan had emerged as a chief architect of blue-
collar support for Nixon. Now, as a member of the Nixon White House, this
former union leader was doing the bidding of the president, denouncing
the claims of suffering by workers as illegitimate and their strike actions
as illegal.

The White House portrayed the truckers as criminals, thugs who
were holding the country hostage to their reckless and selfish demands.
The Justice Department labeled them "dissident drivers" against whom it
would take legal action for conspiring to commit violence and disrupting
trade.[47] In a high-profile meeting, the first reported to the press, Nixon
met with Attorney General Saxbe, Usery, Simon, and Secretary of Transportation Claude Brinegar. On Nixon's orders, Saxbe would take action
against truckers who were participating in the shutdown and blocking interstate commerce.[48] "This handful of truckers is not going to bring this
country to its knees," Saxbe told reporters.[49] Simon echoed Saxbe's tough-
talking condemnation, announcing that the administration would not tolerate "a threat not only to the life and limb but also to the immediate food
supplies of millions of people in our country." "We will not allow any segment of our society to intimidate and threaten workers who desire to do
their jobs," warned the energy czar.[50]

The administration had done all it would, and it would do no more. As Nixon astutely told his advisers, the key thing was not the immediate situation but rather "where we would be six months from now." If the independents got what they wanted from striking, the Teamsters might follow suit, and so, too, would other workers who were experiencing pocketbook pain. Above all, the administration would not, and could not, budge on the rollback. The growing political support for price cuts, plus an ideological aversion, guaranteed that the White House would stand strong in its opposition to this trucker demand.[51]

In a national radio address, after eleven days of silence, Nixon denounced the truckers as nothing more than a "handful of desperados ... In no instance will we tolerate violence from those with grievances." The president claimed the rollback was unnecessary. Calling them lawbreakers, the president promised to bring these outlaws to justice. "Those who willfully break the law can expect no sympathy from those who enforce the law," said Nixon in a short radio address. With these threats, and with the shutdown eating into their pockets, the strike fizzled.

Three days earlier, the House of Representatives authorized the Judiciary Committee to begin investigations into whether Nixon's actions in the Watergate affair merited impeachment. When Nixon ran in 1972, he had hoped to forge a new electoral majority that included the silent majority of working- and middle-class Americans who no longer wanted to vote Democratic. But Watergate crushed these dreams, forcing Nixon to hew to his political right and oppose the kind of economic liberalism that the working classes had come to expect since the New Deal. Pleasing the truckers, and much of the public, meant supporting price rollback, which was anathema to the Right, and Nixon did not have this kind of maneuverability. With a Democratic Congress preparing to impeach him, Nixon needed to retain the support of congressional conservatives, which on energy meant deregulation and market prices.

Flooding the Market

The truckers were back at work, but the fight on Capitol Hill was gaining steam. Jack Carlson, an economist in the Office of Management and Budget, gave voice to the administration's fear that it was losing the battle and the results would be irreversible. To the budget director, Roy Ash, Carlson warned, "We feel overkill is setting in and there is a need to rein in Federal policy and statements and rely more on market forces."[52] These staffers had come to Washington to stanch the growth of the federal government, and now they were faced with the prospect of its dramatic expansion.

The Nixon administration was only the second Republican administration since the New Deal. In contrast to Eisenhower's advisers who came from the ranks of big business and had accommodated themselves to a world of New Deal regulation, Nixon's people had a different ideological makeup; they were Californian entrepreneurs, Wall Street buccaneers, and independent oilmen from Texas. Like William Simon, who had made millions as the head of municipal bond trading at Salomon Brothers, and George Bush, who had struck it rich in the Texas oil fields and in offshore waters, many of them had earned their money and cut their teeth in businesses that were very different from the big bureaucracies like General Motors and AT&T.

By the time Nixon took office, the Chicago school of economics was in the ascendance, lending intellectual credibility to the preference for market solutions instead of government intervention. Few did more to develop the economic science and the political proselytizing that sought to discredit Keynesian economics than Milton Friedman. Born in 1912 to Hungarian Jewish immigrants, Friedman grew up in suburban New Jersey, and were it not for the intervention of the economist Arthur Burns, who taught him at Rutgers University and recommended him for graduate studies at the University of Chicago, Friedman might have become an accountant. Arriving in Chicago in 1932, at the depths of the Great Depression, without sufficient funds for his studies, Friedman stayed briefly. After working in the New Deal and World War II as a government economist and receiving his doctorate from Columbia in 1946, he returned to Chicago, where he would build his career and reputation as a pioneering advocate for monetarism, deregulation, and smaller government.

In 1962, Friedman published *Capitalism and Freedom*, an intellectual treatise intended for the wider public that laid out the case against state authority, bureaucracy, and government regulation. Like many of his conservative colleagues, Friedman was influenced by Friedrich von Hayek's 1944 landmark work, *The Road to Serfdom*, which, written against the backdrop of totalitarianism and collectivism, had warned against the dangers of too much government in a democracy. By the late 1960s, following the passage of the Great Society and the backlash that ensued, Friedman hoped to resuscitate fears of an overweening and inefficient state. Beginning in 1966, he wrote a regular column in *Newsweek* magazine that offered a conservative counterpunch to the side-by-side column of the leading Keynesian Paul Samuelson.

Friedman was affiliated with one of the institutional centers for conservative economic thought: the American Enterprise Institute (AEI), the think tank that positioned itself, with the backing of wealthy donors, as the conservative answer to the liberal Brookings Institution. Founded in 1938 by anti–New Deal businessmen, AEI moved to Washington in 1943 to lobby against the Office of Price Administration and the extension of price controls after the war. Under the leadership of William Baroody Sr., the organization brought together a vibrant right-leaning academic and policy network. The goal was to establish a regular lobbying presence to promote the ideas that government regulations undercut productivity, federal spending triggered inflation, taxes reduced the incentive to invest, and the wage demands of labor unions drove up the cost of living.

At the center of much of this activity was Melvin Laird, the bald-headed master of backroom deals who could be at once ruthless and cunning. As Watergate was engulfing the Oval Office and the embargo was triggering a full-blown crisis, he was sent to the White House to replace John Ehrlichman with the blessing of Barry Goldwater and other Republican congressmen. "We're counting on Mel," said Goldwater. "He's got to make Nixon one of the boys."[53] His influence stemmed not from proximity to the president but rather from his skill at developing, grooming, and institutionalizing a younger group of conservative insiders. Through that process, Laird was making a lasting imprint on the way Washington worked. In 1971, he had helped to raise more than $1 million for the AEI. Laird also cultivated intellectuals and policy experts at the new Heritage Foundation and Georgetown's Center for Strategic and International Studies (CSIS).

These organizations aimed their fire at the Washington establishment, but they were themselves creatures of the Capitol. Edwin Feulner, one of the founders of the Heritage Foundation, got his start under Laird's tutelage in Congress. Born in suburban Chicago in 1941, Feulner went west to Colorado for college, where he became a campus conservative, reading

Barry Goldwater's *Conscience of a Conservative* and Russell Kirk's *Conservative Mind*. As Laird's legislative aide, Feulner helped develop an intellectual platform for the Republican Party. When Laird became Nixon's secretary of defense, Feulner worked for Philip M. Crane, the conservative Republican who had served as director of research for Barry Goldwater's 1964 campaign and then in 1969 won election to fill Donald Rumsfeld's Illinois seat.

In mid-February, just as the energy crisis was descending into total chaos, the conservative members of the House Republicans sought to block the administration from "tilting leftward." Their vehicle was the newly formed Republican Study Committee, the brainchild of Crane and Goldwater.[54] The group's two leading staff members were Feulner and Paul Weyrich. Before becoming president of the Heritage Foundation, Feulner operated through the Republican Study Committee to promote conservative ideas in public policy. With seventy initial members, the committee served as counter to the Democratic Study Group of congressional liberals. There's "a long way to go," Crane acknowledged. Most pressing, they wanted to keep pressure on Nixon to avoid bending to the demands of liberals in Congress. "He is capitulating to the wrong people at the wrong time on the wrong issues," said Representative Edward Derwinski after these hard-line House conservatives met with Nixon on February 6.[55]

They were right to be worried. Occupying the Oval Office was a president who was weakened from his own scandal, a leader who had demonstrated time and again his willingness to deploy the tactics of his liberal opponents if he felt it would advance his personal political standing. As the journalist and former Nixon adviser William Safire explained, "When his back is to the wall, Mr. Nixon tends to adopt the economic suggestions of his Democratic opponents, and with a vengeance." This quality infuriated the Right and even those within the administration like George Shultz and Herbert Stein: "What must disturb these two believers in economic freedom is the President's willingness to make economic decisions for political reasons—that is, to listen to the populist demand to 'do something!'" Nixon's accommodations only made a greater economic mess. "Controls have failed; let's admit it," wrote Safire. Instead, he urged, "Let's consider a capitalist's manifesto: Laissez-fairies of the world, unite! You have nothing to lose but your Keynes."[56]

These Washington conservatives perceived the energy crisis as a crucial test for their ideas about the market and government. Their first task was to block Jackson's energy legislation. Their key principle was the price mechanism. According to their theories, higher prices, set in the market-place, would restrict demand and call forth a greater supply of gasoline. "You do not win popularity contests by saying it, but we need a stiff increase in energy prices in the United States. Higher prices will induce larger do-mestic production of fuels," said the American Enterprise Institute econ-omist and former Nixon staffer Murray Weidenbaum.[57] In contrast, price controls, set by the government below market prices, would stimulate de-mand and stifle supply. To head its project on energy policy, AEI recruited Laird, who, sensing that the president's political chances were in decline, left the White House.

Milton Friedman led the public charge against price controls as the cause of the gasoline shortage. "The current oil crisis has not been pro-duced by the oil companies. It is a result of government mismanagement exacerbated by the Mideast war," he wrote in his *Newsweek* column. Lift-ing controls was essential for ending the shortage and, more generally, for restoring, if not preserving, American capitalism. "It is a mark of how far we have gone on the road to serfdom that government allocation and ra-tioning of oil is the automatic response to the oil crisis," warned Friedman. According to this free-market proponent, the president should hold the line, prevent additional incursions into the private marketplace, and if possible eliminate regulations that dated back to the New Deal.[58]

From the White House, Simon took a hard line, dismissing Jackson's New Dealism as sheer "stupidity." Simon was the public face for the admin-istration; after Nixon, the country looked to the energy czar to see if it could expect more gas, higher prices, or rationing. Very deliberately, Simon cultivated a reputation as a man of action who, according to his former colleagues at the Treasury Department, came across like a "combination whirlwind, computer and slave driver." "I bust their balls, but they know I bust my balls, too," said Simon. He worked fourteen-hour days and pushed his staff, who called him "the Vince Lombardi of energy," just as hard.[59] He projected an image of himself as an entrepreneurial businessman in-stead of a rule-following bureaucrat.

When Simon assumed his post at the Federal Energy Office, it had grown within weeks from just a few staffers to a thousand-employee agency with five hundred regional agents. The great regulatory agencies of the

New Deal era like the National Recovery Administration, the Agricultural Adjustment Administration, and later the Office of Price Administration cultivated a rapport with individual citizens. In contrast, few
Americans ever came to identify with the Federal Energy Office, nor did
its leaders seek such standing. Instead, all power seemed to reside in the
energy czar. Indeed, Simon liked to repeat that when the president gave
him the job, Nixon told him he would have "absolute authority" on par
with Albert Speer in the Third Reich. According to Simon, "Nixon told
the Cabinet that if not for the power that Hitler had given Speer to override the German bureaucracy, Germany would have been defeated far
earlier."[60]

This public persona was part of Simon's effort to discredit the power of
governmental authority even as he was exercising it. Although the Democratic Congress required price controls and allocations, he took every opportunity to stress that the market would do a better job than he ever
could. As he put it, "No group of men could be attacking the problem more
sensibly than we are, but . . . no group of men, we or anyone else, could
ever replace a free market."[61] When, under Nixon's orders, he designed a
rationing program, just as a contingency, each driver would purchase
a ration booklet to offset administrative costs and could sell any unused
coupons for whatever price he could get. As one FEO official said, "There is
nothing to keep anyone from going into the coupon buying-and-selling
business."[62] The ration coupon, with a portrait of George Washington, bore
such a striking resemblance to a $1 bill that it unintentionally could be
used in a bill-changing machine.[63]

Nixon's policy makers did not disguise their preference for market
prices, which they justified as a matter of national security. Under Phase IV
controls, "new" oil could sell at market prices, which rose to more than
double the fixed price of "old" oil. Such a two-tiered system promoted the
opening of new wells, but it also wreaked havoc on the market, distorting
it and creating disincentives for production from old fields. At the worst
possible moment, oil companies took old wells out of production, unwilling to produce at less than market prices. Only the elimination of this system would result in increased domestic production. Higher prices were
the cost the public would have to pay for greater security.

Nixon's advisers were not naive; they understood that any effort to
remove all controls would be politically difficult. Phase IV price controls

were due to expire in April 1974 under existing legislation. Everyone knew that pressure would mount for a further extension, especially if the embargo were ongoing and prices at a peak. George Shultz put it to Nixon directly: "Democrats will want to put the President on the spot rather than vote for price increases in a congressional election year." Controls, he mused, were like the Vietnam War: very easy to march in, but very hard to march out.[64]

The fear of even greater governmental regulation of the oil industry loomed large, especially, of course, among the country's oilmen. Jack Urich, president of an independent California oil company, wrote to a supportive Simon, "Why must honest, respectable and patriotic businessmen be forced to break the law of our land to stay in business because of ill-advised and ruinous mandates from Washington?" After an IRS agent accosted this oil executive, who lived in Nixon's hometown of Whittier, he asked for an investigation. "Put the insolent IRS . . . on notice that they are dealing with harassed and suffering businessmen, not criminals," complained the oilman. Nixon sympathized, "Independents have a case worth looking into."[65]

The RNC's chairman, George Bush, too, understood their set of deep concerns. George Cotton, an acquaintance from Bush's Midland days in the oil fields, wrote to his old friend, "Everybody wants the government to do something about the energy shortage. I don't! . . . Everything but the market place has been tried to solve the 'energy shortage.' And it's the only solution." Bush, too, believed "the freer the market the better."[66] What they meant by a free market was no government interference unless it benefited the industry. These same oilmen had supported import restrictions, for example, when world prices were cheap. But now they lobbied hard against any government rollback of prices or a permanent extension of controls, and they found allies in the White House.

At the core, Nixon's policy makers were motivated as much by ideology as by politics. Simon made his ideological convictions clear. He did not mince words when it came to his views of New Deal liberalism and its proponents. In his memoir, he would write, "If production were dependent on this kind of mind, the human race would still be crawling on its belly in the primeval slime." In a slightly more restrained tone, he proclaimed, "We must lift the deadening hand of government from the many areas of our economy such as energy where overzealous government regulations are now cramping our growth and hopes for the future."[67] These antigovernment ideologues crystallized and articulated this free-market argument from the center of the state regulatory apparatus itself.

The tools they had to combat the energy crisis were classic regulatory measures generated by a Democratic Congress and New Deal statecraft. But even as they reluctantly deployed these statist measures, they repeatedly told themselves and the public that they were illegitimate. By his own account, Simon was a "rotten bureaucrat." In fact, as he explained, he was an "antibureaucrat." Set up in reaction to a crisis, the Federal Energy Office was an "outrage." If Simon had his way, he would "abolish the agency and close its doors tomorrow."[68] After *Time* magazine ran a favorable cover story about him, Exxon's president, John Jamieson, wrote Simon a congratulatory note: "I can sleep better each night knowing that you are the energy czar." But that overstated Simon's power. Simon could not control the political momentum that the energy crisis gave to the Democratic leaders in Congress.[69]

Nixon's advisers made sure to bolster the president's resolve against this legislative onslaught. The budget director, Roy Ash, told Nixon that the energy situation was not, in Ash's words, "a Presidential crisis." It was more like the problem of the previous spring, when a surge in beef prices triggered a short-lived meat boycott. Ash therefore recommended that Nixon "avoid overreacting by getting government into activities that can and will be better done by private industry or by making some inflexible commitments to long term policies." Ash told Nixon this was a job for the private sector: "We must, of course, establish the perception of Federal leadership . . . but we should recognize the problem as essentially a market phenomenon." Ash reassured Nixon, "What the government can most usefully do is remove impediments it has constructed, provide some incentives, and keep out of the way . . . In short, this is not primarily a government problem."[70] All the president's top advisers, including Ash, recommended Nixon veto any energy bill with a rollback provision.

One of the most outspoken opponents was Senator Paul Fannin, the Arizona Republican who was boyhood friends with Barry Goldwater and replaced him during the 1964 presidential campaign. Fannin, having graduated from Stanford University with a business degree in 1930, during the Depression, started a gas distribution business, which he led for the next twenty years, until he became governor. From his perspective, price controls were anathema and the root cause of the fuel shortage. For him, as for economists like Friedman, the price mechanism was the only solution. "Price in the final analysis is by far the best allocator of any resource," Fannin said. Resisting the liberal solution of price controls would "help overcome fuel shortages, increase domestic supplies . . . and keep . . . the labor force employed." Clarence J. "Bud" Brown of Ohio, a conservative Republican in the House, echoed the denunciation, claiming, "This effort in oil is brought to us by the same group of people who brought us the beef shortage."[71]

William F. Buckley, the founder of *National Review* and leading intellectual voice of the conservative movement, shared this dour assessment: "Friedman has said it quite simply . . . The best way to dissipate the crisis is a) get rid of the Federal Energy Office; b) leave the oil companies alone." In the pages of *Newsweek*, Friedman continued his attack. "Lines are forming at those gas stations that are open. The exasperated motorists are cursing; the service-station attendants are fuming; the politicians are promising. The one thing few people seem to be doing is thinking," he complained. "How can thinking people believe that a government that cannot deliver the mail can deliver gas better than Exxon, Mobil, Texaco, Gulf, and the rest?" Buckley concurred. "The only thinkable political intervention would be not here," he said, "but in the Persian Gulf, and this would require not bureaucrats, but soldiers."[72]

Listening to his advisers, Nixon downplayed the crisis. "Don't scare the public on the energy issue anymore," he told his cabinet.[73] Vice President Gerald Ford dutifully informed Americans they were "over the hump." At a news conference, he said that citizens would rather "wait in line to get gasoline than wait in line at the post office for rationing stamps to buy gasoline."[74]

But the administration knew it was not ahead. The loss of Gerald Ford's former House seat in Michigan to a Democrat on February 18, 1974, rattled the White House. Perhaps it was wishful thinking, a way to avoid facing the inevitable impact of Watergate, but to them the message was that the energy crisis was hurting them. With three General Motors factories closed, they attributed the defeat of the Republican candidate to the voters' feeling of being squeezed by inflation and layoffs resulting from the fuel shortage. "We are at the point where we had better make good progress with the energy crisis and keep unemployment at manageable levels," worried George Bush.[75] Nixon told his cabinet the problem was "gut economic issues." "Energy," he said, "is the biggest concern in America today."[76]

Many Americans agreed, insisting that the biggest problem with Watergate was that it distracted Congress from dealing with the very real problems of rising prices and spreading unemployment. One of Henry Jackson's constituents wrote to him, "Wouldn't it be great if Congress had the guts to change the Watergate committee to the oil-crisis committee and really dig into the giant oil companies."[77] Back in his district, Representative Wayne Hays, a Democrat from Ohio, told reporters his constituents know "Simple Simon . . . for the phony and fake that he is." "If we're going to impeach anyone around here it ought to be him," he said.[78]

By the end of February, the gas crisis had become acute. As more drivers turned to panic buying, Senator Abraham Ribicoff said, "Every time they pass a gasoline station they fill up with gas. It is just like a dog beside every telegraph pole."[79] In Maryland, motorists waited for as long as seven hours on lines that snaked around for three miles. The Associated Press lead on February 22 read "Chaos, that's the word for the gasoline shortage." "Another week of this and people will be wild," said a North Carolina man after reaching the front of the line, only to find the gas was all gone. *Newsweek* reported, "The American people seem to be on the verge of psychic rebellion." As Senator Lowell Weicker of Connecticut put it, "Human beings now are acting like animals."[80]

For many, the energy crisis meant more than the inconvenience of gas lines. Millions of children walked to school in the dark after Congress adopted year-round daylight saving time, while some districts closed without enough fuel for buses. Thousands of West Virginia coal miners stayed home from work for two and a half weeks, insisting they did not have enough gas to get to work.[81] While the economy did not come to a complete halt, national production slowed considerably. The auto industry in particular was decimated, and the United Automobile Workers (UAW) demanded a massive public works program. Jackson's energy bill provided an extension of unemployment benefits for those laid off as a result of the energy crisis, which was more than half a million thus far.[82]

The presence of lines in some areas but not in others reinforced the popular belief that the Nixon administration was at best bungling and at worst corrupt. Representative Joseph Maraziti, an otherwise stalwart Nixon supporter, called for Simon's resignation, accusing the energy czar of being either inept or willfully capricious. Only those explanations, it seemed, could explain why New Jersey seemed to be suffering terribly and was "near riot" while gas flowed freely and stations offered complimentary car washes just across the border, in Easton, Pennsylvania, the town of Simon's alma mater Lafayette College.[83] Residents of a northern New Jersey town demanded "relief of this unjust appropriation." "It is unfair that we alone should be forced to sit in a gas line for an interminable wait and all too often for just a small amount of gasoline," wrote housewives from another New Jersey town. The only solution to "reduce anxieties and assure equal distribution of gasoline" is rationing, complained yet another group of citizens.[84]

In the face of long lines, flaring tempers, and a patchwork of confusing local rationing plans, pressure increased on Nixon to support federal rationing. It was not that the public was eager to use coupons to fill up, but the absence of federal leadership appeared to be making the energy crisis worse. "We the AMERICAN PEOPLE are tired of the lack of competent and effective leadership," wrote the Concerned Citizens of Maryland.[85]

Simon knew he was failing when one of his former Salomon partners doubted, or at least did not understand, the Federal Energy Office's public explanations. "Why the dry pumps here [in New York] and elsewhere?" wrote Jonas Ottens to his longtime trading partner.[86] One of Simon's aides conceded, "It's obvious Uncle Sam has goofed. We're driving people nuts with uncertainty about allocations."[87] Governor Robert Docking of Kansas complained to Nixon about the "serious injustice" done to his citizens, claiming that the FEO was "mismanaging Kansas into an acute gasoline shortage."[88] No doubt his constituents shared in this sentiment. The governor of Maryland sued the FEO, charging the agency with underallocating oil supplies to his state. The oil companies, too, were unhappy. Gulf filed suit against the Federal Energy Office on the grounds that its allocation requirements were unconstitutional.[89]

Gas retailers were also furious at the White House. "Where you have taken over control of the fuel with the executive order, you have greatly damaged the free enterprise system, which we thought for so long was what the Republican Party stood for," wrote angry Oregon station owners. Unless Nixon made headway, warned these dealers, "the American public will be for impeachment."[90] Feeling squeezed themselves, retailers threatened their own national shutdown unless they received some profit relief.

With more than a week left in February, already 20 percent of the nation's gas stations had run out of their monthly allocation of gas. To avert a national "pump-out," Simon authorized a price hike of two cents a gallon.

As the gas situation deteriorated, all eyes were on Washington. The Democrats' plan to roll back prices had obvious political appeal. It wouldn't get rid of the gas lines, but it would reduce the pinch in the pocketbook. By now, as many as a thousand Internal Revenue Service agents were performing spot checks on local gas stations to wipe out price gouging. That translated into roughly one agent for every two hundred stations; another thousand were in training.[91] Under the price rollback provision in the energy bill, any consumer could report a perceived violation to a governmental board for investigation.

The House-Senate conferees held unprecedented open hearings on the energy bill, voting 12–4 in favor of a price rollback, which would slash prices on about 25 percent of domestic crude to bring the price of nearly all domestic oil to $5.25 a barrel. On February 20, the Senate took up the bill for a vote. "We're having fist fights and soon we'll be having riots unless we pass this emergency legislation," boomed Jackson.[92] The bill passed 67–32. "They ain't seen nothing yet," boasted Jackson.[93]

The president understood that it was time for a dramatic act. At a cabinet meeting on February 21, Nixon affirmed his resolve to veto. Echoing his supporters, he told his top aides, "Let's not lose sight of our goal to keep government out of people's pockets and off their backs."[94] At a meeting the next day, Nixon urged Simon to ignore the bureaucratic regulations that his office had been required to write and implement. Instead, Simon should take whatever steps were necessary to end the gas lines. He should draw down inventories and shift geographic allocations to end the gas lines in the East and other areas hardest hit.

It was time to flood the market. Ignoring bureaucratic regulations, Simon took a page from his freewheeling days as a buccaneer bond trader to crack the gas lines. In a day and a half, Simon, Gerald Parsky, and Frank Zarb devised and implemented a plan, independent of the rest of the Federal Energy Office staff. To supply the market, Simon increased allocations to twelve states, mostly on the East Coast, and Washington, D.C., and reduced allocations to ten others, mainly in the Midwest.

In a brazen act, Simon dipped into future allocations, even at the risk of greater shortages in the upcoming summer, when demand for gasoline would be at its seasonal high. "We worked for thirty-six hours straight. We called every governor of every state where there were problems. We called every oil distribution line. We worked out the allocations, sent the forms over to the FEO, and I ordered that they sign them," said Simon. "As far as I was concerned and as far as the American gas buyer was concerned, the emergency had been handled successfully." Frank Zarb, who would become energy czar under President Ford, recalled their actions: "We decided to demonstrate to the world that we weren't going to take any shit and would use all the resources at our disposal, politically and economically, to break the crisis before it became unmanageable."[95]

The Crisis Remains

On February 25, Nixon held his first press conference since October to tell the public that "the crisis has passed"; it was now a "problem." He made public his intention to veto the energy bill: "Controls have been tried, and controls have been found wanting."[96] Nixon warned that a price rollback would cause longer lines, lead to rationing, and require tens of thousands of bureaucrats. At the Young Republican Leadership Conference, the president said the rollback was, in a word, "counterproductive."[97] Behind the scenes, he prodded his cabinet to stick to the party line: he had downgraded the crisis to a problem. "Remember we're not 'panting' to the end of the embargo."[98]

The administration put a positive spin on the gas lines. They resulted, said the White House, from a choice to favor jobs over consumer inconvenience. As Herbert Stein put it, the administration made a calculated trade-off to protect employment by granting generous allocations to industry, making automobile driving "bear the brunt of the shortage." Ken Clawson helped to craft this rationale: "The Administration policies saved the Nation from industrial breakdown and resulting soaring unemployment plus kept homes warm this winter."[99] All Nixon's policy makers sang the same tune. "I'm proud of the decision we made," announced Simon. "People . . . would rather wait in line for gas than spend a couple of months or longer waiting in line for unemployment checks." Vice President Ford also toed the party line. The administration "chose between unemployment lines and gas lines. We made the right choice."[100]

Liberals weren't biting. After waiting in line for nearly an hour to fill up his tank, the Senate majority leader, Mike Mansfield, denounced Nixon's pronouncement of an energy "problem" as meaningless rhetoric that would not easily fool the public. "The shortage remains and so does the crisis," Mansfield said, and he called for immediate rationing. Representative Tip O'Neill, the Massachusetts liberal, agreed: "It is all very well for President Nixon to say the energy crisis is over. He doesn't have to wait in gas lines." Senator William Proxmire of Wisconsin proposed the "Let the Big Shots Stand in Line, Too" resolution to compel Washington politicians and top oil executives to fill up their tanks personally.[101]

Grassroots leaders on the left were also quick to challenge the president. "For the people in Chicago and New York and Maryland who are in gas lines for two hours, they still think it's a crisis," protested the Reverend Jesse Jackson. George Meany and Ralph Nader called for the nationalization of the oil industry, comparable to the New Deal's Tennessee Valley Authority (TVA). "The country has been Simonized," said Nader. "Simon wants to go back to Wall Street and tell them, 'I'm the guy who doubled the price of oil.' He's a total phony, a total tool of business."[102]

Nixon had his back to the wall. The president, who earlier in his administration had proven skillful at outflanking his opponents by co-opting their positions as his own, had few good options. On March 1, a grand jury named Nixon as an unindicted co-conspirator in the indictment of seven former presidential aides. He could not afford to lose conservative Republicans whose votes he would have to count on to save his political future. On March 6, Nixon vetoed the energy bill.

Senator Barry Goldwater, who was proving a staunch Nixon supporter, led the fight to sustain Nixon's veto. He and Paul Fannin, the ranking Republican on the Senate Interior Committee, succeeded. The Senate vote was 58–40, a handful of votes short of the two-thirds needed to override Nixon's veto. Some southern Democrats switched their votes, including Senators Long and Bennett Johnston from Louisiana, who had voted for the original measure confident that Nixon would veto it. Two leading moderate Republicans, Hugh Scott and James Pearson, also switched. And Senator John Tower of Texas, who was adamantly opposed to the measure but missed the initial vote, also backed Nixon.[103]

The Democrats controlled Congress, but the energy crisis was exacerbating regional divisions within the party and diluted its numerical superiority. The fuel shortage in the Northeast reinforced this region's support of a liberal agenda. But in the oil-producing states of the South and the Southwest, their energy interests as producers strengthened their increasingly articulate conservatism. In Texas, Louisiana, and Oklahoma, bumper stickers read "Let the Yankee Bastards Freeze in the Dark."[104] With energy prices high and liberal Democrats strong on Capitol Hill, this fight—between government price controls and the price mechanism—was not over. Senator Henry Jackson announced, "Prices are going to go up and up and up. The rollback provision is going to be an ongoing fight."[105]

High prices could quickly trigger unrest and also lead to unpredictable and unexpected coalitions. After the February shutdown, Truckers for Justice, a group of independent truckers in Arizona, formed an unlikely alliance with the United Farm Workers, led by the left-wing labor activist Cesar Chavez. Here were two groups that usually defined the opposite ends of the political spectrum. But now the truckers would not haul scab lettuce or grapes, and the United Farm Workers supported a price rollback for fuel. The administration was aware of this alliance and also knew that organizations of independent truckers received support from various New Left political groups such as the Vietnam Veterans Against the War and the American Indian Movement.[106] As the Domestic Council adviser Michael Raoul-Duval acknowledged, "The bottom line of this is that we don't have a problem now but in the words of Chairman Mao: 'A single spark can set a prairie on fire.'"[107]

On March 18, Saudi Arabia announced the end of the five-month embargo. Even after the shipments started to flow, the geopolitics of oil had been forever changed. Energy prices stayed high; OPEC had raised prices, and it was not inclined to let them drop. America's sense of control over its most fundamental economic resource was gone. Neither political nor economic conditions returned to normal. The success of the embargo came less from crippling industrialized nations, which was not the intention, or even from forcing a permanent peace settlement in the Middle East, which was not obtained, than by announcing in a shocking and powerful way the arrival of resource contests between the First and the Third Worlds that transcended the Cold War and marked a key shift in geopolitical power toward the Persian Gulf. The threat of another embargo was very real, and the pressure for more aggressive government action to deal with shortages and price hikes remained powerful.

The Right understood this new political reality. For many conservatives, Nixon's veto of the energy bill was too little, too late. The conservatives had scored an important victory, but they were hardly winning the war. In an ideological battle, there was no room for compromise. Nixon's pragmatism and political opportunism had opened the floodgates in 1971 with his wage and price controls. Since then, he had agreed to mandatory allocations and created the Federal Energy Office to enforce them. When Simon ordered increased allocations, *The Wall Street Journal* called his actions "absurd." The FEO "continues to pursue the illusion that it can set things right with another round of decrees, when all these do is bring the United States closer to rationing," the *Journal* complained. "There is no way to equalize distress because the price mechanism of the marketplace is inoperative."[108] Young Americans for Freedom led a grassroots campaign across the country against the prospect of future rationing.[109]

Nixon's brand of Republicanism was implicated in all of this. *The National Observer* decried "flaming populists from Richard Nixon leftward." If controls became permanent, "we'd all remain reasonably cold and immobile, and many sensitive Arabs would be overjoyed."[110] In late March, conservatives in the House and the Senate wanted Nixon to use his executive authority to table all price controls due to expire on April 31, 1974. George Shultz reminded Nixon that these were his most reliable supporters. "It may not be wise to leave these people disappointed on every issue," he counseled.[111]

The conservatives were correct. Once controls were in place, they were hard to remove. On May 7, 1974, Nixon signed legislation to establish the Federal Energy Administration (FEA) as a congressionally created agency to replace the FEO. Even with the first oil shock over, the bill Nixon signed granted the FEA a two-year life. Nixon let all other wage and price controls expire at the end of April. But the elaborate system of energy price controls remained in effect, and the FEA assumed responsibility for this regulatory system. At the signing of the FEA Act, Nixon championed the free market as the path toward energy independence. Yet there was no disguising that he was extending the life of a new government bureaucracy that reached deep into the economy.

The Environmental Protection Agency was also spreading its wings with the end of the embargo. Its head, Russell Train, broke with the White House proposals to relax emission standards. "I'm going to fight against them to the last wire, because I don't think they're necessary and I do think they'd do substantial harm," Train said publicly.[112] The country's largest environmental groups, with more than four million members, echoed Train's words. "We will oppose . . . any attempt to sacrifice public health and environmental quality on the altar of the energy crisis or for excess corporate profits," its leaders wrote in an open letter.[113] Given the deep suspicions about the oil industry, the public rejected the idea that environmental regulations caused the shortage. As the executive director of the Sierra Club, Michael McCloskey, noted, "Public opinion has coalesced on questioning the good faith of the energy industry."[114]

William Simon, who became the new Treasury secretary, was alarmed. Nixon was facing a damaging and ultimately fatal challenge to his presidency. The environmental movement was growing, the energy crisis had interrupted the push to deregulate the economy, and now an unfolding recession was likely to accelerate demands for greater government spending. Inflation, which was at a rate of 4.6 percent when Nixon took office, was zooming toward double digits. Unemployment went up from 3.3 percent to 5.5 percent. Dollars were flowing out of the country to pay for high-priced oil. And, with so much public anger at the oil industry, especially as companies reported record gains, repealing the depletion tax break was gaining traction. Simon lamented, "These profits are not exorbitant but I guess you don't get elected to office by saying this."[115]

The first oil shock was over, but conservatives were more worried than ever. On the domestic front, the embargo had taught the lesson that American voters and their representatives in Washington relied on government to attack rising prices and fuel shortages. The foreign policy lessons from the Arab use of the oil weapon were just as frightening. To them, the energy crisis had proven that détente was a failure and that the Soviets had ambitions in this vital region. Furthermore, the crisis also fractured the anti-Communist alliance, creating fissures between the United States and NATO and Japan. The challenge to American support of Israel was a further source of worry.

The White House sought to reestablish its commitment to the twin pillars of stability in this region, Saudi Arabia and Iran. During the embargo, the Saudi Arabian oil minister worked hard to maintain relations with the United States and with the American public, explaining his country's reluctant use of the oil weapon. Even as he led OPEC in taking on the oil corporations, Zaki Yamani understood that the long-term interests of Saudi Arabia rested on growing demand for his country's oil. To hobble the West, and especially the United States, would ultimately hurt his ambitions to have stable Saudi Arabian growth. Moreover, the United States was the Saudis' key military ally against the threat of Soviet power in the Middle East. Secretly, in violation of the embargo, the Saudis had allowed the United States to refuel its Sixth Fleet in the Mediterranean Sea.

Top officials in both countries understood that the heart of this partnership involved the U.S. sale of arms to the Saudis. The purchase of military weapons was the priority for the kingdom. By the summer, the countries had established the Joint Security Cooperation Commission. These arms sales would spur the American defense industry at a time of domestic cutbacks and in effect subsidize production of American arms. This arrangement would also draw American dollars back into the United States that were flowing out of the country to pay for oil.

The foreign policy hawks were not satisfied, especially as Secretary of State Henry Kissinger continued his shuttle diplomacy. Kissinger maintained that the paramount strategy in the Middle East was offering American security to Arab leaders and sidelining the Soviets in these negotiations. Scoop Jackson and Secretary of Defense James Schlesinger vehemently disagreed, preferring instead a buildup of American military presence in the region. Throughout the embargo, Schlesinger had repeatedly pushed for consideration of the use of American force as a real possibility. In December 1973, he had gone so far as to inform the British ambassador to Washington, Lord Cromer, that American intervention was on the table. With the embargo over, Schlesinger redoubled his efforts to craft a new military strategy for the region.[116]

To the conservatives, the energy crisis required a fundamental rethinking of American foreign policy. In February 1974, in an effort to forestall a further deterioration in the Western alliance, Nixon had convened the Washington Energy Conference with leaders from Europe, Canada, and Japan to discuss cooperative solutions to OPEC's show of force. But this was a tepid meeting with few concrete outcomes. Donald Rumsfeld, as the U.S. ambassador to NATO during the embargo, perceived the threat that OPEC's power posed to the anti-Soviet alliance.

The lesson for Rumsfeld and other foreign policy hawks was the failure of détente and the weakness of the Western alliance, as consuming countries worried about their own oil imports and controversy emerged over what the best position was with regard to Israel and the tensions with its Arab neighbors. In February, after he left the White House, Melvin Laird published a scathing and widely read critique of détente's failure to prevent the energy crisis in *Reader's Digest*. "Let's Not Fool Ourselves About U.S.-Soviet Détente" was the title. The Center for Strategic and International Studies' Jack Bridges spoke to more than twenty-five thousand people, including eighty senators and three hundred congressmen. He appeared on the *Today* show, gave talks in Methodist churches, and held coffee klatches in people's basements. He even produced a cartoon with Fred Flintstone, narrated by Charlton Heston, in which Fred appears wearing an empty oil barrel. Hailing from East Texas, educated at Annapolis, trained as a naval officer and engineer, he had a simple message: the United States and its allies were becoming dangerously dependent on Persian Gulf oil.[117]

In the pages of *The New York Times Magazine*, Walter Laqueur, a historian and affiliate at CSIS, wrote a death notice for détente. What remains of the prospects of détente? asked Laqueur. "The short and honest answer is not much." "Détente rests not on a mood, not on good will," he wrote. "It rests on a certain equilibrium of forces. Once the balance is upset, there will be no détente." The Arab embargo had disturbed this fragile arrangement, exposing the vulnerability of the United States and providing incentives to the Soviets to continue to stoke regional instability and the possible use of another embargo. "The basic laws of world politics are usually very simple," he concluded grimly.[118]

The key voice was Admiral Elmo "Bud" Zumwalt, head of the navy, who pushed for the naval buildup in the Indian Ocean as a deterrent to Soviet activity in the region and as a protector of oil delivery from the Persian Gulf to the United States and its allies. In the spring of 1974, Zumwalt announced that he would resign his post. He was being forced out in part for his controversial personnel policies to end racial discrimination in the navy and ease regulations such as those that prohibited long hair, beards, and beer and in part because of his hawkish attitudes. Before stepping down, Zumwalt pushed hard for congressional appropriations to Diego Garcia, a tiny atoll in the Indian Ocean that in his view was crucial as a naval and air support station in the region. As he explained before the House Subcommittee on Foreign Affairs, "It's like the policeman on the beat," an analogy that the Indiana congressman Lee Hamilton and other liberal committee members found repugnant.[119]

Zumwalt's opponents had learned the lesson of a slippery slope in Vietnam. "From our experience in Indochina, we know too well the cost of early, easy congressional and State Department acquiescence to Pentagon demands. We must profit from our past errors," explained Senator Claiborne Pell. Pell co-sponsored a resolution with Senator Edward Kennedy to negotiate with the Soviet Union a limit on naval buildup in the Indian Ocean. "We owe it to ourselves, as well as to all the people of the region, to try preventing yet another arms race," they said.[120] This buildup was forcefully opposed not only by congressional liberals but also by a wide range of policy makers, from post-Vietnam doves to Cold War liberal internationalists. Chester Bowles, the former ambassador to India, said, "Diego Garcia has come to symbolize the most recent example of needless American interference in Asia."

Zumwalt thought these liberals were dangerously nearsighted. "The Indian Ocean has become the area with the potential to produce major shifts in the global balance of power over the next decade," he warned.[121] Just as he was bringing the navy personnel policies into the twentieth century, he was returning to an older nineteenth-century model of American sea power first pioneered by the grand naval theorist Alfred Thayer Mahan.[122]

If the Soviet Union controlled fossil fuels in the Middle East, wrote the journalist James Reston, explaining this doomsday point of view, "then there would be a new concept of military strategy in the world, for the industrial nations would be blockaded, not along their coasts as in the two World Wars, but far away, at the source of oil and power in the Middle East."[123] "We are very rapidly being thrust into a world in which, for the first time, global problems are becoming central," explained Zbigniew Brzezinski, director of the newly established Trilateral Commission that sought to foster a dialogue about what its founders saw as "the growing interdependence" of the world economy, especially among North America, Western Europe, and Japan.[124]

Zumwalt retired in June, issuing a final warning before an audience that included Vice President Ford: "Our Navy has reached a point where the odds are it can no longer guarantee free use of the ocean lifelines to

U.S. and allied forces in the face of a new, powerful and still-growing Soviet fleet."[125] At this moment, Kissinger and President Nixon were in Moscow, hoping to negotiate a second round of strategic arms limitations with the Soviet Union. Some dismissed Nixon's trip as a last-ditch effort to save his presidency and reestablish his strength as an international leader, but for conservatives Nixon's trip represented a dangerous misstep in foreign policy, with the president failing to appreciate the lessons of the energy crisis. On *Meet the Press*, Zumwalt repeated his assertion that America had lost control of the seas. His outspoken comments won him applause from conservatives, including California's governor, Ronald Reagan.

In July, at its annual convention, Young Americans for Freedom sounded a note of despair. Watergate was hampering the president, making him an ineffective champion of the conservative cause, and threatening the electoral future of the GOP. But it was Nixon's foreign policy and economic policies that led to the greatest disappointment and concern. "The conservatives get the rhetoric and the liberals get the action," explained a delegate from Texas. "The Nixon Administration has been a calamitous experience for the American people," said Stanton Evans, the head of the American Conservative Union.[126]

Four days later, the House Judiciary Committee passed three articles of impeachment against the president, and a newly released tape, the so-called smoking gun, implicated Nixon directly in the Watergate cover-up. Barry Goldwater, who had lent strong support to Nixon throughout the controversy, told the president it was time to step down. It was no longer feasible for the wounded executive to lead the country. George Bush delivered the same message, worrying about the damage to the party in the fall elections. To avoid impeachment, Nixon resigned on August 9, and Gerald Ford became the next president.

During the embargo, Washington conservatives had desperately tried to hold the line. They had learned, in the face of the tumult unleashed by the energy crisis, that liberal pressure for regulation from the grass roots and on Capitol Hill was as strong as ever. With energy prices high, and a recession looming, the demands for government intervention would increase. Environmentalists, too, were mobilizing to regain any lost ground, insisting that the end of the embargo made relaxation of the Clean Air Act unnecessary. The prospects of holding off Congress and reversing the

legislative underpinnings of liberalism appeared remote. Milton Friedman captured the challenge moving forward as he saw it. In the long run,
this free-market economist said, it was Nixon's policy decisions that "will
prove to have been more harmful to the nation than the misdeeds he has
been responsible for in Watergate."[127]

4

Finding a Way Out

PRESIDENT FORD AND his advisers entered the White House with a real sense of crisis. Upon being sworn into office on August 9, 1974, Gerald Ford attempted to soothe the nation, reassuring it that the Constitution had worked, that Watergate, as horrible and scarring as it was, would not bring the country down. "Our long national nightmare is over," said the new president in somber tones. But Ford knew that the road ahead would not be easy, not least because of the declining economic situation. The nation had weathered a constitutional crisis, but he and his advisers were fearful of how the country and indeed the free world would fare in the aftermath of the Arab embargo. Oil prices remained four times higher than what they had been a year earlier, inflation was on the rise, and a recession was in the offing. Three days into his presidency, in an address to Congress, Ford said what every American knew to be true: "The state of our economy is not so good."

Heading Toward Disaster

To William Simon, that was putting it mildly. In a cabinet meeting on August 3, days before Nixon's resignation, the Treasury secretary made clear that the free world was facing the greatest crisis since World War II. The problem was not only the oil dependency of the West and Japan but, as Simon suggested, an imploding debt crisis. Petrodollars were leaving the United States, Europe, and Japan, and they were not coming back. Wall Street banks began lending to these governments at a fast clip, financing ever-growing deficits that were putting borrowing countries under fiscal strain. "You are saying the oil situation is unmanageable," repeated Henry Kissinger. "Yes," said Simon. "It will force a massive realignment—you can assess whether that is good or bad for us. Europe is becoming dependent on the Arabs for both oil and money." The Federal Reserve chairman, Arthur Burns, echoing Simon, said, "We are heading toward disaster in the industrial world."[1]

Henry Kissinger, too, believed the situation threatened "the moral and political disintegration of the West."[2] Under heavy debt, Portugal, Italy, and Greece were descending into financial chaos, and the political appeal of Communism was on the rise. Inflation, which was reaching as high as 20 percent, led to the surge of Communist activism in France and Spain as well. By late September, oil-payment deficits, inflation, rising unemployment, collapsing governments, and what the New York Times editorial staff called "a growing danger of social violence" dominated headlines.[3] In the pages of Commentary, Walter Laqueur wrote, "For the general public the energy crisis was over the moment the lines in front of the gas stations disappeared. But . . . the survival of parliamentary democracy will be in doubt in all but a few countries—and there are not that many free countries left even now."[4]

Even Communist China was worried. After Nixon resigned, George Bush asked Ford for an appointment to serve as the United States' official representative in China, which would enhance his appeal as a possible future presidential candidate. From China, Bush informed Kissinger about the deep concern about oil, with Chinese leaders fearing that rising energy prices would destabilize global relations. "Their public backing of the oil weapon notwithstanding," Kissinger replied, "the Chinese are clearly concerned about the implications for them of an economic unraveling of the U.S., Europe, and Japan, and the concomitant rise in relative Soviet power."[5]

The situation within the United States also remained volatile. Energy prices showed no sign of letting up as the country continued to import more oil. Ken Cole, a Nixon holdover and presidential adviser, warned, "We should view this Fall as a potential 'crisis' period in the energy area." The next few months were likely to lead to a "period of unrest and building pressures" as oil prices drove up the cost of living. Cole feared the possibility of another truckers' strike as well as a potential national coal strike.[6] In 1974, work stoppages reached a postwar high; unionized workers in traditional industrial sectors walked off the job, as did garbage collectors, sewer workers, policemen, and many other municipal workers. Americans everywhere were feeling the pinch as wages lagged behind inflation. Protesters in Washington marched with signs that read MILK UP. MEAT UP. BREAD UP. WE'RE FED UP.[7]

The American economy was entering uncharted waters, with energy-driven inflation as only the most graphic symbol of chaos. The economy was beginning its slide into a full-blown recession as unemployment rose and the gross national product stalled. The challenge, as *The New York Times* explained, was how to deal with the unprecedented concurrence of inflation and slow job growth: "The disease of the times is no longer simply inflation nor economic stagnation. It is stagflation." The country had never before encountered this situation. "New diseases, new treatments," counseled the paper.

The Democrats, however, still had the same solutions. Shocks like the Arab embargo drove up inflation, they believed, and the government had to contain the impact. With oil price and allocation controls set to expire in August 1975, Scoop Jackson was already pushing for their extension. That would protect American consumers, and it would also demonstrate to OPEC producers that they did not have power over American markets. William Simon, in contrast, believed that freedom from OPEC could come only through greater American production, and he pushed to remove price controls and allocations as quickly as possible. As one aide put it, their job was to "find a reasonable way out."[8]

All eyes were on the new chief executive. A former football star, naval lieutenant commander, and lawyer, Gerald Ford had arrived in the nation's capital after winning election in 1948 as a representative of Michigan's Fifth District in Grand Rapids, a solidly Republican midwestern area. Starting in 1950, Ford served as a member of the House Appropriations Committee and worked hard to institute fiscal discipline, cut spending, and balance the federal budget. As House minority leader in the 1960s, he opposed Medicare, federal aid to education, and subsidized housing. He and the Senate minority leader, Everett Dirksen, held a weekly televised press conference to take on Lyndon Johnson. Fiscal conservatism formed the core of Ford's political beliefs, along with a tough Cold War stance.

Sitting in the White House, Ford was very much aware of the strength of his liberal opponents on Capitol Hill. Ten days after becoming president, he selected the moderate Republican Nelson Rockefeller as his choice for vice president, much to the chagrin of conservatives inside and outside Washington. If he wanted to boost his influence in Congress, the accidental president believed he would have to draw on the support of all members of his party. Yet Ford made clear he was not a moderate and he was definitely not a liberal. In his first address to Congress, he said, "A government big enough to give you everything you want is a government big enough to take from you everything you have."

On September 8, Ford stunned the country by issuing an executive pardon to Richard Nixon. In part, the new president hoped to heal the country and spare the nation the wrenching ordeal of a criminal trial of a former president. And in part, Ford believed that such a move, as controversial as it was, would allow him and his party the best chance they had to move forward. Laying the investigation of the president to rest, Ford intended to map out a Republican approach to the issues of the day.

Top of Ford's list was energy dependence. On September 23, at the World Energy Conference in Detroit, Michigan, before thousands of representatives from industrial nations, Ford spoke harsh words. "The expectation of an assured supply of energy has now been challenged," he said. Another OPEC price hike, let alone another embargo, would result in a "world in crisis." "Everyone can now see the pulverizing impact of energy price increases on every aspect of the world economy. The food problem, the inflation problem, the monetary problem, and other major problems are directly linked to the all-pervasive energy problem," explained the president. "It is difficult to discuss the energy problem without lapsing unfortunately into doomsday language."[9]

Ford was putting OPEC on notice. "Throughout history, nations have gone to war over natural advantages," warned the new commander in chief. The key to avoiding war—and now he directed his remarks as much to American allies as to the OPEC oil ministers—was to foster a policy of consumer cooperation to check the power of the producing countries. Ford recommitted the United States to Nixon's Project Independence, promising to reduce demand for Arab oil and increase domestic supply through decontrol and deregulation. And he also called for what he labeled "Project Interdependence," an appeal to European and Japanese leaders to avoid acting bilaterally to secure oil from Arab producers.

Secretary Kissinger reinforced the president's resolute rhetoric, delivering a similarly blunt address to the United Nations. Behind closed doors, he had told Ford, "We have to find a way to break the cartel . . . It is intolerable that countries of 40 million can blackmail 800 million people in the industrial world."[10] Publicly, Kissinger said, "Oil prices cannot go up indefinitely. Strains on the fabric and institutions of the world economy threaten to engulf us all in general depression."[11] "What has gone up by political decision can be reduced by political decision," intoned Kissinger.[12] Reporting on the White House's new "hard line," *The Wall Street Journal* saw the president's remarks as "a thinly veiled—and unspecific—threat of possible retaliation against any nation that seriously disrupts the U.S. economy by using oil as a political weapon."[13]

The White House options, however, were limited. With the ending of Vietnam and a war-weary public, there would be no support for a military solution to OPEC prices or future embargoes. Furthermore, the U.S. military did not have the capabilities to project substantial force in the Middle East. And American allies would not endorse the development of a regional presence. A few days after these White House remarks, the leaders of America's industrial allies—Japan, Britain, West Germany, and France—made clear to Kissinger at Camp David their opposition. Secretary of Defense James Schlesinger spent the next several days backtracking, denying the use of force as a policy option.

If Ford was worried about securing supply from abroad, he had equally grave concerns about the prospects of unleashing production at home. The day Ford flew to Detroit for the energy conference, he began the morning with breakfast at the Senate majority leader Mike Mansfield's house.[14] To Mansfield, the leader of the Democrats, the path forward was clear. World oil prices were not going to drop, resources would remain limited, and, as he saw it, price controls would have to stay in place. Rationing, too, might be necessary as a way of distributing this commodity equitably. The embargo was months behind them, but the Democrats' agenda stayed the same: protect the consumer's pocketbook. With inflation on the rise, Mansfield also pushed for a renewal of across-the-board wage and price controls.

The prospect of recession worried Mansfield even more than inflation. At the Detroit conference, Coleman Young, the city's first African-American mayor, elected in 1973, introduced the president. His city's automobile workers were having a hard time keeping up with the cost of living, especially as businesses were scaling back in their investment and hiring. Detroit, along with many other centers of industrial production, was hemorrhaging jobs. According to Young, Mansfield, and the rest of the Democratic Party, only a massive stimulus program could get the economy moving again.

Ford was having none of it. "Inflation is domestic enemy number one," asserted the president. In early October, Ford launched his Whip Inflation Now (WIN) campaign, a voluntary program designed as an alternative to the mandatory controls that the Democrats supported. In a departure from Nixon, Ford firmly rejected compulsory wage and price freezes. Instead, the government distributed WIN buttons all across the country as visible reminders to keep the lid on prices. Ford asked Americans to pitch in. They could conserve energy, plant WIN gardens, recycle, reduce waste, and improve productivity. All these voluntary measures, taken as a whole, were meant to combat rising prices.

The WIN campaign, for all its voluntarism, still smacked of the New Deal. Instead of jawboning American businessmen, William Simon insisted on cutting back government spending, which he believed was crowding out private investment. WIN had come into being before Ford had assembled his full team of advisers; now that they were in place, they made sure to let WIN die a quiet death. The new CEA chairman, Alan Greenspan, William Simon, and Roy Ash, who stayed on as OMB director, all opposed this program. Fundamentally, so too did the president, and he would soon come to regret this policy blunder. Richard Cheney, who joined the new administration, called the WIN campaign President Ford's Bay of Pigs. Underneath this fiasco was a serious lesson: the WIN stumble taught Ford and his advisers the necessity of a more ideologically consistent statecraft.[15]

While Ford had his fair share of seasoned political advisers, many of whom had served with him since his days as House minority leader, he also recruited a coterie of committed conservatives. To them, the energy crisis was their Great Depression. In the 1930s, young, idealistic New Dealers flocked to Washington, each with a letter from Felix Frankfurter in his briefcase; these were the "happy hot dogs" who became the staffers to FDR's brain trust agencies. Like the New Deal, the 1970s witnessed the rise of a new generation of reformers inside Washington, except that these free-market Mohicans, as William Safire called Shultz and Stein, sought to shrink the government rather than expand it. Just as ambitious New Dealers used the Great Depression as an opportunity to carry out a Keynesian revolution, so did these reformers use the oil crisis as an occasion to advance the ideology of their intellectual heroes like Friedrich von Hayek, Ayn Rand, and Milton Friedman.

Steeped in an antigovernment philosophy, they all entered public service with a mission, much as the young New Dealers had in the 1930s. Except now they sought to reduce federal spending, cut deficits, and roll back government regulation. Nixon had promised this reform, but the deficit was growing, and so was the size of the federal budget. The energy crisis was forcing a massive expansion of government involvement in the economy, giving the old Democratic liberals another chance to extend the federal government's reach. With a recession looming and the tide of energy prices rising, these Washington conservatives had their fingers in the dam of a great liberal onslaught. Determined and skilled, Ford's men would fight one budget and legislative battle at a time.

Alan Greenspan, whom Ford appointed chairman of the Council of Economic Advisers, reflected the free-market point of view. Born in New York in 1926 to a stockbroker and a saleswoman, Greenspan was, from an early age, a mathematical whiz. He also had musical talent and attended the Juilliard School, where he mastered the jazz saxophone and clarinet. After a brief stint in a swing band, Greenspan studied economics and established a successful economic forecasting firm. In the early 1950s, he met his first wife, Joan Mitchell, an artist who introduced Greenspan to the philosopher Ayn Rand.

For the next two decades, Greenspan was a regular member of Rand's inner circle. Rand, as a radical individualist, saw self-interest as the moral foundation for capitalism. She wanted to eliminate all government regulation, except for crime control and the courts. Rand derided the "evils of altruism" and argued that big business was America's "most persecuted minority." In Rand's 1966 edited book, *Capitalism: The Unknown Ideal*, Greenspan laid out his own conservative views. "Government regulation is not an alternative means of protecting the consumer," he wrote. "It does not build quality into goods, or accuracy into information. Its sole contribution is to substitute force and fear for incentive as the 'protector' of the consumer . . . At the bottom of the endless pile of paper work which characterizes all regulation lies a gun." Greenspan and Rand had a long collaboration. He read draft chapters of *Atlas Shrugged* before its publication in 1957. In 1974, Rand attended Greenspan's swearing-in ceremony as CEA chairman.[16]

Ford's choice of Donald Rumsfeld as his chief of staff best reflected the new administration's cast of Washington conservatives who had been working within the capital to shift politics and policy rightward. Rumsfeld grew up on Chicago's North Shore in a very wealthy and very Republican community where his father was a successful real estate man. As an undergraduate at Princeton University in the early 1950s, he was popular, ambitious, and captain of the wrestling team. After graduating, he served in the navy as a jet pilot and flight instructor. In the 1960s, as a young congressman, he voted against Great Society and War on Poverty legislation. Ford chose Rumsfeld because he had proven himself a skilled insider who knew how to centralize power and also organize and discipline congressional conservatives.[17]

If history has decisive moments, in hindsight, perhaps none proved more fateful than Gerald Ford asking Rumsfeld to join him. This position catapulted Rumsfeld's career as a leading young Republican who offered a clear vision for how the GOP should run the country, free from New Deal influences. Rumsfeld did not enter the White House with the generational New Deal tool kit that his predecessors, including his old boss Richard Nixon, had. This young midwesterner turned powerful presidential adviser had little faith in wage and price controls, deficit spending, and energy regulations. From his NATO experience, he also understood the challenges of asserting American strength and retaining allied support against the backdrop of OPEC's power and rising oil prices.

Below these cabinet-level conservatives, on the front lines of the fight over energy policy, were Frank Zarb and Michael Raoul-Duval. They were in their thirties, as was Rumsfeld's assistant, Richard Cheney, who in 1974 was thirty-three. When Henry Jackson started his congressional career in 1941, these policy makers were in diapers. Cheney was Rumsfeld's deputy at the Cost of Living Council. After Rumsfeld moved from the White House to the Pentagon in 1975, Ford promoted Cheney to chief of staff. In 1978, he would run successfully for Congress from Wyoming.[18]

In the fall, Ford announced that Frank Zarb would be his new energy czar. Zarb, the son of a Maltese immigrant refrigerator repairman, spent his youth in Brooklyn, where he attended a vocational high school. Noticing an intellectual spark, his teachers encouraged him to go to college. At Hofstra University on Long Island, he studied business and became student body president while his future wife, Patricia, served as vice president. After a brief tour of duty in the army, his next job out of college was pumping gas as a company trainee for the Cities Service oil company. He worked his way up to training service station dealers and to a management position, then left to become an investment banker. In 1971, Zarb took on his first government job as an assistant secretary of labor and then worked closely with Simon at the FEO. More than two decades later, Zarb would serve as the chairman of the NASDAQ Stock Market.[19]

Raoul-Duval also entered politics in the Nixon years. A clean-shaven former Marine captain with a law degree from the University of California, he moved to Washington to work in the Department of Transportation before becoming a staff assistant to President Nixon at age thirty-three. Raoul-Duval handled all of the scheduling and advance work for Nixon's China trip and became a member of Nixon's Domestic Council. During the truckers' strike, Zarb was dispatched to come up with the specifics of the freight rate change and diesel price freeze, while Raoul-Duval's job was to stand strong. As a member of Ford's Domestic Council, Raoul-Duval would take the lead in devising the White House political strategy to fend off the Democrats.

Simon's assistant at Treasury Gerald Parsky, who was the point man on oil, energy, and capital markets, typified these young free-market Mohicans. After working for a Wall Street law firm, Parsky joined the Treasury Department in 1971 to help rewrite tax policy. He quickly proved himself to Simon and to Secretary George Shultz; *Time* magazine dubbed him "Treasury's Wunderkind." Parsky moved with Simon to the Federal Energy Office and then back, becoming, at thirty-two, the youngest assistant secretary of the Treasury. Years later, Parsky would join a global law firm specializing in international tax reform and capital investment with an office in Riyadh and head an investment group with Simon. He would become a close confidant of George W. Bush's adviser Karl Rove, serve as the California director of the Bush-Cheney 2004 reelection campaign, and help craft President Bush's Social Security privatization plan of 2005. The world looked very different three decades earlier when this young GOP insider faced an impressive Democratic opposition, confident in its strength and in its armory a full complement of New Deal regulatory solutions.

In the fall of 1974, as the Democratic call grew louder for a stimulus program, Ford insisted on trimming the budget deficit by pushing for spending cuts and a one-year, 5 percent surtax, both of which would drain purchasing power by taking money out of taxpayers' hands. William Simon maintained this was the proper course of action to stem the inflationary tide and restore economic health. Reducing inflation "will not be achieved without pain," he admitted.[20] Alan Greenspan also argued for substantial spending cuts to break what Ford's team saw as inflationary expectations. Paul Samuelson, the liberal economist, remarked, "I'm not sure that Alan's reckoning with Congress and with elections."[21]

Samuelson was right. Budget austerity did not play well at the polling booths. The 1974 November midterm elections were a complete disaster for the GOP. George Bush had flown more than 100,000 miles as Republican National Committee chairman, and in the fall Ford continued the rally.[22] But the Republicans lost forty-three seats in the House. With 291 seats to the GOP's 144, the Democrats had more than double the number of their opponents. Democrats also controlled the Senate, where they picked up three seats, giving them a 61–39 majority.

The economic conditions in the months leading up to the election led to the devastating losses. The Watergate scandal, combined with Ford's pardon of Nixon, made the favorable Democratic outcome likely. The incoming class was quickly dubbed "the Watergate babies," with the average age in the House below fifty. Nearly half of the seventy-five Democratic freshmen were holding elective office for the first time. But the election took place during what was turning out to be the worst downturn since the Great Depression. Detroit's automakers laid off more than a quarter of a million workers. Many cities fired large numbers of their municipal workforces, most spectacularly in New York City. Under these conditions, the GOP insistence on deficit reduction did not hold up to Democrats' demand for greater spending.

With their strengthened numbers, the Democrats on Capitol Hill would call the shots. The situation, Dick Cheney reflected, was the exact opposite of what Franklin Roosevelt and Lyndon Johnson had faced, when each of those transformative presidents relied on large majorities from their party on Capitol Hill.[23] In the weeks after the election, the Democratic leadership introduced bills for large-scale spending and unemployment relief. They also renewed calls for wage and price controls, as inflation now was running above 12 percent. Each night, the three broadcast news shows reported on the price of sugar, which was up 400 percent in just a year. And the fight was on to extend controls on oil.

The conservationists were gearing up too. In the fall, the Ford Foundation published its report *A Time to Choose*. The notion that Americans could solve their energy problems through voluntary restraint was ridiculous, while the use of market prices to draw down demand, especially among low-income families, at a time of rampant inflation and rising unemployment, would be outright cruel. David Freeman, who led the Ford study, called for energy stamps for low-income families and endorsed the Democratic policy of immediate gasoline rationing along with repeal of the oil depletion tax break. "The social equity implications of high energy prices should be resolved by a national commitment to income redistribution measures," said Freeman. Responding to the threat of oil dependency required improving energy efficiency and conservation through policies such as automotive fuel-efficiency standards and loans to households and small businesses for insulation and other energy-saving equipment. Freeman also supported reform of utility rates and the delay of additional power plants.

These environmentalists favored less consumption, not more production. According to Freeman, the country had to slow down its use of energy, which would benefit the environment and improve international standing among allies who insisted the United States consumed too much. "The fact is that the private interests of energy companies and the broader public interest do not always coincide. What is good for business is not always good for the rest of the country," he wrote. Freeman claimed that gains in efficiency would allow for cutting the rate of energy consumption in half without slowing economic growth. "Energy growth and economic growth can be uncoupled," the report boldly proclaimed.

To the oil industry, *A Time to Choose* became a symbol of left-wing attacks on American capitalism. William Tavoulareas, the president of Mobil Oil, criticized the report "as a formula for perpetual economic stagnation." In an op-ed advertisement, Mobil said the report "offers no choice at all." "It says, in essence, that the search for energy is bad; usage of energy is bad; only 'conservation' is good," criticized the oil company. If the country heeded such advice, Americans would rely on bicycles instead of cars and stay at home for vacations. The result would be "government control over our lifestyles."[24]

Just before Thanksgiving, Ford's press secretary, Ron Nessen, appeared before reporters wearing an upside-down WIN pin. When asked what NIM stood for, he said, "No Immediate Miracles." With unemployment at 6.5 percent and rising, Nessen at last acknowledged that the country was in a recession. But that would not change the president's course of action. The president was going to fight for his conservative principles.

Forcing Congress

In mid-December 1974, Ford's top advisers retreated to Camp David to devise a strategy for stopping liberals in their tracks—or at least slowing them down. Addressing the energy crisis was priority number one. Even as the recession was deepening and unemployment was growing, they saw energy dependence as the bigger threat. Alan Greenspan explained, "National economic policy no longer has the luxury of focusing on the very simple question of whether the unemployment rate is 4½ percent or 6½ percent or regrettably even 8 percent." Instead, "the immediate problem is oil." Unless America could become independent of OPEC, the country would no longer hold its preeminent place in the world, and international stability was uncertain. "The viability of our free institutions" hung in the balance.[25]

The international situation looked grim. The Arab-Israeli peace negotiations stalled, American allies were worried about their own interests, and the United States appeared vulnerable. Henry Kissinger successfully negotiated with Western Europe and Japan to create the International Energy

Agency (IEA) for oil-consuming countries. But this was a toothless organization with no check on OPEC. As Frank Zarb summed it up, "What is
essentially at stake is the economic balance of power achieved by the Western World over the last century and a half."[26] Kissinger warned, "Domination is not the issue; survival is."[27]

Beating back OPEC's power and preserving American independence
required letting American businessmen do what historically they had done
best—produce oil. The way to do this was by lifting domestic price controls,
the oil industry's key legislative demand for 1975. Taking off controls and
removing regulations would stimulate domestic production. "The restora-
tion of American dominance in setting the goals and establishing the price
of energy must be the ultimate objective of our national energy policy,"
explained Zarb.[28]

On January 13, 1975, in a television address from the White House,
Ford told Americans that it was time to restore the price mechanism to
energy. Global fuel prices were at historic levels, leading to double-digit
inflation and driving the economy into a serious recession. But the president said Congress had to allow controls to expire as scheduled at the end
of August. That would enable the price of old oil, which represented about
60 percent of the market, to rise from its controlled price of $5.25 to the
market level of roughly $11 per barrel. In addition, the president asked
Congress to end wellhead price controls for natural gas, allow offshore
exploration and coal conversion for factories and utilities, and ease compliance with clean air standards. Ford also proposed the creation of a strategic petroleum reserve in the event of a future embargo.

These measures made up what Ford called his Energy Independence
Act. The goal was to cut oil imports by one million barrels per day by the
end of the year and two million within two years while boosting domestic
production. Using the bully pulpit of the presidency, Ford said, "Americans are no longer in full control of their own national destiny, when that
destiny depends on uncertain foreign fuel at high prices fixed by others."
Energy dependence, he explained, is "intolerable to our national security."
"It seriously threatens . . . the very existence of our freedom and leadership
in the free world," he said at a press conference.

Two days later, in his 1975 State of the Union address, Ford said the
higher cost of oil was a necessary price to pay for the country's independence. Redrafted in the eleventh hour by Donald Rumsfeld and the presi-

dent himself, the speech shed the chirpy optimism of the WIN campaign. Americans were "self-indulgent," said the president. In addition to reducing reliance on foreign oil, Americans needed to cut back on federal spending, which the president said was too high and was driving up inflation. *The New York Times* described the speech as "the gloomiest delivered by a President since the Depression of the nineteen thirties." Congressional applauses interrupted the speech only a handful of times.[29]

There was little to applaud. If Congress let decontrol go into effect, prices at the pump would increase by at least ten cents a gallon.[30] Ford did support an immediate federal income tax cut of $16.5 billion to spur the economy, but that would not fully offset the drain in purchasing power caused by higher fuel prices and was only about half the size of the larger tax cut Democrats wanted as a response to the recession. The University of Chicago economist Arthur Laffer, who had worked for George Shultz at OMB, told Cheney and Rumsfeld that Ford should sponsor his own massive tax cut, not to stimulate consumption, but rather to provide incentives to invest, which in turn would generate growth and greater government revenue, thereby shrinking the deficit. But Ford's team was not ready to embrace what would become a staple of supply-side economics. They were sticking to their agenda of fiscal austerity. Ford coupled his lukewarm endorsement of a tax cut with his insistence on a one-year moratorium on new federal spending.

Ford's Project Independence was a plan born from ideological conviction. It also reflected the reality that the administration had few foreign policy levers it could pull.[31] At Camp David, Frank Zarb had made an off-color remark in jest: "Let's try the low-cost option—war."[32] A few days later, two thousand Marines staged a practice maneuver off the coast of Sardinia as a trial run for a desert invasion. Vice Admiral Frederick Turner, commander of the Mediterranean fleet, told interviewers, "We don't want to invade, but we are prepared."[33] Kissinger himself escalated the military talk when, in a *Business Week* interview, he said that were OPEC producers to use their power to bring about the "strangulation of the industrialized world," it would be difficult to sit by idly. The Pentagon reported that a U.S. aircraft carrier entered the Persian Gulf on a "familiarization deployment." These actions, however, were largely bluster.[34]

With limited military options, Ford was banking everything on Project Independence. As Irving Kristol, one of the founders of neoconservatism,

explained in a *Wall Street Journal* editorial, "This is a foreign policy program, not a domestic economic program at all . . . It is a program that has
as its purpose the preservation of America's status as a world power, with
the capability of conducting a foreign policy free from blackmail." Unless
American oilmen discovered and pumped more oil out of the ground, in
the face of another shortage or another dramatic OPEC price hike the
United States would have to confront the choice of either military intervention, which seemed unlikely, or capitulating to Arab countries.

Kristol saw catastrophe ahead. Appeasement would mean abandoning
American commitment to Israel and acceptance of the rise of anti-Western
Arab nationalists in the Middle East armed by the Soviet Union. Next
would come the disintegration of NATO as European nations watched the
United States desert its allies and shrink from international obligations.
Once Europe became a part of the Soviet sphere of influence, "we shall be
utterly isolated." "To those of us who have even the vaguest memories of
the 1930s, it is all too chillingly reminiscent," warned Kristol. President
Ford told Donald Rumsfeld that he thought Kristol's analysis was "one of
the finest—so perceptive and wise."[35]

In the pages of *Commentary*, the editors published a hotly debated
article, "Oil: The Issue of American Intervention," that offered an aggressive call for the use of force. The neoconservative author, Robert W. Tucker,
explained that the oil crisis and the absence of a credible military response
represented a turning point in American foreign policy. He was stunned
by "the almost utter irrelevance of military power to a conflict that in-
volves vital interests." Tucker laid out what he saw as a plausible military
solution: the United States could seize a four-hundred-mile stretch of
lightly populated oil fields from Kuwait to Qatar, along the Persian Gulf,
which represented 40 percent of the world's oil reserves and 50 percent of
OPEC reserves. If the Soviets intervened through Iraq, a situation Tucker
deemed unlikely because "the Russians simply do not have the interest
here that we have," then the United States could take over Kuwait as a buf-
fer zone. I. F. Stone denounced the article as "criminal nonsense," a reckless decision on behalf of the editors to publish a piece that would only
incite Arab nations. But the choice to publish was part of a larger effort to
influence foreign policy.[36]

Soon after, an anonymous article appeared in *Harper's Magazine* under
the title "Seizing Arab Oil." It called for the deployment of forty thousand

troops in a ten-year occupation of the oil-rich area in eastern Saudi Arabia. Written under a pseudonym, the Unknown Soldier, it was widely reported to have come from within the Department of Defense. Some speculated that Kissinger was behind it, hoping the tough talk would intimidate Saudi Arabia to put pressure on Iran to moderate prices. There was nothing subtle in its analysis: "The only feasible countervailing power to OPEC's control of oil is power itself—military power." "The policy of appeasement has failed, again," wrote the author. "If Vietnam was full of trees and brave men, and the national interest was almost invisible," the writer continued, "here there are no trees, very few men, and a clear objective." "There is no sense in paying $85 billion a year [on defense spending] for impotence," the anonymous author concluded.[37]

Arab leaders threatened to respond to any invasion by blowing up the oil fields. When James Akins attempted to mitigate the damage by suggesting that only a "madman" would recommend a military intervention, Kissinger fired him.[38] But the military option presented real challenges. As one general put it, "We could do it all right. But would the country stand for it? I doubt it. The 'no-more-Vietnams' trauma is still very powerful. And dangerous. There may come a time when we should move for our national interest and the memory of Vietnam will stop us."[39]

On January 30, 1975, President Ford put his Energy Independence Act before Congress. But how would he force this Democratic Congress to submit to his will? At Camp David, his team had hatched a plan. Under the Trade Expansion Act of 1962, Ford had the authority to impose a fee on a foreign good if an import threatened national security. They saw oil from OPEC as such a case, and so Ford would levy a $3 tax on each barrel of foreign crude. Raising prices, his advisers said, would reduce dependency on foreign oil and send a tough signal to OPEC producers. This executive action would also put pressure on Congress to act, or rather in this case, not to act—to let domestic controls lapse. Ford would back off the import fee if Congress permitted domestic controls to expire and passed his other deregulatory measures. Allowing market prices for American oilmen would increase their production, and the result would be the same: a reduced dependence on Middle Eastern oil.

Through this presidential maneuver, Ford was going for the jugular. Specifically, he was targeting the northeastern liberals who were most dependent on foreign oil and also the ones most in favor of domestic controls. Essentially, he was telling them that either they could let the price of domestic fuel rise, which he promised would lead to greater supply, or he would use his authority to raise the price of the foreign oil they used. By his use of executive power, Ford was outflanking his political opponents in Congress, or at least putting pressure on them. Donald Rumsfeld warned Frank Zarb, "Northeastern Congressmen will fight it like mad."[40] And that was the point.

The president gave Congress a deadline to propose an energy bill that he would sign. He would levy the first dollar of the import fee on February 1 and then two more later in the spring. That way the White House would "turn the heat up gradually," said Zarb.[41] Rumsfeld, as a veteran member of the House, understood that the president would have to use what presidential powers he had at his disposal to offset his weakness on the Hill. As Dick Cheney said to Ford, "We need to find some way to force Congress to act." This was a tool, Zarb later recalled, "to get the Congress moving."[42]

On February 1, Ford imposed the first dollar. Immediately, eight northeastern governors filed a suit challenging his action. The oil industry, in contrast, gave him strong support. The Exxon Corporation "welcomes President Ford's effort to address energy policy . . . [by] relying on market forces to achieve the nation's energy objectives."[43] In public testimony before Congress, John Hill of the FEA laid out the logic directly: "The most efficient way to reduce demand and increase supplies (and thereby reduce imports) is, of course, through the price mechanism."[44] The FEA considered running a commercial with the Statue of Liberty surrounded by oil wells on a chessboard and a foreign hand moving the statue around. An aide explained, "The message is that we are vulnerable to foreign powers."[45] The takeaway was clear: lift controls or be controlled.

Ford, the football player, was driving the ball down the field. He took to the hustings, delivering speeches and holding rallies that had the feel of a political campaign. Meeting with governors, farmers, laborers, and businessmen, he urged the nation to put pressure on Congress. In a single day, Ford traveled from Houston, Texas, to Topeka, Kansas, and back to Washington. "I believe it would be a serious mistake not to make the maximum use of the marketplace to achieve our goals," said Ford. Before six hundred oilmen, he extolled the virtues of decontrol. "The promised land of allocations and rationing would turn out to be a jungle," Ford declared to a cheering crowd. In Kansas, Ford denounced these Democratic solutions, saying that Washington was, like the Land of Oz, full of empty promises.[46]

This feisty approach reflected years of Ford's partisan efforts to advance the GOP's unpopular minority platforms. He knew that his calls for fiscal restraint and higher energy prices were a tough sell, with unemployment levels the highest they had been since World War II. After Ford's mention of the Land of Oz, reporters ridiculed the president, writing a parody of the Scarecrow's song: "I could overcome inflation, Put gas in every station . . . I could hold down grocery prices, Wipe out the oil crisis, . . . If I only had a brain."[47] Ford's approval rating dropped to 36 percent, and 86 percent of the public said they did not like how the president was handling the economy.[48]

The Democrats went on the attack. Henry Jackson said Ford's plans were like "rearranging the deck chairs on *Titanic*."[49] Calling for higher energy prices was the wrong policy. In the Senate, Jackson and Edward Kennedy sought to cripple Ford's executive power, drawing up a bill to block his use of the import fee. On February 19, the Senate passed a joint resolution, 66–28, introduced by Kennedy, to delay the president's imposition of additional oil tariffs.[50]

By using his executive authority, Ford hoped to force congressmen to debate not whether to lift controls but when. "I am accused of trying to ram something down their throats," Ford said in a meeting in the Oval Office with the British prime minister, Harold Wilson. "But if I hadn't, Congress would have continued to drift. Congress is now trying to remove my authority to do it. But I will stick to it."[51] Ford agreed to postpone the second dollar on imports as long as Congress would allow the first dollar to stand. That would also give Congress time to propose what the administration saw as a reasonable energy bill.

The Democrats were not taking the bait. They responded to Ford with an alternative that was nothing short of a New Deal throwback. Representative Jim Wright of Texas and Senator John Pastore of Rhode Island, who had both served in Congress since the 1950s, designed it. Pastore, the son of Italian immigrants, grew up in working-class Providence and symbolized the traditional New Deal commitment to robust government with a strong electoral base in an urban industrial center. At the 1964 Democratic convention, President Johnson had personally picked Pastore to deliver the keynote address in which this diminutive five-foot-four-inch liberal, known as the "gamecock of the Senate," eviscerated Senator Barry Goldwater as beholden to "reactionaries and extremists."[52]

Like Pastore, Wright was a fierce Democratic partisan, and the Texan seized the opportunity to challenge the Republican president. Hoping to rise to a House leadership position, Wright placed the interests of consumers over those of his home state producers just as Lyndon Johnson had done once he assumed the presidency. Wright rejected Ford's strong-arm tactics, telling the press, "Relying on a tariff to cut domestic consumption is roughly analogous to a husband's arranging with a merchant to raise the prices on women's clothing in the hope that his wife could be induced to buy fewer dresses. Such a husband might discover that he has outsmarted himself."[53]

The Wright-Pastore plan read more like a call to arms than a legislative proposal. A mere two pages long, it denounced decontrol and deregulation. Instead, it demanded an extension of mandatory allocations and price controls, along with mandatory efficiency improvements and a massive government energy research and development program. This manifesto was thoroughly steeped in traditional Democratic language and New Deal solutions. Among the goals it laid out were full employment, a prevention of price increases, and rationing. "We reject the fundamental premise of the President's program that the only way to achieve energy conservation is deliberately to raise the price," it stated.[54] As the economy slipped into a deep recession, the Democratic Party, including many of its southern members, was closing ranks.

The battle lines were drawn. The Wright-Pastore plan was unworkable, according to the White House. "The differences are fundamental and far-reaching: philosophically, programmatically and in terms of specificity," said John Hill.[55] Michael Raoul-Duval agreed: "Fundamentally, the Pastore-Wright plan rejects the free enterprise approach of the President's energy plan. They substitute government regulation for price/market force mechanism."[56] The Young Republican Leadership conference urged Ford to "readopt the conservative principles that brought about the massive Republican mandate in 1972, and abandon the liberal policies that have brought the United States to the brink of economic disaster."[57]

The Democrats were riding high, with the Watergate babies leading the charge. The newcomers had run on a platform of political reform, seeking to make the legislative process more democratic and challenging the current system in Congress that gave committee chairmen great powers. Recent congressional reforms allowed for greater participation among all members, including junior members, and gave senior members even less standing. These Watergate babies wielded power through the Democratic Caucus, a body that consisted of the full membership of Democrats, and they sought to rein in the power of the Speaker, the majority leader, and committee chairmen. Nothing and no one were sacred. Wilbur Mills, who had chaired the Ways and Means Committee for more than a decade, protecting the oil depletion allowance and ruling with an iron fist, was forced to step down amid a sex scandal. And three other senior committee chairmen lost their grip on power as well.

On the energy question, these young congressmen took a decidedly liberal position, at times farther to the left than the Democratic leadership. They viewed the oil industry as one of the most privileged special interests, with an ability to distort and pervert the legislative process through lobbying, campaign contributions, and even bribery. There was no greater symbol of the industry's special standing than the oil depletion allowance. Common Cause, the leading organization promoting greater transparency, reported that since September 1973 the oil industry had contributed $350,000 to eight members of the Senate Finance Committee, controlled by Senator Russell Long of the oil-producing state of Louisiana.[58] The freshman Democrats in the House joined the more senior Democratic liberals in their disdain of this much-hated industry tax break, which oil-state senators had successfully defended for nearly half a century.

The young Democratic legislators went after oil depletion. Defying the leadership, they insisted on attaching its repeal to the antirecession tax cut that the Democrats were proposing. That would make it difficult for Congress to block or the president to veto. Al Ullman, who replaced Mills as chair of Ways and Means, the majority leader, Tip O'Neill, and Speaker of the House, Carl Albert, failed to persuade the Democratic upstarts to separate the issues. With Mills out of power, this tax break was especially vulnerable. The same thing happened in the Senate, where Mike Mansfield, the majority leader, wanted to delay the depletion allowance issue for fear that the tax cut would not go through before the Easter recess. But the leadership could not hold the younger members of the party in line, and the measure went forward. Senator Long, chairman of the Senate Finance

Committee, won exemption from repeal for the independent oilmen who produced fewer than two thousand barrels a day. But the larger producers could not be protected.[59]

On March 29, Ford signed the Tax Reduction Act, with the oil depletion repeal intact. Ford had requested a much smaller tax cut, which would have largely benefited the better-off taxpayers. The final tax cut, written by the Democrats, was one-third larger and favored lower- and middle-income Americans. Simon and Greenspan, advocating for fiscal austerity, pushed for a veto. But five days earlier, the Senate had passed a tax cut measure double that of Ford's, and this seemed the best he could do. In the end, Ford knew he did not have the votes to pass an alternate tax cut, so he signed it. Just like that, the oil depletion allowance was gone.

What would happen to the rest of the president's energy agenda? Michael Raoul-Duval made an ideological appeal to Ford. "Shall the United States solve its energy crisis by relying on further government control over the use of energy or will we rely on the private sector and free market forces. In short, will it be government choice or free individual and business choices?" he wrote to the president. Ford needed to stand his ground, for we are "drifting towards . . . compromise."

In the twentieth century, there were two great moments of government expansion, the Great Depression and the 1960s, Raoul-Duval explained. "The energy crisis has given us another opportunity to shift towards the course of increasing government control or, hopefully, in the opposite direction." Raoul-Duval contended that Ford would have a tough time resisting the "powerful momentum, pulling our energy choices towards the sanctuary of government controls." Watergate had weakened the presidency, liberals controlled Congress, and, according to the public, government was always the answer. "We face a Nation scared by their economic crisis and conditioned to expect a government-oriented solution," Raoul-Duval explained. "The center of gravity of the political forces which exist in this country is clearly against a solution to a national problem, such as our energy crisis, which relies on the individual and the marketplace."

Ford was at a historic crossroads. The administration should avoid debates over whether a particular energy proposal would yield a savings of one or two million barrels of oil per day. That was a "technocrats' trap." Rather, Raoul-Duval argued, it was important to stand strong on this "critical conservative-liberal choice." Without Ford's decisive leadership and conviction, and a commitment to decontrol, the administration would find itself retreating from core principles. "We need to maintain a public position of flexibility," wrote Raoul-Duval, "but within the Administration, we should have sharply-defined marching orders."[60]

The Conservative Compromise

Ford's team found the Wright-Pastore plan completely unacceptable. But Congress would not let total decontrol stand. "We walk on Main Street. We don't walk behind fences protected by Secret Service men. We walk with the people, and what the people are talking about is high prices," said John Pastore.[61] The question was whether Ford could work out a compromise. The Watergate babies would make it especially difficult. They came into office ready to fight, and they were standing behind tough measures to keep the lid on prices. Andrew Maguire, a thirty-six-year-old freshman representative from New Jersey, led the charge.

The Ford administration backed away from its original insistence on immediate decontrol and made it clear that it would accept a gradual decontrol plan phased in over several years. That would establish the principle of decontrol. When this concession did not yield much—Jackson said this was simply "inflation on the installment plan"—Ford unleashed a blistering attack on his steadfast liberal opponents.[62] "The Congress cannot drift, dawdle and debate forever with America's future," declared a visibly angry president in a May prime-time televised speech. Unless Congress supported decontrol, America would grow increasingly vulnerable. It was just a few weeks earlier that Ford had ordered the evacuation of the last Americans in Saigon as Communist forces took control of South Vietnam. Importing oil posed a national security threat, and it also siphoned off billions of dollars from the American economy. As a result of this fiscal drain, Americans were losing millions of jobs. In the spring, unemployment peaked at 8.9 percent, with more than eight million people out of work. Ford said he was imposing the second dollar import fee. "I cannot sit here idly while nothing is done," he said.

Ford was deeply committed to decontrol, and the Right, which was becoming increasingly organized, bolstered his views that the country would follow him. New Hampshire's governor, Meldrim Thomson Jr., helped to found the Conservative Caucus to mobilize at the grass roots. As he explained to potential supporters, "For 42 years [since the New Deal] we have been giving up freedom to 'we know what's best for you' liberal bureaucrats and social planners in Washington."[63] Right-wing activists, including Phyllis Schlafly, Richard Viguerie, Joseph Coors, Howard Phillips, Ron Docksai, and William Rusher, publisher of *National Review* and author of *The Making of the New Majority Party*, considered forming a third party.[64]

Within the administration, Ford's right-leaning advisers also backed him. Governor Thomson solicited Dick Cheney to become a member of the Conservative Caucus. While Cheney remained loyal to Ford, he had already clashed with the president over Vice President Nelson Rockefeller, especially on energy policy.[65] Rockefeller, a grandson of the oil magnate John D. Rockefeller and a man who personified the eastern Republican establishment, developed plans for an Energy Independence Agency reminiscent of the great government projects of the past, the New Deal's Reconstruction Finance Corporation, the Manhattan Project, and the Apollo space project. Rockefeller, who as governor of New York had expanded large-scale public projects, typified the Republican accommodation to big government.

Cheney hated this energy idea, claiming that government entry into the oil industry would distort capital markets, increase the deficit, create another large bureaucracy, and be inconsistent with Ford's market ideology. Much to Cheney's consternation, the project gained momentum. As he told Donald Rumsfeld, "I am concerned that a number of people on the staff may not have been as direct as they should have been in voicing their concerns to the Vice President. As is often the case, people are awed by the Vice President and reluctant to disagree with him. This may in turn lead the Vice President to mistakenly assume that they agree with the substance of his proposals."[66] The president lent tepid support to Rockefeller's scheme for a government research project, aware that it would get bogged down in Congress.

In advocating for some sort of gradual decontrol, Ford was not caving; rather, he was attempting to steer a course that would achieve his long-term goal and would not be overturned by a Democratic Congress wanting to avoid presiding over price hikes during an election year. Conservatives might demand ideological purity, but Ford was looking for a realistic path, politically and legislatively, toward achieving the permanent end of New Deal–style controls. He also suffered a blow when the U.S. Court of Appeals ruled that he did not have the authority to levy an import fee. (The Supreme Court would ultimately rule in Ford's favor, but that judgment came too late.)

As the White House was seeking some kind of compromise, Ford let the Right know that he would not abandon his conservative principles. He had an opportunity to demonstrate his resolve against the power of liberals when New York City sank into an unprecedented fiscal crisis. Appealing to the president to bail them out, New York leaders hoped to avoid defaulting. Ford resisted, insisting that the city impose austerity measures. Secretary of the Treasury William Simon steadfastly opposed a bailout. "The fundamental solution to the city's financial problems does not lie at the federal level," said a stern Simon.[67] "We gave them no encouragement," repeated Gerald Parsky, Simon's assistant, in reporting on a meeting with New York City officials.[68]

The president parlayed his punitive policy against New York effectively in national political circles. When a New York delegation failed to squeeze money from the president, the New York *Daily News* headline ran, "Ford to City: Drop Dead." To the delight of conservatives, he used the financial troubles in New York as an opportunity to preach the value of fiscal restraint and the necessity of austerity. This message was crafted as much to placate conservatives, who were growing more interested in the potential challenge to the incumbent from Governor Ronald Reagan, as it was to appeal to the general public.

A few days after the *Daily News* headline, Ford announced a shake-up in his cabinet, which the press quickly dubbed the "Halloween Massacre." Top of the list was the decision to dump Nelson Rockefeller as the vice presidential candidate on Ford's reelection ticket. In addition, Ford replaced James Schlesinger, with whom he had repeated personal clashes, with Rumsfeld as defense secretary. Cheney took Rumsfeld's spot as chief of staff. George H. W. Bush became the head of the CIA. Ford stripped Kissinger of his national security adviser role, a position that went to Brent Scowcroft. With Rumsfeld at the Pentagon and Bush at the CIA, and

Kissinger out of the White House, Ford was installing "his team." On his first day, Rumsfeld said, "Détente must be seen for what it is—a word for the approach we use in relations with nations who are not our friends, who do not share our principles, whom we are not sure we can trust."[69]

On environmental policy, too, Ford demonstrated his right-leaning resolve. Twice he vetoed strip-mining regulation legislation, and he also supported easing restrictions on offshore drilling and nuclear power. He had long opposed these regulations, but now Project Independence gave him additional justification to challenge environmental protection. Amid the recession, critics gained traction in their arguments that greater environmental protections would harm the economy. Ford appointed Stanley Hathaway, the former governor of Wyoming and known opponent of environmentalism, as the secretary of the interior.

On economic policy, Ford took his toughest stand, insisting on a spending freeze. It was up to the White House, said a reassuring Alan Greenspan, to fight for "a program to stem the ever growing presence of governmental intervention into the personal lives of American citizens." At all costs, Ford had to commit to "defending our system in ethical and moral terms."[70] The Democrats were pushing for another tax cut, but Ford said he would veto any measure that did not have corresponding spending cuts. On national television, with the New York City crisis as the backdrop, Ford told Americans, "We must decide whether we shall continue in the direction of recent years—the path toward bigger government, higher taxes, and higher inflation—or whether we shall now take a new direction, bringing to a halt the momentous growth of government, restoring our prosperity, and allowing each of you a greater voice in your own future."

Ford laid out his austerity plan, a stunning political choice as the economy was facing unemployment levels approaching double digits. The rate in New York City, at 12 percent, was inching toward some of the worst levels of the Great Depression, and Detroit's inner city posted an unemployment rate more than double New York's.[71] Ford vetoed a public jobs bill and a housing bill. As promised, he also vetoed a tax cut that Congress put forth without spending cuts.

In the end, the best Ford could do was use the threat of a veto to prevent an even larger stimulus that liberals were calling for. He did not have the political muscle he needed to withstand some kind of stimulus. Under pressure, he had to accept a $9 billion extension of the 1975 tax cuts with only a promise for future spending cuts. Ford also relented on a New York bailout. As the economy continued to slide, and other cities faced difficult cuts, sympathy grew for federal aid. The president understood that liberals were still strong, and the old solutions to economic crisis were hard to purge.

After nearly a year of negotiations, Congress finally delivered an energy bill to Ford's desk in December, the Energy Policy and Conservation Act of 1975. Ford had agreed to a temporary extension of price controls when they expired in August to allow more time for Congress to put forward a bill. The one that wound up in front of the president was not one he liked. It was a price rollback bill, similar in effect to the measure that Democrats had drawn up in the worst days of the Arab embargo. The measure rolled back the price of crude oil by extending price controls to new oil, which had previously been exempt. And rather than expiring, controls would be extended for three more years. The bill gave the president authority to administer oil decontrol incrementally. Each time the White House wanted to raise prices, however, it would have to seek congressional approval.

The Republican leadership and oil-state senators minced no words in telling the president he should veto the bill. Senator John Tower, the powerful Republican from Texas who chaired the Republican Policy Committee, told Ford, "This bill is an absolute and total disaster. It's 180 degrees away from your earlier position. The *New York Times* has called it a victory for Scoop and the Democrats. It means more Arab oil. The consumer savings stuff is bunk . . . It will pay a high price in domestic jobs . . . It is a turning away from energy independence and will wipe out the marginal producer. Mr. President, you get no credit by signing and it's a capitulation to Scoop." Senator Clifford Hansen, Republican from Wyoming, agreed: "I support John Tower 100%. This is a disaster." Dewey Bartlett, Republican from Oklahoma, a former oilman, accused the president of switching midstream: "There is more control, less free market, and we become more dependent upon the Arabs . . . This would be selling the free market and private enterprise down the river."

Senator Charles Percy, a moderate Republican from Illinois, tried to broker peace: "It is not a good piece of legislation, but it does have a bias toward letting market forces work." At least it would remove the indecision that the industry had operated under since controls had begun, by setting a timetable for decontrol. To which Tower retorted, "It would remove the indecision alright. It would stack rigs and stop seismic drilling."[72] The industry agreed. Robert Young of Exxon wrote to Ford to denounce the compromise: "Capitulation would be a more appropriate description." Most of the opposition came from oil- and gas-producing areas of Texas, Oklahoma, New Mexico, Louisiana, California, Arizona, Colorado, Wyoming, Florida, Kansas, and Arkansas.[73]

The president pointed out the political reality that Democrats outnumbered Republicans on the conference committee two to one. "It was a hell of an achievement to get this agreement," he said. Hugh Scott, Republican of Pennsylvania, the Senate minority leader, recommended making the deal. The Republicans who pushed for a veto "were like the last ditch Republicans who opposed Social Security and the party has paid the penalty ever since." Still, the House Republican Policy Committee, made up of the most conservative Republicans, called for a veto, disparaging "the mirage of bargain-basement pre-election energy prices combined, impossibly, with future abundant energy supplies and no-pinch conservation measures."[74]

Ford's advisers were split along familiar lines. Alan Greenspan recommended a veto and tried to persuade Zarb to back down. "By embracing controls now it will substantially reduce and probably eliminate the opportunity to remove controls later," Greenspan argued. More generally, "it will encourage the forces which would extend government direction of the economy and discourage those who would rely on the free market to guide consumption and production."[75] Greenspan also thought that if Ford signed the bill, he would damage what Greenspan saw as the president's key asset: "telling it like it is" instead of opting for political expediency. "Anyone who defends higher oil prices to achieve a necessary long-term economic advantage for the country cannot be pandering to a special-interest electorate," said the CEA chairman.[76]

William Simon pushed most vehemently for a veto. For Simon, this choice was the single most important one Ford would make, signaling his ideological commitment to conservative values. Ford should veto the bill even if that meant a short-term decline in economic growth and an increase in unemployment and inflation in an election year. The long-term costs of the measure far outweighed any other considerations. The bill would produce an uncertain investment climate, deny industry necessary capital at the same time that the end of the depletion allowance also took away capital, and above all pose economic and national security risks. Simon, too, believed that price controls would become permanent. The night before Ford made his decision, Simon called the president after midnight and yelled at him for an hour.[77]

Ford faced a difficult decision. He was personally committed to ending controls, and this bill departed significantly from what he had proposed. Election year considerations did not point in any clear direction. On November 20, the former California governor Ronald Reagan had announced he was seeking the Republican nomination in 1976 and would run a primary campaign to Ford's right.[78] But as much as Ford feared the threat from the hard Right, he also had to run in a general election in which the number of registered Democrats outnumbered Republicans more than two to one. Campaign finance reform reduced Republicans' traditional fund-raising advantage, and the deep recession hurt Ford's ratings. If Ford vetoed the bill, the Democratic Congress would certainly make repeated attempts to roll back oil prices, especially in an election year. At the moment, Senator Jackson looked like a real contender. If Ford accepted the bill, however, then he could take credit for pressuring Congress to take action. At least the Democratic candidate would have a harder time turning energy into an election issue.[79]

At the last minute, the energy bill took a backseat to what had been a core Republican issue since the New Deal, the role of labor and the legislation that sustained its power. Labor leaders were pushing for a bill to make it easier to organize construction sites and shut them down during strikes. This measure would enhance union strength in a key sector of the economy, and its proponents saw it as vital to retaining union power on the shop floor and in the economy as a whole. Organized labor correctly understood the contest over this bill as a test of its political and economic power.

Senator Paul Fannin, who played a leading role on energy, worked hard to defeat this labor bill. Like Barry Goldwater, Fannin had led right-to-work campaigns in Arizona. In the end, Fannin made it clear that he was willing to trade one veto for another. Robert Hartmann, Ford's old-time adviser, recommended choosing to veto one but not both for fear of appearing to veto everything. Ford understood that to satisfy Republicans he needed to veto one of these two bills. "If you intend to veto [the labor bill], hold your nose and proclaim that you have finally persuaded Congress to adopt an imperfect national energy program which can be further perfected next year," advised Hartmann. "The big oil companies' bark will undoubtedly prove worse than their bite."[80]

Ford made up his mind to sign the energy bill. The bill included many of the measures Ford had initially proposed. It created a strategic petroleum reserve, allowed for coal conversion, and delayed implementation of emissions standards. In exchange, the bill required the automobile industry to improve energy efficiency by 40 percent over a decade. At the time, the average gas mileage for new cars was approximately 13 miles per gallon. The new law, with its corporate average fuel economy (CAFE) standards, required automakers to achieve 18 miles per gallon by 1978 and 27.5 by 1985. It also imposed a ban on oil exports to protect domestic supply.

On the most contentious issue of prices, the bill provided agreement on the principle of decontrol to take place over a number of years. Prices of crude oil would rise gradually, and the president had the authority to recommend a faster rate of increase, unless Congress rejected the request. The law also authorized the president to propose decontrol of finished petroleum products, subject to congressional disapproval. It also provided the president with standby authority to allocate and ration in the event of another embargo.

When Frank Zarb and Alan Greenspan announced Ford's decision, the press scored it as a White House defeat. Under the existing system, controls set the price of old oil at $5.25 a barrel, leaving new oil uncontrolled. This bill now mandated a composite price for all oil, new and old, of $7.66. In effect that price required new oil to be rolled back from the current market price above $13 a barrel to $11.28. Reporters asked why, if the president had insisted that national security, energy independence, and economic stability required higher prices, he had agreed to roll back prices and extend controls for more than three years. Zarb suggested that the nation had made recent unexpected gains in conservation, and therefore Ford could sign the bill. Higher prices, Zarb explained, had already worked to slow demand and spur production. Not wanting to portray the administration as caving in, Zarb did not grab credit for a price rollback and denied that one would be substantial. Greenspan, who had been one of the bill's chief opponents, barely mustered a defense.[81]

Ford made peace with his decision. "This legislation represents the most constructive bill we are likely to work out at this time," he said at the signing. Later, Ford reflected that if he could have acted on his own, "I probably would have decontrolled period, immediately." "But that was not the real world. The real world was that I had to deal with the Congress," said the president, who had served for twenty-four years in the House, mostly in the minority. He believed that a "half a loaf was better than none."[82] Several weeks earlier, forty-five senators had voted for a divestiture bill to split up the major oil companies. The strength of anti-oil sentiment spoke to the deep mistrust of the private marketplace and the persistent support for government regulation.

The political Right felt betrayed. Michel Halbouty, an independent oil producer who had been active in the Texas GOP, instantly threw his support behind Ronald Reagan. Halbouty, a legendary wildcatter, had developed a reputation in Washington as the Texan who, since the 1960s, had warned about the dangers of dependence on Arab oil. Senator Tower summoned Halbouty to meet with President Ford and urge him to veto the measure. The wildcatter had done his best, but Ford had other considerations. "I feel the President has caved to the pressure of radical members of Congress, and I fear he has been misled by Frank Zarb to sign this legislative monstrosity for purely political reasons," Halbouty told reporters. "As an American in search of leadership, and a Republican who has stood with his party through thick and thin, I am disgusted."[83] Reagan would be his man.

The Wall Street Journal saw Ford's decision as "the clearest blunder of his administration." "What was bad for Texas was supposedly good for the rest of the nation," editorialized the *Journal*. According to this logic, Ford had traded the Texas primaries for an early win in New Hampshire. Texas was already leaning toward Reagan, perceiving Ford as too liberal. That perception stemmed from his selection of Nelson Rockefeller as his first vice president, the growing federal deficits under his watch, and his granting of amnesty to draft evaders. Still, one White House confidant saw Ford's signing as "the principal reason the dumb bastard got walloped by Reagan in Texas."[84]

Throughout the 1976 primary season, Ford had to beat back Reagan's challenge from the right. To help him, he recruited George Bush's friend James Baker, who had come to Washington to serve in the Commerce

Department. Baker, as a Texas Republican, was perfectly poised to take on Reagan. On domestic policy, the former California governor called for a massive spending cut of $90 billion. That fit with his antigovernment ideology, but it did not play well in the large industrial states of the Midwest and the East, where Ford was able to secure comfortable victories. A critical win for the insurgent candidate came in the March North Carolina primary, where Reagan won based largely on his attack on Ford's foreign policy. In the South and the West, Reagan's message of strong defense, tax cuts, and smaller government had greatest appeal. According to Reagan, the country needed a leader who could break through what he called the "buddy system" in Washington.[85]

Reagan was not the only candidate running as an outsider. That was the theme of Jimmy Carter's Democratic campaign. In the aftermath of Watergate, the Georgia governor used his status as an outsider to push aside more traditional Democratic prospects such as Henry Jackson and Morris Udall. Hamilton Jordan, who would later become Carter's chief of staff, counseled the Georgia governor, "Perhaps the strongest feeling in this country today is the general distrust of government and politicians at all levels."[86] Carter, a Southern Baptist who wore his religion on his sleeve, promised Americans that he would restore respectability to the White House and rebuild trust in government. (He liked to leave out the fact that he had served as the campaign chairman of the Democratic National Committee.)

Even as he sold himself as a new kind of candidate, Carter ran a traditional Democratic campaign. The recession of 1974–75 and its lingering effects left him no choice as millions of Americans were still out of work. He conveyed more skepticism about organized labor than many of his northern colleagues. But Carter understood the need to build on traditional Democratic themes if he hoped to win in the fall. In Congress, Hubert Humphrey and Augustus Hawkins were proposing the Humphrey-Hawkins full-employment bill, which would require a major federal jobs program to keep unemployment no higher than 3 percent. At the Democratic convention in mid-July in New York City, Carter selected the Minnesota senator Walter Mondale, a protégé of Humphrey's and a favorite among organized labor, as his running mate to dispel any doubts the delegates might have. The Texas Democrat Barbara Jordan, one of the most prominent African-American elected officials, delivered a powerful keynote address trumpeting the Democrats as the only party that would respond to the needs of Americans facing hard times.

Ford's top strategists felt that liberal Democrats were out of step with the general public. The day after the Democratic convention, William Simon lambasted the opposition: "The Democratic Party Platform contains so much bigger-and-bigger government." This provided the White House with an opening, explained Simon, for "we should easily be able to shape a Republican program which offers a clear choice." Instead of tempering his conservatism, Ford should run on a platform of "the freedom and dignity of the individual, an emphasis on private enterprise, the need to keep the government within bounds to serve the people (not vice versa)." "In blunt terms," advised the Treasury secretary, "the Carter-Mondale ticket should be forced into clear identification with the spend-spend, inflation-inflation, controls, big government Democratic platform." The president had to stick to his ground and attack "the Democrats' fraudulent and counter-productive emphasis on bigger and bigger government as an instant and permanent cureall to our problems."[87]

With few exceptions, Republican Party regulars stayed with the president and believed that he represented the best hope for conservative free-market ideals. White House officials saw Reagan delegates as "right-wing nuts" who operated on the principle of "rule or ruin," supporting their candidate even though he did not have electoral viability and even though the bruising battle would end up weakening the sitting president.[88] To signal his own political outlook, Ford got rid of Rockefeller from the ticket in favor of the more conservative and acerbic senator Bob Dole. After a brutal primary season, neither candidate had secured enough delegates. Fighting all the way through the August convention, Ford scraped together enough votes to win the nomination.

Ford's 1976 campaign was not simply about outflanking Ronald Reagan. His campaign reflected the genuine beliefs of top staffers in the White House who saw the election as a referendum on the future of American government. Richard Cheney, Ford's new chief of staff, asked Michael Raoul-Duval to map out a conservative strategy for the general election against Carter. Raoul-Duval wrote a 120-page memo modeled consciously on the famous memo that Clark Clifford had written for President Truman in November 1947 in which Clifford had advised Truman to return to his labor-liberal base. Raoul-Duval told Ford to stake out a clear, coherent, conservative alternative to Carter's liberal impulses. "We are in the process of making a choice (consciously or not) between greater self-reliance to govern our lives, or even greater reliance on government," counseled Raoul-Duval. "For many Americans who believe that unconstrained government is a threat to individual freedom, your election in November is a national imperative," he told the president. "For them and for us, the campaign is not simply a fight for power. We are fighting for principle."[89]

In the remaining two months of the campaign, Ford staged an amazing comeback against Carter's postconvention lead of more than thirty points.[90] Only one week before the election, pollsters could not say who would win. Most of the televised debates, in which Ford seemed clumsy and ill-prepared, favored Carter. Even still, Ford had appeal as the incumbent president running against a governor who was largely untested.

The state of the economy, however, made the president vulnerable. Seven million Americans were unemployed after eighteen months of economic expansion. That reflected substantial progress, with unemployment rates dropping from near 10 percent down to just above 7. Throughout the summer, Alan Greenspan had argued against fiscal stimulation, claiming the economy was rebounding and warning that increased spending would trigger inflation and lead to the very recession that the Democratic Congress wanted to combat. But in the fall, unemployment rose back up to 7.9 percent, which, in spite of the White House efforts to stress that this was temporary, the press labeled the "Greenspan pause."[91]

As the Democratic Congress continued to push for increased spending and a jobs program, the president stuck to his message of smaller government and free markets. Milton Friedman, who won the Nobel Prize in Economics in 1976, preached the value of this conservative ideology. The economist told a national audience on NBC's *Meet the Press*, "There are very few taxpayers I believe who think they are getting their money's worth for the forty percent of their income which is being spent for them by government bureaucrats."[92]

Yet the Democratic Party's promise of government assistance in hard times still resonated in 1970s America. As they had for generations, millions of Americans looked to the promise of more government spending to help them through tough economic circumstances. Ford was offering austerity at the worst moment since the Great Depression. A national poll showed Americans trusting Democrats over Republicans to handle economic issues by a two-to-one margin.[93] In November, the aftermath of Watergate as well as Carter's basic promise to have the government help those who were suffering brought out the traditional Democratic coalition. In addition to his victories in the South, Carter won a few large industrial states, including New York, Ohio, Wisconsin, and Pennsylvania.

In the Ford years, conservatives moved from the margins to the center of power, and they had much to celebrate. During the steepest downturn since the 1930s, they thwarted the ambitions of a Democratic Congress. Alan Greenspan and William Simon argued that inflation was a bigger evil than unemployment, and along with other Washington conservatives like Donald Rumsfeld and Richard Cheney they urged Ford to use the threat of the veto to prevent a large stimulus package pushed by Democrats. Simon offered up an argument, which would become commonplace, that public debt "crowds out" private investment, raises interest rates, and reduces confidence in the dollar, and therefore was enemy number one.

The same was true on energy. The plan had not worked out exactly as these Washington conservatives had hoped. When Richard Nixon had created the Federal Energy Office, Secretary George Shultz said to William Simon, "I'm so glad it's you who's heading up the energy bureaucracy. That way it will go out of business, and you'll be able to keep the damage in check." It did not turn out that way. As Simon regretfully explained, "Well, I didn't keep the damage in check—it outlasted me. And Zarb didn't keep the damage in check—it outlasted him. 'We' are all out now, 'they' are all in now, and 'our' detestable bureaucratic creations, devised by 'their' standards, are in place, waiting to be used for purposes 'we' privately deplore." These conservatives had hoped to restore the free market. But as Simon concluded, "It is obvious to me that one does not acquire virtue by becoming a 'better type' of prostitute. Nor, obviously, does one win votes."[94]

Yet they had paved the way for a new future. Even as energy prices remained high, and OPEC seemed unwilling to bend, Congress began the process of decontrol. The FEA stayed intact, and the government continued to set the price of domestic crude oil and gasoline. But the free-market Mohicans had forced Congress to pass legislation that set a timetable for the end of the era of controls. In his last year in office, Ford used his executive authority, granted under the 1975 Energy Act, to decontrol the prices of half of all refined products, including home heating oil. "A year ago if the President had sent me up to the Hill to talk about deregulating the price of home heating oil, I would have been tarred and feathered," said Frank Zarb.[95]

It would be up to Jimmy Carter and the Democrats to take the reins of power and chart the future of policy where Ford and the conservatives had left off.

Part III

Divided Democrats

5

Freeze a Yankee

ON JANUARY 20, 1977, Jimmy Carter became the nation's thirty-ninth president. After swearing his oath of office with George Washington's Bible and delivering his inaugural address, this soft-spoken peanut farmer and his wife, Rosalynn, broke with tradition. Rather than riding in a limousine motorcade, the president and the First Lady walked up Pennsylvania Avenue from Capitol Hill to the White House. This choice reflected Carter's preference for eschewing the pomp and ceremony of his office. Headlines touted him as the people's president. The near-record cold weather, with temperatures in the teens, made this display all the more remarkable. The day the president took office, Washington, D.C., and much of the rest of the country east of the Rockies were in a deep freeze.

On Thin Ice

"Please keep thermostats at 65 degrees—The Management." So read the newly affixed signs hung throughout the White House on Carter's first day.[1] With the extreme cold, the country was facing an acute shortage of natural gas, one that was getting worse by the day, and the president said all Americans had to cut back on heating. The winter was shaping up to be the coldest in nearly a hundred years; forecasts were predicting subzero temperatures and massive snowstorms for the weeks ahead. In Philadelphia, a man attempting suicide failed when he bounced off the frozen ice of the Schuylkill River. Miami had its first snow ever.

Once again the energy crisis was headline news. "1.5 Million Left Jobless, 45 or More Dead in Freeze," reported the Associated Press.[2] Without enough heat and electricity, the major Midwest auto manufacturers shut down, as did thousands of other businesses. The Ohio governor ordered one million schoolchildren to stay home for a month. Minnesota, Tennessee, Virginia, Florida, Indiana, Pennsylvania, and New York declared a fuel emergency, as did New Jersey, where Governor Brendan Byrne asked housewives to leave laundry unwashed and requested that residents take short showers instead of baths. Ordering thermostats turned down, he said the state police would conduct compliance checks. "Damn right we're going to arrest people," snapped his aide.[3]

This was a disaster for the country, and it was a disaster for Jimmy Carter, too. At the time, natural gas provided roughly one-third of all energy needs, and many of the users were in the North. But at least half of the available supply was staying within the southern states where it was produced and where the Federal Power Commission had no authority to set prices. Forty million homeowners and half of the nation's industrialists—all of whom relied on natural gas—cast an expectant glance at the new president.[4] So, too, did the oil patch, where producers were hoping, at long last, to do away with natural gas controls. The only way to get gas to the North, an independent producer told Carter, was to end the "Congressionally-created energy shortages."[5]

Carter agreed. On the campaign trail, this southern pro-business Democrat had pledged support for deregulating natural gas prices. In taking this position, he was choosing to support the interests of southern producers over northern consumers, something that no Democratic president had done since the New Deal had first regulated the industry. With an eye toward securing an electoral victory, Carter promised the governors of Texas, Louisiana, and Oklahoma to "work with Congress, as the Ford Administration has been unable to do, to deregulate." Texas, with its twenty-six electoral votes, had gone for Nixon in 1972. Representative Robert Krueger, Democrat from Texas, the leading champion of deregulation, proclaimed that this pledge helped Carter win his state.[6]

Carter's support of decontrol reflected his position as a centrist Democrat. The peanut planter turned politician decided to run for president after Richard Nixon had crushed Senator George McGovern and his brand of liberalism in 1972. A fiscal conservative, Carter stood to the right of his party's mainstream. Carter built his presidential campaign around his own biography as a "New South" Democrat who would draw on his business acumen as a profitable producer as the basis for a new managerial style of leadership, one that was more pragmatic and less ideological and certainly less interested in traditional Democratic policies. Defeating party stalwarts like Henry Jackson in the primaries, Carter ran on the slogan "A Leader, for a Change." His approach to everything, from the economy to energy to the environment, was, in the words of the journalist David Broder, a kind of "managerial moralism."[7]

For Carter, lifting controls was in fact a moral issue. Above all else, Carter believed in the necessity of conservation. A devout born-again Christian and Sunday school teacher, he held dear the values of self-sacrifice and simple pleasures. Having grown up during the Great Depression in a house without electricity or indoor plumbing, he worked side by side with his father on the family farm. For his inauguration, he shunned traditional formal attire and instead donned a suit he had purchased the week before off the rack in Georgia. In his first presidential address, he preached, "We have learned that more is not necessarily better, that even our great Nation has its recognized limits, and that we can neither answer all problems nor solve all problems. We cannot afford to do everything." Nixon and Ford had defined Project Independence, with decontrol at its center, as a program to boost domestic production; Carter believed the path to independence was to reduce consumption. By lifting controls, he would raise the prices of what Americans paid for their fuel, and that would lead them to cut back.

This kind of asceticism put Carter at odds with the New Deal Democrats who still controlled the party. After his victory, Pat Caddell, the president-elect's pollster, advised Carter to resist the pressure to "resort to old Democratic dogmas." As powerful as Senator Ted Kennedy, Democrat from Massachusetts, and other congressional liberals were, Caddell reasoned, they were becoming increasingly "antiquated and anachronistic."[8] Beating Ford in a close race, Carter had drawn support from traditional Democratic voters, including organized labor and minorities who rejected

Ford's fiscal austerity. Yet Carter's outlook was shaped more by white-collar, middle-class suburban America, including in the Sunbelt areas, where he had a strong showing and which were growing as the industrial core of blue-collar union workers was shrinking. Carter, a religious southern businessman, did not have an instinctive feel for the world of union leaders, nor did he believe that their claims for higher wages and more government spending, let alone more fuel at cheap prices, were justified.

Carter confirmed his preference for market mechanisms when he named James Schlesinger his chief energy adviser after the election. He shared Schlesinger's assessment that the country's overreliance on foreign oil, up from 36 to 42 percent of total use, was the most pressing national problem. In December, OPEC had announced a 10 percent price increase. Americans were paying $34 billion annually to foreign producers, an amount that was just under 10 percent of the federal budget. The Republican economist believed that the path to independence required ending controls and letting prices rise. Northern liberals were irate at the Schlesinger appointment, as were the environmentalists who knew he championed nuclear power. "To people who prize the earth," wrote one journalist, "this is inviting the fox into the chicken coop."[9]

Carter could not completely ignore the large constituents of liberals in his party. If the Left did not like Schlesinger, the Right was furious about the presence of David Freeman on Carter's transition team. As a former employee of the Tennessee Valley Authority and public power advocate, Freeman wanted to extend natural gas price controls to the intrastate market. An independent Texas producer complained, "He is philosophically dedicated to socialism and against free enterprise."[10] The author of *A Time to Choose*, Freeman supported the point of view articulated by Amory Lovins, a physicist and environmental activist, who argued for slowing energy consumption and promoting "soft" energies, like solar and wind power, which were renewable, decentralized, and less capital-intensive.[11]

Carter pledged to environmentalists that he would slow offshore drilling, back away from the controversial nuclear breeder reactor program, support strip-mining legislation, and push for stricter emissions controls. A former nuclear engineer and naval officer, Carter had faith in new technologies to solve problems. After his mile-long, inauguration day walk, the new president watched the rest of the parade from a solar-heated viewing stand.

In his first days in office, *The New York Times* ran a photograph of Carter slipping on the frozen ice in the Rose Garden, a powerful metaphor for the treacherous terrain on which the new president would have to find his footing. As the leader of his party, Carter enjoyed significant majorities in Congress, including enough Democrats to end a filibuster in the Senate and summon a two-thirds majority in the House. But wide cleavages were dividing the party. With a stagnant economy, traditional liberals pointed to jobs, health care, and the protection of labor rights as the key issues of the day, while many younger, recently elected Democrats supported government reform and environmental measures. Still others, including the sizable constituency of southerners, favored fiscal restraint, deregulation, and stronger defense. Navigating the current political landscape would have proved challenging for even the most skillful of leaders, but Carter, as an outsider, operated at a distinct disadvantage. He was the first president with no experience in Washington since Calvin Coolidge.

To the White House, Carter brought with him his so-called Georgia mafia, his group of advisers and confidants from his days as governor. Also known as the "peanut brigade," they sorely lacked a deep understanding of how Congress worked and believed a more democratic and open management style would facilitate policy making and substitute for the kind of heavy-handed presidential persuasion and horse-trading that Carter derided. Jody Powell, who started his career as Carter's driver in 1970 and became press secretary, explained that the White House organization would be more like "spokes of a wheel," with all having direct access to the president. When Hamilton Jordan went into his new office, he discovered a beat-up bike wheel with a note attached to it from his predecessor, Richard Cheney. "Hamilton, Beware of the spokes of the wheel, Dick," it read.[12]

On day one, the deep freeze, and the threat of serious shortages of heating fuel and electricity, forced the new president to jump headfirst into the morass of energy politics. The top priority was to get natural gas into the nation's needy homes, hospitals, factories, and schools. The president wanted the FPC to release natural gas from Texas into the interstate market. But the Republican-appointed holdovers on the FPC hesitated, claiming they had no authority for this action. One member, James Watt, a young Wyoming lawyer who had worked on the staff of the conservative Republican Milward Simpson and for the U.S. Chamber of Commerce, doubted the value of any kind of "Band-Aid approach." Instead, they, along with the nation's energy executives, wanted total decontrol as the solution. Take off the restrictions on interstate gas, and the producers would gladly meet the demand.[13]

Conservatives no longer had their man in the White House, but their thinking had left an important legacy. Milton Friedman held a press conference; the natural gas shortage stemmed from the decision to set prices "not by the free market but by government fiat." "Amazingly," said Friedman, Americans do not "say, 'Boy is this a stupid system.' Instead they say the government should have still more power."[14] "There's no mystery about why production is not booming," said the former Nixon speechwriter William Safire. "The regulators have made it stupid to produce gas . . . In this severe winter, the frozen chickens came home to roost. Never before have we had as dramatic an example of the folly of intrusion into the marketplace by well-meaning regulators."[15] Patrick Buchanan, another Nixon speechwriter, suggested that the only way "to allocate natural gas [is] the same way we ration Cadillacs, Chivas Regal, sirloin steaks, and 21-inch color TV sets—through the price mechanism, the market system."[16]

Texas Democrats joined these conservatives in pushing Carter to live up to his campaign commitment to deregulate natural gas. "There is no one in or out of government smart enough to make price controls work for the long-term benefit of consumers," said Texas's governor, Dolph Briscoe.[17] Senator Lloyd Bentsen joined his fellow Texan Representative Krueger in putting pressure on the White House for a deregulation bill. Personally, Carter favored their view. He believed in the price mechanism. Higher prices set by the market would compel consumers to cut back.

But the political momentum was swinging in the other direction. "There are not ideal circumstances to deregulate gas," James Schlesinger told a conference of anxious mayors whose constituents were facing mounting energy bills.[18] John O'Leary, Carter's appointment as head of the Federal Energy Administration, concurred: "I think there are a number of things we can do short of taking the big stick and whopping the consumers across the face with a price rise."[19] Behind the scenes, David Freeman was working out of Walter Mondale's vice presidential office on emergency legislation along with Alvin Alm from the Environmental Protection Agency and James Flug, a leading liberal lobbyist. All three were well-known proponents of regulation.[20]

On February 2, Carter signed his first piece of legislation, the Emergency Natural Gas Act of 1977. The bill authorized the Federal Power Commission to allocate interstate supplies of natural gas from the West, where it was plentiful, to regions east of the Rockies facing the worst shortages. That was what the liberals wanted. But it also permitted the temporary sale of intrastate gas in the interstate market at unregulated prices until the shortage was over.

On national television, minutes after he signed the emergency bill, Carter delivered a fireside chat. Rather than speaking from the Oval Office, the president appeared in a cardigan sweater, seated in an armchair by a fire in the White House library. After two weeks of talking about how he and the First Lady were wearing long underwear, he told Americans that they would all have to pitch in and lower the thermostats in their homes to fifty-five degrees at night and sixty-five degrees during the day. That was three degrees cooler than Nixon had requested during the Arab embargo.

Americans were facing a "permanent" shortage requiring "sacrifice." The unusual cold would pass, but the underlying domestic shortages and dependence on foreign oil would not. Carter said he was going to introduce a complete energy package within ninety days. "Our program will emphasize conservation," but, he said, what was more important than any government action was the willingness of individual Americans to cut back. "All of us," Carter said, "must learn to waste less energy." To that end, he eliminated door-to-door limousine service for the White House staff.

Congressional support for the natural gas bill was nearly unanimous, given the emergency and temporary nature of the legislation, but the two negative Senate votes, from opposite ends of the political spectrum, were harbingers of the challenges for any permanent energy reform. On the right, Senator John Tower, the chair of the Republican Policy Committee, voted against it, favoring immediate deregulation instead. "If the people are cold in Ohio," he said, "let them put the blame where it belongs. It belongs right here, under the Capitol dome."[21] To his *Newsweek* readers, Milton Friedman criticized what he saw as the absurdity of Washington regulating the price of natural gas and then saying there was a crisis. The situation, he wrote, was like "the story of the young man, convicted of murdering his mother and father, who threw himself on the mercy of the court as an orphan! . . . Economists may not know much; but one thing we do know: how to produce a shortage."[22]

The only other negative vote came from Senator James Abourezk, a Democrat from South Dakota and an ardent liberal named in 1974 as one of *Time* magazine's "200 Faces for the Future," who saw the bill as a sop to the oil industry.[23] He denounced it as a detestable deregulation measure because it allowed gas to be sold in the interstate market at unregulated prices for the duration of the emergency. While he was a lone voice of dissent from the Left, his opposition augured the attacks ahead from Carter's liberal flank.

Immediately, congressional liberals made it clear that they would not accept deregulation as the administration's centerpiece of energy policy. If the current regulatory pricing structure distorted the market, creating incentives for gas to stay within the states where it was produced, then the solution was to extend the federal government's reach, creating one uniform national price. In the House, consumer-area representatives, concentrated largely in urban industrial areas, occupied nearly 40 percent of the seats.[24] They grew their numbers by supporting mandatory conversion from natural gas and oil to coal for industrial users, which won over coal-area representatives. Senators Edward Kennedy and Edmund Muskie sponsored legislation to assist low-income families suffering from higher fuel prices, while at the grass roots Jesse Jackson and his civil rights organization mobilized to prevent Chicago utility companies from cutting off heat to those unable to pay their bills.[25]

These liberals were already angry with Carter for what they saw as his meager economic stimulus package. With 7.5 million Americans out of work, Carter called for doubling public works spending from $2 to $4 billion. But he put forward a $50 rebate for every taxpayer and dependent, amounting to $8.2 billion in tax cuts, as the centerpiece. That approach reflected Carter's commitment to trim government. Organized labor and its liberal allies thought the rebate seemed too cautious and also regressive. George Meany and other top labor leaders made it clear that after Ford's austerity agenda and the tremendous campaign effort of labor in support of Carter this Democratic president should use his muscle to push through a massive $30 billion public jobs creation program.

Labor leaders and other liberals were mobilized on the deregulatory issue. As technical as the details were, opposition to deregulation attracted star-studded support. Paul Newman and Robert Redford financed the Energy Action Committee, which was a liberal public interest group run by

James Flug.[26] Flug represented a new kind of Naderite public interest policy activist. He had graduated from Harvard Law School in 1963, served as assistant to Attorney General Nicholas Katzenbach, and then was legislative assistant and chief counsel to Senator Edward Kennedy from 1967 to 1973, working for judicial and legal reform. As director of Energy Action, he pushed for legislation to break up oil companies, prohibit offshore oil leasing, and regulate intrastate natural gas. Joined by Lee White of the Consumer Federation of America, another veteran of civil rights reform, he turned his attention to energy as a fundamental issue of distributive justice.

These liberals believed that the natural gas shortage was a deliberate ploy by the producers to win deregulation. In early February, Flug told a House subcommittee, "The more people who are cold and out of work and out of school, the easier it is to stampede the nation into a deregulation frenzy."[27] During the debate over the emergency natural gas bill, Flug argued for the need to create one federally regulated natural gas market. The government had to have the authority to allocate gas from Texas to the consuming states. "Why should we close down factories in Maryland to heat homes in Ohio, while intrastate gas is being burned freely in Texas for night hours at shopping centers or at amusement parks?" he asked.[28]

This view of the industry as manipulative, and perhaps even criminal, not only had widespread appeal, but could unite the left-leaning parts of an otherwise divided Democratic Party. Public interest reformers and traditional New Deal liberals shared a dim view of the oil industry and its representatives. Ralph Nader demanded that the Justice Department investigate whether the oil companies, which controlled 70 percent of the natural gas market, had colluded to withhold gas to raise prices. Senator Howard Metzenbaum, an Ohio Democrat, and Representatives John Moss, John Dingell, and Harley Staggers called for an investigation. Two-thirds of the New York City metropolitan area believed the shortage resulted from an industry conspiracy.[29]

Even if the shortage was real, liberals argued, deregulation was not likely to draw out more supply. Given the highly concentrated nature of the major oil companies, these producers had the means to restrict supply and keep prices high. Deregulation would harm low-income citizens who would be unfairly burdened. Senator Hubert Humphrey released a study showing that the deep freeze would cost the nation's households an additional

$139 on their heating bills. The overall increase, surpassing $8 billion, would wipe out most of the benefits of Carter's rebate. Over the objections of the White House, thirty-one liberal members of the House, led by Representatives Morris Udall of Arizona, chairman of the House Interior Committee, and John Seiberling of Ohio, introduced a bill to break up the big oil companies. Their motive was to create more price competition, with an eye toward lowering prices.[30]

Liberals' view on energy policy was out of sync with their attitudes toward the regulation of other industries. Kennedy, Ralph Nader, and other liberals lined up behind the deregulation of the airline, trucking, and telecommunication industries. Although deregulation had supporters on the right, who saw government as stymieing market incentives, these liberals, including young legal reformers such as the Harvard professor and future Supreme Court justice Stephen Breyer, who was serving as Ted Kennedy's special counsel, also embraced deregulation. They believed that in certain industries, federal regulation protected big business and hurt consumers. Industries like the airlines, which were naturally competitive, benefited unfairly from federal regulation that granted monopolies, blocked entrants into the market, and artificially held up prices. The same was true in trucking, in which ICC regulations had the effect of preventing independent truckers from hauling certain goods. In these cases, where powerful players in an industry exerted undue influence on regulatory agencies in order to stifle competitors—a sort of regulatory "capture"— deregulation would bring more competition, benefit small producers, and result in lower prices and better service. If newer airlines, or independent truckers, could compete, they would bring down the prices they charged.[31]

Liberals saw the energy industry in an entirely different light. Unlike the effect in other industries, they argued that deregulating energy, with the decline in resources and the heavy concentration of the industry, would be a calamity for consumers. That was the position of Alfred Kahn, who would soon become the leading advocate for airline deregulation. In 1974, as a member of the New York State Public Service Commission that oversaw local gas utilities, Kahn opposed the deregulation of natural gas, insisting that decontrol would result in a transfer of "tens of billions of dollars" from consumers to producers without calling forth much additional production. "The probable windfall to the industry is a price monstrously out of proportion to the benefits that deregulation might be expected to bring," Kahn instructed Congress.[32] If regulations were not working, the solution was not to resort to the market but rather to devise new policy tools that could establish justice and fairness.

In this cold winter, Carter was skating on thin ice. The energy crisis posed a real challenge for him as he sought to chart a new path for the Democratic Party between regulation and deregulation. Running as the outsider, Carter correctly tapped into the frustrations with post-Watergate Washington. He also sympathized with more conservative members of his party who wanted less government interference in business. But as president he had to appreciate that there was still much that people liked and wanted government to do. If Carter's deregulation of the airlines would bring cheaper fares, that sounded good. Likewise, if regulation of natural gas protected consumers' wallets, that also made sense. Amid economic turmoil and freezing-cold weather, much of the public expected government protection. Rather than being told to conserve, they wanted Carter to offer relief.

The debate among Carter's top staff over whether to support Senator Kennedy's proposal for $200 million in aid to low-income families to avoid fuel shutoffs captured the dilemma. All the president's advisers thought it was a bad idea. It would set a precedent, would be difficult to administer, and would not significantly help. The CEA's chairman, Charles Schultze, objected: "What do we do for an encore? . . . Do we then have a new special program? Do we have fuel stamps if OPEC increases prices again?" They ought to avoid conveying a "'we will take care of every problem' attitude." Yet Stuart Eizenstat, Carter's chief domestic policy adviser, who also opposed the plan, pointed out a basic political reality: "The poor are among your major constituent groups."[33]

While ideologically Carter stood in the center, the interests of many in his party pulled him to the left. The president believed that higher prices for energy were essential for cutting consumption. Everything stemmed from that fundamental position, which comported with Carter's main goal of conservation. But he and his team, especially the more liberal among them, knew that any program that placed a bigger burden on consumers would be hard to sell politically, especially as inflation was on an upward trend.

MEOW: The Moral Equivalent of War

On March 1, Carter submitted legislation to Congress to create the Department of Energy, which would replace the Federal Energy Administration. It was understood that James Schlesinger would head up this new
cabinet-level department. This economist believed in market solutions, but
on its first day the department would inherit twenty thousand employees
currently overseeing the industry and scattered across the government. In
the meanwhile, Schlesinger assembled a small team of economists, lawyers, and Washington staffers in the Old Executive Office Building to work
on Carter's energy policy. The president hoped Schlesinger could devise a
"comprehensive" policy before congressmen and interest groups could chip
away at it.

Publicly, Carter laid the groundwork for a tough policy. The plan,
Carter said in an early press conference, "is going to require substantial
sacrifices on the part of the American people." In repeated public comments, he said that "strict conservation" would be at its heart. The rest of
Carter's team sang the same tune. The Federal Energy Administration's
John O'Leary told reporters that the plan would be a hard pill to swallow.
On ABC's *Issues and Answers*, O'Leary said, "I think that we are going to
have to spend more money on energy, we are going to have to do with a
great deal less energy, comfort levels are going to go down; the 65-degree
home will become a feature of the future."[34] There was no choice. "Without an all-out conservation effort we'll fall off the cliff in the early 1980s,"
said O'Leary.[35]

The thrust of the plan, when Schlesinger confidentially presented it to
Carter, induced conservation by raising the price of energy through a
combination of government-mandated price increases and higher taxes.
Schlesinger had opposed controls in the Nixon and Ford administrations,
but now he switched his view. A veteran in legislative battles, he believed
that getting any energy package through the Democratic Congress would
require bending to the desires of Representative John Dingell, the House
Energy Subcommittee chair, and Scoop Jackson in the Senate, both of
whom were firm proponents of regulation.[36] A deregulation bill would be
a nonstarter, so therefore controls would remain and higher prices would
have to come, if at all, through legislative increases.

The plan consisted of five different areas for legislative action. The first extended natural gas price controls to the intrastate market and raised them slightly; the second called for a tax on crude oil that brought domestic oil prices up to world levels and rebated the revenue to consumers; the third imposed a gas-guzzler tax on automobiles combined with fuel economy regulations more rigorous than those set by the 1975 CAFE standards; the fourth mandated efficiency standards for industry, including utility rate reform, and required conversion from natural gas and oil to coal for industrial users; and the fifth provided homeowners and municipalities with tax credits for conserving energy and switching to renewable energies.

In private, Schlesinger warned the president about the proposal's political pitfalls. He and Carter worried about the threat of energy dependence. But Americans, especially in this inflationary moment, perceived the energy crisis as the higher prices they had to pay. Paying more for less was not a motto around which to galvanize the country, and especially not New Deal Democrats. Labor, consumer groups, and congressional liberals would oppose any price increases. As one of Carter's polling reports put it, "For most Americans, the real energy problem is high prices and corporate misbehavior . . . As long as Americans perceive the energy problem this way, they aren't very likely to endorse solutions that require sacrifice."[37]

Yet, Schlesinger warned, producer groups would also be unhappy, because, even if oil and gas prices rose, they were still subject to controls, including the extension of natural gas controls to the intrastate market. If this proposal went through, the government would fix prices for all natural gas, and producers would howl. Schlesinger also anticipated auto manufacturers and the United Automobile Workers would fight hard against the gas-guzzler tax. And all other business groups would oppose mandatory efficiency standards, coal conversion, and oil and gas taxes, all of which would raise their costs. In short, no one would be happy: liberals liked controls but hated higher prices, conservatives liked higher prices but hated controls, and the public did not want to conserve or pay more.[38]

On April 18, Carter announced his national energy plan. On live television, he told the country that combating the energy crisis was, in William James's famous words, the "moral equivalent of war." Schlesinger had urged the president to adopt this phrase.[39] Delivering what his White House aides called a "sky is falling" message, the president—part Sunday school teacher, part engineer—preached about waste, conservation, and national will.[40] Telling the people that it was his duty to have an "unpleasant talk" with them, he blamed the country's careless consumer habits for energy shortages. "Ours is the most wasteful nation on earth," he said. "With the exception of preventing war, this is the greatest challenge our country will face during our lifetimes. The energy crisis has not yet overwhelmed us," he told the nation, "but it will if we do not act quickly." If the nation did not pass comprehensive legislation, "the alternative may be a national catastrophe." "We will constantly live in fear of embargoes," he warned.

The country did not rally behind the president. "Gasoline: Pay More, Buy Less," read a *Boston Globe* headline in typical coverage of Carter's speech.[41] With warmer weather and the winter emergency behind them, only half the public thought the energy crisis was "very serious," and more than 80 percent believed the president's package would cause them financial hardship.[42] A *Time* magazine reporter explained, "It's going to be tough for a Congressman to vote to punish his constituents when they can't see why. Historically, Americans don't mend the roof when the sun is shining, so there's reason for skepticism on whether Congress will go along with the President."[43]

Almost instantly, the journalist Russell Baker noted that the acronym for the moral equivalent of war was MEOW. The president was attempting to rouse the public to put pressure on Congress, but he would find that task challenging. Americans did not want to give up their cars and their gasoline, said Baker. And they were not convinced they needed to. The programs were not a "pussy-cat affair," Baker pointed out. Quite the opposite. They were tough, and they exacted high costs. It would be hard for even the most skillful and popular of presidents to get them through Congress. Baker suggested perhaps Carter's MEOW would be worse than his bite.[44]

Tip O'Neill, the new Speaker of the House, was worried. The total package, which included 113 separate proposals, was as thick as five telephone books, said O'Neill. "I took one look at it and groaned."[45] The Ninety-Fifth Congress, the *Congressional Quarterly* reported, "could be said to have had two agendas: energy, and everything else."[46] Carter, who made this his top priority, had little feel for how to work with Capitol Hill. In response to the Speaker's insistence that he make calls to key members, the president refused. According to O'Neill, Carter replied, "No, I described the problem to the American people in a rational way. I'm sure they'll realize that I'm right." "This is politics we're talking about here, not physics. We need you to push this bill through," implored O'Neill. "It's *not* politics," responded Carter. "Not to me. It's simply the right thing, the rational thing. It's what needs to be done."[47]

Tip was an old-school, backslapping, cigar-smoking politician, just the kind that Carter deplored. The mistrust, if not outright disdain, was mutual. O'Neill, who got his start in politics campaigning for Al Smith and since then had represented his urban, working-class Catholic constituents as a faithful Franklin Roosevelt Democrat, knew this southern peanut farmer was not one of them. When Carter gave his cardigan speech by the fire, during the winter's deep freeze, O'Neill reflected that no northerner would have used only a single log.[48]

The legislative battle would divide the party, pitting producers in the South against consumers in the North and also setting environmentalists against New Deal liberals. In a widely reported conflict, the environmental advocate Representative Henry Waxman, a California Democrat, accused Representative Dingell of threatening to hold the natural gas bill hostage in his committee unless the White House relaxed its stance toward the auto industry. Given his district in Los Angeles, where smog blanketed the city, Waxman made tougher emissions a top priority. Dingell represented Detroit, and though his committee did not have jurisdiction over it, he found the gas-guzzler tax especially infuriating because it offered rebates for the purchase of fuel-efficient cars, which effectively penalized the domestic auto market by subsidizing the purchase of foreign cars.

In a public letter, Waxman suggested that if Dingell could not see beyond the interests of his Detroit constituents, then the Democrats should reconsider Dingell's position as chair of the Energy Subcommittee. Dingell was furious. A member of the class of 1974, Waxman arrived in the Capitol, at age thirty-five, eager to take on the entrenched system of governance in Congress. Dingell, who had been in office for close to a quarter of a century, deeply resented the challenge: "Your letter is an outrageous insult and I demand an immediate apology." Waxman stood firm and insisted that Congress and the president maintain their commitment to pollution control even if that risked angering Dingell, whose support Carter would need for the natural gas bill.[49]

Environmentalists were also irate over the coal conversion measure, which required increasing coal production by two-thirds before 1985. While the proposal also offered tax breaks for conservation, environmentalists criticized what they saw as the meager support for renewable energies. Tom Quinn, special assistant for environmental protection to California's governor, Jerry Brown, faulted the plan as far too timid: "Large Chevy owners will now have to switch to small Chevies. I don't consider this a sacrifice."[50]

Northeastern liberals and minority representatives had the opposite response, saying that the plan called for too much sacrifice from the people least able to afford it. They feared that the energy package would hurt the poor disproportionately. Harlem's Charles Rangel, who was a founding member of the Congressional Black Caucus and served on the House Ways and Means Committee, would not support the president's energy proposal until he knew how much job creation the White House intended to back.[51] Moreover, these liberals did not trust the administration to return to consumers the crude oil taxes collected. That was especially true after the White House withdrew the $50 tax rebate, deciding that the economy was improving and no longer needed that kind of stimulus.

The idea of raising gasoline prices through taxes angered everyone. In addition to the crude oil tax, Carter requested the authority to impose a gasoline tax if Americans did not decrease their consumption. The measure, which would add approximately five cents per gallon, triggered opposition from all sides. The tax would be "unpopular as hell in Texas," said Senator Bentsen, while Senator Kennedy asserted, "It hits the average worker too hard."[52] Those from auto-producing areas hated it, and it also alienated politicians from rural areas whose constituents had to commute long distances and had no mass transit alternatives.

Carter was failing. The pollster Daniel Yankelovich told the White House, "Americans acknowledge in their minds that there's a problem, but the true meaning and gut reality of it has not yet hit home." Unless Carter was making headline speeches, they did not rank the energy crisis at the top of their concerns. "Without constant reinforcement from you, people unconsciously assume that the problem couldn't be as important and urgent as you said it was," explained Yankelovich. Carter's initial rhetoric, invoking war, did not help, he added. "Such a strong call-to-arms requires vigorous follow through, or else it quickly loses its credibility." Only firm and persistent leadership could generate popular backing. "The energy crisis is remote and unreal, there are no visible signs of it, and most important of all, *you are not talking about it any more*," the pollster pointed out. Instead, Americans were worried about the economy, especially the problem of inflation, which only undercut support for Carter's higher energy prices.[53]

As the Democrats fought among themselves and the public remained unaroused, the Republicans offered their own critique. Along with producer-state Democrats, the minority party faulted Carter's package as anti-growth, placing too much emphasis on conservation and not enough on production. "We can produce our way out of this," said the Senate minority leader, Howard H. Baker Jr. of Tennessee.[54] The thirty-eight Senate Republicans issued a joint response, criticizing Carter's program as "further regulation, further bureaucratization, further government intervention into every facet of the energy program." The only solution would come from "greater reliance on competitive pricing and on the resilience, resourcefulness and the drive of our market system."[55]

In the House, Representative Jack Kemp of New York gave an impassioned denunciation: "The American people are being asked to take it on the chin for what Government policies have done in the energy picture. It is those Government policies which are the greatest causes of the energy shortages we face." Kemp, who was putting together a master plan for GOP-sponsored tax cuts, went on to criticize the program as a massive tax: "The President has asked the American people to sacrifice, to assume the hardship of resolving this crisis, when the American people have not done one thing wrong for which to be penalized." The solution, according to Kemp, was to set prices free: "The most equitable way to determine anything is through the interplay of market forces. Anything else is the biased socioeconomic judgment of a small group of policymakers . . . masquerading as equity."[56]

Many on the right and in industry argued that there were not shortages, only government-created shortages, for which the antidote was lifting regulations. The American Enterprise Institute released a study citing regulatory red tape as the chief obstacle to energy security and prosperity. Oil price controls inhibited an expansion of refining capacity and created inefficiencies in distribution. Extending gas controls to intrastate markets would only make problems worse.[57] "Sadly and ironically," concluded

Melvin Laird, who chaired the study, "the greater the time, attention, and effort devoted to energy problems by the government, the more counter-productive have become our policies."[58]

Throughout the spring, the Right stepped up its attacks. In a *Wall Street Journal* editorial, William Simon, the former energy czar, denounced the Carter plan. "The more the government has tinkered with the intricate marketplace machinery, the worse things have become," wrote Simon. "It is folly to believe that the same people who created this mess can now improve the situation."[59] Simon recorded nationally syndicated daily radio editorials. He also published a book, *A Time for Truth*, which was a repudiation of David Freeman's *Time to Choose* and a fierce attack on government regulation.[60]

Condemnation of Carter's energy plan appeared almost daily in the pages of conservative mass publications. If Carter simply got rid of controls on oil and gas, said the *Wall Street Journal* editors, "we could all quit haggling about energy and talk about something else."[61] The assertion of a crisis was, in their word, complete "nonsense."[62] "What is expressed in the package is worse than a mystical faith that markets work," wrote its editors. "It is—at best—a mystical faith that the government and its experts can sit in Washington and see the future . . . The central ethos of the plan . . . is tinker, tinker, tinker."[63] The conservative weekly *Human Events* echoed that sentiment: "The energy problems which beset us have been created through official bungling and will be solved, if ever, by phasing government out of the energy business."[64] In an article titled "How Liberals Caused the Energy Crisis," *Human Events* laid blame on the "nihilistic cult" of anti-oil-company propaganda, which led to excessive regulations on the energy industry.[65] "Under the Carter proposals," another editorial warned, "swarms of new federal bureaucrats will be monitoring the energy industry, regulating home improvements and supervising the consumer. All those Jimmy Carter promises about de-centralizing the Washington bureaucracy during his election have been chucked for 'Big Massa' government."[66]

The real problem, according to Milton Friedman, was not in the details of Carter's energy proposals; the real problem was the creation of the Department of Energy. Friedman argued, "The typical Federal agency starts small, grows slowly for a while, and then explodes." The DOE could be the "most powerful, and the most harmful, of all Federal agencies. It would control the life-blood of our economic system. Its tentacles would reach into every factory, into every dwelling in the land." Enforcing all the presidential edicts would require a police state threatening both free enterprise and personal liberties.[67] In the popular press, Friedman and the editorial page of *The Wall Street Journal* abhorred what they saw as "creating a monster."[68]

The Right faulted Carter's plan not only because it relied on government but also because it assumed a pessimistic view of the future and would harm consumers. Carter appeared to reproach and condemn Americans, calling for puritanical restraint and a rejection of greedy consumption habits. Friedman rejected the pretense of judgment: "One man's gas guzzler is another man's necessity." He told his readers, "There is simply no special moral issue involved in energy . . . The problem is a strictly technical economic problem."[69] In the House, the Republican representatives David Stockman, a young conservative from Michigan, James Collins from Texas, and Clarence "Bud" Brown from Ohio released a study, claiming that Carter's proposal would restrict production and force consumers to pay for higher-priced substitutes like imported oil.[70] "There is absolutely no logical way deregulation can cost consumers more than the Carter plan," wrote *The Wall Street Journal* after reviewing the Stockman study.[71]

The attack on Carter's energy plan served as a dry run for the antitax, antigovernment arguments of the Republican Right. The American Petroleum Institute's Charles DiBona, who had pushed for deregulation in the Nixon White House, denounced the plan as "basically a tax bill," not an energy policy, saying it would cause "more harm than good."[72] The Heritage Foundation, issuing its own assessment, announced, "There is little doubt that [Carter's plan] will exacerbate the nation's current capital shortage seriously and that there will be a growing dependence on foreign oil as a result of the disincentives to the production of oil and natural gas."[73] Its chief analyst, Milton Copulos, claimed the package would cost each American family more than $5,000 by 1985, constituting "the most significant increase in the middle-class tax burden in our nation's history." He also predicted that the White House would not use taxes for energy development. "The majority of the tax revenues under the Carter plan will wind up in the federal coffers and quite possibly eventually be used for social programs," warned Copulos.[74] *National Review* voiced the concern of many on the right: "Carter and his Democratic Party have an abundance of worthy causes" from Social Security to welfare to financial aid for New York City.[75]

Carter's energy plan made many more enemies than friends. By the summer of 1977, the package had stalled in the Senate. Henry Jackson chaired the newly created Energy Committee. Early on, he expressed concern that Carter's program would trigger a "political firestorm."[76] The energy package got divided between his committee and Senator Russell Long's Finance Committee. Long, a senator from Louisiana, wanted to use his powers to grant tax breaks to the oil industry.

The House, where Tip O'Neill was trying to push the program through, provided a more hospitable forum. As the new Speaker and a fierce partisan, O'Neill wanted a big victory, and he recognized that the best chance for success was to keep the different elements of the Carter proposal together, allowing the full House to vote only on the total package. Environmentalists would favor conservation, liberals would fight for price controls, and coal-producing states would get behind conversion. O'Neill took the unprecedented step of creating a special ad hoc committee to handle the full package and handpicked its forty members. This would allow him, as Speaker, to centralize his power and would also force compromise. The Commerce Committee would mark up the natural gas bill, and the Ways and Means Committee would oversee the tax measures, then each component would go to the ad hoc committee.

To chair the committee, O'Neill selected the Ohio Democrat Thomas "Lud" Ashley. Ashley was a tough liberal who, since he first won election in 1954, represented the auto industry workers in Toledo, Ohio. Known as Mr. Housing, he supported an activist vision of government helping the needy. He had no special knowledge of the oil industry, other than what he knew from his longtime college friend George Bush. Like Bush, he had deep political roots, though their politics were very different. His great-grandfather James Ashley was an outspoken abolitionist and, as a representative from Ohio, helped secure passage of the Thirteenth Amendment. Lud grew up as a committed New Deal Democrat, and his "political godfather," Michael DiSalle, the one who first urged him to run, was the mayor of Toledo, governor of Ohio, and the Washington wage and price administrator during the Korean War. For two decades, Ashley had represented the tens of thousands of auto and other unionized workers in his district.[77]

Ashley understood how Carter's proposals would play to his constituency. Above all, his typical voter wanted to know that he could count on a steady supply of fuel at affordable prices. "He's the guy in Jim and Lou's bar on LaGrange street in Toledo," explained Ashley. "He's an automotive worker; he knows he needs his job, but he doesn't care if he is building gas guzzlers or cars that meet tougher mileage standards; he's Roman Catholic; he's got four kids; he'll accept sacrifices if he is convinced they are evenly shared; when it comes time for vacation, he wants to drive on vacation, and he wants to do it in a family-size car."[78] Ashley supported controls, wanted to keep prices down, and opposed standby taxes on gasoline.

The Ohio Democrat knew that average Americans were not rallying around the president's plan. All they heard from the president was talk of sacrifice and higher prices, and they were hard-pressed to believe that either was necessary. Even with periodic reminders of energy shortages, no groundswell of public support was emerging. On July 13, 1977, a blackout in New York City put nine million people in the dark and stranded thousands of commuters. The blackout lasted for twenty-five hours and led to widespread looting and arson, resulting in what Mayor Abe Beame called a "night of terror." Though it was caused by lightning, which shut down the Consolidated Edison grid, Amory Lovins of Friends of the Earth pointed out that a greater reliance on solar power and other "soft" energies would make Americans less vulnerable to "cartels, mistakes, oligopolies, unions, saboteurs, bureaucrats, acts of God, and Acts of Congress."[79] The next day the lights came back on, and, again, energy shortages ebbed as a source of pressing public concern.

Just before Congress recessed in August, Carter signed a bill establishing the Department of Energy. For all the heated political rhetoric coming from conservatives about the inefficiencies of government and the need to eliminate bureaucratic monstrosities, some of which came from the White House itself, this measure sailed through. The Senate passed the bill by a voice vote, and in the House the vote was unanimous. Within a day, the Senate confirmed James Schlesinger as the first secretary. The nation's politicians saw the creation of a new department as inevitable. Even those most vehemently opposed to government controls and regulation did not block it. The American public wavered in its level of concern about energy, but few politicians would risk appearing not to take this issue, and their responsibility in addressing it, seriously.

The next day, August 5, 1977, the House voted in favor 244–177 on Carter's energy package. Before the vote, Speaker O'Neill appealed to his fellow congressmen to support Carter's plan as a protest against "Big Oil" because "the future of America, the economy of this country, the defense of this nation, are at stake." The final measure included the crude oil tax, the gas-guzzler tax, utility rate reform, and natural gas regulation. The only thing lost was the standby tax on gasoline.[80]

As the House was voting, the president had bought political goodwill from environmentalists by signing two important new pieces of legislation, the Surface Mining Control and Reclamation Act to limit strip-mining and a substantial legislative amendment to the Clean Air Act. Together, their passage constituted a significant advance since the initial burst of environmental legislation in the early 1970s and meant tougher pollution controls and greater government enforcement of environmental regulations.

Getting the package through the House had required compromise, especially on the issue of natural gas regulation. Liberals accepted some upward adjustment in prices, and deregulation supporters agreed to extend controls to the intrastate market. Representative Toby Moffett, a Connecticut Democrat, brokered the deal on behalf of the liberals. A Watergate baby elected in 1974 at the age of thirty, Moffett cut his teeth in politics first as an aide to Senator Walter Mondale and then at the grass roots by forming a Connecticut branch of Ralph Nader's Citizen Action Group. Agreeing to raise prices was just as hard for Moffett as accepting additional regulations was for Representative Charles Wilson of Texas, who knew his constituents would feel as if he had "fed them castor oil." Wilson aptly remarked that Moffett "had to hold his nose a little bit when he swallowed this, and he has a few friends with consumer groups out in the hall who are just as angry with him as some of my producers are with me."[81]

Consumer groups were indeed outraged. Energy Action ran a television ad in Washington, D.C., called "Mugging," in which a man in Arab dress mugged an ordinary citizen in a back alley using a gas nozzle as a weapon. After the mugger had stolen the man's wallet and run away, he took off his robe and headgear to reveal that he was actually an American oil executive. A voice-over warned, "We'd better break up the oil monopoly before it breaks us."[82]

George H. W. Bush working in the oil fields of Midland, Texas, during the postwar boom. (George H. W. Bush Presidential Library and Museum)

LEFT In 1967, Bush arrived in Washington, D.C., for his first term in the House, determined to promote free markets and protect the oil patch. (George H. W. Bush Presidential Library and Museum)

BELOW Nixon inspecting the beaches of Santa Barbara damaged by an oil spill in 1969. The president could not hold back the environmentalist movement. (Richard Nixon Presidential Library and Museum)

TOP In October 1973, OPEC ministers in Kuwait imposed an embargo on oil to pressure the United States into changing its policies in the Middle East. (Associated Press)

ABOVE Secretary of State Henry Kissinger convinced Saudi Arabia's King Faisal to help arrange a ceasefire in the Arab-Israeli War but failed to persuade him to end the oil embargo. (Associated Press)

TOP LEFT The Nixon administration enlisted all kinds of allies in its effort to urge Americans to conserve oil voluntarily. (PEANUTS © Peanuts Worldwide LLC. Dist. by Universal Uclick)

TOP RIGHT Unable to get the oil flowing, Nixon took tougher measures to ensure energy savings. In January 1974, he signed a national speed limit law that would remain in effect until 1995. (Walter P. Reuther Library, Wayne State University)

ABOVE Nixon appointed William Simon as the country's energy czar. Simon, a free-market ideologue, found himself administering a national system of gasoline allocations along with federal price controls. (Associated Press)

The nation's gas retailers had only a fixed amount of gasoline to sell, and most closed on Sundays. (National Archives)

In early 1974, Americans ranked the gas shortage above the Watergate scandal as their number one concern. Fearful of running out of gas, Americans waited in lines that stretched for miles at stations across the country. (Associated Press)

Portland, Oregon, became the first city to introduce an odd-even rationing system, which allowed drivers to purchase gas on certain days depending on the last digit of their license plates. Even so, the city's stations still ran out of gas. (National Archives)

As shortages persisted, some Americans resorted to stealing gas right out of the tank. Others took defensive measures. (National Archives)

Democratic senator Henry "Scoop" Jackson sought to curb the profits of oil companies by forcing them to roll back prices. In televised hearings, Jackson asked oil executives if they had contrived the shortage to raise prices. (University of Washington Libraries, Special Collection)

At a press conference in early 1974, political activists Ralph Nader and Jesse Jackson urged Americans to stop paying their fuel bills as a protest against Big Oil. (Associated Press)

TOP Angry truckers took to the streets in a nationwide strike in February 1974 to demand a rollback in fuel prices. (Associated Press)

ABOVE Lasting for eleven days, the trucking shutdown worsened the gas shortage as strikers blockaded gas distribution centers. Some of the strikers used violence to make sure other truckers stayed off the roads. (Associated Press)

TOP Desperate to achieve calm, Nixon ordered William Simon to release as much gasoline into the market as he could, even though this meant dipping into future months' allocations. The energy czar, who became a recurring figure in the Doonesbury cartoon, announced the crisis was over. (DOONESBURY © 1974 G. B. Trudeau. Reprinted with permission of Universal Uclick.)

ABOVE Nixon met with Arab leaders after the embargo ended. But even after oil started flowing, gas prices remained high and Americans remained vulnerable to another embargo. (Richard Nixon Presidential Library and Museum)

ABOVE President Ford relied on Chief of Staff Donald Rumsfeld and his deputy, Dick Cheney (left), to craft a conservative response to the ongoing energy crisis and fear of dependence. (Gerald R. Ford Presidential Library and Museum)

BELOW Council of Economic Advisers chairman Alan Greenspan (left) told the president that with the country at a crossroads, the administration had to fight for free energy markets. (Associated Press)

In February 1977, within days of taking over the presidency, Jimmy Carter appeared on television wearing a cardigan and seated by a fire, as he appealed to Americans to turn down thermostats and cut back on energy use. (Jimmy Carter Presidential Library and Museum)

Carter urged Americans to pay more for the energy they consumed—and use less of it. (Jimmy Carter Presidential Library and Museum)

James Schlesinger, the first secretary of energy, described Carter's national energy plan as the "moral equivalent of war." (Jimmy Carter Presidential Library and Museum)

This popular record in 1978 captured the tensions between southerners of both parties who wanted to deregulate energy markets and northern liberals who wanted the government to guarantee low prices for consumers. (Courtesy of the author)

Carter, who believed in renewable energy, installed solar heating panels on the White House roof. (Jimmy Carter Presidential Library and Museum)

Carter visiting Three Mile Island after an accident in March 1979 that shattered support for nuclear power. (Jimmy Carter Presidential Library and Museum)

Americans were furious at Carter when the gas lines returned in the summer of 1979, following the Iranian Revolution. (Associated Press)

Some gas stations locked their tanks, as they had no fuel to sell. (Associated Press)

Tensions mounted as Washington, D.C., failed to respond to the energy shortage and rising prices. A gas riot erupted in Levittown, Pennsylvania, when striking truckers protested at local gas stations. (*Bucks County Courier Times*)

The protest turned violent as local citizens joined in with signs that read MORE GAS NOW and NO GAS MY ASS, reflecting the fury over Carter's handling of the shortage. (Associated Press)

"ROSALYNN, IT'S HIM AGAIN"

TOP On July 15, 1979, angry Americans heard their president tell them that they suffered from a crisis of confidence. (Associated Press)

ABOVE LEFT As his relations with liberals deteriorated, Carter faced a serious challenge when Senator Edward Kennedy ran against him in the 1980 Democratic primaries. (The Herb Block Foundation)

ABOVE RIGHT With the second oil shock in a decade, Americans were frustrated by the difficulty of thwarting OPEC's power. (Wisconsin Historical Society)

ABOVE Many Americans demanded the use of force when Iranian fundamentalists seized the U.S. embassy in Tehran in November 1979 and took Americans hostage. (Library of Congress)

BELOW Ronald Reagan at the 1980 GOP convention with former president Ford and vice presidential nominee George H. W. Bush. Reagan's election in 1980 was a triumphal moment for conservative insiders. (Corbis)

TOP Under Reagan, the oil industry received favorable treatment from Secretary of the Interior James Watt, a longtime Washington conservative. (Ronald Reagan Presidential Library and Museum)

ABOVE With Operation Desert Storm in 1991, President George H. W. Bush committed American troops to protecting oil assets in the Middle East after Iraq invaded Kuwait. (George H. W. Bush Presidential Library and Museum)

Strange Bedfellows

This August victory rested on a shaky foundation and threatened to fall apart, especially when the White House became embroiled in a front-page scandal. In the summer, accusations that Bert Lance, Carter's director of the budget and close associate, had engaged in financial improprieties as president of a Georgia bank dominated the news and tarnished the White House image. The scandal, which forced Lance from office in September, raised voters' skepticism about Carter as a new kind of politician who could run government free from corruption. Carter's popularity began a decline from which it would never fully recover and undercut his ability to use his bully pulpit.

Accelerating inflation hurt support for Carter's energy plan even more. Disaffected and suffering hardship, consumers initiated popular movements against rising energy costs. In New Jersey, for example, more than twenty-five hundred families withheld payment on their gas and electric bills to protest rate increases.[83] When Congress returned from its summer recess, less than a majority of voters favored the energy bills. In July 1977, 61 percent of Democratic voters had regarded the package favorably; by September, the number was down to 45 percent. The biggest decline in support for Carter's plan came from the poor, minorities, the less well educated, and the elderly. House liberals fought hard to keep the lid on energy prices, agreeing to as small an increase in natural gas prices as they could negotiate with their political opponents. But the rest of the package, with taxes on crude oil and gasoline, would raise the cost of energy. That was by design, as Carter had wanted it, but that was a tough sell.[84]

The White House knew it was losing. Hamilton Jordan told Carter, "The sense of urgency which was created in the country when our energy proposal was announced faded with the warm summer weather. We cannot create an atmosphere of sacrifice that is politically meaningful if the American people persist in thinking the crisis is not real." His advisers were concerned not only with the energy problem but also with Carter's reputation. If Congress stalled on energy, they believed the president's first year would be deemed a failure.[85]

In the Senate, where producer groups had more power, the opposition mounted an all-out campaign against Carter's energy plan. It would tax

Americans and offer them nothing in exchange, just less fuel at higher prices, they said. In September, in an article for *Reader's Digest* titled "The Energy Crisis: Made in the U.S.A.," Melvin Laird brought the conservative critique to millions of readers: "Many of the fuel shortages which threaten our economy are the product of our own shortsighted governmental policies." The government "should intrude less and permit the market to do its proper work."[86] The U.S. Chamber of Commerce launched a public speaking campaign around the country, spreading the view that the proposal was a tax increase in disguise.[87]

Carter's energy package was in trouble. On October 16, James Schlesinger summed up the situation on CBS's *Face the Nation*: "The basic problem is that there is no constituency for an energy program. There are many constituencies opposed. But the basic constituency for the program is the future."[88] Schlesinger made that proclamation just as the Department of Energy opened its doors. It was not an auspicious beginning.

Liberals fought hard to preserve the New Deal–era price controls on natural gas. The energy lobby, with Senator Bentsen as its chief spokesman, introduced a deregulation bill. Senators Howard Metzenbaum and James Abourezk staged a well-orchestrated filibuster, offering up 508 amendments as a delaying tactic that lasted for thirteen days, including one all-night session, the first since the civil rights era.[89] As it wore on, one White House staffer abjectly said the president's program was now looking like the "moral equivalent of the Vietnam War."[90]

The White House, worried about total failure, led the retreat. Vice President Mondale helped the Senate majority leader, Robert Byrd, use procedural rules to break the filibuster and move past the logjam. Given the president's declining popularity, Carter's team preferred a negotiated compromise to further delay and inaction. The liberals felt burned. "I've been told from the beginning that all governments lie," an angry Abourezk said on the floor of the Senate. "One thing I never thought would happen . . . is that Jimmy Carter would lie."[91]

Now the Senate demolished the Carter program, passing the Bentsen deregulation bill. If the bill became law, controls would soon be gone. A *Time* magazine political cartoon, depicting Carter as Charlie Brown, summed up the president's efforts. As she always did, the conniving Lucy, wearing a jersey that read "Congress," snatched the "energy plan" football away from the hapless Charlie Brown, whose only response, of course, was

"Augh!"[92] In spite of Tip O'Neill's successful maneuvering in the House, the Senate was proving to be a graveyard.

Consumer and labor groups pounced on the Senate deregulation bill as a giveaway to the oil industry. Senators Kennedy and Jackson, along with Birch Bayh, Gary Hart, and Adlai Stevenson III, threatened to stage a "liberal revolt."[93] Kennedy regarded the bill as an "abomination."[94] Labor threw its support behind the House version. "Everybody is in a real ass-kicking mood," Toby Moffett told a *Newsweek* reporter.[95]

The House liberals bore down on Carter. As the House and Senate bills went to a conference committee, the liberals were insistent on regulating natural gas and unwilling to raise prices any higher than what they had already signed off on. And they certainly were not willing to accept deregulation. Toby Moffett demanded a meeting with Carter. "It will be the liberal barons presenting the Magna Carta to King John," said one aide.[96] At the White House, Andrew Maguire told Schlesinger, "Toby and I are not by ourselves. We have 67 other guys in the House who feel the same way."[97] To which Schlesinger famously remarked, "I understand now what hell is. Hell is endless and eternal sessions of the natural gas conference."[98]

Throughout the spring of 1978, the energy secretary worked to broker an acceptable deal. For that, he looked to Scoop Jackson. Jackson had recommended Schlesinger for his job as energy adviser. As much as they disagreed on domestic policy, these two foreign policy hawks agreed that energy dependence weakened the United States. As Carter prepared for a summer summit of industrialized countries to take place in Bonn, America's allies were demanding that the United States cut back on its energy consumption to ease the pressure on global prices. The tension over oil put serious strain on the anti-Soviet alliance. Given his Cold War fears, Jackson wanted to get a bill through Congress that would demonstrate that the United States was serious in trying to curb its energy use. To get a deal, he had to support higher natural gas prices. Critically, he also agreed to a gradual phaseout of controls by 1985. That was a long time off. But still, the decision reflected an acceptance of the free market instead of the New Deal. In making this choice, Scoop was placing his national security concerns over his decades-long commitment to economic liberalism.

Carter accepted this deal for gradual decontrol too. He had given reassurances to the Left that he would support the House version. "I haven't modified my position at all," the president told consumer groups. "Not to my wife at night and not to Jim Schlesinger with the door closed."[99] But now he did. He had always supported decontrol. So, too, had Schlesinger. With Jackson serving as handmaiden, it looked as if they were getting what they wanted. President Ford had agreed to gradual decontrol of oil prices to get his energy bill through. Carter was following in his footsteps. Except he was a Democrat who would have to answer to his party.

Carter's compromise on the natural gas bill and its gradual phaseout enraged the left wing of the Democratic Party. "Rather than play St. George battling the oil and gas industry dragons," said Senator Abourezk, "he has opted for the role of midwife to this economic Frankenstein." The bill, with its phased deregulation, gave the oil and gas industry "the right to plunder the consumer's pocketbook and savings for the rest of this century."[100] The UAW, the AFL-CIO, the Consumer Federation of America, and the Americans for Democratic Action all rejected this kind of compromise, and organized labor mounted strong opposition.[101] William Winpisinger, president of the International Association of Machinists, denounced the deal as "the worst scandal on the American energy scene since the Teapot Dome scandal of the 1920s."[102]

Carter was looking more and more like a Democratic Party leader who had little to offer its hurting constituents. In the last year, the consumer price index had gone up by 9 percent, and the rate of acceleration was increasing each month. Since January, food prices had risen 16 percent, and now energy prices would go up too. Carter was in a bind. He believed that inflation stemmed from too much government spending. Yet the traditional constituents of his party required relief. As much as the Right, and centrists like Carter, railed against government waste, Americans in distress still expected federal largesse. As the journalist William Greider observed, "History tells us that popular opinion moves toward government-imposed solutions in times of economic stress, not away from them."[103]

Carter's relationship with the traditional American Left was reaching a low. In the summer of 1978, labor narrowly lost its legislative fight to make union organizing easier and the penalties for labor law violation stiffer. Carter did not invest political capital in this fight, nor did he fully support the Humphrey-Hawkins employment bill. The bill, as originally introduced in the 1974 recession, committed government to be the employer of last resort, promising a massive economic stimulus and public works jobs program. It represented a last gasp of New Deal liberalism. In early

1978, Humphrey had passed away, and with unemployment hovering at 7 percent labor, civil rights leaders, and liberals faulted Carter for not seizing the chance to get the bill through. Disappointing liberals like Congressman John Conyers, a black representative from Detroit, on Humphrey-Hawkins made them less inclined to fight for the White House's proposal on energy. The 1980 election was more than two years away, but already the United Automobile Workers president, Douglas Fraser, started to talk about a Kennedy candidacy. "I hate to put a limit on it . . . [but] I would think that if in the next six months he (Carter) can't get an upturn, it's too late," Fraser told the *Detroit Free Press*.[104]

Carter was alienating the environmentalists, too, who wanted a bigger commitment to renewable and alternative energies. On the first Sun Day, celebrated on May 3, 1978, Carter tried to appease them by approving plans to explore the installation of solar heating in the White House, as long as it was not an "eyesore," he told his staff.[105] Yet the president was not satisfying this constituency. A bill to protect Alaska's vast tracts of land from development, a measure the White House supported, stalled in Congress, further exposing the weakness of the Oval Office to force through environmentally friendly measures.

If liberals were backing away, the president also could not count on the South. Small independent producers opposed the natural gas compromise, certain that the extension of federal regulation to the intrastate market would stifle them. In the summer of 1978, "Freeze a Yankee" became a fast-selling 45 record. In a folksy twang, the chorus encouraged Texans to "drive 75 and freeze 'em alive." The song mocked liberals like Senator Kennedy for wanting cheap gas while blocking exploration off the East Coast.[106] *The Wall Street Journal* wondered, "How many people in Texas would be singing about freezing the Yankees if they were free to sell them oil and gas at free market rates."[107] The former Texas governor and Nixon Treasury secretary, John Connally, who was a key force in building up the Republican Party in Texas, was an outspoken critic of Carter's energy package and warned against "an overkill of government regulations."[108]

As the fate of the energy package hung in the balance, Americans were tuning in to the new show *Dallas*, which aired for the first time on April 2, 1978, and became an instant success. The hit of the airwaves featured a daring independent oilman in the form of J. R. Ewing. Each episode chronicled the adventures and misadventures of the greedy oil tycoon who was driven by self-interest and yet managed to win audiences' hearts as a villainous hero. Carter was urging the nation to conserve and sacrifice, but Americans were glued to their television sets, watching J. R. Ewing. The show featured displays of wealth rather than discussions of politics, but the message was clear: red-blooded producers would save the United States, or at least entertain the country.

Ewing had a real-life equivalent, and his name was George W. Bush. While his father, George H. W. Bush, was planning his 1980 presidential campaign, considered one of the favorites to win the GOP nomination, the younger Bush was in the very oil business that Carter wanted to reform. A 1975 graduate of Harvard Business School, Bush returned to Midland, Texas, the place of his childhood, where he started an oil company. His younger brother Marvin called him JR after the television show, but Bush had nowhere near the success of the fictional character. Bush liked the world of business, but he was really drawn to politics. He had worked on three of his father's political campaigns as well as the campaigns of two other GOP candidates in Florida and Alabama. In 1978, he embarked on his own political career, running for a seat in Congress and presenting himself as an outspoken critic of Carter's stalled energy plan. Championing the independents, Bush wrote to his father's friend Lud Ashley, as he was managing Carter's energy package, to express his concern. "My worst fear of government tinkering with economic forces is the growth of a troika of big government, big business, and big labor," said a young Bush.[109]

As the final bill came up for consideration, a group of liberal senators, including Kennedy, Abourezk, and Metzenbaum, as well as George McGovern and William Proxmire, allied with conservative Republicans led by John Tower to try to kill it. President Carter ruefully recalled how the "strange combinations of conservative and liberal senators—such as Russell Long and Howard Metzenbaum, John Tower and Edward Kennedy, Paul Laxalt and George McGovern, Barry Goldwater and Floyd Haskell—were fighting the bills."[110] In an open Senate-wide appeal to their colleagues, these unlikely allies joined forces to assert that the natural gas bill that came out of the conference would place "excessive costs on consumers or excessive regulations on producers."[111] In the House, Toby Moffett and Bud Brown led a parallel effort.[112]

It was a bizarre moment in American politics. A Democratic White House was up against an emerging alliance of liberals and conservatives.

These groups defined the polar opposite on the issue of price controls. Opponents of controls believed their numbers were growing and were prepared to hold out, while liberals hoped that another crisis in supply or dramatic spike in prices would tilt the political mood in their favor. In his memoirs, Jimmy Carter reflected on the situation. Liberals "did not want any deregulation of oil or gas prices, the producers wanted instant and complete decontrol."[113] These strange bedfellows had in common only the belief that no bill was better than a compromise.

As the Left and the Right were trying to bury Carter's energy legislation, the president was at Camp David for the historic peace talks between Egypt and Israel. After Carter's intense thirteen-day negotiations with their leaders, Israel agreed to withdraw from the Sinai Peninsula in exchange for Egypt granting formal diplomatic recognition to Israel. The successful negotiation of the peace accords on September 17 gave Carter a needed boost in his approval rating, jumping thirteen points to 51 percent.[114] For Carter, the accord signaled one of his greatest achievements. The White House hailed his accomplishment as the handiwork of a genuine leader. Reporters made much of the fact the president appeared at a press conference in a new dark blue suit instead of his usual hues of gray and light blue. The switch seemed to signal Carter's new toughness.[115] The accord, in addition to allowing Carter to appear presidential, reduced the chances of another oil embargo by calming tensions in the Middle East.

Carter seized the moment to force a final energy bill through. The president reached out to the American business community to drop its opposition to the natural gas compromise. The Independent Petroleum Association of America, the Farm Bureau, and the U.S. Chamber of Commerce remained firmly against the measure. But many large firms, like General Motors, Bethlehem Steel, and B. F. Goodrich, went along, under heavy pressure from the White House, preferring to have the issue resolved. As Amory Houghton Jr. of Corning Glass Works put it, "We need a program."[116]

In the end, most of the large oil producers accepted the bill, recognizing that the future could just as easily bring a Congress even less hospitable to industry interests. If there were another terrible winter, with another natural gas shortage and higher prices, the pressure would increase for permanent controls. And this package at least gave some certainty about what future prices would look like. The majors were also still hoping to win administrative decontrol of oil prices. In addition, the coal interests came out for it, benefiting from the mandatory conversion measures.[117]

The National Energy Act, which Congress passed on October 15, the last day of its session, was not the package Carter had wanted. In its original design, the proposal called for a massive conservation effort. The initial package promised savings of 4.5 million barrels of imported oil a day by 1985; the final pieces of legislation scaled that number back to 2.5 million. To gain passage, the act did not include the crude oil tax or the standby gasoline tax. These tax measures, which would have raised the price of gasoline and heating oil, found no support from a nation of consumers who did not want to pay more for the oil they used. Nor did they see an energy bill as their top priority. As a fifty-six-year-old out-of-work steelworker in Detroit told Carter, "I don't feel much like talking about energy."[118]

The final bill reflected a series of half measures, promoting conservation through a combination of weakened regulations and tax incentives. The coal conversion allowed generous exemptions, and utility rate reform became voluntary. With no requirements to conserve, the act instead provided grants for insulating lower-income homes as well as grants to states to improve the efficiency of hospitals, schools, and municipal buildings. The centerpiece became the natural gas compromise, which no one liked. Even in the last days, an alliance of Republicans, producer groups, and urban consumer area representatives came within a single vote of killing the bill in the House on a procedural ruling. No one was enthusiastic, just relieved to have this year-and-a-half-long battle over.

The White House decided it was time for a makeover. That responsibility fell to Gerald Rafshoon, a forty-four-year-old public relations expert who had worked for Carter on his 1970 race for governor and his 1976 presidential campaign. In the aftermath of Watergate, Rafshoon had advised Carter to act with humility, portraying himself as a thoughtful, trustworthy, moderate man. But now Rafshoon urged Carter to look tough, to exude more confidence and power, even to change the part of his hair. "You're going to have to start looking, talking and acting more like a leader if you're to be successful—even if it's artificial," counseled Carter's adviser. Rafshoon knew Carter was uncomfortable with this approach. "Look at it this way," he told the chief executive. "Changing your position on issues to get votes is wrong; changing your style (like the part in your hair) in order to be effective is just smart, and in the long run, morally good. I know you think it's phony and that you're fine the way you are but that pride, is by far, your greatest political danger."[119] The media, too, was suspect of this attention to style. One political cartoon depicted the White House spin doctors locked behind closed doors "trying to decide what color socks would look the most presidential."[120]

Beyond these superficial changes, the reality, Rafshoon told Carter, was that unless he came out with a serious anti-inflation program, it would be "very difficult for most Americans to be enthusiastic about your Presidency in general and your reelection bid in particular." "It is impossible to overestimate the importance of the inflation issue to your Presidency," instructed Rafshoon. "It affects every American in a very palpable way. It causes insecurity and anxiety. It threatens the American dream."[121]

Carter's relations with his liberal wing were severely strained, and they would only get worse as the president launched his campaign against inflation, which was spiking and would soon hit double digits. On October 24, 1978, in a major televised address, Carter told the nation it was time to cut government spending, slash federal hiring, and reduce the deficit. He promised to use the powers of his office, including the veto, to keep the country on "the path of fiscal restraint." "Reducing the deficit will require difficult and unpleasant decisions," warned the president. He also asked workers to limit their requests for wage increases, insisting that "we must face a time of national austerity." Carter, with his support of gradual decontrol and inflation as his top priority, was sounding a lot like Ford.

As his chief inflation fighter, Carter appointed Alfred Kahn. On the same day, Carter signed the airline deregulation bill that Kahn, as the head of the Civil Aeronautics Board, had pushed to make the industry more competitive and offer consumers cheaper fares. Liberals saw this particular bill as a success, and they had played a key role in its passage. But the attack on government regulation, of which it was a part, fed into a larger conservative antigovernment critique.

Carter's commitment to fiscal restraint was unwavering, further exacerbating tensions with his core constituents. Three days later, on October 27, Carter signed the Humphrey-Hawkins bill. In its final form, it was a pale imitation of its original draft, stripped of its commitment to public spending and pledging instead to fight inflation. To slow inflation and strengthen the dollar, Carter adopted a restrictive credit policy, which risked triggering a recession and rising unemployment. The return of high unemployment would hurt the poor and black Americans first, the groups Carter had to depend on for his reelection. Instead of austerity, liberals in the Democratic Party wanted Carter to open the government spigot.

That was especially true as Republicans were offering their own remedy for an ailing economy. On July 14, 1978, the Senate Finance Committee had begun hearings on the Kemp-Roth tax cut bill. An across-the-board, dramatic cut, it was a new dawn for the Republican Party. As Bruce Bartlett, an aide to Jack Kemp put it, "The Republicans finally had something to offer the voters besides austerity." The tax cut gave tangible benefits to voters who were worn down by the bracket creep that resulted from inflation and disillusioned with the Carter White House. In June, California voters had passed Proposition 13 to cut state property taxes. At the national level, Kemp-Roth became, in the words of Bartlett, "the focal point of a counter-revolution in American politics that will have impact for years to come." Packaged as the Jobs Creation Act and offered up as the Republican alternative to the Humphrey-Hawkins full-employment bill, the Kemp-Roth tax cut promised to enhance capital formation, economic growth, and ultimately tax revenue. Just as important, it functioned on the right as a "consciousness-raising vehicle." Even better, Democrats would have a hard time co-opting this issue, because, as Bartlett pointed out and Carter was experiencing, "their basic present-day constituency (primarily those who consume government revenues rather than producing them) would not stand for it."[122]

The 1978 midterm elections on November 7 confirmed the trouble Democrats were having. Although they retained control of both Houses, the Republicans made gains, picking up three seats in the Senate and fifteen in the House. George W. Bush lost in the general election to Kent Hance, but Hance was a conservative Democrat who ran to Bush's right and would eventually throw his support behind the Republican Party. Dick Cheney won his race for the House in Wyoming, as did Newt Gingrich in Georgia. Both were part of a rising generation of House Republicans who were ideologically sympathetic to the kinds of market-based ideas that conservatives in the Nixon and Ford administrations, including Cheney himself, had promoted.

The election results sent the White House into a panic. "The mood is hostile, suspicious, and in many cases, bitter," reported Pat Caddell. "The electorate has become more volatile and responsive to negative personal campaigns than I have ever seen." Only one-third bothered to vote, with many traditional Democrats staying home as an act of "conscious abstention." "Because the public has lost faith that either party can adequately solve our complicated problems, particularly inflation," Caddell concluded, "the traditional anchors of party and ideology have been lost, the vote itself has become more sport than task and the distance between the system and the electorate is growing greater at an alarming pace."[123]

Carter's bid for the center was not working. He had banked his presidency on his ability to attract college-educated, white-collar, middle- and upper-middle-class voters to a new kind of moderation. "Simply doing slightly better (among them) than in the past is not sufficient," Caddell had told him before the 1976 election. "If there is a future in politics, it is this massive demographic change."[124] After the 1978 elections, *The New York Times* affirmed "the political power of America's middle class, a rapidly expanding segment of the electorate that is tired of being taxed, is frightened by inflation, and is wary of the Federal Government's ability to solve the nation's problems."[125] But they were not enough to secure successful electoral outcomes for Democrats. Carter was unable to convince them that he was an effective leader, and his moderation cost him support among the Democratic base.

The president's top advisers were struggling to map out an effective political strategy for Carter as a post–New Deal Democrat. "We need to counter the charge that President Carter is deviating from Democratic Party traditions," wrote Christopher Matthews, a young speechwriter. The Democratic Party had built its political following because "it has dealt with the nation's problems as they really exist." Like the New Deal, which was a "vigorous government effort to restore economic hope," the president "is using the same pragmatic approach." But, of course, as Matthews knew, the problems were very different: "During the 1930s people lacked confidence in private institutions; today they lack confidence in public institutions. They believe government taxes too much, wastes too much of their money, and interferes too much in their lives," Matthews explained. Roosevelt had navigated between laissez-faire and socialism. Now Carter, too, had to strike a moderate position, "an alternative to extremism." "Instead of massive retrenchment, instead of 'Proposition 13' Kemp-Roth irresponsibility," said Matthews, "he is offering reasonable restraint."[126]

But making government more efficient and less intrusive was neither help-ful in the short term nor particularly rousing as a political platform. Cut-ting back a little, revamping, and restructuring were not as exciting and certainly not as mobilizing as the New Deal and the Great Society.

Two days after the midterms, Carter signed the National Energy Act into law. The mood was one of relief, more than celebration. Lud Ashley remarked that there had been few bills over which people had delivered last rites as much as these. On the campaign trail, Carter had promised to be a new kind of Democrat, moving away from New Deal–era guarantees of cheap energy and toward market incentives. Once in office, he had been forced to move to his left. But now, at the end of this battle, Carter under-scored the market-based philosophy that these measures, especially the Natural Gas Policy Act, reflected. These laws would yield necessary con-servation, Carter said, from incentives that "rely on natural market forces of the free enterprise system to accomplish this purpose. The government regulatory intrusion is minimized." This point of view did not win sup-port from liberal Democrats, nor did it appeal to environmentalists. Both groups wanted Carter to do more.

On December 1, Carter used his executive authority to designate fifty-six million acres of Alaska federal lands as national monuments. Under heavy lobbying from the mining and oil industries, Congress had failed to protect what environmentalists proclaimed was the country's "last fron-tier." Using powers vested in the president under the 1906 Antiquities Act, Carter proclaimed an area larger than the size of Minnesota off-limits to development and in a single gesture doubled the amount of land under the control of the national park system. Only an act of Congress could reverse his decision. But this bold move did little to shore up his base.

The problem for Carter was that too often he sounded like a Republi-can, without that party's confidence and gusto and without the massive tax cuts it was offering. Not only did Carter fail to command loyalty from middle-class suburban voters, he also alienated traditional constituents of the Democratic Party. His first two years in office had not delivered the kind of boost that these left-leaning elements were looking for. And the fight over energy had only made matters worse. In the end, even as Carter continued regulations, he failed to fight hard, or even at all, to provide any kind of tangible rewards. The passage of the national energy bills was not one that a congressman could take back to his district and trumpet as a major success.

Caught between the old liberal labor elements and the changing political realities of Sunbelt suburban voters, Carter was unable to offer an effective platform or rebuild the Democratic Party. His failure on energy politics both was symptomatic of his inability to carve out a middle way and contributed to the further disillusionment with the Democratic Party, one that would only grow when the world experienced its second oil shock in 1979.

6

Hot Summer Mad

IN EARLY 1979, the White House could see the makings of a political disaster. A few months earlier, in October 1978, strikes in the Iranian oil fields set in motion a revolution, which led to the toppling of the shah. On January 16, when the shah left Iran, saying he was going on vacation, the world understood that his rule was over, a fact that posed a particular challenge for President Carter. The United States had relied on the shah to help stabilize world oil markets. The relationship had had its ups and downs, with Iran proving unreliable and often unwilling to facilitate the interests of the United States and other oil-dependent American allies. For years, American presidents had gambled that support of the shah made more sense than any other alternatives. Carter had celebrated New Year's Eve with the shah a year earlier. But this erstwhile ally had lost power, and the prospects for the free flow of oil became uncertain.

Taking the Heat

The Iranian Revolution resulted in the second oil shock in less than a decade. Political unrest in opposition to the shah brought on sporadic disruptions in the oil fields. On December 26, 1978, production stopped for sixty-nine days, and Iran, the world's fourth-largest oil producer, cut off all oil exports. At the time, the United States was importing approximately 800,000 barrels a day from Iran, an amount equal to roughly 10 percent of American imports and 5 percent of total oil consumption. That cut came as the United States was increasing its use, with consumption rising 4 percent in the first three months of 1979.[1] The Iranian shortfall was eased at first by an increase in Saudi Arabian production. But with the world market tight, prices began to increase. On December 17, 1978, the Organization of Petroleum Exporting Countries announced a 14.5 percent price hike.

Higher fuel prices had immediate domestic political consequences. The winter of 1979 was another cold one, and rising costs came on top of an escalating rate of inflation, nearly reaching double digits. In February, an eight-month-old child froze to death in Queens, New York, when the local gas company turned off the heat after the family had failed to pay its utility bill. The death spurred a protest by seventy religious, political, and labor groups to oppose utility shutoffs for those unable to pay.[2] The OPEC price rise made a recession likely as businesses cut costs and the Federal Reserve increased interest rates to slow down inflation.

On the same day that reporters asked Carter about his response to the shah's departure from Iran, they also grilled him on his 1980 budget. Would Carter stick to his fall pledge to fight inflation? Or would he succumb to pressures for some kind of stimulus after the Democratic setback in the 1978 midterms and the run-up to the 1980 presidential campaign? No, Carter said. "The budget commitment will be to control inflation. It will be very austere, stringent, tough fiscal policy."

The pollster Pat Caddell cautioned Carter that he was standing on the edge of a precipice. His survey findings showed a general decline in American attitudes about the future. "Almost half of the American people are now long term pessimists!" exclaimed Caddell. He described his findings as "chilling," "dangerous and debilitating," and "staggering." Caddell saw the country's problem as psychological, even as he noted the impact of inflation on Americans' daily living. Carter had won office in 1976, Caddell reasoned, to heal the country's lingering wounds from the 1960s assassinations, the failure in Vietnam, and Watergate. He compared the nation to someone who had not recovered from trauma: "Because the damage has never been healed a period of anomie prevails—the explosion, even suicide, often comes down the road often apparently out of the blue." Caddell argued that it was essential to tackle "this immense and ethereal monster." "Mr. President," he announced, "I fear if we fail to address this crisis of confidence that history will severely judge our inaction . . . You were elected to restore trust, restore values . . . to first and foremost deal with the spiritual malaise in America." Carter should tackle this "uneasiness over purpose" in his State of the Union speech.[3]

Stuart Eizenstat disagreed. The annual address, broadcast on national television, functions as a "political statement," counseled Eizenstat, who had gotten his start in electoral politics working for Hubert Humphrey, and it needed to signal to Democrats that "the President is still 'on their side.'" That objective was particularly important when budget restraint meant "we can not satisfy the normal desires of important elements of the Democratic Party—blacks, mayors and governors, and labor."[4] In the final version, Carter included a few sentences on affirmative rights and the need for labor law reform, but it was hardly what Eizenstat saw as enough, given the overall message of austerity. "We cannot afford to live beyond our means," said Carter.

The Democratic congressional leaders were horrified. This was the longest period of slow growth that Americans had lived through since the Great Depression coupled with an inflationary surge that was getting worse. The fundamental issue for the president, they believed, was the lack of his tangible successes. Unemployment had declined, but the economy was still doing poorly, and the president's commitment to budget cutting spelled political trouble for traditional Democrats. While expanding foreign aid and defense spending, Carter limited the growth of domestic social programs. In response, Tip O'Neill, who was first elected in 1952, remarked, "I did not become Speaker of the House to dismantle the programs that I've worked all my life for." "The fact is," said the presidential aspirant Senator Edward Kennedy, "the Administration's budget asks the poor, the black, the sick, the young, the cities and the unemployed to bear a disproportionate share of the billions of dollars in reductions in Federal spending."[5]

The strains within the Democratic Party provided the backdrop for formulating a response to the oil situation. Carter was committed to raising the price of domestic oil, and he had tried and failed to achieve that goal in his first energy package through a tax on crude. The Energy Policy and Conservation Act of 1975 authorized the president to raise oil prices administratively as early as June 1, 1979. That would allow Carter to act more deliberately than he had during the protracted natural gas battle. He could raise prices incrementally until they expired in October 1981, or he could do away with controls altogether. His action would stand, unless either congressional chamber vetoed the decision within fifteen days.

Carter's energy secretary, James Schlesinger, gave him some bold advice. Get rid of price controls, get rid of allocations, get the government out of the oil business: "Government regulations will continue to serve as a poor substitute for the competitive dynamics of a marketplace," wrote the secretary. With profit margins fixed at 1973 levels, producers claimed they had little incentive to increase gasoline production. Moreover, the DOE based allocations on historical use in 1972, which did not account for the rapid growth of places like California and prevented the flexibility needed to respond to shortages where and when they emerged. In light of the Iranian Revolution and the likely shrinking supply, Schlesinger predicted the future: "If existing controls are merely revised, the government will remain in the control business . . . When shortages develop under continued controls, the government—instead of the oil companies—will have to shoulder the blame." The prospect of the return of gas lines was worrisome, especially for an administration that had spent much of its political capital on the energy question. The right policy, Schlesinger argued, was for Carter to authorize total and immediate decontrol on June 1.[6]

Lifting controls would prompt a political uprising from Carter's liberal flank. The DOE estimated that the OPEC price rise would add nine cents to every gallon of gas by the end of 1980. With decontrol, that increase would be closer to thirteen cents.[7] "The tension between the inflation problem and the energy problem is tearing us apart," said Alfred Kahn.[8] In addition, Carter would suffer enormous political costs. At a time when the public already thought Big Oil earned too much, Carter would appear to be handing the oil companies large windfall profits. Finally, the president was asking labor to restrain its wage demands to comply with voluntary guidelines. If Carter were determined to use his executive authority to raise prices, then he should do so slowly and incrementally.[9] Schlesinger, too, recognized these political realities. As he told a *Time* magazine reporter, "What I want, and what I recommend, may be two different things."[10]

Liberals in Congress opposed lifting controls ahead of their expiration date, even if gradual and incremental. From their point of view, there would be hell to pay if they went along with Carter. The last oil shock led to a stampede for government intervention in the oil industry, and now the number of congressional liberals was even larger. Since the Arab embargo, Americans knew much more about the Middle East, OPEC, and the threat of the oil weapon. But they still believed the major oil companies controlled, influenced, and manipulated global markets: if a shortage was emerging, it resulted from a Big Oil conspiracy. Already, before evidence of any serious shortfall, Scoop Jackson asked the General Accounting Office (GAO) to investigate. Were oil companies deliberately holding back supply in hopes of future price increases? Jackson wondered.[11]

Representative Toby Moffett, the tenacious consumer advocate, would lead the crusade in the House to block presidential decontrol. In January, Moffett, a junior member of the House, outmaneuvered other congressmen and won the chairmanship of the Government Operations' Subcommittee on the Environment, Energy, and Natural Resources. After his victory, he announced he would take on Big Oil and order an investigation into "the operations of the oil cartel."[12]

As vocal and loud as liberals were, conservatives were just as vociferous. The battle lines were drawn. Leading members of the GOP, joined by oil-state Democrats, offered the view that the public should blame the government for any shortages that developed. The Heritage Foundation issued a report explaining that the regulatory regime of the last decade impinged on American production, with serious economic and national security costs. Gerald Parsky, William Simon's assistant during the Arab embargo, called for immediate decontrol. "Controls on gasoline prices should not be relaxed . . . they should be eliminated," asserted Parsky in an editorial. "The day of cheap, abundant oil is over . . . We should concentrate on enlisting market forces and the pricing system to solve our problem."[13]

Conservatives also argued for rolling back costly and counterproductive environmental restrictions. These opponents of regulation pointed to the fight over the construction of the Tellico Dam, which environmentalists claimed would make the snail darter, a small fish, extinct, as a leading example of how environmentalism unnecessarily curtailed energy supplies.[14] Strip-mining legislation, which Carter had signed in 1977, inhibited coal production, as did tougher emissions standards. Under Carter, the Environmental Protection Agency had permitted states to set more rigorous levels for allowable pollutants. Nuclear plants and hydroelectric facilities encountered siting problems, further limiting domestic supply. Carter's defense of the Alaskan wilderness from oil companies offered another example of backward energy policy.[15]

Caught between the Left and the Right, Carter decided to take the political heat. In mid-March, he told congressional leadership that he was going forward with phased decontrol to begin on June 1. Within the month, he would go public with his decision. "I'd rather do that and accept the political blame than spend another two years arguing with you about what ought to be done—when you know what ought to be done," he said.[16] To balance this move to market prices, he would propose a windfall profits tax to recoup half of the gains oil companies would earn as a result of decontrol and use the funds for alternative energy research, mass transit, and payments to lower-income families to help with higher energy bills.

Carter felt convinced that the oil situation threatened American national interests. Despite the ambition of Project Independence, the United States was now importing about half of daily use, with the majority coming from OPEC. Oil imports burdened the economy by adding to the trade deficit and weakening the dollar, especially as OPEC continued to raise prices. In addition, America's growing reliance on imports made Carter's negotiations with its allies difficult. Oil dependence could also diminish the United States' standing in international relations, forcing compromise on its commitment to Israel.

Carter's decision on oil reflected a larger rethinking of Middle East foreign policy within the White House. Carter's more hawkish advisers were pushing for a bigger military presence in the Persian Gulf as the next crucial arena in the Cold War. In early 1977, the special NSC analyst Samuel Huntington wrote an influential memo, suggesting that this area was the site most likely for a test of wills between the two superpowers.[17] "U.S. interests there continue to grow as Western access to oil becomes more important," according to this analysis. "The possibility of conflict, potentially involving the USSR, remains higher there than in other parts of the world." Of concern was the limited ability to react to any regional threats. In short, "the U.S. would face the greatest difficulty projecting power into the Middle East."[18] In August 1977, the NSC, under the direction of Zbigniew Brzezinski,

wrote Presidential Directive 18, which Carter signed, endorsing the idea of a limited contingency force in the Gulf.

Huntington, a Harvard political science professor, and Brzezinski, his NSC boss, espoused a hard line on the Soviet Union, rejecting the policy of détente. They also dismissed the conventional wisdom that modernization, as envisioned by Cold War economists like W. W. Rostow, worked everywhere and that economic growth would lead to political liberalization. Moreover, they did not believe that democracy, or a form of it, better promoted stability. They supported the cause of human rights, especially in the Soviet Union, but that did not translate into withdrawing backing of autocratic regimes elsewhere. Above all, they feared that Middle East instability created an opening for the Soviets who were projecting influence in Afghanistan, South Yemen, and Ethiopia. They also appreciated that the Middle East would become especially important as the United States, and even more, Western Europe and Japan, became almost totally dependent on oil from this region. At the same time, intelligence told them that the Soviets would reach their peak oil production in 1980 and thereafter they would need to increase imports.

A rapid deployment force to respond to Third World crises won favor among the hard Right and hawks like Henry Jackson. In addition, a group of younger Democrats, including Senators Sam Nunn of Georgia and Gary Hart of Colorado, also supported defense spending and a rapid deployment strategy as part of an effort to craft a post-Vietnam-era foreign policy. But a new militarism hardly dominated the Democratic Party, and the administration made little progress in putting this Middle East plan into operation.

After the toppling of the shah, Brzezinski appealed directly to Carter to see the historic significance of events. Suffering from internal political conflicts, countries extending from Bangladesh and Pakistan to Yemen and Iran were experiencing an "arc of instability," which could allow for the rise of new powers friendly toward the Soviets. The result could be devastating; it "would mean a fundamental shift in the global structure of power." If the new Iranian regime sympathized with the Soviet Union, it would mean "the most massive American defeat since the beginning of the Cold War."[19]

This White House hawk went public, warning in speeches and in the pages of mass-circulation magazines of troubles ahead. "I'd have to be

blind or Pollyannish not to recognize that there are dark clouds on the horizon," Brzezinski wrote. There was a new threat to the United States, with Iran as only the most visible and recent example. In an interview with *Time* magazine, he explained, "An arc of crisis stretches along the shores of the Indian Ocean, with fragile social and political structures in a region of vital importance to us threatened with fragmentation. The resulting political chaos could well be filled by elements hostile to our values and sympathetic to our adversaries." As the *Time* magazine article, which could have been written by Brzezinski himself, concluded, "Instability itself is contagious, and the opportunities for exploitation are increasing."[20]

After the shah fled, the president, following the advice of his hawkish advisers, sent a carrier-led task force from the Philippines to the Persian Gulf. But the doves in the State Department and his vice president, Walter Mondale, prevailed upon him to turn the ship around in the middle of the South China Sea. The decision, a critical William Safire wrote, produced "the first example of no-boat gunboat diplomacy. We showed a naked flagpole."[21] Irving Kristol announced in *The Wall Street Journal* "the end of an era for American foreign policy." Without Iran as an ally, the likely outcome would be "the effective expulsion of American power from the entire Middle East."[22]

By February, Brzezinski persuaded Carter of the importance of a greater military presence in the Gulf. The need for a new command structure, one devoted to the Middle East, reflected Brzezinski's belief that this was as serious a moment as the immediate postwar years at the start of the Cold War. Just as George Kennan had laid out the logic behind the need for President Truman to commit the United States to reconstructing Europe as a way to contain the Soviet Union, so, too, did Carter have to make a similar commitment in the Persian Gulf. In this stage of the Cold War, the Middle East joined Europe and East Asia as vital areas, and all were interdependent because of the heavy reliance on oil. Brzezinski began weekly meetings of the NSC to develop a new Persian Gulf security framework and push for a new strategic command devoted exclusively to the region.[23]

The new Khomeini regime, which took over on February 11, 1979, ended the oil field strikes, and on March 5 the country renewed shipments. But the new regime would not produce oil at its previous level. Turmoil among the radical Left continued, conservative religious leaders worried about the speed of modernization that oil revenues would make possible, and the absence of Western participation in the country's oil production, after foreign technicians left and the government took control of the industry, posed technical challenges.

The situation worsened when Saudi Arabia announced a major cut-back in production. As President Carter was finalizing the peace treaty between Israel and Egypt, which he would announce at Camp David on March 26, Saudi Arabia was cautious about appearing too friendly during this Middle East peace process. Its leaders also worried about the United States' commitment to regional stability in the wake of the shah's demise. The United States had been a longtime ally of the shah's, but Carter insisted that the United States would stand aside. "We have no intention, neither ability nor desire, to interfere in the internal affairs of Iran," said Carter at a news conference. Pointing to the experience in Vietnam as a failure, Carter said the United States would not repeat the mistake.

The Saudi cutback resulted in a tightening of the world oil supply, which fueled price increases, especially on the spot market, where oil traded at prices several dollars a barrel above OPEC levels. In the wake of the Arab embargo, the major international oil companies owned less of the international oil they distributed, and therefore they had to accept the production and price levels set by OPEC producers. Moreover, the percentage of oil offered by OPEC on the spot market, as opposed to set under long-term contracts with the majors, had increased, adding volatility to the market.[24]

Even as the oil situation deteriorated, the chances for a more aggressive U.S. military policy appeared hard to implement. While Saudi Arabia, America's chief ally, eagerly sought the purchase of arms from the United States, which Carter helped to arrange, allowing Americans access for a military base proved problematic. Brzezinski, along with James Schlesinger and Secretary of Defense Harold Brown, argued for a greater naval presence in the Indian Ocean. Carter sent an additional aircraft carrier to the Persian Gulf, and he let Moscow know that the United States regarded the Persian Gulf as "a vital U.S. interest" and would use force if necessary. Realistically, though, the commander in chief faced constraints.[25]

On April 5, Carter delivered disconcerting news to the country: "Our national strength is dangerously dependent on a thin line of oil tankers stretching halfway around the earth, originating in the Middle East and around the Persian Gulf—one of the most unstable regions in the world."

The instability in the Middle East, the growing consumption of fossil fuels, and the dim prospects for any alternative energies were making the United States vulnerable. The nuclear accident at Three Mile Island days earlier revealed the problems of this technological fix. "What can we do?" Carter asked. Step one said the president was to decontrol oil prices. He would start the process on June 1. This policy was essential to reduce consumption and stimulate domestic production. "I'll give it to you straight," he said. "Each one of us will have to use less oil and pay more for it."

Carter was relying on his executive authority to raise prices. It would be up to Congress to decide who should keep the profits. Carter proposed a windfall profits tax to fund alternative energy research, with tax revenues directed toward mass transit and the poor as well. Carter could not hope to win support from the Right, whose leaders like Jack Kemp denounced any new taxes. But he hoped that the tax would buy support from the Left and from many other congressmen who would be eager to figure out ways to spend the extra revenue, especially in a time of budget austerity.

Instantly, the liberals went on the attack. Carter's windfall tax was not enough to subdue their anger over decontrol. Kennedy decried the move as a sellout to Big Oil, which would hurt low-income families.[26] "It will force the poor to choose between food, medical care, and keeping warm," he blasted. He and twelve other liberals, including Senator Jackson, co-sponsored a bill in the Senate to extend mandatory price controls for two years and give the president authority to extend them until the end of 1982.[27]

In the House, the president faced even stiffer challenges from liberals, consumer advocates, and organized labor. Ellen Berman of the Consumer Federation of America said, "At a time when inflation is raging at 14 percent and the President asks workers to limit their wage increases to 7 percent, it is the height of hypocrisy to remove price controls from the oil industry." Toby Moffett claimed that Carter's decontrol decision was a "declaration of war on the Northeast."[28] On May 2, led by Moffett, the liberal Democrats on the House Commerce Committee came within one vote of blocking Carter's decontrol decision.[29]

Carter's action set into motion a bruising battle, which would make the president vulnerable from all sides. While the Left jabbed at the president for proposing to raise prices, even if incrementally, the Right was arguing that the elaborate system of price controls and allocations, which would stay in place until 1981, guaranteed a major shortage of gasoline. And Carter was making their argument for them. "Excessive federal government controls must end," the president declared when he announced his decontrol decision. "The federal bureaucracy and red tape have become so complicated, it is almost unbelievable."

Carter's centrist agenda satisfied few in Congress and did not generate much enthusiasm from the public. He believed that raising prices was unavoidable—"I did not make the decision that I announced because I expected it to be pleasant or popular. I made it because it's right, and it's necessary, and it's in the best interest of our Nation"—and he also believed he was demonstrating leadership, which his adviser Jerry Rafshoon said was "our biggest weakness." "The issues are not even that important—nobody's got any better answers to inflation or energy than you do," counseled Rafshoon. "People in 1980 are going to vote for whomever they think has the best chance to lead us out of our troubles."[30] But Carter seemed less like a leader than a technocratic problem solver.

Except his solutions did not work. Or at least they did not fix the problem at hand. Just as he was announcing a price rise, gas lines started forming on the West Coast. On May 5, after beginning his day in Iowa, in what was an unacknowledged start to his reelection campaign, the president flew to Los Angeles, California, where the energy issue was making front-page headlines. As states east of the Rockies were having a harder time importing oil because of the Iranian situation, the flow of oil to states to the west declined. Motorists, panicking that they would be caught with empty tanks, were rushing to fill up at the pumps, where gas lines stretched five hundred cars long. When the president arrived, his motorcade had to drive twenty miles out of its way to fill up its tanks.[31]

The president came to California to view the situation on the ground, but he used the occasion to fight his battles back on Capitol Hill. Rather than addressing the frustration of those on the newly forming lines, he called out liberals in Congress for nearly blocking his decontrol of oil: "The reason for the gas lines and terrible inconvenience here . . . is that we have failed to be prepared." Launching a direct attack on his liberal wing, he announced, "It is time for responsible national leaders in the Congress and elsewhere to forget about extending controls."

To Carter, the solution was to let the price mechanism work. In response to the gas lines, Carter said there was nothing he could do: "There are simply no easy answers—no answers that do not involve higher costs for energy and using less energy." It was up to Californians. "I want to ask drivers in this area to resist the urge to try to keep their tanks full at all times," the president pleaded. The only thing that would help was to let prices rise and get the government out of the energy business. Conservatives, of course, agreed.

Energy Is Our Vietnam

As the first shortages appeared, in the spring of 1979, the California Energy Commission's chairman, Richard Maullin, reported chaos on the gas lines: "People have got into fights. Gasoline station attendants have been hit with pipes."[32] A week after Carter's visit, the situation grew worse. "If there was more order and less fear, we'd be able to get by," Maullin said. "But people are freaking out."[33] As panic buying spread, the average sale fell from eight gallons to three. Topping off, as it was called, meant that motorists were carrying nearly a month's supply of gasoline in their tanks, draining the local inventory.[34] Desperate for fuel, drivers put leaded gasoline in unleaded tanks, which destroyed their catalytic converters. The result was the worst smog Los Angeles had experienced in years.[35]

Day after day, headlines told of lines getting longer. Some news stories made it sound like a party. According to one account of an all-night gas station, drivers "spent their time drinking wine, smoking marijuana, talking with people in other cars, flitting between the few tailgate parties that sprang up and just generally hanging out." But the reports also captured a deep sense of anger: "Everyone in line was alternatively cursing the oil companies and cursing President Carter, the most likely fall guy in their eyes."[36]

As NO GAS signs littered local landscapes, anger could turn to resignation. The majority of Americans believed that the oil companies engineered an artificial shortage that would disappear once prices went higher. The number who blamed Big Oil for the shortages was even higher than during the Arab embargo. The most common rumor was that fully loaded tankers were waiting offshore until prices went up. In Gardena, California, one resident said, "It's a fix. The gas companies are taking advantage of us."

With politicians unable to extract more gasoline from Big Oil, then perhaps drivers had to surrender. "Why don't they just raise prices and we can forget the whole thing?" asked another driver. "When gas goes up to $1.50 a gallon, then we won't have any more lines," said a Bakersfield driver. "Carter is powerless."[37]

Liberals did not want to go down without a fight. Toby Moffett appeared on CBS's *Face the Nation* to demand that the White House use its authority to force greater oil production and make oil refineries operate at capacity.[38] Moffett, along with Senator Howard Metzenbaum, wanted the General Accounting Office to uncover the truth. They wrote, "It is our suspicion that once again the American people are being manipulated by oil companies, that the shortage is contrived, not real, and that the purpose is to justify the higher prices that have spiraled relentlessly upward since January."[39]

Senator Kennedy, Carter's greatest potential rival in the 1980 primaries, was unforgiving in his attacks. Kennedy pointed to Carter's decision on decontrol as evidence of uncaring. In a commencement address at Howard University, the African-American college in the nation's capital, Kennedy went after the president, wondering, "Is it fair to ask those who are poor to pay a much larger proportion of their income for energy than those who are affluent?" Kennedy saw the energy issue as a matter of equity and distributive justice. "What possible gain can there be from an energy policy whose primary effect is to boost the already ample profits of the oil industry, put millions of consumers through the wringer, and sharpen the class divisions of our society?" asked the presidential hopeful.[40]

California's governor, Jerry Brown, another Democratic presidential contender, also capitalized on the gasoline shortages to tarnish Carter's reputation. In early May, Brown spoke at a massive antinuclear rally in Washington, where sixty-five thousand protesters gathered to challenge the president's environmental record. Also in attendance was Jane Fonda, who starred in *The China Syndrome*, which was released just before the Three Mile Island accident and, with its plot of corporate cover-up and political incompetence, echoed the public's deep mistrust of Washington and the energy industry to manage the nation's resources. She and other activists faulted the Carter administration for being, as Stu Eizenstat described it, "entirely pro-nuclear" and insufficiently committed to solar energy.[41]

The liberals were turning up the heat on the White House. On May 22, Moffett led a successful effort to get the House Democratic Caucus to vote in favor of extending mandatory controls into 1980, which its members did by a margin of two to one. With the exception of the majority leader, Jim Wright from Texas, the entire Democratic leadership came out against the president's move to decontrol. This defection stemmed from the Democrats' belief that Big Oil and the OPEC cartel made the market non-competitive, and they had to protect consumers. "Will it be the guys in the rooms in Abu Dhabi who determine the price of oil in the United States?" asked Moffett.[42]

In a public letter to Carter, Moffett and Andrew Maguire, who had received more than ten thousand letters complaining about rising costs, claimed they were responding to "a growing public sentiment for restraints on rapidly escalating energy prices."[43] In private, Moffett told Carter, "There's nothing I'd like better than for you to go to my region next year in good political shape, but unless there's a dramatic change, I don't see how it can be done. You're facing a *revolution* up there on energy."[44] When asked if he would support Kennedy in 1980, Moffett replied, "Immediately."[45] By late May, Pat Caddell was reporting that Kennedy was leading Carter in the polls.[46] The presidential assistant Les Francis told the White House, "The President's policy on decontrolling oil prices may, in fact, make extraordinary good sense. However, its political costs continue to mount."[47]

Carter had no plan to get rid of the gas lines. Hendrik Hertzberg drafted a speech for Carter, which reflected this deficiency. Sounding a now familiar White House theme, the speech alternated between blaming the excesses of consumers and the inaction on the Hill. "We have indulged ourselves," Hertzberg wrote. "We have buried our heads in the sand. We have let our divisions and our selfishness paralyze our will to get together and deal with our energy problem." The tone was strident. "From an energy point of view, this country is fat, flabby and short-winded." Taking aim at ordinary Americans, the speech continued, "Every time you get in your car, please ask yourself: Is this trip necessary?" Oil lobbyists came in for ridicule, as did congressmen who did not fight harder against the oil companies. When the president had summoned the nation's leaders to a war on energy dependence, "the Congress responded with the moral equivalent of going AWOL."[48]

Eizenstat killed the speech, at least for the time being. He told Hertz-berg, "This is totally [the] wrong thrust . . . This fails to explain *why* there is a shortage." He advised Hertzberg not to "blame the driver." And he also criticized the attack on Congress: "This is the worst thing for a country looking for an answer and getting nothing but finger-pointing."[49] Charles Warren, whom Carter appointed his special liaison to California on the gas situation, reported that the lines existed because the shortage was real and closer to 20 percent rather than the 7 or 8 that the DOE was report-ing.[50] Still, Jody Powell said Americans were responding to the energy cri-sis in a selfish fashion that was making the shortage worse. "Me first, last and always. Give me mine, and to hell with the rest of the country," Powell told the press.[51]

Carter struck the wrong note. In a one-hour NBC special on the gas lines, he defended decontrol as the only useful policy response.[52] He said there was no magic wand he could wave to make the lines disappear. In-stead, he urged conservation and sacrifice, and to set an example, the White House unscrewed every other lightbulb, turned up the summer thermo-stats to eighty degrees, removed many window air-conditioning units, and encouraged employees to take the stairs instead of the elevator.[53] This re-proving tone did not play well. Moffett, who was now considering a run for the Senate in 1980, told a group of United Automobile Workers, "The Ad-ministration seems to think that working people are like spoiled children. Maybe it's the Baptist schoolteacher element."[54]

On June 1, President Carter's phased oil decontrol went into effect. This plan designed a government-mandated pricing system for three categories of oil, each roughly one-third of the market. "Old" oil, which was crude oil discovered before 1973 and under price controls sold for approximately $6, would sell at roughly $13 a barrel. "New" oil, crude discovered after 1973, would move incrementally from its current price of $13 to world prices. Another third from smaller wells, also known as stripper wells, would sell at the market price, which was around $16. Controls would ease until their expiration on October 1, 1981. The day before he implemented this plan, Carter met with fifteen oil executives to urge greater production in ex-change for these higher prices.[55]

To avoid getting steamrolled by the liberals in Congress, Carter turned to Republicans. More than 100 of the 159 House Republicans backed decontrol.[56] Looking to Republicans for support was becoming a regular political habit. Republican votes had proven decisive on the sale of fighter planes to Saudi Arabia, natural gas deregulation, and budget cutting. But Carter reaped little political gain from these policies. Carter's phased decontrol placated neither the oilmen nor the conservatives, especially as the president was pushing for a windfall profits tax, while it cost support from liberal Democrats.

Most problematic, decontrol did nothing to end the lines. By mid-June, many eastern states were facing gasoline shortages. Drivers rushed to the stations fearful that supply would run out and angry that government was not taking more action. Allocations made the situation worse by preventing the shifting of oil from rural areas that had plenty of supply while depriving fuel-starved cities. Frank Moore, head of the Congressional Liaison office, told Carter, "The people believe most of the problem is attributable to dishonesty and chicanery on the part of energy industries . . . In their view, the government is a co-conspirator in the hoax."[57] A White House staffer reported the general refrain: "When gas gets to be 'X' dollars a gallon—there will be plenty of it. The oil companies are just trying to rip us off, and Carter is letting them get away with it."[58]

Within the White House, a sense of confusion and chaos pervaded. The president's advisers dubbed their nightly meetings on energy the "five o'clock follies." Carter understood the damage that the energy question was causing. In a meeting with the Democratic leadership, he said, "The future of the Democratic Party is tied to energy. It could cost us control of the Senate and the White House. It could be the issue that puts the Democrats out of power for a very long time."[59] OPEC was expected to raise prices again at the end of June, which, Eizenstat told Carter, "will add to the sense of despair and lack of control which the public seems to feel about the energy issue."[60] As Representative Morris Udall grasped, voters might be inclined to sweep incumbents out of office if the gas lines persisted: "I think this has . . . potential—for an angry electorate to say something's wrong and we want change."[61] Twenty-four Democratic seats were up for election in the Senate, allowing for the real prospect of losing that chamber in 1980.

The president's standing with the public plummeted. *The New York Times* and the Gallup survey released polls showing that Carter's job approval rating was at its lowest point, lower than at any point for Presidents Johnson and Ford. The *Times* poll also showed Carter's personal rating as a negative, which, as Eizenstat put it, "was really bad news." Caddell warned Carter that these results were alarming, suggesting that the "frustration with the President is moving toward personal hostility as opposed to indifference or disappointment." Reversing negative personal ratings was much more difficult than reversing negative job approval ratings. The implications for 1980 were clear.[62] "Energy affects the life of every goddam American, and most of them are mad at us," a senior White House aide told *Newsweek*. "Energy is our Vietnam," another aide said.[63]

Solar power emerged as the White House's solution. "A strong solar message and program," Eizenstat told Carter, "will be important in trying to counter the sense of hopelessness which polls are showing the public feels about energy . . . From both a substantive and political standpoint, solar and renewable resources are the only really bright spots on an otherwise bleak energy horizon."[64] Eizenstat explained, "I'm quite convinced Congress and the American people want a Manhattan-type project on alternative energy development. There is almost a desperation on this issue."[65] Eizenstat thought that a big and bold program would help to offset the political cost of decontrol. "A strong and vigorous commitment to solar can help us in getting the Congress and the public to swallow the more bitter pills of decontrol and generally increasing prices," this adviser hoped. To make the White House commitment credible to environmentalists, Carter had to promise that as much as one-fifth of the country's energy would come from solar and other renewable energy sources by the year 2000.[66]

Carter had to act before Congress stole his political thunder on this issue. In the House, the Solar Caucus had obtained a near majority. As gas lines grew, momentum for a massive government research program for alternative energies gained steam. Solar energy was broadly popular, but support for all kinds of alternative energies surged. In January, Representative William Moorhead, a Pennsylvania Democrat, had introduced a $2 billion spending bill to subsidize synthetic fuels. Initially, the bill drew little interest, but by June congressmen were rushing to line up behind it.

The White House wanted it both ways. It wanted a substantial program for which it could take credit, score political points, and trigger genuine conservation of fossil fuels. However, as Eizenstat explained, it was cautious about creating a "big government concept" that would be "too expensive, coercive, and relies heavily on mandatory government programs."[67] Eliot Cutler, Carter's energy adviser in the Office of Management and Budget, worried that congressional liberals would propose a program that was too costly and would not work. He told Eizenstat, "We need to seize leadership on alternative energy development . . . in order to avoid not only serious political damage, but also the possibility that genuinely bad and very expensive investment decisions will be made by a Congress in panic."[68] Cutler, as a former legislative aide for Senator Edmund Muskie and then counsel to the Senate Subcommittee on the Environment, had helped to draft the seminal pieces of environmental legislation, including the Clean Air Act and the National Environmental Policy Act. Yet he was concerned that Congress would produce a massive pork barrel energy bill, which might lead to boondoggles and could trigger a backlash against the environmental cause.

On June 20, Carter unveiled his solar energy proposal, beginning with a dedication of a new solar system at the White House. Just as Benjamin Harrison introduced electric lighting in the White House in 1891 before it was commercially viable, so, too, was Carter installing a solar heating system in the West Wing. Visible from Pennsylvania Avenue, the thirty-two solar roof panels demonstrated the White House's backing of this alternative energy.[69] To spread solar technology, Carter called for spending $1 billion in fiscal year 1980 to fund research, create a Solar Bank within the Department of Housing and Urban Development, and provide homeowners with loans to finance solar installations. "We will build a more self-reliant and a more secure nation for the generations to come," he said.

The vision was at once grand and small, futuristic and quaint. If every household installed a solar heating unit, America would again be strong and independent. As he told Congress, "No foreign cartel can set the price of sun power; no one can embargo it. Every solar collector in this country, every investment in using wind or biomass energy, every advance in making electricity directly from the sun decreases our reliance on uncertain sources of imported oil, bolsters our international trade position, and enhances the security of our Nation." The stakes of switching to solar power were high. "When we speak of energy security, we are in fact talking about how we can assure the future economic and military security of our country—how we can maintain the liberties and freedoms which make our Nation great," announced the president. The White House hoped the solar message would shore up Carter's political standing, especially among environmentalists. The White House invited Denis Hayes of the World-watch Institute and Gary DeLoss of the Environmental Policy Center to attend the announcement.[70]

Perhaps the solar panels might generate good publicity, but they could not contain the fury bubbling up from the gas lines. Carter went directly from the dedication ceremony to deal with the threat of the nation's inde-pendent truckers to shut down at midnight. Already, these truckers were staging demonstrations in thirty states. "When they're not making money, they get very hostile," said a spokesman.[71] In Tuscaloosa, Alabama, a striker shot and critically wounded a trucker's wife who was riding in the passenger seat.[72] Fearing a total shutdown and more violence, Carter took a page from Nixon's handling of the 1974 strike and denounced their actions. "Violence and lawlessness will not be tolerated under any circum-stances. Murder, vandalism and physical intimidation are criminal acts, and they will be treated as such," said a stern Carter. "We will do whatever is necessary to see that those truckers who want to work are not threatened by either violence or intimidation."

Undeterred, the strike began officially on June 21. Facing diesel fuel shortages as high as 40 to 45 percent, the truckers blamed the Department of Energy for having given priority allocation to farmers for their planting season.[73] Moreover, federal price controls no longer regulated diesel fuel at the pumps, which was selling for more than a dollar a gallon. "What we really need is a price rollback," explained a spokesman for the Indepen-dent Truckers Association, which now had thirty thousand members.[74] Since the start of 1979, prices had gone up by over a third, fuel became scarce, and as many as one-fifth of independent truckers had gone bank-rupt.[75] It was like "being crucified on the cross of inflation," said a group of Chicago truckers.[76] In a repeat of the Arab embargo shutdown, the truck-ers blockaded interstates, targeted gasoline terminals, and refused to drive. Within a day, the strike took at least 40 percent of the major carriers' hauling capacity out of commission.[77]

The truckers wanted Washington to act. They expected assistance from a Democratic president and a new government agency of twenty thousand employees, all dedicated to solving the energy crisis. Carrying three-quarters of the nation's livestock and fresh produce, they reasoned that a shutdown would put pressure on the White House. "There will be one hellacious uproar heard in Washington" when consumers found bare shelves at the markets, said one trucker.[78] "Shut off the fuel, shut off the trucks and people get hungry. Then something will happen," explained another hopeful driver. "Sure they're going to yell at us, but that's what we want. We want them to scream and yell. We want them to yell at the Governor and the President," said the president of the Council of Independent Truckers of New Jersey. Another trucker broadcast over his CB, "It's time the Government stopped pushing the American people around."[79]

On June 21, the first day of the official shutdown, President Carter announced he was sending a bill to Congress to deregulate the trucking industry. He had supported this measure as a follow-up to his airline deregulation, condemning what he saw as "a mindless scheme of unnecessary government interference and control." With little to offer the truckers to alleviate their immediate needs, he chose this moment to formally request Congress to deregulate. He pointed to many examples of what he saw as government-created inefficiency in the trucking business. While ICC rules allowed certain truckers to transport bananas and others pineapple, only some could transport bananas and pineapple combined. Some could carry two-gallon cans of paint but not five-gallon cans. Truckers going from Denver to Albuquerque had to make a detour of several hundred miles through Salt Lake City. This was a historic bill, said Carter, intended to "reduce the red tape and the excess regulations that have strangled and straitjacketed the trucking industry of America for the last 40 years." Carter saw this measure as an important step to "lift the heavy hand of Government regulation from the American free enterprise economy."

Carter's announcement did nothing to resolve the situation on the nation's highways. The independent truckers were the main supporters of deregulation—they had been demanding it since the first oil shock—yet they stood on the verge of riot. As self-employed workers who got paid by each load they hauled, they saw the precipitous rise in fuel costs come straight out of their profits. As in 1974, they demanded a government rollback of prices and an increase in fuel. George Oberg, president of the New England Independent Truckers Association, wrote to President Carter on the day of his deregulation message: "We feel if we are ignored by you and the members of Congress, that we as a non-violent organization will no longer be able to restrain the radical element which surrounds us."[80] Senator Kennedy warned the White House that unless Carter took deliberate steps to help the truckers immediately, "tensions could escalate and result in violence."[81]

The strike was already escalating. Police reported shootings, destruction of property, and intimidation in dozens of states. Commerce slowed across the country, with as many as seventy-five thousand truckers refusing to drive. Transportation in California came to a standstill as fruits and vegetables perished on the vine.[82] The Midwest livestock markets shut down.[83] In Maryland, four strikers, brandishing a sawed-off shotgun, forced a trucker off the road and then robbed him.[84] In Alabama, Governor Fob James told truckers to arm themselves: "It's time to put the billy back in the billystick. I'd put a shotgun beside me and go . . . and I'd kill anybody that tries to stop me."[85] In Washington, eleven state truckers associations held a press conference, announcing, "We face now a national crisis of untold proportions, a crisis that lies firmly now in the lap of the government."[86]

By design, the truckers' strike inflamed the fuel shortage. The allocations for June were already running low. "There is a panic at the pumps," said a New York representative of service stations. "It's the worst it's ever been."[87] "I had to step between two people," said the owner of a New York Mobil station. "After waiting on line they got into an argument right at the pumps, about who was cutting in front."[88] Automotive stores reported an increase in sales of siphons and gas-tank locks.[89] *The New York Times* ran a daily column, Notes from the Gas Line, giving an instant sense of permanence about this new way of life. Motorists were waiting as long as five hours, with the majority of stations shutting down early, if opened at all.[90]

On June 23, a gas riot erupted in Levittown, Pennsylvania, a working-class suburb of Philadelphia, when twenty truckers blockaded an intersection, flanked by four gas stations, to protest the fuel shortage. One striker, with American flags adorning his truck, stood on his hood, egging the protesters on. Local residents joined the truckers, chanting, "More gas! More gas!" They threw rocks, beer bottles, and cans at the local police. The crowd grew to two thousand, and the police arrested 69 people for disorderly conduct. On the second night, the riot turned more violent, resulting in the nonfatal shooting of an eighteen-year-old. The crowd set two cars on fire and vandalized the local gas stations.[91] Police arrested 127 demonstrators. Two hundred and forty-four people suffered injuries, many from dog bites from the Philadelphia K-9 Corps, which had come to calm the situation.[92]

"Social disorder in Levittown? The postwar era really has ended," wrote George Will in the pages of *Newsweek*. The famous catchphrase from the award-winning movie *Network*—"I'm as mad as hell and I'm not going to take this anymore"—was coming to life. Levittown, the icon of postwar suburbia, symbolized a whole way of living, built on the assumption of cheap and plentiful fuel. Now it was going up in flames, all because of a gas shortage, one that its citizens doubted was real. NO GAS MY ASS, read the posters that citizens displayed as they rioted.[93]

At the White House, Vice President Mondale met with truckers in the Roosevelt Room. He told them the administration would fight to reform regulations and raise shipping rates.[94] But that was not enough. "Nothing has been resolved," said their spokesman William Hill. "We were given Government promises only. Our people can't run trucks on promises. All trucks should stay parked."[95] Michael Parkhurst, another veteran from the embargo shutdowns, explained, "A lot of independent truckers are now ready to lose their trucks and even burn them in protest of White House ineptness."[96]

Amid the chaos, the Department of Energy stood helpless. Its representatives did not claim to have solutions. "It's really a psychological problem," explained a DOE spokesman.[97] As one federal energy official told *The New York Times*, "We're trying to improve the overall supply problem, but, as for these local problems, I don't know what else we can do."[98] The local problems were spiraling out of control. In New York, fights on gas lines resulted in two murders, one man stabbed to death in front of his pregnant wife; another person was shot in the head while waiting on line in Dallas.[99]

With 90 percent of the New York City metro area's stations closed, Governor Hugh Carey denounced Carter and the DOE. "I want the energy people in Washington to tell us where the gas is and to use the special Federal authority to prevent price gouging and hoarding," Carey insisted.[100] The New York congressional delegation, which demanded a White House meeting, accused the DOE of shortchanging the state. Senator Daniel Patrick Moynihan said, after the New Yorkers met with Vice President Mondale, "If they just go on giving us explanations about why nothing can be done, they're explaining this Administration out of office." "I have never seen the delegation so upset, angry, and excited," New York City's mayor, Ed Koch, told reporters. "They're enraged because they don't believe the facts—or the alleged facts—coming out of Washington."[101] Koch described the situation as "the worst political mood since Vietnam, and in some ways, even worse because it's more immediate."[102]

By the end of June, Carter and his team of energy advisers had no defenders and many detractors. The House minority leader, John Rhodes, an Arizona Republican, said, "The people are puzzled. They are angry. They don't understand why this has to be, and frankly, I don't either."[103] Democrats also attacked the administration. Twenty-six House Democrats demanded that Carter get rid of Schlesinger, pointing to the "failures of the Department of Energy" and the "lack of public and Congressional confidence in its leadership."[104] "Nearly every government attempt to manage the shortage seems to backfire or break down in confusion," explained an analysis in *U.S. News & World Report*.[105] A report in *Time* magazine charged that "the Department of Energy has set up a hideously complex allocation system," one that left many groups from farmers to truckers to motorists scrambling for fuel.[106] On ABC *World News*, a correspondent portrayed the DOE as "one of the villains."[107]

Carter was sinking fast in the polls. One angry Long Island driver snapped, "I think the gas companies are holding back and I blame the government for letting them."[108] "Carter Kiss My Gas" became a popular bumper sticker.[109] According to an ABC News–Louis Harris poll, Carter trailed behind Ronald Reagan as a presidential hopeful, 51 to 43 percent. Among Democrats, 58 percent supported Kennedy with only 31 percent backing the president.[110]

A climate of gloom descended on the White House. Carter, who had just returned from a successful arms treaty negotiation with the Soviets, was about to depart for Japan, where he would attend a summit of the top seven industrial democracies. The prospects for this meeting were much dimmer. OPEC was expected to announce another substantial price increase, which was likely to worsen unemployment. "All the summits in the world aren't going to make Jimmy Carter popular," a domestic adviser told *Newsweek*. "People want gas and they want lower prices."[111] Another Carter aide said, "You can see a sort of malaise economy with no growth, inflation and no end in sight. It is an extraordinarily depressing prospect we face because of energy."[112]

Blaming Americans

On June 28, 1979, while Carter was in Japan, OPEC announced a massive price increase, the largest since the 1973 Arab embargo. The press redubbed the Japanese meeting the "Khomeini Summit." Since January 1, OPEC had raised prices by 50 percent. (And prices were up 1,000 percent since the start of the decade.) Saudi Arabia proved unable to moderate the more hawkish OPEC members, including Iran, who saw their chance to make a big play. Oil would now sell at up to $23.50 a barrel. The headlines in American newspapers were devastating. According to all reports, the increase guaranteed a recession and would result in the loss of at least 9 million jobs. The *CBS Evening News* calculated that the average family's bills would go up by $490.00. "It's a catastrophe," said Alfred Kahn.[113]

The political consequences for Carter seemed clear. In Boston, on the day of the OPEC announcement, Massachusetts labor leaders and progressive Democrats staged a dump-Carter protest, one of many draft-Kennedy campaigns springing up around the country.[114] Given the likely rise in unemployment, congressional Democrats demanded the White House increase spending and not delay. These groups found Kennedy more attractive than the incumbent. At its annual convention, the executive director of the NAACP, Benjamin Hooks, reported that the Massachusetts senator could garner more black support than Carter.[115] According to *The New York Times*, White House insiders saw the gas crisis as fatal to Carter's reelection prospects. "This one can finish him," one of the Georgia advisers said. "The American people are mad—hot-summer mad."[116]

"This would appear to be the worst of times," Eizenstat wrote to Carter in Japan. "Nothing else has so frustrated, confused, angered the American people—or so targeted their distress at you personally, as opposed to your advisors, or Congress, or outside interests." Eizenstat pointed out the latest polls had Reagan and Kennedy ahead of Carter by several points. The truckers' strike was not ending, gasoline lines were spreading in the Northeast and the Midwest, and violence continued. The riot at Levittown made headlines across the country. Gas retailers were threatening to shut down unless the DOE allowed them to increase their prices. As the July 4 congressional break approached, the Hill was tremulous. "Members are literally afraid to go home over the recess, for fear of having to deal with very angry constituents," Eizenstat reported. Governors, too, were feeling the pressure. The state of Maryland sued the DOE for misallocating gasoline, and more states were expected to "follow that politically popular route," said Eizenstat.[117]

Eizenstat gave the president clear marching orders. Carter should cancel his post-summit vacation in Hawaii, come back to the White House, and address the American public in a prime-time speech upon his return. "With that type of involvement," asserted Eizenstat, "we can regain the initiative and rise above much of the confusion and bureaucratic tangling now occurring." Carter had to take tough actions, though, and it would not be easy. He told the president, "You must address the enormous credibility and management problems of DOE which equal in public perception those which State or Defense had during Vietnam." Eizenstat warned Carter, "The similarities between problems of credibility and political opposition from the left are real."[118]

The DOE was coming under fire from all sides. Secretary Schlesinger himself joined the chorus. From Japan, he told the press, "There would be no lines if there were no price and allocation controls."[119] Secretary of the Treasury Michael Blumenthal concurred. He told a reporter, "The more I'm in the Government, the more market-oriented I become. No bureaucrats with pins at the Department of Energy, trying to figure out how much gasoline each gas station in the country should get, can set out a way to distribute gas in this country."[120] Walter Heller, former chairman of the Council of Economic Advisers for President Kennedy, said, "I've heard it said that if God wanted us to have gasoline, he would never have created the Department of Energy."[121]

What was Eizenstat's solution? Blame OPEC: "We have a better opportunity than ever before to assert leadership over an apparently insolvable problem, to shift the cause for inflation and energy problems to OPEC, to gain credibility with the American people, to offer hope of an eventual solution, to regain our political losses." According to Eizenstat, Carter should "use the OPEC price increase as the occasion to mark the beginning of our new approach to energy." Eizenstat sensed that the mood of the country was shifting. As much as Americans mistrusted Big Oil, they had also come to feel bullied by Middle East oil producers. Tapping into that, he advised that "a statement which goes light on OPEC or a commitment to synthetics and other domestic initiatives will not convince the public that anything is different, that we are embarking on a new effort, or that there is hope that the energy problem will be solved, or that we will ever stand up to OPEC (which Americans want even more than cheap gasoline)."[122]

Carter had to lead the nation. His push for a windfall profits tax was paying off, and the bill was gaining traction in Congress, especially as the major oil corporations announced another quarter of record profits. On June 28, the day Eizenstat sent his memo, the House passed a windfall tax bill, which was substantially bigger than what Carter had proposed. Two days earlier, the House had passed a $3 billion synthetic fuels bill. An even bigger commitment of resources was working its way through the Senate. According to Eizenstat, Carter had to claim these initiatives as his own. He also had to push for the creation of an energy mobilization board to speed up energy projects like pipelines and research facilities and to eliminate "all of the normal regulatory tangle that slows such projects down." The analogy, said Eizenstat, was the War Production Board during World War II. Such a board would demonstrate that Carter regarded the production issue "as one of highest national security." "With strong steps we can mobilize the nation around a real crisis and with a clear enemy—OPEC," he wrote.[123]

Blaming OPEC was gaining popular support, reflecting a sense of frustration and failure. "Here we are in the U.S., getting strangled," said one New Jersey driver. "The greatest country in the world is stifled by a few sheiks."[124] The New York state senator John Calandra had a solution: "Retaliate in kind." "The Arab nations destroy our standard of living . . . forcing the United States of America to a brink of a recession," Calandra told Carter. American foreign policy should insist on a "quid pro quo," a food-for-crude campaign to punish oil-producing countries by raising the price of American wheat exports and cutting off supply to OPEC.[125] From the gas lines, citizens expressed the same sentiment. "Why don't we balance food policy against oil policy? Whatever it is that we sell to OPEC nations, why don't we raise our prices when they raise oil prices? . . . It beats going in there and taking the oil," explained a Southern California motorist.[126] In the Midwest, in grain-growing country, bumper stickers read, "A Bushel of Grain for a Barrel of Oil."[127]

The Food for Crude campaign spoke to the desire to defeat an enemy. In Trenton, New Jersey, a local disc jockey locked himself inside the broadcasting booth and played the Top 40 Bobby Butler song, "Cheaper Crude or No More Food," for almost twelve continuous hours. When the owner threatened to fire him, listeners flooded the station's phones with calls of support.[128] The New Jersey state senator S. Thomas Gagliano wrote to Carter, "This Food for Crude concept is meeting with overwhelming applause by the people at the grass roots level." He saw it as the only just and effective solution to the "strangulation of our people by OPEC."[129]

Senator Patrick Moynihan jumped on the bandwagon and advocated "a sustained effort to break the OPEC cartel." Specifically, he called for the creation of a wheat-exporting authority, essentially a wheat cartel consisting of the United States, Canada, and Australia that would threaten the oil-producing nations.[130] The New York City councilman Nicholas LaPorte wrote to Carter, agreeing with "Senator Moynihan's contention that OPEC is waging economic warfare against the United States . . . These sheiks and other OPEC leaders are using their illegal cartel to retaliate against American foreign policy. Such blatant blackmail against a country and a people with whom they are ostensibly at peace is not acceptable."[131]

To the American public, Carter looked weak. At the Tokyo summit, he joined the leaders of the other six industrial democracies in issuing its first collective denunciation of OPEC for its price hike. But that reproof was little more than a paper tiger. The same evening, news reports carried the story that Libya would be cutting its oil exports for several years to punish the West.[132] Within the administration, at the NSC Persian Gulf meetings, Zbigniew Brzezinski was pushing for a "perceptible military preponderance," especially in light of the summer shortages and their impact on the president's capacity to govern. As the NSC military adviser William Odom later commented, "Iran and the growing Soviet influence in the Gulf region became inextricably linked to U.S. domestic politics."[133] The impression was of a president who could not stand up to OPEC.

The latest ABC-Harris poll showed Carter's positive job performance rating at 27 percent, lower than Richard Nixon's just before he left office. His negative rating was the lowest on record since polling had begun. Nearly three-quarters of the public lacked confidence in him as a leader. More than 80 percent of the public disapproved of how Carter was handling inflation and the energy situation. "The mood here is like the last days of the Nixon presidency," said one White House staffer.[134]

The gas lines made a mockery of the upcoming July 4 holiday weekend.

As Americans prepared to celebrate Independence Day, they seemed beholden to a few Arab sheikhs and Big Oil manipulations. Shortages of gas besieged thirty-five states, with urban areas in the East suffering the most. Headlines told of disaster. "Like some biblical plague, the nation's energy problems just keep multiplying," said *Newsweek* in its lead story. "The Great Energy Mess" ran as *Time*'s cover story.[135] Rumors continued to circulate about tankers waiting offshore. The latest twist was an alleged report of oil companies dumping oil and gas in the desert. On *CBS Evening News*, the correspondent Terry Drinkwater tried to find the source of the rumor. Though he could not, he concluded, "The less we know, the more we suspect."[136]

Carter's team went into action. By July 3, Eizenstat, Rafshoon, and Hertzberg had a draft of a speech ready, which Carter, who was back in the White House, was to deliver two days later. His advisers told the president he should summon the nation to a war against energy dependence. "The tone of this speech is stark," they explained. "We have purposely used the war analogy repeatedly. We feel that the crisis with OPEC is an effective hook for this." The president needed to rally the public. "We are now in a decisive fight for the independence and security of our nation. The battlefield is energy," the draft read. Carter had to provide a succinct review of the rapid increase in imports and cost, the Iranian Revolution and the cutoff of oil production, and the decline in American production. He should tell the public, "The shortage is global. It is real. And because there is a shortage, there are gasoline lines." Carter should acknowledge the inconvenience of the lines but then make the larger stakes clear, saying, "Our very independence is in danger. The threat is not military but economic— but it is no less real, no less serious, no less grave." Carter also had to demonstrate resolve. It was time for the nation "to break its bondage to the whims of OPEC ... It is now our solemn duty to mobilize ... for ultimate victory in the energy war." Mobilization meant conservation, a federal investment in alternative fuels, and a windfall profits tax to fund those initiatives.[137]

On July 4, Carter canceled the speech. The networks had granted a time slot for it and announced all week that Carter would be giving a speech on July 5. But Carter did not like what his team had come up with. The draft included some passages, explained the advisers, that "speak to the crisis of spirit that we have discussed with Caddell et al."[138] So, for example, the draft explained, "Our most serious problem is not a material one but a spiritual and psychological one. An atmosphere of fear, futility and foreboding has clouded our response to the energy crisis at hand."[139] But Carter wanted more. Having received counsel from Caddell for months on the "malaise" that made the nation nearly ungovernable, Carter, the born-again Christian, wanted to address this spiritual crisis head-on.

Carter convened what correspondents began calling a "crisis summit" at Camp David. The plan was to give a major address on Sunday, July 15, after ten days of consultation, or "mountaintop musings," as the press dubbed them, with the nation's political, academic, religious, and other top public leaders. Carter was seeking a deeper exploration of his problems of leadership and, as he and Caddell saw it, the problems with the nation.

The Camp David summit was a crucial moment in the 1970s debate over liberalism. For over a week, different political factions gathered to give Carter advice. From the president's own ranks, the energy secretary, Schlesinger, and the Treasury secretary, Blumenthal, represented the moderate, market-oriented approach. They counseled Carter to scrap petroleum allocations and decontrol prices. Schlesinger argued the crisis situation demanded something radical; he titled his memo to the president "A Bold Stroke to Deal with Gasoline Lines and Controls." "I urge you to consider a dramatic proposal," he wrote to Carter on July 5. "Your economic and energy advisers generally agree that decontrol of gasoline prices would end gasoline lines," wrote Schlesinger. "In short, controls do little to assist consumers, while saddling many of them with massive inconvenience from lines." Echoing his January predictions, he told the president, "American citizens generally are frustrated by the inability of the Government to deal with gasoline lines."

Schlesinger was alert to the political problem that ending controls posed for the Democrats. "Decontrol of prices, with direct regressive impacts on the poor, would alienate traditional Democratic constituencies—labor, consumer interests, blacks, and liberal representatives," he acknowledged. But Schlesinger thought there was a "way of pre-empting criticism from liberals." He told Carter that after decontrolling gasoline prices, he should tax oil companies and institute a gasoline tax, using the money "to cushion the blow of higher energy prices on the workingman and lower income citizens." The government could use the tax revenue for direct aid to the poor for energy costs and to reduce payroll taxes. Schlesinger made his case: "A combined program of decontrol, a tax on oil companies, and a progressive program of assistance to workers and lower income citizens is bold, imaginative, and capable of broad-scale political support. It would demonstrate willingness to take decisive action in the face of crisis."[140]

This was historic: the administrator of a massive program calling for its immediate dismantlement. Schlesinger believed controls were inefficient and thought the nuclear development program within DOE was much more important for long-term security. As a politician, he knew controls were losing their credibility as an effective policy tool. He knew, too, that his usefulness to the administration had run its course. Carter should accept his resignation, and he should get rid of controls as a way to contain damage to the department, if that was possible. As Frank Moore confirmed for Carter, "Neither Secretary Schlesinger nor his Department enjoys any support in Congress." Instead, the Hill regarded both with a total "lack of confidence."[141] "I'm afraid I'm not willing to trust the Department of Energy," Leon Panetta, the Democratic California congressman, had said when the gas lines first appeared.[142]

The summer lines were undermining faith in government. Moore explained to Carter, "The forces opposing deregulation are losing rather than gaining ground. They expected to gain public support as gas prices rose. Instead, the public has largely ignored the high prices and focused on the misallocations that cause spot shortages. They blame the latter problem on poor government regulation."[143] According to the *Washington Post* editors, that meant Washington should get rid of them: "The solutions do not lie in more tinkering with the allocations or in an elaborate system of rationing . . . The uneasiness and uncertainty is caused by the government's attempts to do the distributing instead of letting the market operate."[144]

The liberals at Camp David disagreed. Getting rid of controls would be political suicide for Carter. The gas lines might have damaged the DOE's credibility, but if Carter ended controls and prices shot up, that would be politically disastrous. Vice President Mondale articulated that point of view most strongly and won support from Hamilton Jordan, Charles Schultze, and Stuart Eizenstat.[145] The economist John Kenneth Galbraith, who was the grandfather of price controls, spoke strongly in favor of retaining them. More than thirty years after Galbraith had designed the World War II price controls, he still believed this policy tool was essential to restrain corporations and distribute income and scarce commodities equitably. Organized labor, also represented at Camp David, shared that view as well.[146]

Many liberals refused to abandon nearly half a century of experimentation with price controls, especially during a time of sky-high inflation. As Carter was meeting at Camp David, the prominent public intellectual and New Deal champion Arthur Schlesinger Jr. laid out why the Democrats had to retain controls in order to hold together their New Deal coalition. At the Americans for Democratic Action convention, a bastion of liberal politics, Schlesinger said, "The Carter administration's remedies are based on the theory that we can best cope with our problems by turning them over to the private market and keeping the government out of it. This is the conservative theory. This is the establishment theory. This is the Republican theory." Schlesinger, the liberal historian, argued that this was a losing political strategy: "The Democratic party will never succeed as a timorous, respectable, standpat, conservative, private-market, pro–oil company, anti-government party, luxuriating in alibis of public impotence." Instead, the party had to renew its "commitment to the poor and the powerless."[147] Mark Green, a leading public interest advocate, echoed Schlesinger. According to Green, the poorest 10 percent of Americans paid out almost 30 percent of their spending on energy.[148] While Carter deliberated at Camp David, Kennedy supporters were launching a nationwide direct-mail fund-raising campaign to draft their liberal champion.[149]

As a New South Democrat, a small entrepreneur, and an advocate of self-reliance and restraint, Carter was wrestling with the future of his party. At Camp David, he heard from other young New South Democrats like Arkansas's governor, Bill Clinton, who was also trying to carve out a post–New Deal agenda for the Democratic Party. Carter had won the support of professional suburbanites and rural Protestants. Yet he recognized that the party had not yet sufficiently reconstituted itself. He could not have won in 1976 without the support of unions and blacks, and he would still need their votes in 1980. Carter represented a party in transition but one not yet fully formed.

So what would Carter do? In addition to the advice of Eizenstat to blame OPEC and Schlesinger to decontrol, Carter heard from Pat Caddell.

To his mountaintop retreat, the president brought Caddell's thoughts on the crisis of confidence, which the pollster had worked up into a memo. Caddell, a twenty-nine-year-old Roman Catholic who had attended a parochial high school in Florida before heading off to Harvard, believed deeply in the profound alienation and psychic distress of the American public. At the summit, he handed out James MacGregor Burns's book on leadership. Burns, a leading presidential scholar, asserted that successful presidents mobilized citizens for greater moral purpose. Carter also consulted with the sociologist Robert Bellah and pondered the work of Christopher Lasch and Daniel Bell, all of whom affirmed Carter and Caddell's desire to address the country's current cultural climate.

This spiritual approach was risky. In a Gallup poll, as Carter was considering his options, Americans reported on what they saw as the most important problem. Slightly more than half said it was inflation, one-third said energy, and only 4 percent listed moral decline.[150] Many in Carter's inner circle rejected this psychological tack. Vice President Mondale believed Carter had to tackle the mounting economic crisis, of which the gas lines were only the most visible manifestation. Don't be "an old scold or a grouch," Mondale told Carter, but instead take on the pressing economic concerns of many Democratic constituents.[151] "Dealing with the recession without refueling inflation is likely to be the topic most on Congressional minds," Alfred Kahn told Carter.[152]

Jerry Rafshoon, Carter's chief image maker, was even more direct. He wrote to Carter, "If we give the speech that Caddell has proposed, it will be counterproductive to what we are trying to do. It could even be a disaster." Rafshoon's deputy and director of the speech-writing office, Greg Schneiders, laid out the argument that Rafshoon would make, almost verbatim, to the president. "It's an interesting academic treatise. But people want Jimmy Carter to do something, to be a President, to be a leader—not to philosophize about it," Schneiders told Rafshoon. "It would be nice if everyone thought the President talked about some interesting and unconventional concepts. More likely, the reaction would be 'bullshit.' He kept us waiting and watching for ten days to produce this? What's he going to *do* about the problems?" In words that Rafshoon repeated to Carter, Schneiders wrote, "People don't want to hear Jimmy Carter *talk* about our problems and they certainly don't want to hear him whine about them."[153]

Carter's staff recognized that this speech would be a major moment in the run-up to the 1980 election. They feared the challenge from the president's likely rivals. "People are not turning to Kennedy or Connally because they seem attuned to the crisis of confidence in the country—they're turning to them because they look like the solution to the crisis," insisted Schneiders. As Rafshoon told Carter, "You inspire confidence by being confident. Leadership begins with a sense of knowing where you're going. The Caddell speech sends all the opposite signals." "Each self-deprecating remark and each negative comment about America" would cause problems for Carter, predicted Schneiders. Rafshoon warned the president, "We'd hear them thrown back ad nauseam during a campaign."[154]

At last, Carter was ready to speak to the nation. Sixty-five million Americans tuned in to see what the president had to say. Appearing in a dark suit and talking in somber tones, Carter told Americans that there was little he, or the government, could do. "All the legislation in the world can't fix what is wrong with America," he said. The problem was fundamental. "It is a crisis of confidence," Carter explained. The consequences were serious: "The erosion of our confidence in the future is threatening to destroy the social and the political fabric of America." Unable to make the gas lines go away, the president was changing the conversation. He believed that to be an effective leader, to lift the country upward, he had to lead listeners on a collective journey of soul-searching. Carter, the Sunday school teacher, was delivering a sermon.

As tempers flared over the fuel shortage, the president blamed American consumers. Carter responded to the gas lines by criticizing the country for self-indulgence and overconsumption. Because Americans had little optimism about the future, said Carter, they turned instead to mindless consumerism. "Too many of us now tend to worship self-indulgence and consumption. Human identity is no longer defined by what one does, but by what one owns," lamented Carter. The president sounded like a preacher urging his congregants to lead more purposeful lives. "We've discovered that owning things and consuming things does not satisfy our longing for meaning," he said. "We've learned that piling up material goods cannot fill the emptiness of lives which have no confidence or purpose."

The nation could regain its faith by fighting for energy independence in what Carter defined as a moral, cleansing crusade. "On the battlefield of energy we can win for our nation a new confidence and we can seize control again of our common destiny," he asserted. Carter implored Americans to exchange their profligate ways for patriotic self-sacrifice: "I'm asking you for your good and for your nation's security to take no unnecessary trips, to use carpools or public transportation whenever you can, to park your car one extra day per week, to obey the speed limit, and to set your thermostats to save fuel." To cut dependence on foreign oil, he set import quotas for 1979 and 1980. "Beginning this moment," he declared, "this Nation will never use more foreign oil than we did in 1977." Conservation would redeem American souls while also freeing them from energy dependence.

Carter also said the government would undertake a massive initiative to develop alternative fuels. He called for the creation of an energy security corporation to stimulate the production of synthetic fuels. This investment would yield 2.5 million barrels of synthetic fuels a day by 1990 to replace roughly 30 percent of oil imports. Carter reiterated his commitment to solar energy. He also called on utilities to switch back to coal and away from oil. An energy mobilization board would facilitate completion of essential energy projects.

On the issue of the gas lines, Carter did nothing. Carter chose to continue with the gradual decontrol of oil prices and retain allocations. He feared the liberal wing of his party. Plus he worried about the impact of a price hike, which would unsettle markets. Alfred Kahn confirmed for Carter that removing price controls would end the lines but at too high a cost: "I cannot quarrel with your rejection of immediate decontrol."[155] Every additional penny at the gas pump would extract $1 billion from consumers, a substantial drag given the recessionary conditions.[156] The clearest indication that Carter ruled out total immediate decontrol came with the rumors that James Schlesinger was going to lose his job. Already John O'Leary, his deputy, had resigned.[157]

Carter and his young advisers like Caddell were hoping they could refashion the Democratic Party around a new kind of centrism. They sought to move past a Johnson-era Great Society liberalism that made Democrats vulnerable to defection from white middle-class constituents in the suburbs and in the South. Carter wanted to create support behind a modified form of government involvement in the economy, one where federal funds stimulated technological development. At the same time, he wanted to scale back the regulation of prices. This approach resulted, however, in a middle course that offended liberals yet did not please conservatives. As Christopher Matthews explained, "He is not a traditional liberal. He is not a traditional conservative. The result: the President finds himself with clear-cut opposition but only fuzzy support. He finds himself with substantial philosophical opposition, and with no philosophical constituency of his own." Two and a half years into his presidency, with his popularity at a low, Carter was still in search of a following behind a "positive, pragmatic centrism."[158]

After the speech, Carter did take one immediate action, and that was to get rid of James Schlesinger. All spring, Rafshoon had been telling Carter to fire someone to demonstrate leadership: "As far as I can tell there is only one issue on which this country is totally united: the need for you to fire some people." "Nothing would do more political good for you right now," counseled Rafshoon, "than to shake up your Cabinet and your staff . . . People want you to act like a leader and leaders make tough decisions and stick with them even when it hurts. Leaders occasionally fire people."[159] Congressional liberals were calling for Schlesinger's resignation, while conservatives wanted to get rid of the entire Department of Energy. As the Republican national chairman, Bill Brock, said, the DOE was "a major contributor to our current crisis and should be abolished."[160]

Shortly after his speech, Carter let go five cabinet secretaries, including Schlesinger. Carter also formally gave Hamilton Jordan, his young Georgian adviser, the title of chief of staff. This "born again cabinet," as the press dubbed it, appeared to some as an effective political strategy, enabling Carter to run his reelection campaign as an outsider, even as he occupied the Oval Office. By purging his administration, the political scientist Nelson Polsby noted, Carter could campaign against his administration and, by extension, against Washington.[161]

But the president was still accountable for the long lines. And firing Schlesinger did nothing to make them disappear, nor did appeals to conservation and promises of alternative energies in the future. The shake-up came across as an act of scapegoating rather than an assertion of leadership. The *Philadelphia Inquirer* editors faulted Carter: "The appearance today is of a petulant President, blaming his staff and his Cabinet officers for what's gone wrong."[162] "This seems to have been the result of someone's telling the President it would make him look bold, but he has come off not looking very stout. I'm afraid many people see it as instability," said Majority Leader Jim Wright. Senator Ted Stevens, the Republican whip, questioned Carter's mental health.[163]

The speech did little to give Carter a sustained boost in the polls. A *Newsday* poll found that 82 percent of Long Island residents gave Carter negative job approval ratings. Of the 69 percent who watched the speech, almost two-thirds said the speech did not make them any more confident in Carter as a leader, believing that the speech was "aimed at increasing the President's popularity but didn't offer any new ideas of dealing with the energy crisis." As the *Los Angeles Times* editorial page put it, "Carter is right. There is a crisis of confidence in his administration. What has been happening this week intensified it." According to the *Denver Post* reporter Kenneth Walsh, "People . . . are just too skeptical of Carter and the federal government in general to be turned around by one much ballyhooed speech, a couple of follow-up addresses on energy and moving new names into top executive organization charts."[164] According to an ABC News–Harris survey, Carter's job approval rating went up after the speech, to 33 percent from a low in June of 25 percent, and then slid back down. The reporter Adam Clymer was not surprised. As he explained, "One lingering problem is that previous Carter gains have not lasted." On personal confidence, even fewer regarded Carter favorably.[165]

Carter's problems ran too deep. No single speech, courageous and bold as it might have been, could have reversed the judgment that Americans had reached.[166] In their minds, Carter was failing to lead the country, or at least failing to address their immediate concerns. Some may have appreciated the president sermonizing, speaking to them in an elevated fashion and providing a public moral cleansing. After the speech, the White House received an outpouring of appreciation in favorable letters and phone calls, along with the brief uptick in the president's polling numbers. But the speech could not erase the double-digit inflation that was gripping the nation. Nor could it convince the public that the president had handled the gas situation well. Indeed, a majority still thought the energy shortage was artificial, and by the summer of 1979, many believed that Carter's administration was to blame.[167]

The gas crisis of the summer shone a harsh light on the administration's perceived competence. The General Accounting Office conducted a study of the Energy Department and concluded that the "DOE has not been able to provide the Congress and the public a credible and convincing explanation for the reduced supplies of gasoline. In the absence of such an explanation, cynicism and suspicion have become widespread, and public confidence in the Government's ability to deal with the situation has been severely eroded." The GAO found the public's lack of trust well-founded. "Notwithstanding the Nation's experience during the 1973–74 Arab oil embargo," the report concluded, "the Department accomplished little in planning for and dealing with subsequent energy shortages, especially the current one." In particular, the GAO faulted the DOE for its failure to collect reliable information on supplies and instead using weekly statistics published by the oil industry itself, which contributed to doubts that the DOE served the public's interests.[168]

At the height of the 1970s energy crisis, with gas lines snaking for miles and riots erupting at service stations, the government was stalled in its efforts to design an energy policy that would free the country from its energy dependence. The tensions between Carter and liberals, the emergence of a vocal Right, and the presence of intractable inflation stymied progress. Under political heat from his left, especially as the 1980 primary season approached, and concerned about galloping inflation, which ran as high as 11 percent, Carter retained the price and allocation system, even as all commentators and the president himself agreed it was broken. Firing Schlesinger, therefore, did little to restore public confidence. The failure to prevent or end the gas lines seemed to confirm the conservatives' arguments that government was inefficient and Washington was unable to handle the energy situation. In response to the president's speech, Ronald Reagan told the press, Carter "cannot divorce himself from the problem by shifting the blame to the people."[169]

Part IV

Blaming Government

7

Running on Empty

THE DAY after his prime-time sermon, Carter took to the stump. In the face of deep public skepticism, the president seemed undeterred. Before a crowd in Kansas City, with his shirtsleeves rolled up and his voice raised, he said he was proposing an "unparalleled peacetime commitment, an investment of $140 billion, for American energy security, so that never again will our nation's independence be hostage to foreign oil." This was Carter's biggest initiative, promising a solution to future shortages with a massive government program for alternative energies funded by a windfall profits tax on oil companies. Notwithstanding the president's enthusiasm, the political adviser Les Francis warned Hamilton Jordan, "Our biggest political risk in the energy area is that we will continue to look like we don't know what we're doing."[1]

Putting on the Brakes

Just as the chief executive was calling Americans to battle, oil began to flow more rapidly from the Middle East. Saudi Arabia announced an increase in oil production, and within a couple of weeks the panic stopped. As quickly as they had appeared, the lines evaporated. At the end of July,

Carter's legislative liaison, Frank Moore, explained, "Now that gas lines have disappeared, the 'heat' seems to be off. Instead of the willingness to act we saw two weeks ago Members and Senators seem more inclined to discuss and debate."[2]

Moreover, few trusted the government to run this kind of development program successfully. Even if Americans liked the idea of synthetic fuels, of American technology and ingenuity saving the country, the gas lines had subjected the administration to widespread criticism. The president's track record was not very good. Carter was calling for a twelve-year public charter for the Energy Security Corporation (ESC), which could lend billions of dollars to private industry to develop coal liquids, coal gases, biomass, shale oil, and unconventional natural gas. The White House boasted of an endeavor as spectacular as putting a man on the moon; indeed, the amount of money Carter was asking for was more than double the Apollo project. But after the long lines of the summer, the public had little confidence that government could do it, or do it better than private enterprise, a perspective shared on both the left and the right and in the middle.

Even more problematic, Carter alienated his potential congressional supporters, especially environmentalists who opposed his emphasis on synthetic fuel production instead of solar energy and conservation. Carter looked kindly on solar initiatives. But solar power alone would not cut imports substantially, and certainly not anytime soon. Even in its most expansive provision, Carter's proposal would subsidize the annual installation of solar heating in 150,000 homes.[3] Conservation also lacked the capacity for the president to demonstrate leadership. And talk of sacrifice, even as it resonated with Carter's moral sensibility, made him politically vulnerable. "I think we ought to express our faith in America by making the energy pie bigger and bigger," challenged Representative Charles Grassley, a Republican from Iowa.[4]

The White House turn to synthetic fuels and coal infuriated the environmentalists. They feared that synthetic fuel production, while boosting the power supply of the United States, would roll back much of the progress in environmental regulation and lead to an increase in carbon dioxide pollution. Carter also pushed for utility companies to convert from oil to coal, which would also cause harm to the environment. In Kentucky, as he continued his post-speech stumping, Carter boasted, "The United States is the Saudi Arabia of coal." The amount of coal in the United States was enough to guarantee electrical generation for over a century. And American shale contained more oil than all of Middle Eastern reserves. Senators Mark Hatfield, an Oregon Republican, and Wendell Ford, a Kentucky Democrat, proposed amendments to substantially weaken the anti-strip-mining legislation that Carter had signed in August 1977 and allow states greater flexibility in ignoring regulations.[5] "This is Armageddon for the environmental movement," said the Sierra Club.[6]

Instead of building a broad coalition of the different factions within his party, Carter seemed to be angering each one of them, pushing them farther apart. As Carter was turning his back on environmentalists, he remained on shaky ground with traditional elements of the Democratic Party. Labor continued to rally behind Senator Edward Kennedy, the Massachusetts liberal, especially as inflation climbed higher and the economy slipped deeper into recession. More than a year before the 1980 election, Democrats were abandoning the president. The Detroit representative John Conyers of the Congressional Black Caucus withdrew his support from Carter, accusing the president of breaking all his promises to blacks and cutting every domestic program.[7]

Carter did not help himself when he appointed Paul Volcker the new head of the Federal Reserve. Many on the left feared that the appointment of Volcker, who had made his anti-inflationary views clear as president of the New York Federal Reserve Bank, reflected a White House choice to battle inflation over unemployment. Instead of a major spending initiative or jobs program to stimulate the economy, which liberals sought, Volcker preferred the tightening of the money supply to halt the upward inflationary trend, which was now running at an annual rate of over 11 percent. Thus far, Carter's approach to inflation relied on a tepid combination of jawboning and budget belt-tightening while the Fed raised interest rates, none of which had yielded the administration much success. The Volcker appointment suggested a new focus on serious monetary restraint. With millions of Americans struggling through stagflation, this choice did not sit well. Vice President Mondale opposed Volcker, as did the AFL-CIO and the Keynesian economist Walter Heller.[8] On his handling of the economy, Carter's approval rating slipped lower, with 83 percent of those surveyed giving him a negative score.[9]

Carter's energy policies further compounded the fallout with the Left. In August, the United Automobile Workers launched its Campaign for Lower Energy Prices, demanding that the president reimpose price controls. To these Americans, bringing the oil companies to heel mattered more than the promise for future production of alternative fuel.[10] Carter's program of oil decontrol was pushing prices up, and the synthetic fuels programs threatened to increase the deficit while serving as a subsidy to the energy industry. With the exception of his support of the coal industry, Carter did not link his synthetic fuels program to jobs creation. Nothing in Carter's energy agenda responded to pressing pocketbook issues.

Even stalwart proponents of government research and development, including Senator Henry Jackson, were putting on the brakes. Before the August recess, Jackson told the president that he could not support a massive undertaking. "We have to make a beginning," said Jackson, "but we don't have to . . . go off the deep end." Jackson was prepared to request $3 billion in the 1980 budget, still a large amount, but small compared with the president's request for $22 billion as an initial, first-year installment. Jackson worried about where the funding would come from for the program, especially as the fate of the windfall profits tax remained uncertain. The House had passed a huge tax in late June, at the peak of the gas lines, but it looked as if the Senate would pass something half the size, if it passed anything at all. Other committee members shared in the reluctance to commit future funds without any evidence that such spending would actually yield results and lower American dependence on imported oil. "A wish and a hope and a prayer—that's all it amounts to," said Senator Howard Metzenbaum.[11]

Senator Gary Hart, a younger member of Congress from Colorado whose support Carter might have hoped to count on, typified the resistance to a program costing billions of dollars for technologies that were not proven and could harm the environment. Hart, who had run George McGovern's campaign in 1972, had won election to the Senate in 1974. A rising star who served on the Budget, the Environment and Public Works, and the Armed Services Committees, Hart fused fiscal conservatism and strong defense with environmentalism. He voiced one of the earliest warnings about acid rain, which scientists were identifying as a pollution threat from emissions. As much as he wanted to reduce the reliance on imported oil, Hart doubted that the ESC was the way forward. "It's too much, too soon," said Hart. "It is a good program for the 1990s, not something you have to pass in the summer of 1979. We might create a monster we can't get rid of."[12]

The synthetic fuels debate fanned the flames of the so-called sagebrush rebellion, an antigovernment conservative movement growing in the West. Wyoming, Montana, Colorado, and other resource-rich western states worried that the ESC would construct plants in the West, where federal lands made up a significant portion of the territory, and would use a substantial amount of scarce water. Some like Hart feared the damage to the environment, while others were concerned about limits on regional development. Environmental legislation of the 1970s had designated much of this area as wilderness regions to slow development by ranching, grazing, and mining interests. And the ESC threatened greater reduction of state control over these lands. Frank Moore explained that Senators Alan Simpson and Malcolm Wallop, Wyoming Republicans, had "the fairly typical 'rape of the West' concern." Richard Cheney, the state's sole representative, shared their views.[13]

Other conservatives were quick to condemn Carter's proposal for a new government corporation. Representative David Stockman, the young conservative Republican from Michigan, explained, "Congress lacks the time, knowledge, and technical expertise . . . and thus is inherently incapable of making detailed choices of particular technologies . . . We should look once again at the potential for supporting the marketplace as the means for making these critical decisions."[14] No government intervention was necessary, according to Senator Mike Gravel, who represented the Alaskan oil interests. "Greed motivates the world," he said. "If we will just unleash the greed, then we will solve our energy problems."[15]

The Right lashed out at Carter's initiatives as an "energy boondoggle," as Milton Friedman put it. "President Carter, if we cut through all the rhetoric, has proposed solving the energy problem by turning control of the production and distribution of energy over to the people who run the post office, administer Amtrak, [and] produce long gas lines," chastised Friedman.[16] The Wall Street Journal concurred. "The President has weighed the merits of either getting the government out of the energy business or getting it more deeply in. He has chosen to get it further in, on a massive, almost unbelievable scale," wrote the editors. "The real Jimmy Carter has finally stood up, on the far left of the Democratic Party."[17]

Carter responded by qualifying the public nature of the ESC, adding his own coda to the growing chorus about government's incompetence. Carter insisted that the Energy Security Corporation would not reside within the Department of Energy: "It will be outside the Federal Government, outside the Federal bureaucracy, free to use its independent business judgment." The idea was to assume the financial risk at the start of these ventures while relying on the best talent from private industry to develop new technology, resources, and plant capacity. "This assistance has been designed to *stimulate the private sector, not to supplant it, and to assist the marketplace, not overwhelm it*," explained Carter's staff.[18] Jerry Rafshoon told Carter to further stress the role of private industry. "We are *not* proposing another government bureaucracy," Rafshoon reiterated, "but rather a publicly chartered private corporation. People still don't seem to understand this."[19]

Carter's synfuels proposal not only spawned more enemies than friends but also reignited the alliance of Left and Right, which had united against the president's earlier energy initiatives. "There's a liberal-conservative coalition building here against a giant program," explained Representative Stockman.[20] The U.S. Chamber of Commerce and Common Cause, for example, were working together against a synthetic fuel corporation. The White House faced opposition from "the very liberal and very conservative wing of both parties," explained Frank Moore.[21] Senator Hart compared the ESC to setting a prairie fire to cook a sage hen, while Stockman denounced the spending as nothing more than handing out money to special interests. "Instead of a great synfuels crusade, you will have a middle-sized pork barrel," predicted Stockman.[22]

The president's grand vision of synthetic fuels as the solution to foreign oil dependence was falling flat. "Have you taken into account the OPEC gun at our head?" Senator Lawton Chiles, a Democrat of Florida and a proponent of an all-out investment, asked his colleagues.[23] But the go-slow approach had greater support. Instead of $88 billion over ten years, the Budget Committee supported a total commitment of $20 billion.[24]

Hart had indeed considered the so-called OPEC gun aimed at Americans, and he wanted to confront the threat directly. Hart was committed to nuclear nonproliferation, and he supported the SALT II treaty with the Soviet Union that Carter, with the help of Secretary of State Cyrus Vance, put before the Senate in the summer of 1979. But Hart also believed the United States had to devise a new defense policy, including a new kind of military and weaponry, for the Middle East. Specifically, he pushed for building up sea-based strength. On NBC's *Today* show, during the height of the summer gas lines, while Carter was convening his Camp David summit, Hart said that the United States might have to intervene militarily to secure the flow of oil from the Middle East. In an address to the Air Force Academy, he cautioned, "We may be forced to use military force to preserve the oil flow."[25]

Senator Henry Jackson and other neoconservatives agreed. The production of synthetic fuels was nothing compared with the potential strength of the American military in securing America's future. The stakes were simply too high to be left to this kind of hopeful technological fix, especially as they believed the Soviets were flexing their muscles in the Middle East. Right after Carter's speech, Ben Wattenberg, a close ally of Jackson's and a leader in the neoconservative Coalition for a Democratic Majority, put pressure on Carter to counter the Soviets' perceived regional strength. "It's time to stop America's retreat," announced Wattenberg in the pages of *The New York Times*. The United States had to "unlearn some of the 'lessons of Vietnam,'" counseled Wattenberg. America should no longer stand as a "helpless giant," unable to defend its interests.[26]

In his farewell address, before departing from public office, James Schlesinger sounded the alarm, warning that the fate of "all free nations, indeed freedom itself remains dependent for the immediate future on access to the oil resources of this volatile region." Combined with the instability, most visibly in Iran, the "regional preponderance of Soviet military power" posed a grave danger to the United States. For someone like Schlesinger, who had devoted his career to assessing the Soviet threat, the Middle East was the most recent chapter in the Cold War, where the Communist superpower could bring the United States and its oil-dependent allies to their knees. "Soviet control of the oil tap in the Middle East would mean the end of the world as we have known it since 1945 and of the association of free nations," Schlesinger feared.[27]

Carter shared the belief that energy dependence was first and foremost a national security threat. The appointment of Charles Duncan as the new energy secretary reflected that thinking. Duncan, who had worked briefly as a roustabout in the Texas oil fields before joining the Coca-Cola Company and rising through the ranks to become its president, had most recently served as deputy defense secretary. Duncan was a prudent choice, someone who commanded respect in the business community and within Washington. And he shared Schlesinger's sensibility about the national security threat of energy dependence on the Middle East. But without sufficient support from his party, Carter could not increase military spending for the region.

By the fall of 1979, it looked as if Carter's energy agenda were in shambles. As the economic news worsened, the leading energy issue, especially for liberal Democrats, continued to be the high cost of fuel. Labor representatives joined with Ralph Nader and senior citizen groups to form the Citizen Labor Energy Coalition, and on October 17 they organized "Big Oil Day" protests in cities across the country to draw attention to the hardship caused by gasoline and home heating bills. This protest came on the six-year anniversary of the start of the Arab embargo. These groups continued to point to what they believed to be the extortionist profits Big Oil squeezed from consumers' wallets. No matter that these corporations now exerted less power in setting market prices; their profits, bigger than ever, condemned them in the eyes of liberals who were seeking greater protection for their constituents as prices rose and paychecks shrank.[28]

In the House, Representative Toby Moffett, who kept constant pressure on the White House about energy prices, introduced a measure to extend the life of price controls. The proposal went down to defeat, 257–135, with Democrats divided on the issue. The next day, the House voted to end the price controls on gasoline by a close vote of 191–188, with 130 Republicans joined by 61 Democrats, mostly from oil-producing states. However, in an instant, Washington could line up behind liberal policies if lawmakers saw it in their interest to do so, especially on an issue as visceral and visible as gas prices. After the oil companies announced record-high quarterly earnings, Speaker O'Neill called the profits reports "absolutely a disgrace to the nation—it's sinful—an absolute and utter disgrace."[29] Immediately, the House reversed its decision, 225–189, to decontrol gasoline prices at the pump. In the face of rising profits, price controls still had appeal.[30]

One week later, foreign affairs intervened to save Carter's synthetic fuels program. On November 4, Islamic radicals took sixty-six Americans hostage in Tehran. The shah had arrived in New York for cancer treatment after Henry Kissinger persuaded the Carter administration to grant entry to this long-standing American ally. In response, and fearful that this was the beginning of American intervention into their internal politics, student radicals seized the American embassy, setting in motion what would become a 444-day diplomatic crisis.

The Iranian situation instantly transformed the debate over Carter's energy program. The Energy Security Corporation had made more enemies than friends. But Frank Moore recommended that Carter use the hostage crisis as a way of garnering support, telling reluctant environmentalists, like Senator Edmund Muskie, "Our dependence on foreign oil poses an extreme threat to our national security. A defeat of this bill at the very time I am negotiating for the release of U.S. citizens in Iran would provide an important psychological edge to the Iranians who provide a substantial portion of our imported oil."[31] Scoop Jackson reversed course, insisting that only by passing the synfuels bill could the United States "rid itself of the bondage imposed by OPEC, the economic bondage, the increasing threat to our national security."[32]

Days later, the Senate voted in favor of a bill committing $20 billion to synthetic fuels, with a promise of $68 billion more over five years. That budget was twice as large as the total worth of Exxon. "Voters want action on energy; they don't really care how much it costs," said Representative Millicent Fenwick, a Republican from New Jersey. With Americans in captivity, politicians jumped at the chance to demonstrate their resolve, claiming the program would replace roughly 20 percent of oil imports within fifteen years.[33]

Alfred Kahn saw the hostage situation as an occasion to push for a major gasoline tax. Kahn, as well as many other economists, believed the only way to reduce consumption was by substantially raising the tax on gasoline at the pump, which Kahn now justified as a matter of national security. Testifying before Congress, he said the tax had to be "big enough to have a real effect on people's consumption so we can say to Iran, 'Keep your oil.'" He suggested "something dramatic—25 or 50 cents a gallon." The cost of a gallon of gas had gone up by roughly 31 cents in 1979, nearly doubling in a year and surpassing the dollar-a-gallon mark.[34] A 50-cent tax would be on top of that increase. Kahn wanted to return the revenue in the form of a payroll tax cut, but few heard that part of his proposal.

The gasoline tax idea sparked a firestorm. The antitax movement was gaining steam, and this White House proposal was moving in exactly the wrong direction. The public was outraged. Newspapers carried the story, and Americans sent furious letters to Washington. "Think about it before you hurt the little man any more," signed "a frustrated citizen and voter."[35] An angry woman who lived in suburban New Jersey had traded in her "fully paid for gas guzzler" for a new car with better mileage. Now she felt betrayed by reading about the possibility of a "dramatic tax." "We are just about making ends meet," she explained. "An additional tax of 25–50 cents/gallon would make it impossible to drive to work to earn an honest living rather than welfare . . . Please!" She implored Kahn to "consider us middle class, hard working, self-respecting people before adding such an insurmountable burden to our lives . . . Are you trying to denigrate the suburban Americans to requiring welfare?"[36]

Letters of protest poured in from across the country. Many pointed out their dependence on driving cars to get to work. Almost all mentioned the difficult economic times. The missives had a desperate quality to them, born of months of frustration over the economy and resentment of a government that seemed unable to offer any relief. "We are only lower middle class people who if gas goes up will just have to cut down on food," another housewife pleaded. "Or do they want us all to sit home and go on welfare?"[37] A small number wrote in support, inspired to sacrifice because of the hostage situation: "Let's do this so we can become independent of foreign oil . . . It makes me angry and it hurts to see our flag burned and our citizens held hostage in Iran."[38] But the vast majority registered their deep dissatisfaction with the White House.

As Carter stood paralyzed, unable to free the hostages or combat energy prices, Senator Kennedy formally declared his candidacy for the Democratic presidential nomination two days after the embassy seizure. The issue, he said, was Carter's incapacity to lead. Exhibit A was the energy situation. In every early campaign stop, he faulted the president for initiating oil decontrol at the moment of record profits. Exxon increased its profits by $1.1 billion, and Texaco's were up 210 percent from the previous year. If he were president, he would return to controls.[39]

A week later, on November 13, Ronald Reagan threw his hat in the ring. Reagan put his endorsement of the Kemp-Roth tax cut at the center of his presidential candidacy. As a contender in the 1976 Republican primaries, Reagan had proposed a $90 billion cut in government spending, a proposal that brought him endless grief as it became clear that such cuts would exact painful political costs. This time around, Reagan placed his faith in tax cuts rather than spending cuts, as did House and Senate Republicans. According to Jack Kemp, who gained fame as a champion professional quarterback and now represented working-class Buffalo, cutting income taxes would give individuals greater incentives to work, allowing taxpayers to keep more of their earnings, and would result in economic growth, which would then eliminate inflation, restore productivity, and reduce unemployment.

Reagan sold himself as the anti-malaise candidate. He framed his entire speech as a rebuttal to Carter's summertime address. An ever buoyant Reagan assured his viewers, "The crisis we face is not the result of any failure of the American spirit . . . It is a failure of our leaders." He rejected the notion of a countrywide illness. "In recent months leaders in our government have told us that, we, the people, have lost confidence in ourselves; that we must regain the spirit and our will to achieve our national goals," said Reagan. "Well, it is true there is a lack of confidence, an unease with things the way they are," Reagan said, as he wound up for the knock-out punch. "But the confidence we have lost is confidence in our government's policies."

Reagan put Carter's energy failures front and center: "If you ever had any doubt of the government's inability to provide for the needs of the people, just look at the utter fiasco we now call 'the energy crisis.'" In contrast to Carter's appeal to sacrifice, Reagan offered a picture of an abundant future. "First we must decide that 'less' is not enough," he told his television audience. "Next we must remove government obstacles to energy production. And, we must make use of those technological advantages we still possess. It is no program simply to say 'use less energy.'" Displaying what would become his signature optimism, Reagan promised, "As President I will not endorse any course, which has this as its principal objective." As the Senate was voting on the synthetic fuels bill, Reagan attacked Carter's proposal for a government-funded program head-on. "Putting the market system to work for these objectives is an essential first step for their achievement," insisted the free-market champion. In a refrain that would become a staple in his campaign rhetoric, he concluded, "Additional multi-billion dollar federal bureaus and programs are not the answer."

Send in the Marines

If the Carter administration appeared powerless on the domestic front, the hostage crisis might give the president an opportunity to show strength abroad. The November hostage seizure set off an instant public clamor for the president to act. At a rally in Washington, D.C., crowds gathered, bearing signs saying DEPORT ALL IRANIANS. GET THE HELL OUT OF MY COUNTRY. At a bar near the Marine Corps base in Quantico, Virginia, a bartender sold T-shirts that portrayed a Marine with a bayonet pointing at an Iranian hiding between a pouch of money and an oil barrel. The caption read "How much is the oil now?" "We can tell by the way our own public's acting that this is not going to be tolerated much longer," said one military veteran.[40] At California State University, Fresno, college students led a protest with banners reading "Send in the Marines."[41]

Politicians in Washington also sounded the call for a swift response to defend the prestige of American power abroad as well as to preserve access to Middle Eastern oil. Representative G. William Whitehurst, a Virginia Republican, sponsored a bill to deport the fifty thousand Iranian students in the United States. Representative Larry McDonald, a Georgia Democrat and a recently elected conservative, urged the president to take "whatever action necessary," including military intervention. "If that means armed action, then do it," McDonald said, arguing, "The oil fields could be taken with a relatively small military action."[42]

Gary Hart, as a leading spokesman for a stronger military commitment in the Gulf, capitalized on the hostage crisis to push for a new Democratic national security strategy. Images of American hostages blindfolded and flags burning aroused a sense of patriotism and a call to arms. Sam Nunn, the young Georgia senator, suggested the events in Iran made an increase in military spending "politically much more palatable and acceptable now."[43] The context for spending was no longer just the Cold War but also oil interests, said Hart. Increasing the American military presence in the Persian Gulf and protecting overseas oil supplies were the objectives. Iran made clear "dramatically the need for flexibility, mobility and presence." The United States "cannot be entranced with Europe, NATO."[44]

Those geopolitical concerns persuaded even outright opponents of

Vietnam-era intervention. Senator Frank Church, a Democrat from Idaho and chairman of the Senate Foreign Relations Committee, said, "The highly volatile and unpredictable politics of the Middle East, the wave of hysteria in the Islamic world, the explosive possibilities of countries like Saudi Arabia and Iraq—all of these have led to a mood that we must be prepared to take action to protect vital interests." He was even more explicit in his willingness to commit troops, insisting, "The vital interests of the United States, Western Europe, and Japan in Saudi oilfields would necessitate military action if our interests were threatened." Church, a leading critic of military interventionism, felt confident that his peers shared his views: "If that required organization of strike forces, there would be strong support for this on Capitol Hill."[45]

Carter had to balance the demand for a decisive display of force against the reality of the limited military options available. Immediately, Carter banned oil imports from Iran and deported illegal Iranian students. But the U.S. military did not have local bases from which to operate, nor did the air force possess the necessary air rights to make local operations easier. The Pentagon's planning for a rescue operation revealed such basic flaws as the inability to read maps of the sand dunes and the lack of necessary methods of concealment, including the appropriate combat dress for desert landscapes instead of for jungles and forests. Moreover, bulking up an American presence in the Gulf suffered from the significant military cuts since the ending of Vietnam as well as an unwillingness for the central commands of Europe and the Pacific to shift priorities. Operating under constrained budgets, the various forces resisted additional demands on their resources.

The Soviet invasion of Afghanistan on December 24, 1979, when eighteen hundred Soviet tanks and eighty thousand troops crossed the border, dramatically accelerated the debate over the proper foreign policy in the Gulf. In the face of such a bold move by the Soviets, the assessment from the NSC was not good. On the day of the Soviet invasion, David Aaron, deputy national security adviser, told Zbigniew Brzezinski, "somewhat to my surprise" the army was "not currently fully capable of conducting division-size operations." To get 100,000 men into the Gulf would require nearly a month at best.[46]

In early January, Carter cut off American grain shipments to the Soviet

Union and placed an embargo on high-technology transfers. The president also recommended a boycott of the 1980 Summer Olympics to be held in Moscow. More important, he asked the Senate to postpone consideration of the SALT II treaty for ratification. Finally, Carter called for a reinstatement of registration for the draft.

Within the White House, Brzezinski and his assistant William Odom pushed Carter to take a firm stand. They were both fiercely anti-Soviet. Having served as a military liaison stationed in East Germany, Odom had developed an acute sensitivity to life under Communist rule. He shared that with Brzezinski, who was born in Warsaw, Poland, and whose father served as a Polish diplomat in the early years of Nazi Germany and then in the Soviet Union during Joseph Stalin's Great Purge, before immigrating with his family to Canada. In response to the experiences of the Vietnam War Odom believed in having clear objectives for action that served the United States' strategic interests. Odom felt certain that the Soviet invasion into Afghanistan fit that definition, especially as the Soviets' demand for oil was growing at a rate twice that of the Americans'.[47]

With the Soviets in Afghanistan, the threat grew that they could extend their reach into the Persian Gulf and close off the Strait of Hormuz, a narrow passage between Iran and Oman providing entry from the Persian Gulf into the Indian Ocean through which oil tankers traveled.[48] According to Odom, it was time for the United States to establish a Middle East command: "All the arguments raised against it (backlash in the region, etc.) have been undercut . . . by events in Iran and Afghanistan."[49] Odom worked with Samuel Huntington, who was back at Harvard, to design what would be a major presidential address on the Persian Gulf situation.

As the White House formulated its response, the 1980 election was heating up. In May 1979, George H. W. Bush had declared his candidacy for the Republican nomination. Bush had been preparing for a presidential run for years, believing his strength lay in bringing together different strands of the Republican Party. Through his father, Prescott Bush, the Wall Street investor turned politician, and his own Yankee upbringing, Bush had natural connections to the establishment wing of the Republican Party. After thirty years in Texas, he spoke without a southern drawl, didn't have a herd of cattle, or even a cowboy hat.[50] Still, Bush, the independent oilman, had cut his teeth in Texas politics, where, in spite of his personal style as the buttoned-up New England country-club Republican, he had embraced the new kind of Sunbelt conservatism. That was especially true on matters of economics and regulation, which had served Bush well as chairman of the Republican National Committee. To run his campaign, Bush turned to James Baker, who had established a political action committee, the Fund for Limited Government, in support of his friend.

Bush understood better than most the dangers of the Persian Gulf. In a fall speech at the National Press Club, before the hostage seizure, he discussed what he saw as "the shocking vulnerability of America's strategic forces." He opposed the SALT II treaty, and he shared the conservatives' fear of the Soviets expanding their power and reach, especially in the Middle East. "The Persian Gulf could become the scene of a second and more deadly Cuban missile crisis," said Bush.[51] "This time we may be the first to blink," he cautioned. If the Soviets took advantage of regional instability and moved into the area, they could "present us with an impossible choice—either we yield a critical source of oil to their control, or we risk nuclear catastrophe."[52] In October, before another audience, Bush repeated the call for an increased military presence. "Our ability to obtain crude oil from the Persian Gulf," he said, "will hinge upon our willingness to bolster our defenses and strengthen our allies."[53]

Many on the Republican Right shared the sense that the Middle East reflected a danger zone for the United States, in large part because of the opportunity it created for Soviet influence over a region that these policy makers believed was vital to American and allied interests. Donald Rumsfeld, Ford's secretary of defense, had left government and was serving as the chief executive of the Illinois-based Searle corporation, a multimillion-dollar pharmaceutical firm. Rumsfeld remained active within Republican circles, and many considered him likely to return to national politics. In November, after the embassy takeover, Rumsfeld shared the alarm of his fellow conservatives. "We can sit around with our fingers in our ears hoping things will turn out all right, or we can rearm," he said in a public speech. "If you haven't liked the Soviets when they were inferior to us militarily, you'll like them even less when they are superior. They are becoming increasingly adventuresome, increasingly feisty, and increasingly successful. And remember, they don't believe anything we believe in regarding basic democratic freedoms."[54] At the Republican National Committee meeting in January, days before Carter was scheduled to deliver his State of the Union address, Rumsfeld warned that the president was leading the U.S. military down "the path towards inferiority."[55]

A sense of national decline pervaded conservative critiques. The neo-conservative military strategist Edward Luttwak, who supported the seizure of Saudi Arabian oil fields through the use of force, harshly described the United States as no longer "in business as the countervailing super-power." "The last several years have witnessed a shipwreck in America's reputation as a valid protector, with the Tehran hostage crisis itself lethally damaging our prestige," declared Luttwak in the editorial pages of *The New York Times*. "Most of the Moslems anywhere near the Soviet Union will simply accept the fact that the Russians are the new masters of their fate, as other great foreign empires were before them."[56] The American Enterprise Institute fellow Emile Nakhleh worried that "America is no longer a dependable ally." As he put it, "Gulf leaders have difficulty accepting the argument that military power has its own limitations and that the safety of a few hostages is more important than a country's honor." He claimed one leader told him that America had become "a superpower in decline."[57]

In the eyes of his critics, Carter was acting like a coward at a major turning point in global history. Rowland Evans and Robert Novak criticized "Jimmy Carter's restraint in this cauldron of world conflict."[58] The *Wall Street Journal* editors argued, "The American reaction should be military—not of course attempting to reverse the outcome on the land in Afghanistan, but making sure that further thrusts will face an effective counterforce." Given "the dramatic change in the military balance over the world's most strategic choke-point," Carter had to respond with more than economic sanctions and the withdrawal from the Olympic Games.[59]

The stakes were high when, on January 23, Jimmy Carter delivered his 1980 State of the Union address. With conviction and resolve, Carter told the country, "The Soviet invasion of Afghanistan could pose the most serious threat to the peace since the Second World War." As the president explained it, the growing dependence of industrial democracies on Middle Eastern oil combined with the Soviet military power in the region and the regional instability, which amplified the Soviet threat, required a new foreign policy. More than just an immediate response to an unexpected crisis, the need for a new foreign policy doctrine reflected the outgrowth of a long debate over the response to the energy crisis. In clear terms the president mapped out American policy toward the Gulf in what became known as the Carter Doctrine: "An attempt by any outside force to gain control of the Persian Gulf region will be regarded as an assault on the vital interests of the United States of America, and such an assault will be repelled by any means necessary, including military force."

With this declaration, the United States began moving toward a new era in foreign relations, even as the Cold War still reigned. The announcement of the Carter Doctrine grew out of a traditional Cold War conflict. The Soviets had invaded neighboring territory, and the United States responded. But the Carter Doctrine itself represented a significant shift in the direction of a new set of foreign policy priorities very different from what had shaped the Cold War: protecting energy resources in the Persian Gulf with force, contending with Islamic fundamentalism and militarism, and containing the threat of terrorism.

The morning of his State of the Union address, Carter met with the congressional leadership. They would have to approve Carter's request for a substantial increase in the military budget to allow the United States to expand its regional presence, acquire bases, and solidify relationships with allies. In the short term, that meant securing military access to Oman, Kenya, and Somalia and increasing foreign aid to countries the White House and the NSC defined as essential to carrying out the Carter Doctrine. Frank Moore explained, "We cannot contain Soviet expansion without the support of developing countries in Asia, Africa, and Latin America." And the spending had to increase: "The funding levels are too low; you cannot address problems of the '80s with '79 dollars."[60] While regional powers feared the presence of American troops on their soil, they eagerly welcomed aid and arms.

Carter's efforts to chart a new course did not redound to his political advantage. Two days before he announced the Carter Doctrine, the primary season had officially begun with the Iowa caucuses. For the moment, the nation rallied behind the embattled president during this foreign policy crisis, and Carter came out on top. In light of the hostage situation, Carter announced that he would not leave the White House to campaign. But his attempt to remain above the fray proved untenable. The start of a presidential election season greatly intensified the blowback to his speech, with even stronger and more polemical attacks. It was impossible for Carter to do or say anything outside the prism of the election.

Carter's tough-sounding rhetoric did little to appease the Right, which

was hankering for a dramatic response to Iranian terrorists and to the Soviet Union. Representative John Rhodes of Arizona, the House Republican
leader, accused the president of being too soft. "There was a lot of sabre
rattling but not much in the sabre," said Rhodes after the State of the
Union. Carter's strong statement on the Persian Gulf did nothing to dull
his conservative opponents' critiques. "The defense part of the speech was
excellent, but it hardly sounded like it came from someone who canceled
the B-1 bomber, fought the neutron bomb and who campaigned to cut the
defense budget," ribbed Senator S. I. Hayakawa, a California Republican.
"It comes a little too late for him to suddenly see the need for national security," criticized Representative Philip Crane of Illinois, the conservative
Republican who was running in the 1980 Republican primaries. "If that's
the new Carter Doctrine, it's obvious to me we are in for the same old
palaver," retorted Minority Whip Robert Michel, representative of Illinois.[61] Carter reversed the decline in defense budgets that began under
President Nixon, but Republicans belittled his efforts. By attacking Carter
for not doing enough, Republicans hoped to appeal not only to GOP members but also to the conservative wing of the Democratic Party.[62]

The biggest attack came from Ronald Reagan, who had suffered a loss
to George H. W. Bush in Iowa. In designing his campaign, Bush had stolen
a page from Carter's 1976 playbook, working hard to plant the seeds of his
nomination with an early primary victory. Amid the hostage crisis, Bush
came across as the trustworthy, experienced statesman, and voters re-
warded him over his rivals. To regain momentum, Reagan escalated his
right-wing assault, especially on the foreign policy failings of the president. With an eye to the upcoming South Carolina primary, which as the
first race in the South would give Reagan a chance to shore up his conservative base, he went on the attack. He said that Carter's failure to take more
deliberate action to free the hostages invited the Soviet invasion: "I cannot
doubt that our failure to act decisively at the time this happened provided
the Russians with the final encouragement to invade Afghanistan." Reagan went a step further, lambasting the president as "either deceitful or a
fool" if he believed his tough talk in the State of the Union address would
impress either the Soviets or the Iranians.[63]

From the president's left, Kennedy wasted no time in denouncing the
president's "exaggerated militarism." After losing in Iowa, Kennedy sought
to breathe new life into his campaign. Five days after the State of the Union

address, on January 28, he delivered a dramatic speech at Georgetown University in which he distanced himself from the Carter Doctrine. He preferred instead a "measured response," believing that diplomacy would "prove less hazardous and more effective than a unilateral and unlimited American commitment" in the Gulf. He challenged the notion that the Soviet invasion represented the greatest danger to American security since World War II, arguing, "Exaggeration and hyperbole are the enemies of sensible foreign policy." Kennedy called for a United Nations commission to investigate the Iranian charges against the shah. Staking out a position to the far left of the president, Kennedy sounded his support for traditional liberal measures from equal rights for women to national health care to wage and price controls.[64]

On the campaign trail, Kennedy said it was time for the United States to confront its "petroleum paralysis." "The clearest way to send a signal to the Soviets right now would be to end our dependence on Persian Gulf oil," boomed the Massachusetts senator.[65] Kennedy wanted to achieve this goal with Roosevelt-era interventions by ordering immediate gasoline rationing. This would be a liberal program of shared sacrifice, one that would release Americans from their reliance on foreign oil and slow the accumulation by Big Oil of what Kennedy called "unconscionable" profits.[66] Issuing ration coupons, Kennedy's campaign aides explained, would reduce American daily consumption of crude oil by 1.7 million barrels, which would then eliminate the need for Middle Eastern oil imports. Campaigning in New England, the area most dependent on Middle Eastern oil, Kennedy urged mandatory conservation. As he put it during a campaign stop in Maine, "I believe people would rather use a little less gasoline in their cars than spill the blood of young Americans to protect OPEC pipelines."[67]

Carter did not back down. In his budget requests for 1981, the president asked for an increase of more than $15 billion in military spending, bringing total military spending to almost $143 billion. The increase was essential, Carter said, for ensuring that American troops would be ready for action in an "uncertain and sometimes hostile world." Carter also requested more than $8 billion for domestic energy initiatives.[68] (The total budget was almost $616 billion.) His requests for greater spending on defense and on energy ranked as the two largest increases, which Carter justified as necessary in light of recent events. These were essential, said

Carter, especially given that in 1979 the United States had spent $64 billion on oil imports.[69]

For all his new toughness, Carter could not generate public support. He had set a deadline for Soviet withdrawal from Afghanistan of February 20, which came and went. The 1980 Lake Placid Winter Olympic victory for the American ice hockey team over the Soviet Union offered a temporary salve to the perceived wounds of American military might. But soon voters were giving Carter negative approval on his handling of defense policy, as they did on the economy and on energy matters.[70] And the Right was unrelenting. George Will described Carter's response to Iran and the Soviet Union as an "agenda of appeasement," while William Safire charged the president with "rewarding terrorists."[71]

Carter suffered a further drop in his prestige as he came under constant criticism from American allies in Western Europe. Eager to ensure access to oil from the Gulf, these countries threatened to pursue what Henry Kissinger derisively called "divisible détente."[72] The National Security Council's William Odom worried that in the wake of Afghanistan each country might make its own overtures to Middle Eastern countries and to the Soviet Union, which would result in a "spectacle of disarray." In a direct challenge to American Middle Eastern policy, the French president, Valéry Giscard d'Estaing, toured the Arab world, suggesting that France might be prepared to grant recognition to the Palestine Liberation Organization as part of a two-state solution.

Throughout 1980, even as the campaign and budgetary fights complicated his efforts, Brzezinski worked hard to implement a new policy. As he explained in an official NSC report, "The theme we propose is that the Soviet invasion of Afghanistan must focus our attention on a major new order of politico-economic-military threat to the non-communist world security—Soviet domination of Middle East oil." Just as Truman's policy makers had feared the Soviet control of the central European breadbasket after World War II, so, too, did the current acts of aggression pose a serious risk to industrial democracies, believed Brzezinski. "The willingness of the Soviets . . . to use their own military strength in this geographic area, strongly indicates that the Soviets are willing to take aggressive moves in an area that is vital to us but merely of interest to them," explained a top-level NSC memorandum.[73]

The real threat to the United States came less directly from the cutoff of oil to the nation than from the potential cutoff to its allies. "The effect of Soviet control of those resources, either through overt military action or by internal subversion or political intimidation, would destroy the free market economies and dissolve our alliances in Europe and East Asia," asserted the NSC. Only the United States had the capacity to provide the necessary military strength in the region; therefore, national security required a redirection of military power to Southwest Asia. "Because no one else can," concluded Carter's national security advisers.[74]

Brzezinski believed that the concern over Soviet strength in the Middle East had to condition the response to the hostage crisis. An aggressive strategy against Iran might propel that country into the Soviet orbit. "What really ties our hands about acting forcefully to retrieve our hostages," an NSC report explained, "is the risk of driving Iran toward the Soviets or creating chaos which the USSR can exploit." The fears that regional instability would redound to Soviet advantage, much as the unemployment and hunger had fueled Communist strength after World War II, were very real: "We cannot be seen to be supine to an act of lawlessness directed at us, but we do not want to drive the Iranians into a close relation with the Soviets." And yet, as the NSC advisers acknowledged, the cost of inaction could be high: "In reasserting our leadership we must avoid the Scylla of perceived over-reaction—which leads our fearful friends and Allies to pull back from us, and the Charybdis of passivity—which reinforces the image that America has lost its capacity to control events." The NSC summed up the policy dilemma: "Inactivity and drift in our efforts to resolve the hostage crisis is undermining respect for the United States in the region and worldwide. At the same time, it is essential to emerge from this crisis without driving Iran into the arms of the Soviet Union."[75]

The prospect for a successful military rescue did not seem good. If a rescue attempt led to bloodshed, that outcome might push the Iranians and other countries that much closer to an alliance with the Soviets. That development would endanger American allies who depended on Middle Eastern oil. And if a rescue mission failed, it could "severely damage American prestige."[76] Carter's advisers were divided on the proper course, with the NSC pushing for a rescue operation, in spite of the risks, and Secretary of State Cyrus Vance counseling against it.

The White House understood that Americans were growing restless. By February 1980, 64 percent of Americans approved of sending troops to the Middle East to "protect our oil sources."[77] As much as the world praised Carter's restraint, the lack of action damaged the perception of the United States' strength. With the primary season heating up, Reagan and Bush began openly criticizing the president's handling of the hostage situation. Reagan, in particular, with support from neoconservative circles, mapped out a menacing narrative of interlocking events, beginning with the fall of the shah, a Soviet brigade in Cuba, the fall of the Somoza regime in Nicaragua, the taking of the hostages in Iran, culminating in the Soviet invasion of Afghanistan, holding Carter responsible for all. With the hostages still in captivity, the president's approval ratings, already low, slipped further.[78]

On April 24, 1980, under the cover of night, eight helicopters took off from the USS *Nimitz* in the Indian Ocean and headed to rescue the American hostages in Tehran. The military developed the plan in secrecy over several months, and now Carter was ready to act. After three of the aircraft encountered technical troubles hundreds of miles away from the nearest base, the president agreed to abort the mission. As the aircraft prepared to fly back to the *Nimitz* from the meeting point outside Tehran, sandstorms blocked visibility, and two of the aircraft collided, resulting in the deaths of eight American servicemen. The next day the president announced the grim news.

The aborted rescue attempt amplified the perception of Carter's diplomatic weakness. The president's tough-sounding rhetoric in his State of the Union speech mattered little in comparison to the servicemen who died in the botched attempt he had authorized and the hostages who remained in captivity, to say nothing of the Soviets making a major power play in the region. Reagan stepped up his campaign trail attacks and accused the president of actions "bordering on appeasement."[79] Robert Tucker and his neoconservative allies continued to push for militarizing the Gulf, insisting American power in the region "must be quite visible and have the air of permanence."[80]

Carter's back was up against the wall. Under siege from all sides and fighting a bruising budgetary battle, on March 1 Carter had designated the MacDill Air Force Base in Florida as the Rapid Deployment Joint Task Force headquarters. The NSC also began laying out the rationale for preemptive strikes in the region. Yet, in the context of the 1980 election, this historic shift in American policy caused the president political problems.

Carter's foreign policy was alienating much of his own party, while it did little to placate his conservative opponents, who were on the attack.

Energied-Out

At the time of the failed hostage rescue, the number one issue weighing on Americans' minds was the economy. The inflation rate had reached a stunning 18 percent, and Americans were hurting. Carter was desperate to take steps to slow the inflationary spiral, and he told the country that inconvenience, discipline, and austerity were all necessary to saving the Republic. "There certainly are not any painless answers," he announced to a national television audience. "Our whole society, the entire American family, must try harder than ever to live within its means." In this speech, Carter called for spending cuts, and he also proposed further restrictions on credit. When asked if fiscal and monetary restraint would trigger a recession and higher unemployment, the Federal Reserve chairman, Paul Volcker, said, "Yes and the sooner the better."[81]

Tip O'Neill had blocked Carter from delivering his austerity address before Congress. The Speaker did not want to appear on national television applauding what one White House aide described as "draconian" cuts to the programs that he and other Democrats had devoted their careers to building.[82] They expected that a Republican like Ronald Reagan would call for these kinds of cuts, but they could not accept these tough measures from a member of their own party, and certainly not during an election year. Carter was betraying the very principles of the New Deal coalition that had elected him at a time when voters were suffering.

Even as he was dropping in the polls, Carter was shifting the political center of the campaign debate to the right. "This is the last gasp of Democratic liberalism," said Representative Stephen Solarz, a Democrat from Brooklyn, New York, who opposed the president's proposed cuts to cities and the disadvantaged.[83] The budget "is not just a bunch of numbers. It is a political philosophy," explained Solarz. It was not a move that would help the party: "Why should we try to out-Republican the Republicans? And if we do, why should voters support fake Republicans in November, rather than the genuine article?"[84]

On March 25, 1980, Carter lost the Connecticut and New York primaries to Ted Kennedy. If Ford had told New Yorkers to "drop dead," said Kennedy, then Carter was telling them to "die slowly." The solution to a troubled economy was not austerity or what liberal critics called "Volcker's shock therapy." Instead, the Kennedy camp advocated boosting urban spending, cutting defense, attacking monopoly pricing in food, housing, health care, and energy, and imposing mandatory wage-price controls, which Kennedy had featured as the key part of his agenda in the run-up to his primary wins.[85]

As much as economists and Washington policy makers hoped to relegate this New Deal tool to the dustbins of history, ordinary voters held fast to this Band-Aid measure. A *New York Times/CBS News* poll reported that 65 percent of Americans favored controls as the way to halt inflation, cutting across political and ideological lines. As the reporter E. J. Dionne noted, the public "likes wage and price controls a lot better than it likes the Government pushing up interest rates as a way of fighting inflation. These folk also prefer controls to policies that allow unemployment to rise."[86] For the average American, as well as for many liberal Democrats, blaming businessmen for driving up costs served as a ready explanation for galloping inflation; bringing them to heel was the necessary remedy.

On April 2, 1980, President Carter signed the Crude Oil Windfall Profit Tax into law. For a brief moment, the president aroused the kind of popular support that had propelled him into the White House four years earlier. The final measure split the difference between the House version and the Senate version, which had passed in December, and anticipated raising approximately $227 billion in revenue between its immediate enactment and 1991, when it would terminate.[87] Forty leading labor unions endorsed the final bill and had lobbied for its passage. At its signing, Carter gave profuse thanks to Brendan Byrne, the governor of New Jersey, who had led a citizens committee for a windfall profits tax. Labor and consumer groups were hopeful that the revenue, which would go into the general revenue stream, would subsidize energy costs for low-income families and thereby offset some of the cuts in unemployment benefits and other welfare measures.

The largest single tax passed on a single industry, this historic measure hardly signaled a victory for liberalism. Carter had used his executive authority to scale back price controls, over the objections of liberals, and the oil interests and their lobbyists recognized that only the passage of a

profits tax would make that policy stick. Senator Russell Long, chairman
of the Senate Finance Committee, remarked with candor, "It's the price we
have to pay in order to have decontrol."[88] It was, in essence, a vote for more
government to obtain less government. The New York representative Bar-
ber Conable understood the nature of this bargain. "The issue here," said
Conable, ranking minority member on the Ways and Means Committee,
"is not so much taxation as deregulation." "The tax is basically a political
tax," said Representative W. Henson Moore, a Republican from Louisiana.
"Politically it was determined to have decontrol, and it was determined
that you had to have a tax to support that."[89]

For conservatives, in the middle of an election season, the windfall
profits tax was a political godsend. Even though Carter stood in the center
and embraced an austerity agenda that angered many liberals in his own
party, Reagan and fellow conservatives used the tax to show that the president was still too far to the left. Centrism, they said, was just a cover for
tax-and-spend liberalism. The tax was further evidence, said the Republican Right, that the administration had no effective energy policy. The
windfall profits tax, according to Reagan, would cut domestic production
by 840,000 barrels a day. The American Petroleum Institute's Charles Di-
Bona agreed, pointing to the possibility that states would make matters
worse by passing their own state-level profit taxes.[90] The economist Paul
Craig Roberts dubbed it the "weakness tax," while the *Wall Street Journal*
editors renamed it "the close-the-wells tax," one that was sure to hamper
America's ability to free itself from imported oil.[91] Reagan promised to
eliminate the tax, if he were president, and also to remove remaining price
controls immediately. "Turn the energy industry loose in the marketplace," explained Reagan, reflecting his approach to governance more
generally.[92]

For Reagan, the solution to all the country's ills, from energy shortages
to inflation to recession, was a massive income tax cut. Reagan never wavered in his commitment to a vision of supply-side economics, in which a
massive tax cut would diminish the power of government and thereby
stimulate growth, nor did his advisers. "I think we will win," remarked Jude
Wanniski, "because we have truth and light on our side. This is the only
campaign, Republican or Democrat, in which you will find this kind of
intellectual ferment."[93]

Reagan's insistence on a historic tax cut came in for criticism, including from George Bush, who was trailing Reagan in the primaries. Just before the Pennsylvania primary, Bush launched an assault on Reagan's "economic madness," premised on what Bush called "voodoo economic policy." In Pittsburgh, where steelworkers were suffering from a slowdown in the economy, Bush said, "Governor Reagan is promising to cut taxes by 30 percent, balance the budget, increase defense spending and stop inflation all at the same time. His solution for the energy crisis is simply to drill more wells in Alaska—a state in which he claims there is more oil than all of Saudi Arabia." "Now that's a list of phony promises," Bush told his audience. Instead, the country should return to the "fundamentals of economics," by which he meant an increase in productivity, cuts in federal spending, and a moderate tax cut.[94] On April 22, Bush upset Reagan in the primary, where voters were uncertain that Reagan's Sunbelt optimism would resuscitate a recessionary economy.

In truth, the ideological distance between Reagan and Bush was not very far. Even if Bush called for a smaller tax cut, both shared a commitment to a supply-side point of view, which had come to define the Republican Party. Rejecting the New Deal and the Great Society, with those programs' emphasis on consumption and equity, Bush, Reagan, and other GOP candidates, with the exception of John Anderson, who was running as an independent, believed the key to the country's renewal and strength lay with stimulating America's productive potential.[95] Even as their specific policy prescriptions varied, "at the heart of the embryonic new consensus is concern about lagging productivity," explained the journalist Sidney Blumenthal. As he summed it up, "Cut taxes to stimulate growth, limit government spending to give the private sector greater scope in its endeavors, encourage accumulation of capital for investment in new machinery, and remove from the books government regulations that inhibit free enterprise."[96]

Republicans were closing ranks, throwing their support behind Reagan as the candidate most likely to defeat President Carter and return Republican rule to the White House. When Gerald Ford made it clear he would not enter the race, many Nixon-Ford-era advisers, including Dick Cheney and Donald Rumsfeld, endorsed the former California governor. They had known and worked with Bush. But in 1980, when trust in Washington was running low, Reagan was a useful front man, one who could sell their brand of antigovernment conservatism while drawing on the behind-the-scenes strength and talent of those who knew their way around the Capitol. To head a new economic policy advisory group, Reagan appointed William Simon, who worked with Caspar Weinberger, Alan Greenspan, Irving Kristol, Donald Rumsfeld, George Shultz, and Murray Weidenbaum, all veterans of the last Republican administrations in office.[97]

Reagan's team included supply-side evangelists like Wanniski and George Gilder who were certain that only a massive tax cut would restore fiscal and moral rectitude to government. There were also former Ford advisers like Simon and Greenspan who placed greater emphasis than the New Right on halting government spending to spur greater capital investment. Young congressional Republicans like Jack Kemp, David Stockman, Trent Lott, and Newt Gingrich, who understood the political appeal of tax cuts and the elimination of certain kinds of government spending, also rallied behind Reagan. "I came in as a balance-the-budget, root canal austere Republican," said Kemp. "Then I looked around and realized . . . people will vote for hope over austerity." Reagan served as the vehicle for a new conservative agenda that promised smaller government, a return of growth, and renewed optimism.[98]

This group of Reagan supporters constituted what the journalist Nicholas Lemann called a GOP government-in-waiting. In addition to their ideological orientation, they all had one thing in common: they were Washington insiders. These were policy makers who had been working for years inside the federal government, waiting patiently since Gerald Ford's defeat for another opportunity to seize control of the White House and shift public policy toward market-based solutions. In the eleven years since Nixon had taken office, institutions such as the American Enterprise Institute and the Center for Strategic and International Studies had become powerful players, influencing political debate and public policy. Melvin Laird's years of institutional building were paying off. As Lemann reported, this group of conservatives was "in place and ready to take power in a Republican Washington." Few, as Lemann pointed out, were early Reagan supporters, but all knew which government agencies and regulations they wanted to scale back, if not dismantle.[99] As Charls Walker, a Business Roundtable lobbyist and Reagan adviser, explained, "You have to know what to do and how to do it, know how to work Congress and work the bureaucracies. I'm very excited about the prospects of a Reagan presidency."[100]

As the Republicans were gaining strength, Carter was hemorrhaging support. In April, he lost the Pennsylvania primary to Kennedy. His stance on the economy and energy drove away liberals who were looking for some old-time New Deal magic to tackle the nation's problems. In a speech to the Cook County Democrats in Chicago, Scoop Jackson warned against Carter's brand of centrism. "The root of our problem," said this party war-horse, "is the widespread perception, by millions of Americans, that the Democratic Party is no longer what it once was: that it is no longer the Party of Roosevelt or Truman; that it has cut itself adrift from traditional Democratic constituencies; that it no longer offers a coherent and compre-hensive program for social progress at home." Though Jackson did not refer to the president directly, he made it clear that Kennedy was a better leader to carry forward the Democratic mantle. "When a large number of work-ing people believe that the Democratic Party has reverted to the policies of Herbert Hoover, we are in trouble," said Jackson. The Reagan camp, sens-ing defection, approached him about the possibility of a foreign policy cabinet post should Reagan win in November, but Jackson turned them down. As he told them, "I still believe in the New Deal."[101]

With his political support crumbling, the president was able to enjoy one last victory on energy policy, a stunning one in fact. In late June, Con-gress passed the Energy Security Act, creating the U.S. Synthetic Fuels Corporation. The act authorized $88 billion over twelve years, with $20 billion available in the first five for loan and price guarantees to private industry to build ten synthetic fuel plants for liquid coal, shale, and tar. In addition, the act allocated $3 billion for a solar bank to subsidize the in-stallation of solar energy equipment in residential and commercial prop-erties. The measure also provided $1.2 billion to produce gasohol from crops and agricultural waste. Finally, the act authorized filling the Strate-gic Petroleum Reserve (SPR), which was still largely inoperable, at a faster rate to make the United States less susceptible to supply interruptions or dramatic price hikes.

The president signed the act into law on June 30 in a quiet South Lawn ceremony. For all the White House's bluster and the bill's bipartisan support, there was no public celebration and little media coverage. Even as it had received substantial backing across the political spectrum, few cheered its enactment. Environmentalists and other liberals opposed what they perceived to be a giveaway to big business. Indeed, the only enthusiastic champions of the newly created government corporation were the utilities, pipelines, and energy companies who intended to borrow funds to construct plants. Exxon executives led the way in this new field.

Environmentalists were especially angered by this massive commitment to alternative fuels. They believed the production of fuel from coal gasification and shale oil would result in unacceptable environmental costs, including the large-scale quantities of water necessary for the manufacturing process. "The socioeconomic impacts are so staggering they are almost beyond imagining," said Paula Phillips of the Environmental Defense Fund. Environmental groups promised to unleash mobilized protest against synthetic production on par with antinuclear campaigns. "We are going to face tremendous opposition from the environmental movement," acknowledged Exxon's chairman, Clifton Garvin Jr. "And I'm not certain that we will prevail."[102]

The U.S. Synfuels Corporation received criticism not just from the Left but also from the Right, who saw this creation as yet another unproductive example of costly government involvement. According to conservatives, the government should not pay for solar panels and bike paths, let alone large commercial ventures that should instead be developed in the marketplace. "Put simply, policies at the state and federal levels have effectively hamstrung attempts to develop domestic reserves, and in doing so have helped tighten the OPEC noose around our necks," explained the Heritage Foundation's Milton Copulos.[103]

In reality, Congress had made sure that little was likely to come from the act. Three days before Carter signed the measure, the House had killed the bill to create the Energy Mobilization Board (EMB), which would have expedited construction of new energy plants and eased environmental restrictions. "Before we built the door to our energy future . . . we went and locked it and threw away the key," complained John Dingell. As a result of what was now becoming a regular thorn in the president's side, an alliance of the Left and the Right had defeated the bill in the House 232–131. The environmentalists lobbied heavily against it, fearing the EMB would override existing regulations and warning of the disaster that would ensue if this bill became law.[104] "Our own liberals joined with the Republicans to vote it down," a dismayed Dingell explained.[105]

Conservatives opposed the EMB as another expansion of federal authority, even for the sake of speeding up approval of energy projects. Opponents wore buttons reading, "Even More Bureaucracy," insisting the EMB would add rather than cut red tape.[106] Representative Robert Bauman of Maryland, a leading Republican conservative, said the bill was "fascism, pure and simple."[107] Ninety-five Republicans who had previously supported the measure voted against it. According to Tip O'Neill, the GOP wanted to prevent the White House from staging a dramatic July 4 energy Independence Day celebration as planned. At a minimum, they were not eager to give Carter any more victories.[108]

Republicans were gearing up for their convention in Detroit, where Ronald Reagan formally won the nomination. Talking to the nation from the heart of the Rust Belt, Reagan rejected Carter's "energy policy based on the sharing of scarcity." "Those who preside over the worst energy shortage in our history tell us to use less," Reagan said, "so that we will run out of oil, gasoline, and natural gas a little more slowly." In contrast, the GOP candidate asserted, "The Republican program for solving economic problems is based on growth and productivity." "The present administration seems to believe the American people would rather see more regulation, taxes and controls than more energy," said a hopeful Reagan. Instead, "America must get to work producing more energy." On the floor of the convention, delegates wore campaign buttons that read "A Democrat Shot J.R.," offering their answer to that summer's much-sensationalized mystery of who tried to kill J. R. Ewing on the *Dallas* season finale cliff-hanger.[109] For Reagan's supporters, the shooter of America's most well-known oilman was obvious.

In Detroit, the GOP used the energy crisis to question the legitimacy of the entire liberal project: "The federal bureaucracy is busy from coast to coast allocating gasoline, setting building temperatures, printing rationing coupons, and readying standby plans to ban weekend boating, close factories, and pass out 'no drive day' stickers to American motorists—all the time saying, 'We must make do with less.' Never before in the history of American government has so much been done at such great expense with such dismal results." The Republican platform called for the immediate decontrol of all prices as well as the repeal of the fifty-five-mile-per-hour speed limit, which the GOP saw as the most visible and irritating symbol of the mandate to "conserve . . . through government fiat."[110]

To strengthen his appeal, Reagan selected George Bush as his vice presidential running mate. Willing to temper his moderate support of women's issues and civil rights, Bush had a long history of conservative voting on deregulation, defense, and tax cuts, which reinforced the views Reagan was espousing at the head of the ticket. Few had done as much as Bush to build up the GOP in the South; Bush had also demonstrated strength in industrial states like Pennsylvania, and, above all, his Washington experience would be an asset to a new Reagan administration. As much as Reagan ran as an outsider, he understood that to be effective, he would have to rule as an insider.

In mid-August, Democrats met in New York City to nominate Carter as their candidate. Kennedy had won only ten primaries to Carter's twenty-four. Carter was the sitting president, and Kennedy could not shake the lasting doubt surrounding the circumstances of the death of his female passenger, Mary Jo Kopechne, when he drove off a bridge on a 1969 summer's night in Chappaquiddick, Massachusetts. At the convention, where he had much popularity, the senator's supporters pushed to place him at the forefront. When their efforts to get Carter's delegates released from their commitments failed, Kennedy at last withdrew.

This battle down to the wire served as a reminder of the great unease that existed within the Democratic Party about their choice. As Republicans enthusiastically embraced their candidate as the new champion of conservatism, Democrats grudgingly accepted theirs as the only option available. The tensions between Kennedy and Carter were palpable when the senator refused to join Carter in a show of unity on the podium at the end of the convention. As Kennedy took the stage, the delegates were much more enthusiastic in their cheering for him than they were for the person who would run for reelection.

On the campaign trail, Reagan hammered away at Carter's energy policy as an example of overzealous and counterproductive government intervention. "The truth is, America has an abundance of energy, but the policies of this Administration consistently discourage its discovery and production," said Reagan in a Cleveland campaign stop.[111] In Youngstown, Ohio, addressing coal and steel workers, Reagan expressed the view that air pollution has now been "substantially controlled." As president, he promised to "see to it that EPA has leaders who know and care about the coal industry." Reagan said that "these 1970 rules have helped force factories to shut down and cost workers their jobs . . . and they will certainly slow the use of coal."[112] Again and again, Reagan announced that the economy suffered from too much government regulation. Removing regulations would restore economic health, result in job creation, and prevent another energy shortage.

Energy became front-page news in late September, when war broke out between Iraq and Iran. Iraq, with its Soviet-supplied military units, had superiority over Iran, especially once the United States suspended its shipment of parts replacements for the military equipment the defense industry had sold to the shah. Fearful that the Khomeini regime would attempt to incite political unrest in Iraq, Saddam Hussein launched an attack on Iran. Although prompted by regional concerns, this conflict had large-scale geopolitical implications. Sixty percent of the world's oil traveled through the Strait of Hormuz, which became vulnerable to shutdown, a prospect that could create chaos for Western nations and Japan. The United States offered the use of surveillance planes to Kuwait, Oman, and the United Arab Emirates as a way to deter Iranian attempts to blow up oil fields.

To the Right, the Iran-Iraq War highlighted the shallowness of the Carter Doctrine. As *The Wall Street Journal* posited, "It is quite conceivable that if the U.S. had a strong presence overshadowing the Persian Gulf this war would have never started." If not a threat to the nation's supply, then once again the war was a sign of national weakness and presidential failure. According to the *Journal*, it would take the Eighty-Second Airborne at least two weeks to arrive on the scene in the Middle East, and even then that installation would not sufficiently augment the eighteen hundred Marines and 170 warplanes deployed after the Soviet invasion. In contrast, the Soviets could rapidly dispatch fighter planes from their bases in Afghanistan. To counter this power, the United States needed to have its own bases in the area and a stronger navy. The Rapid Deployment Force was nothing more than a "charade."[113]

The outbreak of war only seemed to confirm what the oil expert Walter Levy called the "decline of the West." Given the inability of Carter and the rest of the members of the International Energy Agency to respond to the doubling of prices in 1979, Levy concluded that the year's actions illustrated and indeed contributed to "the impotence of Western power and the failure of national and international leadership." The future, according to Levy, looked bleak. The petrodollar problem, with rising balance-of-trade deficits, the incapacity of consuming countries to plan effectively for stable demand, and the internal strife in the Middle East all exacerbated the weakened position of the United States. "The world, as we know it now," Levy wrote, "will probably not be able to maintain its cohesion, nor be able to provide for the continued economic progress of its people against the onslaught of future oil shocks—with all that this might imply for the political stability of the West, its free institutions, and its internal and external security."[114]

As the 1980 election neared, Reagan attacked Carter more directly, denouncing the president for accepting the "humiliation and disgrace" of the hostage crisis.[115] He said that a regional military presence would have dissuaded Iraq from invading Iran. The United States had to send the military into the Gulf, including ground forces or an effective air defense to protect oil fields, as well as supply fully armed F-15s to the Saudis and substantial aid to Pakistan. "A mood is building for rearmament," according to The Wall Street Journal.[116]

During the only presidential debate of 1980, which took place one week before the election, Reagan turned to the energy issue to hammer home his point that government did not work: "I just happen to believe that free enterprise can do a better job of producing the things that people need than government can. The Department of Energy has a multibillion-dollar budget in excess of $10 billion—it hasn't produced a quart of oil or a lump of coal or anything else in the line of energy."[117] Blaming regulations for the limited production of domestic sources of energy, Reagan said that the federal government also stifled offshore drilling and delayed the creation of nuclear facilities.

The energy issue was useful as a battering ram against the incumbent, with voters preferring Reagan's promise to act tougher abroad and promote greater production at home. In oil-producing states, Reagan won sympathy for his support of oil drilling and eliminating controls. In Texas, an overwhelming majority of voters maintained Carter had not done enough to "encourage American oil companies to produce more oil." The polls showed that more people believed that Reagan could reduce dependence on foreign oil than Carter could. In general, though, just before the election, only 3 percent of voters cited energy as the most important problem facing the nation, down from 31 percent in June 1979. "We're all energied-out," a Portland, Oregon, housewife and Reagan supporter explained. "We've heard about it for such a long time and maybe people are just tuning it out . . . Maybe people had enough with the whole energy thing."[118]

The 1980 election, which took place a week after the debate and on the one-year anniversary of the hostage seizure, gave Reagan a substantial victory over the president. The former California governor won 489 electoral votes to Carter's 49. Top-level GOP advisers started talking about a Reagan revolution. The reality was less clear: Reagan had captured only slightly more of the popular vote, 50.8 percent, than Carter had in 1976 and substantially less than Nixon had in 1972. John Anderson did not win any electoral votes but had stolen some of the support from Carter, who had more of a chance of appealing to independents. Although Republicans retook control of the Senate for the first time since 1954, Democrats retained control of the House. Nevertheless, the election shook the country.

In the House, a number of the Watergate babies lost their seats, including Andrew Maguire, who had been an outspoken critic of Big Oil and a liberal thorn in Carter's side. Along with a handful of these young liberals, many of whom had displaced Republicans to win their seats, the election witnessed the downfall of some New Deal–Great Society liberal stalwarts. Harley Staggers, the West Virginia representative who had served the interest of his coal miner constituents since 1948, lost to a Republican, as did Al Ullman of Oregon. Both had helped broker a deal on Carter's energy package in the House. No one had played as leading a role in Carter's energy agenda as Lud Ashley, Bush's longtime friend, who had represented the working-class interests of his Ohio voters since 1955 but now lost to his Republican contender. In the Senate, Birch Bayh, Frank Church, Gaylord Nelson, and George McGovern, all of whom had shaped and defended liberalism for decades, also lost their seats to Republicans.

The clock was ticking before Reagan and the Republicans would take over. On December 2, Carter signed the Alaska National Interest Lands

Conservation Act, setting aside more than 100 million acres of Alaskan wilderness from any kind of development, including oil drilling. The final act was not as strong as the White House and environmentalists would have liked, but the president decided to support a weaker measure in order to get the bill passed. "We thought we were better off to get it done . . . Waiting for another Democratic president just wasn't worth the candle," explained Representative Morris Udall, chairman of the House Interior Committee and leader of the conservation forces.[119] Congress also passed the Comprehensive Environmental Response, Compensation, and Liability Act of 1980, known as the Superfund Act, which gave the EPA the power to clean up polluted sites that posed environmental hazards.

These last-minute gains did not move Democrats any closer toward a strong political position. The song remained the same. During Carter's four years in office, many of the economic challenges confronting the nation caused enormous problems for a Democratic Party that had been built around boosting consumption. Austerity, energy conservation, inflation, and other new issues of the day created immense friction with key segments of the coalition on which any Democratic president depended, splitting northern liberals from the suburban middle-class and from southern conservatives. Republicans, who at least rhetorically offered a stark alternative that centered on radical deregulation, articulated a response to the nation's energy crisis that helped solidify, rather than divide, their coalition and that propelled their man into the White House.

Carter had hoped a show of force in the Middle East and a high-profile program for alternative energies would chart a course to a more secure energy future and to his political success. Yet Carter came up short. After the election, he signed Presidential Directive 63 to codify a new "Persian Gulf Security Framework." But 1980 ended not with a celebration of this new path toward energy independence. On the stump, Carter's foreign policy did not go far enough to squelch the attacks from the Right, especially as American hostages remained in captivity in Iran, to be released only as Ronald Reagan was being sworn in. And the U.S. Synthetic Fuels Corporation had few enthusiastic backers even as Congress passed it. Democrats held their noses as they moved forward with Carter's initiatives, while Republicans pounced on the administration, using his energy policies as a symbol of his incompetence and allegedly leftward bias. The measures Carter managed to get through, as historic as they were, did little to shore up his base. Thus even when Carter was winning on policy, he lost on politics. By the end of 1980, Carter and the energy program he had supported were running on empty.

8

I Can't Drive Fifty-Five

A WEEK INTO his new presidency, on January 28, 1981, Ronald Reagan signed his first executive order to end price controls. "The 1970s were the Dark Ages of America's energy history . . . Happily, the 80s seem to see [the] emergence," remarked the American Petroleum Institute's Charles DiBona.[1] On the campaign trail, Reagan had talked about many policies, from anti-Communism to tax cuts to welfare, but he tackled energy first. "With a single stroke," commented a Dallas, Texas, journalist, "Ronald Reagan ended the Problem of the Seventies."[2] "The long national nightmare of energy regulation is over," wrote a *Washington Post* reporter in a parody of President Ford's inaugural remarks about Watergate, adding, "In his first major political decision as president, Ronald Reagan has pardoned the oil companies."[3]

Freeing the Market

To a generation that had lived through the twin oil crises of the 1970s and the resulting dramatic expansion of government, the political symbolism was unmistakable. "Deregulation Debut," announced the lead, front-page story of *The Washington Post*.[4] Only 15 percent of domestic crude oil was still selling at controlled prices, and controls were set to expire in October. But Reagan spared no rhetorical flourishes. "For more than 9 years," Reagan declared, "restrictive price controls have held U.S. oil production below its potential . . . [and] have also made us more energy-dependent on the OPEC nations—a development that has jeopardized our economic security and undermined price stability at home." In addition to price controls, Reagan ended the complex system of gasoline allocations. At last, he was ridding the economy of the final vestiges of Nixon-era market interference.

The oil industry reacted to the decontrol decision with the same grandiose claims of a new American-led, free-market era. "The President's action is an expression of confidence in the ability of the competitive enterprise system to solve problems," hailed William Douce, president of Phillips Petroleum Company.[5] Removing price controls was at once a testament to American production and an act of national pride. As *The Wall Street Journal* put it, "It is a myth to say that America is running out of gas. All that is required is sufficient price incentive to search further and deeper."[6] Through this executive action, Reagan gave concrete meaning to his inaugural declaration "Government is not the solution to our problems. Government is the problem."

Reagan's decontrol move set the stage for a fundamental shift in energy policy. The president explained that his action, effective immediately, would remove any uncertainty about whether controls would be lifted permanently once they expired. "The days of control are over," a White House aide explained. "Controls are ruled out now and in the future . . . It is better to have people making money looking for oil than it is to have them making money by lobbying Washington."[7] Reagan also wanted to allow power companies and manufacturers to avoid tough clean air laws, to delay the implementation of more rigorous auto emissions standards, and to stall the adoption of alternative energy sources, except nuclear, which the White House favored.

As co-chairs of his Energy Task Force, the new president tapped David Stockman, the newly appointed budget director, and the Texas oilman Michel Halbouty. Their agenda was simple. "We want more production. More, more, more," explained Halbouty, a petroleum geologist and Houston engineer who had become a loyal Reagan supporter in 1975 after Ford extended the Nixon price controls.[8] "There also should be a fundamental revision of all the environmental laws of the 1970s," said Stockman. "They've got rules that would practically shut down the economy if they were put into effect."[9]

To chip away at the remaining 1970s energy regulations, Reagan, who ran as an outsider, relied on longtime Washington insiders. Murray Weidenbaum, a Nixon economist, suggested a radical approach: a one-year ban on all new regulations, to give what he called a "breather."[10] As seasoned policy makers, they came into office better prepared for bureaucratic and legislative battles, hoping to avoid what *National Review*'s Richard Brookhiser called the "aimlessness of much of Richard Nixon's first term," which they believed resulted from a "paucity of programmatic advice."

To remedy that, the Heritage Foundation prepared a monumental treatise, *Mandate for Leadership*, which Brookhiser called an "Owner's Manual for the Federal Government . . . To be sure, a manual for conservative owners." Milton Copulos, who authored the energy section, did not mince words: "The Department of Energy should be abolished." The Interior Department report, written largely by James Watt, who would soon become this agency's secretary, was no less striking with its "aggressive" approach to mining, leasing, and drilling.[11] These ambitious blueprints circulated around Washington before Reagan swore the presidential oath.

Within the White House, Reagan created the Task Force on Regulatory Relief, chaired by Vice President Bush, "to cut away the thicket of irrational and senseless regulations." C. Boyden Gray, the chief counsel of the task force, told a U.S. Chamber of Commerce audience, "If you go to the [regulatory] agency first, don't be too pessimistic if they can't solve your problem there. If they don't, that's what the Task Force is for."[12] As his chief of staff, Reagan appointed James Baker, who had run Bush's primary campaign, because, as Baker put it, "Reagan would need someone who knew the ropes in Washington."[13]

Liberals in Congress were not happy with Reagan's reliance on decontrol and deregulation to guarantee American access to affordable energy. Given the ongoing Iran-Iraq War in the Middle East, the possibility for a major supply interruption remained, which would lead to a price spurt. Senator Ted Kennedy, with help from consumer groups, prepared a report, "Oil Price Decontrol and the Poor: A Social Policy Failure."[14] Even as gas lines and soaring prices from the summer of 1979 left Americans feeling hopeless about the government's ability to check the power of Big Oil, the public had not developed any newfound confidence in the oil industry to manage the supply situation any better. Joel Jacobson, the New Jersey commissioner of energy and longtime consumer advocate, refuted the logic offered up by the Reagan White House: "The gasoline shortage of 1979 was not caused by Government interference with the free market. It was caused by an acquisitive industry manipulating the market to serve a voracious appetite."[15]

On the Hill, liberals retained a strong presence, even with their numbers diminished. If gasoline prices surged, the pressure would grow in Congress, particularly in the Democratic-controlled House, still dominated by northeastern liberals, to renew the authority for controls and extend them beyond their October expiration date. Scoop Jackson was no longer the chair of the Senate Energy Committee, but along with members from energy-consuming states he fought for the maintenance of controls. Representative Toby Moffett, joined by Senator Howard Metzenbaum and the Consumer Federation of America, filed a suit in federal district court to overturn Reagan's executive decontrol action. "I intend to take whatever steps are available in the Senate to see that this tragedy does not befall the American people," declared Metzenbaum.[16]

But President Reagan was firmly in the saddle. On February 5, before a national audience, in a prime-time Oval Office speech, the new president announced his plans for a historic 30 percent tax cut and massive budget trimming. The need to act was urgent, said Reagan. "We are threatened with an economic calamity of tremendous proportions and the old business-as-usual treatment can't save us . . . We forgot or just overlooked the fact that government—any government—has a built-in tendency to grow." In contrast to Franklin Roosevelt's federal relief, public works, and jobs program, Reagan put forth his market-oriented blueprint for a new era of growth; his budget cuts would stop inflation, while, according to his supply-side view, his tax cuts promised jobs and more money in people's pockets.

When Reagan delivered his detailed budget proposal to Congress, the implications for energy policy were clear. David Stockman was riding herd as he sought to squeeze as much spending out of the budget as possible. Conservation was out, production was in, and nuclear power alone received hefty government backing. The president proposed steep reductions in the DOE and the Federal Energy Regulatory Commission (which had replaced the Federal Power Commission under Carter). He also eliminated funds for emergency gasoline rationing. When questioned, the new energy secretary, James Edwards, explained, "I really think that the marketplace and the industry itself are better qualified to distribute these products than any agency that we could set up."[17] The White House was turning the clock back to before the Arab embargo. On March 4, a federal district court denied the liberals' request for an injunction blocking Reagan's executive decontrol order.

As Stockman wielded his ax to knock down programs, the White House put in place the proper personnel to fight bureaucratic battles from the inside, turning to a team of energy conservatives. James Edwards, the former governor of South Carolina and new energy secretary, promised to "work myself out of a job." A dentist and committed Republican whose southern constituents had thrown crucial support behind Reagan, he had no experience in the energy field, except as a proponent of a nuclear-reprocessing facility in his home state.[18]

Reagan looked to James Watt as his choice for secretary of the interior. An ideological darling of the New Right who embodied the antigovernment sentiment of the sagebrush rebels, Watt was in fact a Washington insider who, at age forty-two, had spent his professional career pushing for deregulation as a legislative aide and a lobbyist on Capitol Hill and as a member of the Nixon and Ford administrations. In 1976, he founded the Mountain States Legal Foundation, defending business interests against federal public landholdings. At his public appointment, which *The Washington Post* described as more like an "uncoiling," Watt denounced "environmental extremists [who] . . . would deny economic development" and would fight to "lock up from utilization our resources."[19] As interior undersecretary, Reagan appointed Donald Hodel, who had known Watt since the early 1970s. Like Watt, Hodel attacked environmentalists as "prophets of shortage" who were nothing more than "anti-producers, anti-achievers . . . dedicated to bringing our society to a halt."[20]

Perhaps no one signaled the new direction of energy policy better than Anne Gorsuch of Colorado, Reagan's selection for the EPA, who was known for wearing fur coats, smoking two packs of cigarettes a day, and driving a car that got bad gas mileage.[21] If the environmental revolution had changed America, she had missed the boat. Both Watt and Gorsuch set out to dismantle the regulations of the previous decade. As Watt put it, he would change "several hundred" regulations so completely that no one "would ever change them back because he won't have the determination that I do."[22] After a short time in office, Gorsuch bragged that she cut the book of clean water regulations from six inches down to half an inch. She made it clear what rules her staff should and should not enforce. As one EPA official explained, "The entire organization is suffering from a paralysis from the top down."[23] These deregulators were in position to stop what *The Wall Street Journal* called "the suffocating creep of the bureaucracy over business."[24]

Inside the White House, Reagan appointed Danny Boggs as his special assistant for energy matters. After having worked for Robert Bork in the solicitor general's office, Boggs served on the Federal Power Commission under Watt. During the Carter years, he honed his legislative skills as minority counsel to the Senate Committee on Energy. Boggs came to the White House with a vast and detailed knowledge of energy laws, along with a passion for deregulation. Few knew the regulatory apparatus from within the halls of power better. The job of these energy conservatives was not easy, but they knew where to look to thwart government regulation. Even if they could not achieve legislative rollback, with Democrats still in control of the House, they could make progress by slashing budgets, defunding agencies, and impeding bureaucratic enforcement.

On August 13, 1981, after a herculean effort by Stockman, James Baker, and their allies, Reagan signed his historic budget and tax acts, which took a sledgehammer to federal spending and slashed income taxes. This was, by some estimates, the greatest single departure in public policy since Franklin Roosevelt's New Deal, resulting in $35 billion cuts in spending and a lowering of tax rates by 25 percent. Given that nearly half of federal spending went toward Social Security and other entitlements, which, along with servicing the national debt, Reagan had declared untouchable, and another quarter went toward defense, which Reagan also said was off-limits, that meant that the cuts, by and large, had to come from the regular operations of the government and grants-in-aid to the states. EPA's pollution control budget dropped 46 percent, for example, and its staff declined by 40 percent. The amount allocated for research was cut in half.[25] The hope was that with less revenue to fund federal functions, from social services to environmental regulations to industry oversight, the era of government expansion would stall.

Days before he signed these bills, Reagan fired striking federal air traffic controllers, which signaled just as radical a departure from the New Deal and accelerated the steady weakening of union power that had been taking place for more than a decade. The era of political bargaining, where the nation's political leaders served as a balancing wheel in the marketplace, was done. In 1980, the percentage of workers in unions—one-quarter of the workforce compared with the peak of one-third in the 1950s—started on an irreversible downward trend from which it would never recover. The political retreat from the support of organized labor was part of a worldwide movement in this moment of global stagnation and economic upheaval. Whereas the economic crisis of the 1930s had resulted in an era of bigger government, greater regulation, and stronger labor protections, the 1970s had generated an international thirst for freer markets.

But even as the White House and its allies championed this rightward turn, lawmakers on Capitol Hill in both parties were reluctant to shed all New Deal regulations. In the wake of these August victories, when Reagan pushed for the immediate decontrol of natural gas, not due to expire until 1985, he encountered enormous pushback. The AFL-CIO and the Citizen Labor Energy Coalition led a national campaign against natural gas decontrol, going door-to-door and holding mass meetings in scores of congressional districts. Energy Action explained that a family earning $20,000 would pay more in higher gas bills than they would save through the Reagan tax cuts.[26] Millions of Americans would have to choose "between eating or freezing," warned a United Steelworkers spokesman.[27] Representative John Dingell, who still chaired the House Committee on Energy and Commerce, said that natural gas decontrol would happen only "over my dead body."[28] Fearing failure and political reprisals, the Republican senator James McClure said that the Senate Energy Committee would not take up a natural gas measure anytime soon. "A lot of Democrats are licking their chops, hoping we will introduce the bill because they want to run against it," said an Energy Department staff member.[29]

The Washington veterans of the twin oil shocks found it hard to purge the belief that government would have to "do something" if confronted with a future energy crisis. On September 30, the day that legislative authority for oil price controls lapsed, the Republican-controlled Senate Energy

Committee approved a standby petroleum allocation bill by a margin of 13–4. If and when the country faced another serious energy crisis, politicians on Capitol Hill wanted the White House to have the authority to act. If there was another scramble for fuel, no one wanted his constituents to miss out. On October 29, the Senate approved the measure by a wide margin, 85–7. A similar bill for renewed standby controls passed the House on December 14, though with a smaller margin, 244–136.[30]

The White House opposed this power, and the proposal stalled in conference committee. "There is no way the government can allocate resources to every little farmer in America," Secretary Edwards told reporters.[31] Danny Boggs cautioned the presidential adviser Martin Anderson that they needed to "get Congress to diminish its lust for legislation."[32] On December 17, Reagan made a big play and announced his official recommendation to do away with the Department of Energy. He proclaimed, "The government will no longer try to manage every aspect of energy supply and consumption." Boggs explained that the department "represents a fundamentally misguided view of the government's role in the energy matters . . . we should act to make it clear that the government will now no longer be exercising that type of control."[33] But even as the White House was pushing its decontrol agenda, politicians on Capitol Hill were less willing to take a risk. In March 1982, Congress overwhelmingly passed the standby measures that came out of conference and also threw support behind an increase in funds for low-income energy assistance and weatherization, which the Stockman budget had scrapped.

Congressional Republicans lobbied Reagan hard to sign the standby price control bill. Republican leaders argued that the measure, as written, provided enough discretionary authority for Reagan to use the emergency powers in a way that he saw fit, including not using them at all. They believed it was better than what they could get in a crisis. James Watt explained to the president that many Republicans and even some cabinet members worried that "political pressure at the time of a crisis could be almost irresistible, and may result in passage of a more disruptive and inefficient law."[34] Big oil companies favored the bill for the same reason, maintaining that the statute gave them some predictability about what would happen in the event of another energy shortage. The majority leader, Howard Baker, along with Robert Dole and James McClure, personally pleaded with Reagan to sign the bill.

As they left the Oval Office, waiting in the hallway were Trent Lott, Tom Corcoran, and James Broyhill, the lone voices of opposition. Dole said to Broyhill, "You boys can go home. We've already had the signing ceremony." Undaunted, this group of conservatives appealed to Reagan on ideological grounds. Corcoran "urged the President to veto this attempt to put the Federal Government back in the business of regulating petroleum." The bill, he warned, will put citizens "back at the mercy of bureaucrats and K Street lawyers. The American public . . . deserve[s] better than to suffer again from the same mistakes made by past administrations."[35]

As the ranking Republican member on the House Energy and Commerce Committee, Broyhill commanded respect, and he had proven himself a loyal foot soldier. A deeply committed conservative Republican from North Carolina who had first won office in 1962, Broyhill saw Reagan's presidency as a chance to shift public policy. He explained, "I find myself on the side of trying to restrain government spending, of trying to make sense out of the government regulations to ensure that we leave adequate funds in the hands of working people and make programs in such a way so that the states can operate them."[36] In the president, he found a sympathetic ear.

On March 20, Reagan vetoed the bill. "This legislation grew from an assumption, which has been demonstrated to be invalid, that giving the Federal Government the power to allocate and set prices will result in an equitable and orderly response to a supply interruption," said the president. Reagan assured the country that he had adequate authority to protect national security. "What I do not have, do not want and do not need is general power to reimpose on all Americans another web of price controls and mandatory allocations." There is no "magic federal plan," explained Reagan. The supply interruptions of 1973–74 and 1979 led to higher oil prices, said Reagan, "but they did not cause gas lines and shortages. It took government to do that."

In reporting on the veto, an NBC Nightly News reporter summed up the decision: "The President said the marketplace, not federal controls, is the way to deal with shortage."[37] "With his veto of a bill giving the White House standby power to allocate oil supplies in a crisis, President Reagan has made it plain that dogma is the man's best friend," quipped the Los Angeles Times.[38]

Reagan won. Twenty-four Republicans and three Democrats changed their votes to sustain the president's veto. The triumphant president thanked the Senate for what he characterized as "an expression of confidence that our marketplace and the good sense of the American people provide our best lines of defense against any future interruptions." This represented a historic departure, said Reagan. "America has recently embarked upon a new path in energy—a path that is leading us toward greater production, expanded storage and reduced reliance upon foreign energy sources." In short, this vote promised "greater energy independence."

On the heels of this victory, Reagan introduced his bill to dismantle the DOE. "Through constant overregulation of energy producers and industries in the past, the Department of Energy shackled our drive to increase domestic production," said the president. Joseph Wright, the OMB's deputy director, explained that the goal was to eliminate "a compulsion for Government to 'do something' to solve every problem, a compulsion that did not benefit the nation or its consumers."[39] Reiterating this philosophy, Danny Boggs told the cabinet, " 'Running out' of energy is not the problem . . . This nation and the world have ample resources, if used properly under a free market regime, to avoid the dire predictions of energy starvation."[40] Overall, Boggs instructed, "We have taken the view that energy security is best derived from stockpiling of oil, and from market competition."[41]

In August 1982, Reagan signed the Energy Emergency Preparedness Act, a substantially rewritten and watered-down bill that signaled Reagan's success in freeing the market. Stripped of allocation and price control authorities, this measure instead emphasized the need to fill the Strategic Petroleum Reserve at a faster rate. According to the president's advisers, the SPR would provide all the insurance the nation required against any future supply interruptions. "Restoring America's energy security has been a top priority since I assumed office," Reagan began. "As a result of the policies of this Administration, the vulnerability of the United States and our allies to possible shocks from supply interruptions is significantly lessened." He announced the authorization of $6 billion for the SPR. "In view of this very positive energy supply situation, there is no compelling need now for the Administration to consider energy a top-priority issue," Danny Boggs noted.[42]

Reagan got rid of controls at the right time. The American economy had entered a serious recession, which reduced demand for energy and

softened the supply situation. Paul Volcker's monetary disinflation policies at the Federal Reserve triggered a spike in unemployment. With the
economy undergoing a sharp contraction, energy demands fell substantially, leading to a buildup of inventories and easing the pressure on prices.
That, in turn, took the heat off Congress. "The Administration has been
frightfully lucky," said James Schlesinger.[43]

Even as the recession spelled political trouble for Reagan, the White
House pointed to declining oil prices as one piece of good economic news
that the GOP could highlight, capitalizing on transformed market conditions by explaining that they were a result of deliberate policy. The White
House, according to Danny Boggs, should claim credit for the president's
"controversial and courageous decision" for decontrol. By his action, the
president had "freed American producers and consumers from a confin-
ing web of regulations." Where Carter's attempts at "pious exhortations"
had failed, Reagan had succeeded. "The inherent power of the free market
worked almost exactly as predicted, and it has been a major reason we can
look forward to lower inflation and better economic performance," proclaimed Boggs. "We replaced a known clunker of a regulatory system for a
venture with a system of freedom that had not been tried."[44]

Charles DiBona, who had reluctantly crafted energy controls for
Nixon, championed their demise: "If you look at the whole sweep of this
thing, you've got to conclude it's a tremendous achievement. It's dramatic
evidence of the way the marketplace can solve these problems without
governmental intervention."[45] "The energy crisis, like its fellow 'crises,' was
not a genuine problem at all, but a product of Carter's—and liberalism's—
blunders and conceptual deficiencies," asserted *National Review*.[46]

The triumph over this sense of crisis derived, too, from Reagan's stepped-
up commitment to militarize the Gulf. The White House made clear its
plan to deregulate markets at home and protect them abroad. Douglas
Feith, Reagan's new Middle East expert on energy security, explained in
the pages of the Heritage Foundation magazine, "There is no need for U.S.
policymakers to fear the oil weapon." Feith, who was the son of a Holo-
caust survivor and had worked for Richard Perle and Admiral Elmo
Zumwalt, counseled Reagan to take a tough line. It was in the Saudis' and
other OPEC producers' interest to sell oil to the United States and its allies.
"If a regime is really capable of self-destructive fits of oil weaponeering,
Americans must either live without it or act against it," counseled Feith.[47]

Fundamentally, as Feith told Richard Allen, his boss at the National Security Council, the United States should not overestimate OPEC's power. "From the point of view of U.S. foreign policy," said Feith, "it is critical to recognize that oil is a commodity essentially similar to cocoa, tin, and pigs' bellies. It is subject to the laws of supply and demand, as are all commodities in trade, and one need not ingratiate oneself to any oil regime in order to buy oil."[48]

The concern for Feith was less OPEC's power than the threat of Soviet influence in the Persian Gulf. The United States had to establish a solid base of power in the region so as to prevent the Soviets from becoming what Dennis Ross, in the State Department's Policy Planning Staff, termed "an arbiter of oil flows."[49] Rather than putting out brush fires or engaging in what one neoconservative strategist called half wars and half policies, the Reagan team wanted to establish a credible strategy of deterrence, putting in place sufficient disincentives for the Soviets to interfere.[50] On *Face the Nation*, Reagan's new defense secretary, Caspar Weinberger, made it clear he would go all out for a major buildup.[51]

Reagan's foreign policy team wanted to solidify a "strategic consensus," a policy whereby the United States formed an alliance with moderate Arab countries against the Soviet Union and Islamic fundamentalists.[52] In the fall of 1981, Reagan had pushed through a sale of American military planes with an Airborne Warning and Control System to the Saudis. The assassination of Anwar Sadat that fall served as a startling reminder of the rise of Islamic fundamentalism as a real threat to ruling families. The Saudi elite knew they could pay a price for an alliance with Americans, and yet they also required protection from Americans to stay in power. To retain their position and to defend their oil production and distribution, they relied on Western technology and arms. For the president, the arms sale signaled an important step in shoring up the Saudis' commitment to repelling Soviet advances in Southwest Asia.

The sale marked the beginning of what the *Washington Post* reporter Scott Armstrong characterized as a "new theater of war."[53] Neoconservatives believed that the United States should have retained ownership of these weapons. But the president reassured those who feared that the weapons could wind up in enemy hands in the event of the collapse of the Saudi regime. "I have to say that, Saudi Arabia, we will not permit to be an Iran," Reagan said. "There is no way—as long as Saudi Arabia and the

OPEC nations . . . provide the bulk of the energy that is needed to turn the wheels of industry in the Western world—there's no way that we could stand by and see that taken over by anyone that would shut off that oil." The United States was there for good.

Going Global

In early 1983, OPEC's oil ministers lowered the price of oil to $29 a barrel, the first price cut in its history. As the recession worsened, it became clear that OPEC had overplayed its hand. The price hikes of the preceding decade, along with public policy, triggered the adoption of conservation practices by industry and by individual consumers, which led to a 25 percent gain in energy efficiency. The price spurt had also spurred the discovery of new oil in Mexico, Canada, Venezuela, and the North Sea. To gain market share, these non-OPEC producers cut prices. At first, OPEC ministers resisted, but as the glut grew worse, they too slashed their prices.[54]

The creation of the futures market for oil hastened OPEC's loss of control over the pricing of this international commodity. On March 30, 1983, the New York Mercantile Exchange (NYMEX) and the Chicago Board of Trade began offering sales of crude oil futures. A futures contract gave the buyer the right to purchase oil at a specified time at a guaranteed price. Given the price volatility of the 1970s, these contracts allowed buyers and sellers to hedge their risk—but at a cost. In exchange for providing liquidity, traders became "paper refiners," deciding the future price of a barrel of oil.

This financial innovation undercut OPEC's power. NYMEX floor traders in the World Trade Center replaced OPEC as the price setters. Whereas once the major oil companies and, most recently, OPEC had established the price for this commodity, now traders in front of computer screens set prices in the open market. The introduction of futures contracts, along with the switch from long-term contracts to spot sales, which now accounted for more than 50 percent of transactions, allowed for greater fluctuations in price.[55] The major oil companies, which had once made their money through the discovery and drilling of oil, also became investors who earned income speculating on the future price of global oil.

None of this was good for the oil patch. As prices slipped, the prospects for domestic production dimmed, and very quickly drills shut down, oil prospecting slowed, and Texas underwent a contraction greater than the rest of the economy. In Midland, the heart of the Permian Basin, where the young George Bush had gone to seek his fortune in 1948, the turnaround came quickly. In 1981, this energy-rich area ranked fifth in the nation for per capita income, with the Permian Basin responsible for 20 percent of all national crude production. But as prices tumbled, production dried up. In October 1983, the First National Bank of Midland, which had handed out easy loans all through the boom, collapsed, ranking as one of the largest American bank failures in history. As one reporter put it, "What had been a gravy train for drillers had in a short time become a nightmare."[56]

A reenergized environmental movement made matters even worse for the domestic energy industry. In the 1982 midterms, Republicans suffered as a result of the recession, and the House Democrats strengthened their numbers. That encouraged a pushback against Reagan's EPA budget cuts and an attack on his policy of regulatory nonenforcement. James Watt, Anne Gorsuch, and James Edwards all left the administration. In June 1983, Representative Henry Waxman introduced legislation to regulate acid rain production, an issue that was gaining traction.

With domestic energy producers suffering, they appealed to their friends in the White House for relief. As they had done with Eisenhower, they wanted protection against imports as world prices were slipping. But this time no help was forthcoming. Danny Boggs spoke out strongly against any kind of protectionist policy for the industry, seeing it as a complete contradiction of Reagan's free-market agenda. "Our general energy philosophy has been that the federal government cannot set a more suitable price than the market," Boggs told Edwin Harper, the OMB deputy director.[57] Any assistance, Boggs concluded, "would be an extremely bad idea, not only in practical effect, but because it is completely antithetical to the President's energy philosophy."[58]

Rather than coming to the defense of domestic producers, as had every administration in the twentieth century, the Reagan White House was willing to accept the greater globalization of the country's energy supply. Reagan was less interested in curbing the nation's appetite for black gold and more determined to protect U.S. access at home and abroad to the needed supplies, placing his faith in the market and, if necessary, in the strength of the American military to provide a stabilizing force in the Persian Gulf. The day after the Midland Bank failure, Reagan underscored the United States' commitment to the free flow of oil abroad. "I do not believe the free world could stand by and allow anyone to close the Straits of Hormuz and the Persian Gulf to the oil traffic through those waterways," the president announced in response to a recent escalation of the Iran-Iraq War.

In January 1983, the White House launched the Central Command for Southwest Asia. This command, with 300,000 troops, replaced the Rapid Deployment Joint Task Force and signaled a firm commitment by the United States to deploy force in the Persian Gulf if necessary. To keep the Western and Japanese economies churning required steady supplies of fuel. If that meant securing them from this hostile area, with guns and soldiers, then the United States was getting ready.

The immediate concern was the Iran-Iraq War. Ongoing hostilities brought instability and uncertainty. On the one hand, foreign policy makers were hoping that the war would be fought to a stalemate. If either side won, that created the possibility of an imbalance of power and the emergence of a single country capable of dominating the region. When the war had begun, Henry Kissinger reportedly said, "The only regrettable thing is that both cannot lose."[59] On the other hand, with neither side able to bring about victory, the prospect of terrorist acts, especially on oil, became more likely. Repeatedly, the Iranian government threatened to shut the Strait of Hormuz. In response, Iraq warned that it was prepared to bomb Iran's oil installations. Both sides engaged in the Tanker War, firing missiles on ships that were carrying war matériel and oil exports through the Persian Gulf.

To maintain a balance of power in the region, implementing Kissinger's vision, the United States supplied arms to both sides in the conflict. In practice, that meant the United States had to help Iraq avoid defeat while maintaining neutrality. When Iran appeared to be gaining momentum, Reagan sent Donald Rumsfeld, whom he appointed special envoy to the Middle East, to go speak with Saddam Hussein to try to stabilize the situation. Charles Hill, an aide to Secretary of State George Shultz, explained to the White House, "U.S. diplomatic strategy toward the Iran-Iraq war is designed to deter escalation that could threaten U.S. interests in unimpeded access to Gulf oil and the security of Gulf oil producer states, to deal with a crisis that closes or threatens, imminently, to close the Gulf or cut off access to oil supplies, and to bring the war to an end, eventually."[60] In the short term, the United States had to discourage attacks on shipping and in the long term prevent the "Soviet exploitation of the current unstable environment in the region."[61]

As the Iran-Iraq War escalated in 1984, the United States appealed to its allies to develop reserves and commit to quick usage of them in the event of an attack on shipping and possibly the closing of the strait. "I needn't tell you the disastrous impact such actions might have on the world energy situation, the world economy, the international financial system, and the stability of key oil-producing states in the region," Reagan cabled to the British prime minister, Margaret Thatcher.[62] In the event of a full-blown crisis, the White House planned for an early drawdown of the SPR.[63]

By now, Reagan was presiding over a strong economic recovery. This return to prosperity was fueled in part by the collapse of oil prices, which freed money for greater investment and consumption in other goods. As Reagan geared up for his reelection campaign, he could claim it was "Morning in America." Even as blue-collar workers were not regaining their position as quickly as those at the top, and many families maintained their standing only with married women entering the workforce, Reagan championed what he hailed as a dramatic rebound. Gone was the age of limits; here was endless possibility.

In September 1984, just before the presidential election, the rock star Sammy Hagar released his song "I Can't Drive 55." The song rose in the charts as millions of Americans turned up the music to celebrate the fact that America's energy quagmire finally seemed to be over; driving slow and conserving energy were things of the past. "Go on and write me up for 125. Post my face wanted dead or alive. Take my license and all that jive," shouted Hagar. "I can't drive 55." Four years after Reagan had defeated Jimmy Carter, railing against his economic and foreign policies, the president claimed victory over the energy crisis, economic stagnation, and international impotence and ran a strong campaign for reelection. The fifty-five-mile-per-hour speed limit, which Reagan promised to abolish, seemed a relic of an earlier era when past presidents had stood idly by amid the country's decline.

In his reelection bid, the GOP leader was pleased to face a Democratic

Party deeply divided and incapable of offering an effective response to Reagan's boast of economic recovery. Democrats did not have a candidate who could match Reagan. Scoop Jackson, who for decades had combined a tough foreign policy with domestic liberalism, had passed away in 1983. The former Minnesota senator Walter Mondale carried on the liberal torch, but he did not have the kind of record that could insulate him from charges that he was weak on defense. The Colorado senator Gary Hart, who was more of a hawk, failed to excite traditional New Deal constituencies who were leery about where he stood on domestic issues. When Hart, who promised to inject "new ideas" into the Democratic Party, faced off against Mondale in a primary debate, the Minnesotan turned to his rival and, echoing a popular Wendy's advertisement attacking its competitors, asked, "Where's the beef?" Mondale secured the nomination, but with the economy booming, he trailed behind Reagan in the polls.

In November, Reagan won a resounding victory over Mondale. The president collected more electoral votes than in any other election, with Mondale winning only his home state of Minnesota. After his lopsided landslide, Reagan claimed that the nation had voted in favor of his free-market approach to domestic problems, building on his campaign arguments that his policies had brought recovery. As the economy continued to gain steam, conservatives became even more strident in their celebration of the market.

Nothing seemed to demonstrate the success of Reagan's policies more than the dramatic collapse of energy prices. The Californian had come into office promising the beginning of a new era of abundance. The way to get there was less government. Instead of regulations and restrictions, the unfettered market would provide the energy Americans wanted and needed, even if that meant a greater reliance on foreign oil, and the U.S. military, to guarantee that supply. In the mid-1980s, OPEC was struggling to maintain its international standing. As a percentage of world production, OPEC's share had fallen from more than half to under one-third as non-OPEC producers offered oil at cheaper prices.[64]

In 1985, the Saudis formally accepted what had become the new reality. Instead of an official OPEC price, the government went its own way, linking prices to the spot market and offering "netback deals," which guaranteed profit margins to those who would purchase their oil. To raise revenue and reverse its declining market share, Saudi Arabia flooded the market at reduced prices. In the winter of 1986, prices completely collapsed in a downward spiral from $24 to $12 a barrel. Adjusted for inflation, prices dropped to almost pre-embargo levels.

The precipitous fall threatened to devastate the domestic oil producers. Walter Levy warned about the dangers of such a sharp decline. Even as he had feared the power of OPEC just a few years earlier, Levy was concerned that the price collapse would wipe out high-priced American production and render the country more vulnerable. "Oil," he wrote, "is not just another commodity whose availability over time can be assured by the play of free market forces."[65] "We are sowing today the seeds of our next energy crisis," warned James Schlesinger.[66] They feared that Texas producers would not recover, resulting in an ever greater reliance on imported oil.

At this moment, Vice President Bush flew to the Middle East to meet with the Saudi king, hoping to get an agreement to stabilize prices. As Bush was starting to think about the 1988 election, he understood the visit would play well among domestic oil producers who were suffering in his home state of Texas. This former driller knew the industry from the inside out and also from his son George W. Bush, who had launched his own wildcatting business in West Texas with little success. Since his support of oil import quotas in the Eisenhower years, the vice president maintained that the destruction of the domestic oil industry imperiled national security. Before leaving on the trip, Bush warned, "I think it is essential that we talk about stability and that we not just have a continued free fall like a parachutist jumping out without a parachute."[67]

The White House backed away from this overtly protectionist position, concerned that Bush's statement sounded too much like a call for government rescue. "We believe the way to achieve stability is to let the free market work," said the deputy press secretary, Larry Speakes.[68] Reagan made it clear that his administration would not interfere with these market dynamics. George Shultz said, "Oil is a very important commodity but I'm a believer in the market so I'll stay with that." He also said, "We aren't unsympathetic to the oil patch but we still think we can't correct the price fall by government intervention . . . We think market forces should settle this."[69] The economist Philip Verleger, a student of the renowned oil expert Morris Adelman, put it more bluntly: "The notion of crawling on hands and knees to ask the Saudis to cut their production is unspeakable, awful and stupid."[70]

The White House hailed the price collapse as "one of the most benefi-cial things that's happened to mankind in 13 years."[71] Falling prices brought lower inflation and interest rates, and they contributed to rapid growth, increased consumer purchases, and the rejuvenation of the auto industry. They also improved the international economic standing of the United States by reducing the balance-of-payments deficit. Moreover, Rea-gan's foreign policy team believed that declining prices would cause damage to the Soviets as their foreign currency reserves disappeared. The energy crisis, which had started thirteen years earlier with the Arab em-bargo, appeared over.

With oil flowing, the White House furthered its retreat from govern-ment interference. In April 1986, the U.S. Synthetic Fuel Corporation shuttered its doors. Four months later, the White House ordered the re-moval of the solar panels Carter had installed. *The Wall Street Journal* edi-tors suggested they be placed in the Smithsonian museum "as a reminder to Americans that any number of futile methods of solving the 'energy crisis' were attempted before the right one, price decontrol, was finally adopted."[72] These decisions symbolized an end to the Carter-era search for alternative energy. The nuclear disaster at the Chernobyl plant in the So-viet Union, which occurred in 1986, closed off discussions about nuclear power.

In 1987, Congress voted to allow states to set higher speed limits, end-ing the fifty-five-mile-per-hour speed limit and fulfilling one of Reagan's long-standing campaign promises. Nobody had to drive fifty-five any-more. The automobile industry started to introduce oil-guzzling minivans and sport utility vehicles, which were not covered by existing CAFE stan-dards. With prices at the pump so low, the energy-intensive economy was going ahead at full speed.

The energy market appeared to vindicate Reagan's entire approach to governance. The Reagan recovery, made possible in part by low oil prices, gave conservatives an opportunity to crow about the success of their free-market ideas. William Simon, the former energy czar, was living proof. When he left the Ford administration, Simon was "broke." Having placed his investments in a blind trust before entering government, he found that their value had significantly eroded. But in the 1980s, Simon, along with his old White House assistant Gerald Parsky, ventured into the new world of leveraged buyouts, profiting from the deregulation of financial markets under Reagan. Alongside his lucrative business, Simon, who served as president of the conservative Olin Foundation, pushed for privatization of government programs, ranging from Social Security and public schools to the TVA and the United States Postal Service.[73]

Confidence in the market remained even after the stock market collapse on October 19, 1987. Black Monday, as it was called, was the single largest one-day decline in the history of the Dow Jones. Yet the White House issued a statement, assuring the country and the world that the "underlying economy remains sound." Even as budget deficits grew to unprecedented levels, business hummed along.

Thanks to the deregulation of the financial markets, the high rates of interest, and floating currencies, foreign capital rushed in to American capital markets. Whereas William Simon and Alan Greenspan had argued in the 1970s that the growing federal deficit would lead to crowding out in the financial markets, the emergence of a global capital market meant that foreign capital would underwrite the deficit, which had tripled since Reagan had entered office. No longer did it seem that the nation's politicians had to choose between balancing a budget and financial solvency. With the help of an enormous infusion of Japanese investment in U.S. Treasury securities, the government could pay its bills.[74] Simon himself was at the vanguard of forging ties to Japan, where investors helped to finance the soaring American deficit. Alan Greenspan, too, did his part to sustain an era of low inflation as the new chairman of the Federal Reserve. James Baker, as Treasury secretary, worked to establish and insulate the strength of the dollar, even as Third World countries suffered under debt accumulated in the 1970s to pay for their oil imports.

At the end of the Reagan presidency, a different vision of the market, and of energy in particular, had taken hold, replacing the one that shaped America in the late 1970s. Policy makers believed in the power of global markets to produce the oil that the nation needed. They paid tribute to the free market, which, even as it meant the decimation of the domestic industry, supplied low-cost energy. Added to this import bill was a commitment by the U.S. military power to keep the oil markets open.

The so-called free flow of oil came with its own price. Several days prior to the 1987 stock market crash, Iran had launched an attack on two American-owned supertankers. These were in fact Kuwaiti tankers that had been reflagged as American for the purpose of the U.S. Navy providing military escort through the war-torn Gulf. American policy makers had hoped that this show of force would not only dissuade Soviet involvement but also intimidate Iran, a calculation that proved false. On Black Monday, the United States retaliated with an attack on Iranian oil installations. At a White House press conference the next day, reporters peppered the president with as many questions about the Persian Gulf as about the stock market. When one reporter asked Reagan how long the United States would remain in the region, he responded, "As long as it is necessary."

Reagan complemented the fleet of warships in the Gulf with a strong investment in the Strategic Petroleum Reserve, which the Department of Energy characterized as "America's Energy Insurance." By this time, the SPR had enough supply in the event of a total cutoff from OPEC for a hundred days, or for more than a year in the event of an Arab OPEC embargo. The SPR and the DOE's plans for its use "serve as powerful deterrents to the possibility that the free flow of crude oil could be used again as a political weapon against the United States."[75]

Vice President George Bush understood that the future of American energy policy rested on the free flow of oil abroad and unfettered markets at home. As this Texas oilman prepared for the 1988 election, he could run on Reagan's economic record. Many conservative social policies remained controversial, even among Republican voters. The New Right promoted a constitutional ban on abortion, prayer in school, education vouchers, and the privatization of Social Security, but according to internal polls for Bush these policies had, at best, mixed appeal among many middle- and working-class voters, the so-called Reagan Democrats, who were still essential to a victory in a presidential race. The claim to deliver prosperity through free markets, however, was a winning issue. Lower taxes, reduced domestic spending, and deregulation were at the core of Republican politics. Traditional economic issues, said Bush's pollsters, have "a strong appeal to the Republican grassroots and the general electorate—as Ronald Reagan proved in 1980 and 1984." The key to the 1988 election, Bush's advisers concluded, was to run against "Jimmy Carter's 'malaise.'"[76]

To assume the Republican mantle, Bush received assistance from James Baker, who stepped down from the Treasury Department to run the campaign of his longtime friend and political ally. Robert Mosbacher, one of the nation's richest independent oilmen and another old friend from Houston, served as finance chair. All three made their wealth off the Texas oil fields where they worked together planting the seeds of the GOP. In 1970, both grieving from the loss of their wives to cancer, Baker and Mosbacher threw their energies into Bush's failed Senate campaign against Lloyd Bentsen. They had supported Bush in every race since. Even as these Texans headed the GOP effort to install Bush as the next president, they understood that American energy policy lay with global markets and American military strength. In his acceptance speech at the GOP convention, Bush said, "There are millions of young Americans in their twenties who barely remember the days of gas lines and the unemployment lines." The message was clear: the energy crisis was over, and the future was bright.

As Bush promoted the new direction he and Reagan had taken America, Michael Dukakis, the Massachusetts governor and Democratic candidate, tapped Senator Bentsen as his running mate. Bentsen was a conservative Texas Democrat who supported Reaganomics, the MX missile, aid to the contras, school prayer, and opposition to federally funded abortions. "The days of litmus test liberalism are finished," reported David Broder. More significant, though, than his conservative credentials were the twenty-nine electoral votes in Texas that this popular senator could bring.[77]

The selection of Bentsen harked back to 1960, when John F. Kennedy had selected Lyndon Johnson to balance the ticket. The specific appeal of Bentsen was not so much a southern strategy as a western one, or as one pollster put it, a petro strategy.[78] The collapse in oil prices hit Texas hard, where unemployment had reached levels not seen since the Great Depression and, at 10 percent, still hovered at nearly double the national average. "What makes it especially worse for George Bush is that he was an oilman and he hasn't been able to deliver," said Bentsen. Acknowledging the strategy, he said, "Texas, Oklahoma, Colorado, California—that's where I'll be." "We just don't have an energy policy, and now we are seeing the consequences. The rise in imports is over 40 percent, and we're going to be worse off than we were in 1973–1974," warned this Texas Democrat.[79] In 1970, Bentsen beat out Bush, and the Bush camp was worried, especially in rural Texas. "It's door-to-door warfare," conceded the GOP consultant Karl Rove.[80]

The year 1988 was different. This time the oilmen decided they would benefit most from a Bush victory. Even as Bush had to declare himself an "environmentalist" and promised to take on issues like acid rain under pressure from middle-class voters, his victory as president would likely yield favorable tax breaks for the oil industry. It would also mean that Bentsen, who was simultaneously running for reelection as senator, would continue as chairman of the Senate Finance Committee, from which he would write beneficial tax laws.

Texas oilmen believed that their better days were behind them. In the summer of 1988, the Iran-Iraq War came to an end, which would bring an increase in global oil production and Middle East stability. Moreover, during the race, Bush was forced to support a halt on offshore drilling under pressure from environmentalists, who, nevertheless, endorsed Dukakis. Greater global production, declining domestic prices, and increased environmental restrictions would likely result in a heavier reliance on imports. "Our vulnerability to price or supply blackmail by the world's oil producers is a growing threat," warned the Ford energy czar, Frank Zarb. But, as he acknowledged, few were listening.[81]

Making the Middle East Secure

In 1989, when George H. W. Bush became the forty-first president, Americans were importing more oil from the Persian Gulf than ever before. If every president since Richard Nixon had promised to free the United States from its energy dependence on insecure oil, this project had completely failed. The domestic oil industry had collapsed, and Americans were relying on imports for more than half of their energy needs. Since the bottom dropped out from under oil prices, domestic production had sunk by two million barrels per day, while demand was up nearly 10 percent. Americans were using as much oil as they had in 1973. Even as the transportation sector, which used nearly two-thirds of all oil consumed, had become more efficient, there were fifty million more cars on the roads.[82]

In many ways, 1989 looked a lot like 1969. Imports were growing, the domestic industry was declining, and energy producers were facing ever greater restrictions as environmentalism picked up strength. The historic parallels were even more striking after the *Exxon Valdez* oil spill. On March 24, 1989, an oil tanker heading from Alaska to California struck a reef, resulting in the largest American oil spill to date. Approximately eleven million gallons of oil spewed into the waters, greatly exceeding the damage of the Santa Barbara spill twenty years earlier. The *Valdez* accident derailed efforts to allow drilling in the Arctic National Wildlife Refuge (ANWR) in Alaska. Elsewhere, like the Santa Barbara spill, it gave momentum to other environmental measures, including the Clean Air Act amendments to address the problems of acid rain, urban smog, and global warming, especially with Democrats in control of Congress.

The die seemed cast against domestic production. Bush issued a moratorium on offshore exploration. Republicans from California and Florida who were up for reelection in the 1990 midterms and faced growing public opposition to drilling welcomed this move. The majors did not fight against the ban, because they were already investing more in overseas exploration. As in the Nixon years, environmentalism appeared to have growing bipartisan support. "I have never seen a more difficult—often hostile—political climate than we have today," said Charles DiBona.[83]

Unlike during the Nixon years, however, Bush's foreign policy team accepted the reliance on Persian Gulf oil, especially as the Cold War came to an end. In the 1980s, Mikhail Gorbachev, in response to an ailing economy, made worse by plummeting oil prices, undertook reforms to ease government control of the economy and make the political system more open. The Soviet leader signed arms treaties with Reagan and then with Bush. When Bush took office, the Soviet hold on the Eastern Bloc was slipping. The army withdrew from Afghanistan, and in a historic moment, witnessed around the globe, the leadership accepted the collapse of the Berlin Wall and German reunification, along with the overthrow of Soviet-backed Communist governments in Eastern Europe. In December 1989, Gorbachev and Bush officially declared the Cold War over.

In June 1990, a Central Intelligence Agency report announced that energy independence should no longer be a goal of American foreign policy. Bush appointed James Baker his secretary of state and Dick Cheney the secretary of defense. In the Ford administration, both men had seen OPEC and its influence over oil markets as a potent threat. However, with OPEC in retreat and the end of the Cold War, they no longer regarded imports as much of a national security risk as they once had. Even as the United States relied on Persian Gulf imports, and its allies more so, the country was unlikely to face a resource scarcity. The CIA report found the chances of major disruptions small and predicted relatively steady prices.

In the remote possibility of an embargo, the threat of price shocks would not be as great because prices were so low.[84] They had recovered somewhat from their nadir in the mid-1980s, but at the moment gasoline was cheaper than almost any other liquid, including bottled water.

Security mattered more than independence. But what would happen when and if the United States had to use force to keep the Gulf open remained unclear. By the summer of 1990, there were signs everywhere of looming unrest in the Middle East, particularly coming from Iraq. The day after Bush announced the offshore moratorium on drilling, Saddam Hussein told *Wall Street Journal* reporters that another Middle East war was "inevitable."[85] He also made it clear that he was prepared to use the "oil weapon." James Schlesinger warned the White House that Iraq's aggression could bring instability to the region and pose an unacceptable threat to American security.[86]

Iraq was facing serious hardships that made the possibility of Hussein's aggression more likely. In its long war with Iran, Iraq had racked up substantial debt. Bush supported giving aid to Iraq in the hopes of stabilizing this country and easing it into a more reliable trading partner. But Hussein was after something bigger. He believed he needed to raise oil prices, which had plunged in the first part of the year from $22 down to $16. Raising prices would allow him not only to pay off debt but also to maintain the country's sizable military of one million men out of a population of eighteen million. With the conclusion of the Cold War, Hussein desired to become the next regional superpower, with oil providing the means to shift the global balance of power. Moreover, Hussein believed that the Cold War's ending reduced the threat of regional disputes triggering a third world war and therefore provided greater leeway for local conflicts.

With his desperate need of cash, Hussein sought to prop up oil prices and enforce production quotas, which Kuwait was regularly violating. He wanted to establish an OPEC price at $25 a barrel. Saudi rulers feared that any price higher than $18 would result in the loss of market shares, spur alternative energies and non-OPEC supplies, and erode the value of their heavy investment in American refining and retail, which made them sensitive to the impact of rising prices. Hussein accused Arab countries of a U.S.-led conspiracy. "If words fail to protect Iraqis, something effective must be done to return things to their natural course," he said. After a parliamentary proposal that he be elected president for life, an emboldened

Hussein announced, "Iraqis will not forget the saying that cutting necks is better than cutting means of living."[87]

When Hussein failed to get compliance from Kuwait at an OPEC meeting, he sent 100,000 heavily armored troops to the border. Not only would the troops provide intimidation on the price question, but Hussein also desired to acquire greater access to the Persian Gulf coastline and to disputed reserves, both under Kuwaiti control. It was in Kuwait, seventeen years earlier, that OPEC oil ministers had acted in unison to impose the Arab embargo. If OPEC could no longer use its collective power to influence the market, then Hussein was willing to resort to weapons.

On August 2, Saddam Hussein ordered his troops into Kuwait. President Bush was well placed to understand the threat. His company, Zapata, had built Kuwait's first offshore oil rig. Three decades later, the United States and its allies were more dependent than ever on oil from this region. The Persian Gulf supplied just over one-quarter of the total daily world consumption. The president announced that the United States, which purchased roughly 10 percent of its oil imports from Iraq and Kuwait, would embargo oil from both states and impose economic sanctions.

The central issue came down to whether the Iraqi invasion would discourage Saudi Arabia and other Middle Eastern countries from using their excess capacity to offset the losses. "With massive military buildups in striking distance," explained the DOE's deputy director Henson Moore, "chances are that . . . [they] will be hesitant." As Moore, the former Louisiana congressman, summed up, "Iraq would be in a position to achieve through military threats what OPEC has been notoriously unable to accomplish voluntarily. Production could be held in check and world crude oil prices could rise substantially above pre-war levels."[88]

On August 8, Bush told the country that he had dispatched the Eighty-Second Airborne Division of the U.S. Army and units of the air force as part of Operation Desert Shield. The military took up defensive positions in Saudi Arabia to dissuade Hussein from invasion. "My administration, as has been the case with every president from President Roosevelt to President Reagan, is committed to the security and stability of the Persian Gulf," Bush asserted. He explained the threat that came from Hussein's control over the region's oil supply, not just to the United States, but also to the rest of the world. "The sovereign independence of Saudi Arabia is of vital interest to the United States," he stated bluntly.

Bush's actions received broad support. Following the Iraqi invasion, the United Nations Security Council had voted unanimously on a resolution to call for the immediate retreat of Iraqi forces. In the United States, sending troops won endorsements from across the political spectrum, including from liberal Democrats such as Howard Metzenbaum and Les Aspin who had been critics of the Carter Doctrine.[89] For the time being, Operation Desert Shield was a defensive campaign, meant to prevent Iraq from pushing into Saudi Arabia.

While the military was on the ground in the Gulf, the White House mobilized on the home front. The key objective was to prevent a return to the liberal policies of the 1970s—intervention in the domestic oil market and the possibility of price controls. Bush's advisers saw the failures of energy policy in the 1970s and the market success in the 1980s as the best case in support of doing nothing. Richard Schmalensee, one of Bush's top economic advisers, believed the public had learned this lesson too: "Veterans of gas lines and other unnecessary rationing devices will reckon the costs of this system to have been high." It was imperative to resist the political temptation for action.[90] "It is absolutely critical that we not repeat some of the stupid mistakes of the 1970s," said another senior White House official. "If we got price controls, then we would have to worry about artificial shortages and gas lines. Nobody should want that again."[91]

The calls for some kind of government action came quick. More than two dozen senators requested that Bush establish a federal task force to monitor gas prices at the pump, which had shot up in the days following the invasion. Senator Joseph Lieberman, a Democrat from Connecticut, whose first political job was interning for Abraham Ribicoff, spoke out loudly. "The oil industry of this country is plundering us just as Saddam Hussein is plundering Kuwait," he said to the news cameras.[92] Lieberman denounced the price increases, saying that consumers were being "ripped off on a massive scale." Congressman Philip Sharp, a Democrat from Indiana first elected in 1974, remarked that Hussein "may not be the only greedy person in this picture." Citizen Action's Edwin Rothschild called on Americans to boycott the highest-price gas station in their local communities.[93]

Rhetorical attacks against the oil industry played well. "They have become the Darth Vader of corporations," said Celinda Lake, a Democratic political consultant. "It's open season on them for politicians." A *Wall*

Street Journal poll revealed that in the wake of *Valdez* only 6 percent of Americans had trust and confidence in the industry. With the upcoming midterm elections, both parties worried about rising fuel prices. The president, too, got in on the action: "I'm asking the oil companies to do their fair share. They should show restraint and not abuse today's uncertainties to raise prices."[94] "The administration sees the need now for some low-level populism," remarked Kevin Phillips, a Republican political strategist.[95]

Yet there was broad agreement that price controls were not the solution. "We at DOE have no authority to dictate prices, nor should we," Henson Moore told the press. "The lesson of the 1970s is that it's better to let markets do the work, even if they sometimes overreact, rather than trusting in some bureaucrat sitting in his office," explained John Sawhill, who had briefly headed the Federal Energy Administration and then the U.S. Synfuels Corporation.[96] The *New York Times* editors agreed: "If regulators tried to roll back prices, they would create severe shortages reminiscent of the tortuous gas lines of the 1970s."[97] Instantly, the Interstate Commerce Commission let independent truckers increase their rates.

Conservatives did not want any market interference, and they criticized Bush for even mentioning the need for restraint. "There's no conspiracy," said Philip Verleger of the Institute for International Economics. "It is the market at work."[98] Already Bush was doing too much. "U.S. policy is now beautifully designed to boost demand for oil (e.g. by jawboning oil companies to keep pump prices down) and restrict supply (the embargo). With enemies like that, OPEC doesn't need friends," explained Alan Reynolds of the Hudson Institute.[99]

The White House worked hard to prevent what Henson Moore described as "legislative energy mischief."[100] On the issue of price controls, the White House stood firm. Moore said there would be no reversal of the Reagan policy to "let the market do it."[101] Glenn Schleede advised the administration to take a hard line: "Members of Congress and the media have a strong tendency to overreact to energy crises or perceived crises and to demand government actions." He knew this better than most. As the assistant to Michael Raoul-Duval on Nixon's Domestic Council, he had helped craft the policy response to the Arab embargo. Now he warned the Bush White House, "There are relatively few effective actions—other than diplomatic and military—that the government can take. As demonstrated in 1973–74 and 1979–80, government can take actions that are very counterproductive."[102]

On August 20, Bush, in signing National Security Directive 45, made it clear that the United States would uphold its regional commitment to Saudi Arabia. "The United States will defend its vital interests in the area, through the use of U.S. military force if necessary and appropriate, against any power with interests inimical to our own," he declared.[103] With troops already stationed in the region, this affirmation was more than rhetoric. As the president told his cabinet, "The stakes are . . . clear: US reliability, the potential domination of Gulf energy resources with all that would entail, international order in what I call the post-postwar era."[104] Before a joint session of Congress, on September 11, 1990, where the president laid out his commitment to a "new world order" free from terror, Bush issued a firm warning to Hussein: "We will not let this aggression stand."

Hussein's actions made clear what many energy conservatives had long believed: the necessity of American troops to bring stability and security to this region. The idea of "pillars" in the Middle East had come undone, as one of James Baker's aides, William Burns, explained: "Neither Iran nor Iraq is likely to aspire to the role of a U.S. 'pillar' anytime soon, and Saudi Arabia isn't strong enough." Moreover, "we cannot foster a free-standing balance of power among Iran, Iraq, and the Gulf states given the ambitions and relative weight of the first two." These experts recognized that the regimes themselves were not stable given the concentration of power in the hands of an autocratic ruling elite in countries that were rife with ethnic and religious tensions. These facts, as the foreign policy makers understood them, meant the United States would have to provide security. "The Iraqi invasion has made explicit what was long an implicit reality, namely that the U.S. is the ultimate guarantor of Saudi Arabia's security. While arms sales can improve Saudi Arabia's deterrent capabilities, they cannot match the power of either Iran or Iraq," concluded Baker's assistant.[105]

With the situation on the ground uncertain, crude prices on the spot market climbed to more than $40 a barrel. At the pump, a gallon of gasoline increased by nearly one-quarter to just over a dollar. With a growing recession, the Senate minority leader, Robert Dole, appealed to Bush to order a drawdown of the Strategic Petroleum Reserve. "The United States is paying the price," he said. "Asking our economy to shoulder the additional burden of unnecessarily high oil prices is not required."[106] But the White House refused, seeing a drawdown as an unwarranted intervention. "Price is not the trigger," an administration official told *The Washington Post*.[107] Instead, the White House pointed to the rise in prices as evidence that the market was working. The president of the New York Mercantile Exchange echoed that view. As he put it to Bush, "The price increases to date appear to be consistent with the energy market's attempt to find a new equilibrium based upon its perception of supply and demand."[108]

The White House would rely on what Bush's assistant Ede Holiday called "market incentives and U.S. foreign policy initiatives." Holiday made sure the message got circulated throughout the administration: the oil industry did not profiteer, and the White House would not take any action. As she explained to the presidential assistant Andy Card, "The sharp price increases following the invasion are attributable to uncertainty in the markets, with the markets working as might have been expected . . . The industry has not benefitted from runaway profits."[109] Holiday reassured gasoline retailers, "We do not anticipate any need for the federal government to control the allocation or price of oil in the domestic or world market . . . The oil disruptions of the 1970s have taught us that price controls and rationing systems distort markets and intensify disruptions rather than resolve them."[110]

Even as prices shot up, the domestic industry was in decline. American oilmen could not compete with low-cost producers abroad, especially as they faced more environmental regulations. On November 15, Bush signed a major amendment to the Clean Air Act, the first since the 1970s. By now, Washington no longer assumed the country would reach energy self-sufficiency. "Energy independence is neither an achievable or useful goal," wrote the DOE's Linda Stuntz in a planning memo. The major oil companies concurred. A Chevron newsletter explained, "They cannot make the United States self-sufficient in energy in the foreseeable future."[111]

The rest of Bush's team agreed. The NSC saw independence as "elusive," while the CEA saw it as "undesirable." "No feasible combination of domestic or foreign energy policy options can fully relieve us of the risk of oil dependency," said Bush's advisers. In fact, the situation was likely to get worse: "America's and the world's oil dependency on Middle East suppliers is likely to grow, and as the current crisis demonstrates, with major implications for our foreign, economic, and defense policies."[112]

Guaranteeing oil sources from around the globe, with military protection if necessary, would necessitate what the NSC called "real improvements in energy security." The NSC, under Brent Scowcroft's direction, reflected on the history of American energy policy since the Arab embargo: "For seventeen years, American Administrations have sought to balance the economic and environmental benefits of increasing reliance on imported oil against the foreign policy and military costs of dealing with threats to the free flow of oil, in particular from the Persian Gulf." The country had to accept the new reality that independence was unattainable. "Secure supplies of energy are essential to U.S. prosperity," he asserted, and from that fact flowed foreign policy commitments: "The concentration of 65 percent of the world's known oil reserves in the Persian Gulf means we must continue to ensure reliable access to competitively priced oil, and have the capability to respond to any major supply disruption."[113] The Carter Doctrine was coming to life.

Throughout the fall, the president made it clear that he would not accept any solution short of total Iraqi withdrawal from Kuwait. On November 8, Bush ordered 200,000 more troops to the region. A week later, American and Saudi forces staged a joint exercise, Imminent Thunder. On Thanksgiving, the president traveled to visit the troops in Saudi Arabia. Delivering a speech on America's commitment to the Gulf, he shared those views in *Newsweek*. "We cannot allow any tyrant to practice economic blackmail," he wrote. "Energy security is national security, and we must be prepared to act accordingly."[114]

As the president inched closer to the use of force, congressional opponents pushed for reliance on sanctions instead. The hope was that as Iraq suffered the effects of the economic embargo, Hussein would come under greater pressure to retreat. Bush wanted the support of Congress but understood the issue was becoming polarizing. In the 1990 midterm elections, Democrats held on to their majority, increasing their numbers by one in the Senate and seven in the House. Paul Wellstone, the newly elected senator from Minnesota who defeated the Republican incumbent Rudy Boschwitz, wrote to Bush, urging him "to stop the momentum towards war." Wellstone said, "Taking democracy seriously means that the people of this country . . . must ultimately decide whether we will go to war."[115] Passing this letter on to Robert Dole, Bush told his congressional ally, "Batten down the hatches!"[116]

Reliance on sanctions instead of force had support not just from liberals but also from foreign policy hawks who feared the possibility of a power vacuum in the region. Sam Nunn, the chairman of the Senate Armed Services Committee, held hearings in the late fall where Zbigniew Brzezinski, Paul Nitze, Edward Luttwak, and James Schlesinger testified that the president should give sanctions more time to work.[117] These experts had long worried about the balance of power in the Middle East. They were concerned that the use of force might result in the collapse of the Iraqi regime, which in turn would leave Iran unchecked. Moreover, they feared that an American military action would trigger uprisings against moderate Arab regimes and incite terrorism against the United States.

These hawks believed that a defensive posture in the Gulf was absolutely necessary to protect the region's oil. The issue was not the price of gasoline at the pump but rather, as Schlesinger explained it, strategic. "We cannot allow so large a portion of the world's energy resources to fall under the domination of a single hostile party," the former energy and defense secretary told Congress.[118] But the question of how to ensure stability in the region remained. Henry Kissinger believed it was essential for the United States to use force for the sake of shoring up moderate Arab allies, sustaining American influence in the region, and preventing another Arab-Israeli War. But Schlesinger argued that the use of force would bring more instability, not less.

Within the White House, Secretary Cheney made a clear case to use force. To him, the issue was simple: "Aggression begets aggression."[119] And now he, and not Schlesinger, was the secretary of defense. Unless Hussein "is stopped today," said Vice President Dan Quayle, who played a leading role in making the case to the public, "a nuclear armed Iraq will control the bulk of the world's energy supply tomorrow, thereby holding a gun to all our heads." Quayle warned the Republican governors' conference, "Saddam Hussein desires to use its vast wealth to become the leader of an Arab superpower armed to the teeth with weapons of mass destruction."[120]

The United Nations had voted to authorize the use of force if Hussein did not retreat by January 15. As the UN deadline for Iraqi withdrawal grew close, President Bush shared his long-term vision with Richard Nixon. "Should Iraq withdraw from Kuwait, we will still have the task of restricting Iraq's military capabilities and constructing security arrangements to ensure stability in the Gulf," Bush wrote the former president. The real political challenge, Bush told Nixon, came from Congress. In the wake of Vietnam, this body, under Democratic control, sought to assert its right to decide whether to commit American troops. It was in Congress, explained Bush to a knowing Nixon, "where there are continuing concerns with war powers, where many in the Congress want to have the opportunity to decide whether force is used, and on the policy of whether and if so when to move from sanctions to a policy of liberation."[121]

By early December, the United States had amassed overwhelming power in the Gulf. In his testimony before the Senate Armed Services Committee, Chairman of the Joint Chiefs of Staff Colin Powell explained that the number of troops and the amount of equipment were "comparable to moving the entire city of Richmond, Virginia." To impress his audience with the enormity of the operation, Powell pointed out that the total cargo was equal to two and a half times the size of the Berlin Airlift.[122] The White House argued that sanctions would not dislodge Hussein, who had proven his willingness to subject his population to a subsistence economy. Time, they claimed, was on his side as he would continue to strengthen his fortifications and weaponry.

The White House message resonated with Americans who, by a large majority, supported the deployment of troops and military action. According to a *Newsweek* poll, Americans supported Operation Desert Shield not just to preserve oil but primarily because they feared the prospect of Saddam developing nuclear and chemical weapon capacity. Whereas 60 percent insisted on Hussein's withdrawal from Kuwait, 78 percent worried about his ability to develop weapons of mass destruction. Quayle's message was getting through. Only 31 percent favored military action to lower oil prices.[123] James Baker also argued that repelling Hussein was necessary for protecting the "lifeline" of the American economy. "If you want to sum it up in one word, it's jobs." Even as a small antiwar protest chanted, "No blood for oil," military action made sense to a public that had witnessed what they saw as the outsize growth of OPEC power.[124]

When Congress returned in January, the White House and its supporters made a last-minute effort to win approval. Bob Dole lashed out at his colleagues: "While even the UN has mustered the will to take strong and decisive action, Congress has been AWOL."[125] As the UN deadline of January 15 approached, he said, "It's time for all Americans—especially the U.S. Congress—to express our support for President Bush and the brave young men and women of Operation Desert Shield."[126] With the deadline imminent, Congress voted for a joint resolution authorizing the president to use force. The vote was close in the Senate, where less than 20 percent of Democrats supported the measure. In the House, only one-third of Democrats voted in favor.

On January 15, Bush authorized the use of military action to expel Iraq from Kuwait. The NSC directive began, "Access to Persian Gulf oil and the security of key friendly states in the area are vital to U.S. national security." The NSC charge spelled out the narrow goals of Iraq's expulsion from Kuwait and also cited broader goals of destroying Iraq's capabilities to manufacture weapons of mass destruction. If Iraq were to use these weapons or support their use by terrorists, then "it shall become an explicit objective of the United States to replace the current leadership of Iraq." The same goal applied if Iraq were to destroy Kuwait's oil fields.[127]

On January 16, the United States, with its 500,000 troops, led an international coalition of airstrikes against Iraq in Operation Desert Storm. On the same day, the White House authorized a release of the Strategic Petroleum Reserve to "reassure the world market," said the energy secretary, Admiral James Watkins. Watkins oversaw the drawdown of 1.5 million barrels of oil per day over the next month. The purpose was to demonstrate what Watkins called the quick and efficient ability to move oil to market. He coordinated the action with IEA countries. The goal of the coordinated release, as the International Energy Agency explained, was to thwart "heightened uncertainty and volatility in the market."[128]

To authorize the drawdown, Bush had to assert there was a potential energy supply shortage that constituted a "severe" interruption. Still, Bush made it clear that the administration would not intervene in directing the supply. When Henson Moore inquired as to whether the DOE should draft allocation rules for the SPR, the Office of Management and Budget immediately stepped in. "Someone needs to call the Admiral or Henson and tell them issuing these regulations is not in the Administration's interest. These draft rules should not even be drafted because they would surely be leaked to Congress," cautioned the OMB. Instead the executive office staffer asserted, "All analyses and experiences with this issue clearly points to the need to let the efficient and impersonal market-place allocate the oil through a competitive bidding process." To do otherwise "would be a political and economic disaster," he concluded.[129]

The White House did not expect prices to rise any further. Price hikes had already taken place, and with a downturn in the economy demand for oil had decreased. Moreover, OPEC production, even without oil from Iraq and Kuwait, was higher than before Iraq's invasion. The futures market might respond to the outbreak of hostilities, but given the excess supply a price surge was unlikely. The White House press secretary described the SPR drawdown as a "precautionary measure, taken in concert with our IEA partners, designed to promote stability in world oil markets." In fact, with the start of hostilities and the announced drawdown, prices fell to pre-embargo levels of $21 a barrel. "The problem of expensive oil went away when the bombers went in," explained a *New York Times* reporter.[130]

Critics pointed out that the true cost of a gallon of gasoline, with military expenses included, amounted to $5.50.[131] Instead of troops, environmentalists demanded government investment in wind, solar, and other renewable sources of energy. The government spent daily several times as much on the Gulf War as it did on energy efficiency research.[132] Instead of subsidies for the oil industry and drilling in environmentally sensitive areas, the country had to use less oil. "We cannot continue drilling and burning our way into the future," the Sierra Club's Michael Fischer wrote to President Bush.[133] "A policy based on the security of the oil industry is not the same as a policy to make the American economy less dependent on oil," said Peter Berle, president of the National Audubon Society.[134]

Environmentalists argued that real security would come not from a long-term military presence in the Gulf but rather through conservation. "Security favors those nations which are most efficient in their use of energy, and those which are least dependent upon any one source of supply," the leaders of all major environmental groups told Bush. Above all, the number one priority had to be an increase in automobile fuel efficiency given that cars and light trucks used six million of sixteen million barrels of daily oil consumed. The improvements since 1975, when CAFE standards began, resulted in savings greater than ten times what proponents of ANWR promised this drilling would yield. "In one step you will reduce global warming, enhance national security, reduce CO_2 emissions and urban pollution, save consumers money, and reduce demands to destroy sensitive natural environments," they wrote.[135]

But the Gulf War revealed the new direction of American energy policy. Instead of policies to promote the conservation of resources, the country was relying on oil from abroad. On February 20, the White House released its National Energy Strategy, which it characterized as a "successful policy of market reliance." Market reliance now meant oil from overseas, protected, if necessary, by force. "A goal of the National Energy Strategy is to reduce the U.S. vulnerability to oil supply disruptions. Yet the Strategy acknowledges that the U.S. is part of an energy interdependent world," read the report.[136] Three days later, on February 23, President Bush ordered a ground attack on Iraqi troops.

The war ended only a hundred hours later. With the strongest military in the world, the United States easily repelled Iraqi troops and prevented Hussein from controlling the region's oil supplies. In American history, the use of force to guarantee open markets and free trade was nothing new. William Appleman Williams, the famous diplomatic historian, wrote of President McKinley and his cabinet's decision to go to war in Cuba a century earlier, "They did not want war per se, let alone war in order to increase their own personal fortunes. But their own conception of the world ultimately led them into war in order to solve the problems in the way that they considered necessary and best." Walter LaFeber, too, remarked in speaking of William McKinley, "Although he did not want war, he did want what only a war could provide: the disappearance of the terrible uncertainty in American political and economic life, and a solid basis from which to resume the building of the new American commercial empire."[137]

During the war, Bush had not asked Americans to sacrifice, and few saw any need to do so. According to a Gallup poll, only 3 percent turned down their thermostats, and the same small number said they were carpooling or buying a gas-saving car. As cars had become more efficient, Americans were living farther from work and traveling greater distances. Gasoline consumption had risen nearly 20 percent since the 1973 embargo. Americans used twice as much oil per capita as Europeans.[138] "Americans see cheap, abundant, reliable energy as a biblical and constitutional entitlement," explained a gasoline retailer representative. "If you're born in America and you don't have cheap energy available at any time, day or night, then some-body is beating up on you."[139]

Several months after the war ended, James Schlesinger believed the country had missed an important opportunity. "Since we presently seem to be working on securing a New World Order in the Middle East, then once again we have escaped the implied obligation to do something about our energy habits and our growing dependence on Middle East supplies," he told reporters. Having fought the energy battles throughout the 1970s, he understood the political reality: "Given the history of political capital that has been invested in energy policy and the apparently low returns at least politically from those investments, it's not surprising that adminis-trations back off. Remember, we are talking about the habits of the Ameri-can people. Moralists may find these habits reprehensible, but the public finds them satisfying." Therefore, he concluded, "as a society we have made a choice to secure access to oil by military means."[140]

In the war's aftermath, Presidents Jimmy Carter and Gerald Ford ap-pealed to Congress to pass energy legislation: "The need for new initiatives on energy policy is dramatized by our growing dependence on foreign oil, a dependence which jeopardizes our economy and endangers our secu-rity." The cost of fighting the Gulf War and maintaining a military force in the region was high. Oil imports accounted for half of the trade deficit, and the prospects for the domestic oil industry seemed dim. In May 1991, when *Dallas* aired its final episode, few Americans were still tuning in. According to Carter and Ford, to reverse its dependence, the country had to invest in energy savings and set new CAFE standards. "We must do more," these two presidents urged.[141] But as James Schlesinger remarked, "It's a hell of a lot easier and a lot more fun to kick asses in the Middle East than make sacrifices and practice conservation."[142]

Conclusion:
A New Project Independence?

SOON AFTER GEORGE BUSH declared victory in the Middle East, he received a package at the White House from an old friend, Kenneth Lay. Lay was sending the president a signed copy of Daniel Yergin's *Prize*. Within Yergin's encyclopedic narrative of the history of oil, Lay called special attention to the chapter on World War II, which chronicled how crucial the American supply had been to the Allied victory. At a time when the United States was importing so much of its oil, and the country had just gone through a war to protect this access, Lay underscored the centrality of energy to the country's security. "Anyone reading this section of the book," he wrote, "has to conclude that the United States must regain control of its energy future if it is to continue to be a great world power." Bush responded, "I share your deep concern about the energy future of America."[1]

The solution was to produce more in the United States—the same dream of energy independence that Richard Nixon had first described. Lay, as president of Enron, one of the large natural gas pipeline companies, was urging Bush to deregulate electricity. Since the 1970s, he and Bush, and many other Washington insiders, had promoted and pushed for deregulation as the path toward greater independence. To these Texas energy men, the country's future required taking energy out of the hands of Washing-

ton politicians and returning it to the West Texas oil patch, the Appala-
chian coal mines, the offshore Gulf of Mexico, the natural gas pipelines,
and wherever else American producers could turn a profit and thereby
ensure the United States remained a supreme global power.

Today it looks as if that dream is coming true. Thanks largely to the
revolution brought by hydraulic fracturing, oil imports are down, prices
have plummeted, and there is no shortage of domestic energy. Known as
fracking, this practice has thus far eluded much Washington regulation.
The story of fracking—with the North Dakota boomtowns, the surge
in prospecting, the rapid reversal in domestic oil production—is as dramatic as when Bush sought his fortune in the West Texas oil fields. Once
again, it seems, Americans can count on an abundant future with an
endless supply of affordable energy. As Morris Adelman, the leading oil
economist of the last century, put it, under the right market conditions,
"resources, like other assets, are not found but made."[2] The increase in
production from 5.6 million barrels of oil a day in 2010 to 9.3 million barrels today—nearly the same level as the 1970 peak production—appears to
offer living proof. At last, the United States has solved its dependence
problem.

Or so it seems. There is a huge volatility in energy markets that makes
the future uncertain. And not just since the sudden tumble in energy
prices in early 2015. The history of energy since George H. W. Bush left office has been a seesaw, a story of ups and downs. When prices drop, consumption increases, and the energy problem remains. It was after the 1991
intervention in the Gulf that Americans saw a spike in the country's energy use, with the spread of big SUVs that were exempted from CAFE
standards. In 1975, SUVs accounted for 1.8 percent of the market, rising in
1987 to 6.3 percent. By 2002, large sport utility vehicles made up one-
quarter of the domestic car market.[3] After the 1995 repeal of the fifty-five-
mile-per-hour speed limit law, Americans drove fast. With gas prices so
cheap, they also drove more, moving farther away from the cities and commuting longer distances. In 2005, Americans drove almost three times the
number of miles as they had thirty years earlier.

By this time, with rising consumption, Americans were importing
nearly two-thirds of their daily oil needs. As the United States was using
ever more energy, so, too, were India and China as these countries were
rapidly industrializing. With growing demand, an abundant supply once

again turned into a global crunch, and the result was a surge in prices. By 2008, the cost of a barrel of oil was back up to where it had been in 1979.

With prices so high, the race was on to discover new sources of energy. These high prices spurred the fracking revolution, seemingly fulfilling the market mentality that Lay, Bush, Reagan, and their cohort had done so much to promote. In 2015, the seesaw reversed itself again. With the huge supply in American oil production as well as the global recession, there has been another dramatic decline in prices.

At best, the future is unpredictable. The price collapse is likely to reduce the drilling frenzy, even if it does not wipe fracking out altogether. And OPEC will remain a large player in the global oil market. Even as the percentage of oil we import from the Middle East is down substantially since 1991, we have fought another large-scale war in Iraq. The American public might display some greater reservation about our military presence in the region, but it is unlikely, especially given the ongoing unrest and instability, that we will abandon our commitment to Persian Gulf security anytime soon.

There is also the likelihood that the fall in prices will risk ending gains in conservation, energy reform, and the commitment to discover and develop renewable alternatives as happened in the 1980s. Regardless of whether Americans become independent of foreign oil, they are still highly dependent on fossil fuel. In that sense, we are living with the failures of the 1970s to craft public policies to induce conservation and promote alternative energies.

Will we address the long-term problems of energy security, stable growth, and climate change? The lesson of the 1970s does not provide much optimism. In the summer of 1973, just months before the Arab embargo, as he watched OPEC's power on the rise, Henry Jackson sounded an unheeded alarm to his countrymen, warning about the growing dependence on foreign oil. Attuned to the geopolitics of oil, he urged a massive investment in alternative energies. "We have already waited far too long to increase our options," he wrote in *The New York Times*. "We must abandon myopic indecision and make a determined start on alleviating this increasingly critical situation." Though his concern was the reliance on oil imports, his warnings about "the danger of doing nothing" were prophetic then and remain so today.[4] The challenge with energy policy, as the failures of the 1970s made clear, is the lag between short-term costs and long-term benefits, a lag that presents a basic political problem. History offers a cautionary tale for politicians hoping to tackle this issue.

Throughout the 1970s, Americans' unwillingness to pay more for their energy presented policy makers with a fundamental obstacle to construct-ing long-term policy. As James Schlesinger lamented as he was struggling to push through Carter's energy package, "The basic constituency for the program is the future."[5] To Schlesinger, the future looked bleak, especially at the end of the George H. W. Bush administration, when Americans chose military action in the Middle East over conservation. And even for this strategy, too, of securing oil through military means, Americans were not willing to pay, instead opting to finance military expenditure through deficits.

The rise of antigovernment sentiment has compounded Washington's inability to deal with twenty-first-century energy challenges. This hostility to government resulted in part from the unsuccessful efforts to solve the energy crisis of the 1970s. As governor and as the GOP presidential candi-date, Ronald Reagan told the country that the problem was not a shortage of gas but rather a surplus of government. As soon as Jimmy Carter un-veiled his proposal, Reagan, who was already gearing up for his 1980 run, went on the attack: "The Carter plan represents massive Government in-tervention in the energy economy. It will lead to more shortages and higher prices, more inflation and a depressed economy."[6] Once he was in office, Reagan launched a frontal assault on the Department of Energy, which was his way of saying the country did not need any government interven-tion, just private industry.

As the story of the 1970s shows, Washington policy makers failed to solve the energy crisis because the political power of consumers led to holding down prices even as environmentalists called for conservation. They failed because of the equally powerful position of producers that in-hibited the commitment of resources to new kinds of technology. And they failed because of a new idea that there was no room for government to play an effective role.

History does offer some glimmer of hope, however. Several changes since the Reagan era make some kind of sustained public commitment possible. The biggest change comes from the rise of global warming as a major source of concern. That problem, unlike short-term shortages or spikes in costs, is ongoing and will not disappear. While some deny global warming, most acknowledge the need for comprehensive action. The 1970s also offers another ray of hope if one considers the strength, endurance, and expansion of environmental regulation. This movement has not been strong enough to stop fracking. Far from it. But the concern over global warming—growing out of decades of environmental activism, research, and policy—has resulted in a sustained effort to find paths to a less fossil-fuel-dependent future. In the 1980s, energy researchers put their designs in drawers, where they collected dust; today, there is a full-scale and well-funded effort to create energy solutions for the future. This undertaking is not likely to evaporate even as oil prices fluctuate.

Two other long-term changes since the 1980s make the prospect of addressing energy challenges more likely. The end of the Cold War allowed for a greater presence of American troops in the Middle East without fears of Soviet reprisal, yet it has also opened up possibilities for broad-based international cooperation. While Third World countries who are now on the path of rapid industrialization are unlikely to sacrifice growth, especially when per capita the United States contributes a much greater amount of carbon to the earth's atmosphere, the absence of an East-West divide does create opportunities for global initiatives.

In addition, the Democratic leadership has now embraced environmentalism much more resolutely and uniformly than in the past. This became clear in the House passage of the Waxman-Markey bill, as compromised a measure as it was, to set a cap on the emissions of greenhouse gases. In 2008, after Barack Obama's election to the presidency, the Los Angeles congressman Henry Waxman replaced John Dingell as the chairman of the Energy and Commerce Committee. This reflected the culmination of a struggle between different parts of the party that started after Waxman's election in 1974, when, as a junior congressman, he took on Dingell, challenging this traditional Detroit-based Democrat to put environmental issues at the center of the party's agenda. The passing of the gavel to Waxman signaled a fundamental, even if incremental, shift of priorities.

It is true that thus far global initiatives to regulate greenhouse gases have failed, and the United States has been unwilling to participate in binding obligations. And it is also true that Waxman's bill went down in defeat in the Senate. But proponents will not stop their efforts. As much as the overall history of the 1970s tells a tale of shortsightedness, divisions, and opposition, twentieth-century American politics are punctuated with examples of dramatic and lasting reform, including much of the environmental regulation of that period.

The energy crisis of today is not another Pearl Harbor, taking us by surprise. Moving Americans beyond their dependence on fossil fuels, especially in the transportation and power plant industries, where most of the greenhouse emissions come from, will prove difficult. The energy industry, as a young George Bush knew, is risky business. That is true not just for the wildcatter but for the Washington politician. But past challenges point the way toward new solutions. For a successful energy policy, policy makers will have to protect jobs as they push for conservation and renewable energies, supporting programs that unite and rally workers, consumers, and environmental activists rather than dividing and alienating them. As they craft new policies, the country's leaders have to promote the idea of independence from fossil fuels as a public good, as something that this nation, as part of a global community, must pursue for a prosperous, healthy, and secure future.

Notes

The notes do not include citations to presidential public remarks, which are all available at the University of California Santa Barbara's American presidency project website, www.presidency.ucsb.edu.

Abbreviations

GBL   *George H. W. Bush Presidential Library and Museum, College Station, Texas*

BOS	Michael Boskin Files
CAB	Cabinet Affairs
CEA	Council of Economic Advisers
CONG	Congressional Files
COS	Chief of Staff
FUL	Craig Fuller Files
GBC	George Bush Collection
GEA	Kristen Gear Files
HAS	Richard Haass Files
KOR	Paul Kornfonta Files
LAY	Kenneth Lay
MEL	Eric Melby Files
NSC	National Security Council
PAW	Public Affairs White House
PC	Political Correspondence
PF	Personal Files
SHM	Richard Schmalensee Files

SMZ   Counsel's Office, John Schmitz Files
SUN   John Sununu Files
WHO   White House Office of Records and Management, Alpha Files
ZAP   Zapata Oil Files

GFL   *Gerald R. Ford Presidential Library and Museum, Ann Arbor, Michigan*
    CAN   James M. Cannon Files
    CHY   Richard B. Cheney Files
    DOW   Dorothy Downton Files
    DUV   Michael Raoul-Duval Files
    FRD   Max L. Friedersdorf Files
    GRN   U.S. Council of Economic Advisers, Alan Greenspan Files
    HRT   Robert T. Hartmann Files
    HRTP Robert T. Hartmann Papers
    HWI   James F. C. Hyde Jr. and Stephen Wayne Interviews
    JON   Jerry Jones Files
    NES   Ron Nessen Files
    PCR   President Ford's Committee Records
    PHF   Presidential Handwriting File
    REI   A. James Reichley Interview Transcripts
    SEI   L. William Seidman Files
    TIM   William E. Timmons Files
    ZRB   Frank G. Zarb Papers

JCL   *Jimmy Carter Presidential Library and Museum, Atlanta, Georgia*
    BAU   Patricia Bauer Papers
    BRD   Lisa Bourdeaux Files
    BRZ   Zbigniew Brzezinski Papers
    BUT   Landon Butler Files
    COM   Office of the Assistant to the President for Communications
    CPD   James Copeland Files
    DPS   Staff Offices, Domestic Policy Staff
    EIZ   Stuart Eizenstat Files
    GOV   Staff Offices, Cabinet Secretary and Intergovernmental Affairs
    JOR   Hamilton Jordan Files
    KHN   Office of the Special Adviser on Inflation, Alfred Kahn
    MRE   Frank Moore Files
    NWS   News Summary Files
    NSA   Office of the National Security Advisor–Zbigniew Brzezinski Material
    OCL   Office of the Congressional Liaison Files
    OCS   Office of the Chief of Staff Files
    ODM   William E. Odom Files
    RAF   Gerald Rafshoon Files
    SLG   Stephen Selig Files
    SND   Greg Schneider Files

RNL   *Richard Nixon Presidential Library and Museum, Yorba Linda, California*
    CM   Commodities
    EPO   Energy Policy Office
    FEO   Federal Energy Office
    FG   Federal Government Organizations
    HAIG   Alexander M. Haig Jr.
    HOOP   David C. Hoopes
    MRD   Michael Raoul-Duval
    POF   President's Office Files
    PPF   President's Personal Files
    SMOF   Staff Member and Office Files
    SF   Subject Files
    TN   Transportation
    UT   Utilities
    WHCF   White House Central Files
    WHSF   White House Special Files

RRL   *Ronald Reagan Presidential Library and Museum, Simi Valley, California*
    BOG   Danny Boggs Files
    BLD   Ralph C. Bledsoe Files
    DPC   Special Assistant to the President, Domestic Policy Council
    MAR   William F. Martin Files
    NSCF   Executive Secretariat, National Security Council, Subject Files

TAP   *Thomas L. Ashley Congressional Papers, Center for Archival Collections, Bowling Green State University, Bowling Green, Ohio*

WSP   *William E. Simon Papers, Lafayette College Special Collections, Easton, Pennsylvania*

Introduction: An Energy Pearl Harbor

1. John Updike, *Rabbit Is Rich* (New York: Alfred K. Knopf, 1981), 3.
2. Stephen A. Wakefield, "The Fuel Crisis: An Energy Pearl Harbor," *Public Utilities Fortnightly*, Dec. 6, 1973, 29–33.
3. "For Gasoline, Little Is Certain but High Prices," *New York Times*, April 29, 1974, 51.
4. Paul Friedlander, "Energy for the Great American Motorist," *New York Times*, Dec. 16, 1973, J23.
5. Joyce Porter et al. to Nixon, Feb. 13, 1974, RNL, WHCF, SF, CM, box 22.
6. "Dear Senator: This Has Gone Far Enough," *U.S. News & World Report*, March 11, 1974, 31.
7. John Kenneth Galbraith, *American Capitalism: The Concept of Countervailing Power* (Boston: Houghton Mifflin, 1952), 167.
8. Milton Friedman, "A Monstrosity," *Newsweek*, May 2, 1977, 20.
9. Henry M. Jackson, "The Danger of Doing Nothing," *New York Times*, June 28, 1973, 47.

10. "Dateline Washington: Unified Energy Policy?," *American Legion Magazine*, vol. 95, no. 2, Aug. 1973.
11. Matthew Wald, "Why America Still Hates the Words 'Energy Policy,'" *New York Times*, Feb. 17, 1991, E4.

1: In Search of Oil

1. Bush to Tom McCance, June 25, 1950, GBL, GBC, ZAP, PF, box 4.
2. Bryan Burrough, *The Big Rich: The Rise and Fall of the Greatest Texas Oil Fortunes* (New York: Penguin, 2009), 264.
3. "The Natural Gas Story," n.d., GBL, GBC, ZAP, PF, box 6.
4. Bush to Ashley, May 26, 1953, GBL, GBC, ZAP, PF, box 4.
5. Martin V. Melosi, *Coping with Abundance: Energy and Environment in Industrial America* (New York: Knopf, 1985), 254.
6. "The Natural Gas Story." They also worried that this ruling would challenge the role of the Texas Railroad Commission, which, since the 1930s, had limited the rate of production in the oil fields, thereby placing a floor under prices. See William R. Childs, *The Texas Railroad Commission: Understanding Regulation in America to the Mid-twentieth Century* (College Station: Texas A&M University Press, 2005).
7. Bush to R. S. Brenhand Jr., Dec. 2, 1957, GBL, GBC, ZAP, PC, box 1.
8. Melosi, *Coping with Abundance*, 255.
9. Valenti to Bush, Feb. 21, 1963, GBL, GBC, ZAP, PC, box 1.
10. George H. W. Bush, statement, Aug. 17, 1970, GBL, GBC, CONG, box 1.
11. Melosi, *Coping with Abundance*, 249.
12. George H. W. Bush, remarks in defense of oil import program, May 27, 1969, GBL, GBC, CONG, box 1.
13. Bush to Richard Mack, April 14, 1968, GBL, GBC, CONG, box 1.
14. Daniel Yergin, *The Prize: The Epic Quest for Oil, Money, and Power* (New York: Free Press, 1991), 589.
15. K. C. Clarke and Jeffrey J. Hemphill, "The Santa Barbara Oil Spill, a Retrospective," in Proceedings of the Sixty-Fourth Annual Meeting of the Association of Pacific Coast Geographers, University of California, Santa Barbara, 2001.
16. Samuel P. Hays, *A History of Environmental Politics Since 1945* (Pittsburgh: University of Pittsburgh Press, 2000), 25–26.
17. Robert Bendiner, "Man—The Most Endangered Species," *New York Times*, Oct. 20, 1969, 46.
18. "Fight for Survival," *New York Times*, Jan. 4, 1970, 152.
19. The National Environmental Policy Act of 1969.
20. "Heading Off an Energy Crisis," *Nation's Business*, July 1971, 26–28.
21. F. Ritter Shumway, "The Energy Crisis: The Whys and Wherefores," *Vital Speeches*, Jan. 15, 1971, 209–12.
22. "Too Good to Last?," *Forbes*, Nov. 1, 1969, 29–30.
23. F. N. Ikard, "Criticism, Policy, and Reality: A National Energy Policy," *Vital Speeches*, Aug. 1, 1971, 625–28.
24. Lawrence A. Mayer, "Why the U.S. Is in an 'Energy Crisis,'" *Fortune*, Nov. 1970, 74–77, 159–64.

25. "8000 Jam 1st Teach-In, Cheer Critics of Gov't," *Environmental Action*, Jan. 31, 1970, 1.

26. "Pollution Fight Gains in Colleges Here," *New York Times*, Feb. 23, 1970, 1, 25.

27. Yergin, *Prize*, 589.

28. "Man-Made Fuel Crisis," *New York Times*, Oct. 2, 1970, 33.

29. Mayer, "Why the U.S. Is in an 'Energy Crisis.'"

30. According to Samuel Hays, 60–70 percent of those who appeared on the list would lose at the polls. Samuel P. Hays, *Beauty, Health, and Permanence: Environmental Politics in the United States, 1955–1985* (New York: Cambridge University Press, 1989), 463.

31. Eric Hirst, "Energy Versus Environment," *Current*, April 1973, 50–56; "The Growing Gasoline Gap," *Time*, April 16, 1973, 88; "America's Energy Crisis: Ways People and Companies Beat It," *U.S. News & World Report*, Sept. 10, 1973, 53; "3 of 4 Americans Get to Work by Car," *U.S. News & World Report*, Dec. 31, 1973, 12; "The Painful Change to Thinking Small," *Time*, Dec. 31, 1973, 18–22, 25.

32. Allen J. Matusow, *Nixon's Economy: Booms, Busts, Dollars, and Votes* (Lawrence: University Press of Kansas, 1998), 150.

33. Comments made at the American Mining Congress Coal Convention, May 17, 1971, quoted in David R. Toll and Richard X. Donovan, "Toward a New National Energy Policy," Nov. 9, 1972, RNL, WHCF, EPO, box 24.

34. Flanigan to John Ehrlichman, George Shultz, et al., July 7, 1972, RNL, WHCF, EPO, box 43.

35. Richard H. K. Vietor, *Energy Policy in America Since 1945: A Study of Business–Government Relations* (New York: Cambridge University Press, 1984), 211.

36. George S. McGovern, "Toward a Sound National Energy Program," n.d., RNL, WHCF, EPO, box 56.

37. DiBona to Ehrlichman, Henry A. Kissinger, and George P. Shultz, March 27, 1973, RNL, WHCF, EPO, box 22.

38. Medders to Nixon, Jan. 20, 1973, RNL, WHCF, EPO, box 48.

39. Richard Fairbanks to Ehrlichman, Feb. 1, 1973, RNL, WHCF, EPO, box 26.

40. Flanigan to Nixon, Dec. 28, 1972, RNL, WHCF, EPO, box 43; Lay to John Rafuse, April 11, 1973, RNL, WHCF, EPO, box 22.

41. Schaefer to DiBona, April 15, 1973, RNL, WHCF, EPO, box 34. On Jackson's presidential ambitions, see Robert G. Kaufman, *Henry M. Jackson: A Life in Politics* (Seattle: University of Washington Press, 2000).

42. Fraser to Nixon, April 24, 1973, RNL, WHCF, EPO, box 73.

43. "Sargent Says Mass. Must Go on Energy Diet," *Boston Globe*, April 18, 1973, 1.

44. Amory B. Lovins, letter to the editor, *New York Times*, June 8, 1973, 38.

45. S. David Freeman, "Is There an Energy Crisis? An Overview," *Annals of the American Academy of Political and Social Science*, Nov. 1973, 2, 10.

46. David S. Painter, "From the Nixon Doctrine to the Carter Doctrine," in *American Energy Policy in the 1970s*, ed. Robert Lifset (Norman: University of Oklahoma Press, 2014), 67.

47. Yergin, *Prize*, 591.

48. Walter J. Levy, "Oil Power," *Foreign Affairs*, July 1971, 652–68.

49. Painter, "From the Nixon Doctrine to the Carter Doctrine," 63–64.

50. Ronald Schiller, "It's Time to Face the Energy Crisis," *Reader's Digest*, Jan. 1973, 71–76.
51. James E. Akins, "The Oil Crisis: This Time the Wolf Is Here," *Foreign Affairs*, April 1973, 469.
52. "Oil, Gas Resources Dwindling: U.S. Faces Crisis," *Washington Post*, Oct. 5, 1972, F1.
53. Akins, "The Oil Crisis," 482; "Top Energy Expert: James E. Akins," *New York Times*, April 19, 1973, 53.
54. Yergin, *Prize*, 591.
55. "Exxon Stations on 2 Toll Roads Are Limiting Sales," *New York Times*, June 20, 1973, 87; "Gasoline: A Step Toward Rationing," *Newsweek*, May 21, 1973, 76; "The Gasoline Shortage—When Will It End?," *U.S. News & World Report*, July 2, 1973, 29; "Enough Gasoline After All—If . . . ," *U.S. News & World Report*, July 23, 1973, 36.
56. Al Richman, "The Polls: Public Attitudes Toward the Energy Crisis," *Public Opinion Quarterly* 43, no. 4 (Winter 1979): 576–85.
57. "The Gasoline Shortage: Real or Contrived?," *New York Times*, June 8, 1973, 51.
58. "Senate Asked to Order Probe of Gas Crisis," *Boston Globe*, June 2, 1973, 1; "Is the Shortage Serious?," *New York Times*, June 10, 1973, 216.
59. Richman, "Polls"; "Gas Gap: More Taxes?," *Newsweek*, June 11, 1973, 87; "What's Being Done as Gasoline Shortages Grow," *U.S. News & World Report*, June 18, 1973, 78; "The Shortage Hits Home," *Time*, June 25, 1973, 85; "Back Come the Trustbusters," *Time*, July 23, 1973, 74; "Did the Oil Giants Rig Prices?," *U.S. News & World Report*, July 30, 1973, 27; "Rollbacks and Rationing," *Newsweek*, Sept. 17, 1973, 65.
60. "Is the Big 'Shortage' Just Gas?," *Newsweek*, July 2, 1973, 59; "Energy Crisis: Second Look," *Nation*, Feb. 19, 1973, 229–30.
61. "Fresh White House Moves to Cope with Energy Crisis," *U.S. News & World Report*, July 9, 1973, 21–22; "A Plan of Attack on the Energy Crisis," *Business Week*, June 30, 1973, 26; "Shortage Hits Home"; "America's Energy Crisis," 52.
62. Knauer to Love, July 18, 1973, RNL, WHCF, SF, FG 6-25 (EPO), box 1.
63. "Mobil Oil Co. Discontinues Gasoline Ads," *Washington Post*, June 22, 1973, 3.
64. "The Gasoline Shortage Hits the Media," *Business Week*, Aug. 11, 1973, 129.
65. Cole to Nixon, Aug. 7, 1973, RNL, WHCF, SF, FG 6-25 (EPO), box 1.
66. Gergen to Haig, Oct. 1, 1973; Gergen to Bruce Kehrli, Sept. 24, 1973; both in RNL, WHSF, SMOF, HAIG, box 13.
67. Love to senior advisers, Sept. 6, 1973; David Parker to Love, Sept. 13, 1973; both in RNL, WHCF, EPO, box 2.
68. Ed Thompson to Love, July 24, 1973, RNL, WHCF, SF, FG 6-25 (EPO), box 1.
69. J. A. Vickers to Love, Sept. 5, 1973, RNL, WHCF, SF, FG 6-25 (EPO), box 1.

2: Coming Up Dry

1. Love to Kissinger, Oct. 14, 1973, RNL, WHCF, EPO, box 24.
2. Nicholas C. Proffitt, "Faisal's Threat," *Newsweek*, Sept. 10, 1973, 35–37.
3. "Arab Oil Policy Means a Crisis for the U.S.," *Chicago Tribune*, Sept. 16, 1973, 1.
4. On Kissinger, see Jeremi Suri, *Henry Kissinger and the American Century* (Cambridge, Mass.: Harvard University Press, 2007).
5. Robert Dallek, *Nixon and Kissinger: Partners in Power* (New York: Harper Collins, 2002), 525.

6. On the embargo, see Rudiger Graf, "Making Use of the 'Oil Weapon': Western Industrialized Countries and Arab Petropolitics in 1973–1974," *Diplomatic History* 36, no. 1 (Jan. 2012): 185–208.

7. "Cutoff in Oil to U.S. Ordered by Libya," *New York Times*, Oct. 20, 1973, 37.

8. "Victims Police Arab Oil Embargo," *Los Angeles Times*, Nov. 18, 1973, J1.

9. "The Oil Crunch to Come," *Christian Science Monitor*, Oct. 17, 1973, 1.

10. "Faisal Lecture," *Washington Post*, Nov. 12, 1973, 4.

11. U.S. Congress, Senate, Committee on Foreign Relations, Subcommittee on Multinational Corporations, *Multinational Corporations and U.S. Foreign Policy*, 93rd Cong., 2nd sess., June 20, 1974, 447.

12. Dallek, *Nixon and Kissinger*, 535.

13. Stanley Karnow, "Jackson's Bid: Walking the Long Road to the White House," *New Republic*, May 25, 1974, 18.

14. Joseph Kraft, "Secretary Henry," *New York Times*, Oct. 28, 1973, 267.

15. Robert Sherrill, "Casing the Democrats: Senator Jackson Enters Right," *Nation*, Feb. 1, 1975, 105–11.

16. Juan Cameron, "Scoop Jackson Comes Down with Presidential Fever," *Fortune*, June 1974, 236.

17. "U.S. Airlift May Exceed Soviet Aid," *Los Angeles Times*, Oct. 17, 1973, 3.

18. Buchanan to Nixon, Nov. 5, 1973, RNL, WHSF, SMOF, HAIG, box 9; "Bush Assails Carter Criticism of Nixon," *Atlanta Constitution*, Oct. 31, 1973, 7.

19. Love to Nixon, Oct. 27, 1973, RNL, WHCF, EPO, box 24.

20. John McLaughlin to Haig, Nov. 14, 1973, RNL, WHSF, SMOF, HAIG, box 10.

21. Ibid.; Concerned Citizens of Eastern North Carolina to Nixon, Feb. 8, 1974, RNL, WHCF, SF, CM, box 22.

22. Buchanan to Nixon, Nov. 5 and 10, 1973; Shultz to Nixon, Nov. 5, 1973; all in RNL, WHSF, SMOF, HAIG, box 9; Gergen to Haig and Ronald L. Ziegler, Nov. 2, 1973, RNL, WHSF, SMOF, PPF, box 102.

23. "A Still Unexplained Challenge of Nerves," *New York Times*, Oct. 28, 1973, 207.

24. Memo: Energy meeting with state and local elected officials, Nov. 7, 1973, RNL, WHSF, SMOF, POF, box 93.

25. "President Is Open on Gas Rationing," *New York Times*, Nov. 18, 1973, 1.

26. Memo: Cabinet meeting notes, Nov. 6, 1973, WHSF, SMOF, POF, box 93; Stein to Shultz et al., Nov. 9, 1973, RNL, WHSF, SMOF, HAIG, box 10; "Rationing, Tax— or White Market?," *Time*, Dec. 3, 1973, 38–39.

27. Kissinger to Scowcroft for Haig, Nov. 16, 1973, as quoted in Graf, "Making Use of the 'Oil Weapon,'" 205.

28. "U.S. Says Oil Cut Will Not Alter Mideast Policy," *New York Times*, Nov. 22, 1973, 1.

29. News Summary, Dec. 3, 1973, RNL, WHSF, SMOF, POF, box 69.

30. "Fuel Cuts Expected," *New York Times*, Nov. 25, 1973, 28.

31. See, for example, the letters from Mrs. Sheila Roalf's second-grade class, Petersburg, Va., Nov. 18, 1973, RNL, WHCF, SF, UT, box 10.

32. Nixon to girls and boys (Va.), Dec. 11, 1973, RNL, WHCF, SF, UT, box 10.

33. Mildred Ellis to Love, Dec. 1, 1973, RNL, WHCF, EPO, box 16.

34. Yankelovich to Shultz, Nov. 29, 1973, RNL, WHCF, SF, UT, box 5; "Oil and Gas

Executives Gave at Least $5 Million to Nixon's Re-election Campaign," *Boston Globe*, Dec. 2, 1973, 33.

35. Mrs. Maurice Frolich to Nixon, Nov. 29, 1973, RNL, WHCF, EPO, box 16.

36. Mrs. J. E. Carlisle to Nixon, Nov. 30, 1973, RNL, WHCF, EPO, box 17.

37. News summary, Dec. 19, 1973, RNL, WHSF, SMOF, POF, box 69.

38. "Will Everyone Hold at Fifty?," *Newsweek*, Nov. 26, 1973, 84.

39. "Where the Tradeoffs Come in the Energy Crisis," *Business Week*, Nov. 17, 1973, 66.

40. H. C. Wehmeier to Love, Nov. 30, 1973, and Joe Jennings to Love, Nov. 30, 1973, RNL, WHCF, EPO, box 16.

41. Ed Ertman to Love, Nov. 29, 1973, RNL, WHCF, EPO, box 17; "Congress Veto over Rationing Voted," *New York Times*, Dec. 15, 1973, 18.

42. Members of the Eau Claire County Welfare Rights Organization to Nixon, Nov. 27, 1973, RNL, WHCF, SF, CM, box 22.

43. Eliot Marshall, "Gas Rationing," *New Republic*, Nov. 24, 1973, 11.

44. "Minorities Are Hardest Hit by Energy Shortage," *Philadelphia Tribune*, Jan. 5, 1974; "Blacks to Be Hit Hard by Energy Crisis," *Washington Afro-American*, Dec. 18, 1973; Vernon E. Jordan Jr., "The Energy Crisis and the Ghetto," *Florida Star*, Dec. 8, 1973, all in RNL, WHSF, SMOF, HAIG, box 19; "Blacks Fear Layoffs and Rising Costs in Energy Crisis," *New York Times*, Jan. 26, 1974, 15; Vernon E. Jordan Jr., "The Energy Crisis: For Blacks, a Disproportionate Burden," *New York Times*, Feb. 9, 1974, 29; Goodlett to Nixon, Feb. 4, 1974, RNL, WHSF, SMOF, HAIG, box 19.

45. "House Vote Bars Giving Indochina Oil for Military," *New York Times*, Dec. 15, 1973, 1; Jack R. Hill to Love, Dec. 3, 1973, RNL, WHCF, EPO, box 16.

46. Nanine Bilski to Love, Dec. 5, 1973, RNL, WHCF, EPO, box 16.

47. Mrs. Peter Green to Love, Nov. 30, 1973, RNL, WHCF, EPO, box 17.

48. Ash to Haig, Nov. 14, 1973, RNL, WHSF, SMOF, HAIG, box 8.

49. Simon to Haig, n.d., RNL, WHSF, SF, FG 6-25 (EPO), box 1.

50. William Safire, "Who's What Around the White House," *New York Times Magazine*, Nov. 11, 1973, 39.

51. "The Gordian Knot of Gasoline Prices," *Business Week*, Dec. 15, 1973, 23.

52. Parsky to Simon, Dec. 5, 1973, WSP, ser. IIIA, drawer 13, folder 29.

53. Tom Korologos, Dec. 19, 1973, RNL, WHSF, SMOF, POF, box 24.

54. News summary, Dec. 19, 1973.

55. "Drivers' Choice: Cut Gas 10% or Face Rationing," *New York Times*, Dec. 23, 1973, 105; "No Rush to Car Pools, Mass Transit or Two-Wheelers," *New York Times*, Dec. 26, 1973, 48.

56. William E. Simon, *Face the Nation* interview, CBS, Dec. 16, 1973, WSP, ser. IIIA, drawer 13, folder 38.

57. Press conference of Henry A. Kissinger and William E. Simon, Jan. 19, 1974, WSP, ser. IIIA, drawer 13, folder 39.

58. Senator Robert J. Dole, Dec. 8, 1973, RNL, WHCF, SF, UT, box 6.

59. Hudnut to John C. Sawhill, Jan. 9, 1974, WSP, ser. IIIA, drawer 13, folder 16; press conference of William E. Simon, Jan. 23, 1974, WSP, ser. IIIA, drawer 13, folder 39; "Drivers in Daytona 500 Begging for Gasoline, Too," *New York Times*, Feb. 17, 1974, E14.

60. Simon to Weinberger, Jan. 29, 1974, WSP, ser. I, drawer 1, folder 18.
61. Kehrli to Haig, Nov. 30, 1973, RNL, WHSF, SMOF, HAIG, box 9; Kehrli to Haig, Dec. 1973, RNL, WHSF, SMOF, HAIG, box 15.
62. "The Energy Crisis Turns Ugly," *Science News*, Dec. 22–29, 1973, 391; "Painful Change to Thinking Small," 19.
63. "Energy Office Flooded by Suggestions, with 90% Preferring Rationing of Fuel," *New York Times*, Jan. 7, 1974, 18.
64. News summary, Dec. 13, 1973, RNL, WHSF, SMOF, POF, box 69.
65. "House Rejects Energy Bill After It Passes the Senate," *New York Times*, Dec. 22, 1973, 1, 10.
66. "The Angry Truck Driver: 'We've Got to Show 'Em,'" *New York Times*, Dec. 5, 1973, 1; "The New Highway Guerillas," *Time*, Dec. 17, 1973, 33.
67. Studs Terkel, "Truck Power: A Steel Hauler Speaks Out," *New Times*, Dec. 28, 1973, 20–27; "Ohio Protest Goes On," *New York Times*, Dec. 6, 1974, 1; "The Great Truck Blockade," *U.S. News & World Report*, Dec. 17, 1973, 18; "New Highway Guerillas."
68. Harry Maurer, "Organizing the 'Gypsies,'" *Nation*, Jan. 11, 1975, 12.
69. Susan Sheehan, "On the Road with a Bedbug Hauler," *New York Times Magazine*, Nov. 12, 1972, 36. On trucking, see Shane Hamilton, *Trucking Country: The Road to America's Wal-Mart Economy* (Princeton, N.J.: Princeton University Press, 2008). See also D. Daryl Wyckoff and David H. Maister, *The Owner-Operator: Independent Trucker* (Lexington, Mass.: Lexington Books, 1975); John Richard Felton and Dale G. Anderson, eds., *Regulation and Deregulation of the Motor Carrier Industry* (Ames: Iowa State University Press, 1989), 14–37; Charles R. Perry, *Deregulation and the Decline of the Unionized Trucking Industry Labor* (Philadelphia: Industrial Research Unit, Wharton School, University of Pennsylvania, 1986); Interstate Commerce Commission, *The Independent Trucker: Nationwide Survey of Owner-Operators* (Washington, D.C.: Bureau of Economics, Interstate Commerce Commission, 1978).
70. Sheehan, "On the Road," 36.
71. Ibid.; Donn Pierce, "Those Truck Drivin' Men," *Esquire*, Dec. 1972, 322.
72. Maurer, "Organizing the 'Gypsies,'" 11.
73. "Pennsylvania Road Is Blocked as Truckers Protest Fuel Cost," *New York Times*, Dec. 4, 1973, 51; "Truck Driver-Owners Block Highways in Five States," *New York Times*, Dec. 5, 1973, 34; Maurer, "Organizing the 'Gypsies,'" 11; "Transportation Department–Related Federal Actions on Trucking Industry Problems Arising from Energy Shortage" (background paper, Feb. 8, 1974), RNL, WHCF, SMOF, MRD, box 16; news summary, Dec. 5, 1973, RNL, WHSF, SMOF, POF, box 69.
74. Cabinet meeting notes, Dec. 5, 1973, RNL, WHSF, SMOF, POF, box 93.
75. Claude S. Brinegar to the governors, Dec. 6, 1973, RNL, WHCF, SMOF, MRD, box 16.
76. News summary, Dec. 6 and 7, 1973, RNL, WHSF, SMOF, POF, box 69.
77. E. J. Bondhus (Colo.) to Love, Dec. 5, 1973, RNL, WHCF, EPO, box 16.
78. Jefferson Cowie, "Nixon's Class Struggle: Romancing the New Right Worker, 1969–1973," *Labor History* 43, no. 3 (2002): 257–83.
79. News summary, Dec. 10 and 12, 1973, RNL, WHSF, SMOF, POF, box 69.
80. Maurer, "Organizing the 'Gypsies.'"

81. "Truckers Adopt 'Demo' Weapon," *Boston Globe*, Dec. 10, 1973, 19.

82. Terkel, "Truck Power."

83. William Simon, press conference, Jan. 3, 1973, WSP, ser. IIIA, drawer 13, folder 39.

84. Alvin Snyder to Haig, Jan. 28, 1974, RNL, WHSF, SMOF, HAIG, box 16.

85. Bush to Simon, Dec. 18, 1973, WSP, ser. I, drawer 1, folder 26.

86. "Shoppers Stock Up on Toilet Paper," *Wisconsin Rapids Daily Tribune*, Jan. 10, 1974, 2; "The 'Shortage' of Bathroom Tissue: A Classic Study in Rumor," *New York Times*, Feb. 3, 1974, 29.

87. "Even Without Gas Rationing—Headaches Pile Up for Drivers," *U.S. News & World Report*, Dec. 31, 1973, 11–12; Judith Viorst, "A Day at the Pumps: A Nostalgic Look at the Energy Crisis," *Redbook*, June 1974, 38–40.

88. "The Gas Price Rise Was for Our Own Good," *New York Times*, Jan. 6, 1974, 23; "Half-Gallon Gas Price Seen," *New York Times*, Feb. 9, 1974, 32.

89. News summaries, Dec. 19, 1973, Jan. 15–16, 1974, RNL, WHSF, SMOF, POF, box 69.

90. "An Interview with William E. Simon," Jan. 6, 1974, WSP, ser. IIIA, drawer 13, folder 39.

91. U.S. Congress, Senate, Committee on Government Operations, Permanent Subcommittee on Investigations, *Current Energy Shortages Oversight Hearings: The Major Oil Companies*, 93rd Cong., 2nd sess., Jan. 21, 1974, 113–14; "Oil Companies Tell Senators Gap Is Real; Conservation and Alternative Fuels Urged," *Wall Street Journal*, Jan. 22, 1974, 2; "Top Oilmen Term Fuel Crisis Real; Senators Dubious," *New York Times*, Jan. 22, 1974, 1, 26; "Oil Profits Up 46% on 6% Volume Rise," *New York Times*, Jan. 23, 1974, 1, 21; Joseph Kraft, "Drubbing the Oil Companies," *Washington Post*, Jan. 24, 1974, 29; "Angered Oil Men Dispute Charges of Senate Critics," *New York Times*, Jan. 25, 1974, 1; "Oil Carpeted," *Economist*, Jan. 26, 1974, 56–57; "The Shortage: What Ticks Off John Doe," *National Petroleum News*, Feb. 1974, 36–38; "'Big Oil' Under Attack: The Crackdown Taking Shape in Congress," *U.S. News & World Report*, Feb. 4, 1974, 14–16; news summary, Jan. 22, 1974, RNL, WHSF, SMOF, POF, box 70.

92. Johnson to Simon, Jan. 12, 1974, WSP, ser. IIIA, drawer 13, folder 42; "Unit of Gulf Bought Ringling," *New York Times*, Jan. 22, 1974, 53.

93. News summaries, Jan. 21–24, 1974, RNL, WHSF, SMOF, POF, box 70.

94. "New Shape of the U.S. Oil Industry," *Business Week*, Feb. 2, 1974, 50–55; "Oil: A Catalyst for More Cooperation?," *Business Week*, Feb. 9, 1974, 24–25.

95. News summary, Jan. 24, 1974.

96. News summary, Feb. 5, 1974, RNL, WHSF, SMOF, POF, box 71.

97. "Jackson Sees Overriding of a Veto on Energy Bill," *New York Times*, Feb. 19, 1974, 20.

98. Ruth King (Boulder City, Nev.) to Nixon, Feb. 7, 1974, RNL, WHCF, SF, CM, box 22.

3: Turning Right

1. "Wife of Energy Chief Works at Saving Fuel," *Wisconsin State Journal*, Dec. 23, 1973, WSP, ser. VIII, drawer 48, folder 31; William E. Simon, *A Time for Truth* (New York: Reader's Digest Press, 1978), 54.

2. Dallek, *Nixon and Kissinger*, 557.

3. "The Times They Are A-Changin'," *Newsweek*, Feb. 18, 1974, 19–22.

4. "Trucker Spokesmen: No Guarantees," *Austin American-Statesman*, Feb. 5, 1974,

15; "Texas Truckers Dump Problems on Briscoe's Aides," *San Antonio Express*, Feb. 4, 1974, 1; "Truckers' Strike: Food Supplies Threatened," *Dallas Morning News*, Feb. 3, 1974, 1; "Truck Drivers Stopping in Texas for Protest," *Fort Worth Star-Telegram*, Feb. 3, 1974, 1, all in WSP, ser. IIIB, drawer 22, folder 37.

5. William S. Heffelfinger to Claude S. Brinegar, Feb. 4–6, 1974, RNL, WHCF, SMOF, MRD, box 16; news summary, Feb. 4, 1974, RNL, WHSF, SMOF, POF, box 71.

6. Simon to governors of each state, Feb. 2, 1974, RNL, WHCF, SMOF, MRD, box 16.

7. Schubert to Michael Raoul-Duval, n.d., RNL, WHCF, SMOF, MRD, box 16.

8. Shapp to Nixon, Feb. 2, 1974, RNL, WHCF, SF, TN, box 2.

9. "The Times They Are A-Changin'."

10. UPI report, Feb. 3, 1974, RNL, WHCF, SMOF, MRD, box 16; "Gov. Shapp Urges Truck Tie-Up Halt," *New York Times*, Feb. 4, 1974, 1, 22.

11. Michael Raoul-Duval Notes, Feb. 3, 1974, RNL, WHCF, SMOF, MRD, box 16.

12. President's remarks regarding negotiations on the stoppages, Feb. 9, 1974, RNL, WHSF, SMOF, HAIG, box 43; Raoul-Duval Notes, Feb. 3, 1974.

13. UPI report, Feb. 3, 1974.

14. Heffelfinger to Brinegar, Feb. 6, 1974; Leslie W. Bray Jr. to Raoul-Duval and Walter Scott, daily report on truck work stoppages, morning edition, Feb. 6, 1974, both in RNL, WHCF, SMOF, MRD, box 16; news summary, Feb. 7, 1974, RNL, WHSF, SMOF, POF, box 71.

15. Francis W. Niland, Department of Justice summary, Feb. 7, 1974, RNL, WHCF, SMOF, MRD, box 16.

16. UPI report, Feb. 6, 1974, RNL, WHCF, SMOF, MRD, box 16.

17. Bray to Raoul-Duval and Scott, daily report on truck work stoppages, evening edition, Feb. 6, 1974, RNL, WHCF, SMOF, MRD, box 16; Charles G. Rodman to Haig, Feb. 5, 1974, RNL, WHSF, SMOF, HAIG, box 19; "Truckers' Strike Idles Auto Workers," *New York Times*, Feb. 5, 1974, 52; "Charter Flights Carry Beef to the East Coast," *New York Times*, Feb. 6, 1974, 20.

18. News summary, Feb. 4, 1974; Case to Simon, Jan. 30 and Feb. 4, 1974, WSP, ser. IIIA, drawer 13, folder 17.

19. "Gas Fever: Happiness Is a Full Tank," *Time*, Feb. 18, 1974, 35–36; "The Times They Are A-Changin'."

20. Sonny Kleinfield, "Hey Buddy, Can You Spare a Gallon?," *New Times*, March 8, 1974, 14–15.

21. "Van Snarls Traffic as Driver Leaves It in Trucker Protest," *New York Times*, Feb. 7, 1974, 26.

22. Niland, Department of Justice summary, Feb. 7, 1974; press conference of William Saxbe, Feb. 8, 1974, WSP, ser. IIIA, drawer 13, folder 40.

23. "Truckers' Tie-Up Cutting Supplies," *New York Times*, Feb. 5, 1974, 1, 21; news summaries, Feb. 5–6, 1974, RNL, WHSF, SMOF, POF, box 71; Bray to Raoul-Duval and Scott, daily report on truck work stoppages, evening edition, Feb. 7, 1974, RNL, WHCF, SMOF, MRD, box 16.

24. News summary, Feb. 2, 1974, RNL, WHSF, SMOF, POF, box 71.

25. "One State's Response to Gasoline Panic," *U.S. News & World Report*, Feb. 4, 1974, 16; "Energy: How Much Worse?," *U.S. News & World Report*, Feb. 11, 1974, 20; "Do-It-Yourself Rationing," *Economist*, Feb. 16, 1974, 50–51; "Gas Fever."

26. Press conference of William E. Simon, Feb. 8, 1974, WSP, ser. IIIA, drawer 13, folder 40.
27. News summary, Feb. 6, 1974, RNL, WHSF, SMOF, POF, box 71; "Byrne Announces Mandatory Plan of 'Gas' Rationing," *New York Times*, Feb. 9, 1974, 1; "Governors Act, Washington Says It's for the Best," *New York Times*, Feb. 10, 1974, 183.
28. Shapp to Nixon, Feb. 8, 1974, RNL, WHCF, SF, TN, box 2.
29. News summary, Feb. 4, 1974; Richman, "Polls."
30. Clawson to Haig, Feb. 9, 1974, RNL, WHSF, SMOF, HAIG, box 19.
31. George P. Shultz testimony, Feb. 4, 1974, RNL, WHSF, HOOP, box 5.
32. Haig to Nixon, Jan. 18, 1974, RNL, WHSF, SMOF, POF, box 25.
33. News summary, Feb. 4, 1974.
34. Thomson to Nixon, Feb. 6, 1974; Thomson to James Falk, Feb. 6, 1974, both in RNL, WHCF, SF, TN, box 2.
35. News summary, Feb. 6, 1974; Simon to Nixon, Feb. 6, 1974, WSP, ser. I, drawer 1, folder 19; Judy Bachrach, "William Simon, the Energetic Czar," *Washington Post*, Jan. 13, 1974, 1, 2.
36. William Safire, "Do Something!," *New York Times*, Feb. 14, 1974, 41.
37. Remarks of Deputy Press Secretary Gerald L. Warren, Feb. 7, 1974, RNL, WHSF, SMOF, HAIG, box 43.
38. "Angry Truckers Reject Deal," Associated Press, Feb. 9, 1974.
39. News summary, Feb. 8, 1974, RNL, WHSF, SMOF, POF, box 71.
40. Bray to Raoul-Duval and Scott, daily report on truck work stoppages, evening edition, Feb. 7, 1974; "Strike of Truck Drivers Makes 75,000 Jobless," *New York Times*, Feb. 6, 1974, 20.
41. Charles G. Rodman to Haig, Feb. 5, 1974.
42. Moules to Nixon, Feb. 8, 1974, RNL, WHCF, SMOF, MRD, box 16.
43. Heinz to Nixon, Feb. 6, 1974, RNL, WHCF, SF, TN, box 2.
44. Shuster to Nixon, Feb. 6, 1974, RNL, WHCF, SF, TN, box 2.
45. Timmons to Haig, Feb. 6, 1974, RNL, WHSF, SMOF, HAIG, box 19.
46. Interview of Peter Brennan on the *Today* show, Feb. 7, 1974, RNL, WHCF, SMOF, MRD, box 16.
47. Clawson to Haig, Feb. 7, 1974, RNL, WHSF, SMOF, HAIG, box 17.
48. "Most Truckers Still Idle," *New York Times*, Feb. 9, 1974, 1.
49. "Saxbe Bids Governors Act," *New York Times*, Feb. 4, 1974, 22.
50. Press conference of William E. Simon, Feb. 5, 1974, WSP, ser. IIIB, drawer 22, folder 37.
51. Raoul-Duval, Memo, Oval Office meeting, Feb. 8, 1974, RNL, WHCF, SMOF, MRD, box 16.
52. Carlson and Terrence R. Colvin to Ash, Jan. 29, 1974, WSP, ser. IIIA, drawer 13.
53. Nick Thimmesch, "The Back-Room Master in Waiting: Melvin Laird, the Professional Politician Who Launched a Thousand Compromises, Now Waits to Launch a Thousand More," *Washington Post*, May 5, 1974, 25.
54. "70 in House Form Conservative Bloc," *Chicago Tribune*, Feb. 18, 1974, 2; "GOP Group Moves to Stop Nixon from 'Tilting Leftward,'" *Boston Globe*, Feb. 18, 1974, 14.

55. Roland Evans and Robert Novak, "Conservatives and the Nixon 'Sell-Out,'" *Washington Post*, Feb. 16, 1974, 19.

56. Safire, "Do Something!"

57. "Energy Men Find Nixon Plan Weak," *New York Times*, Nov. 27, 1973, 57.

58. Milton Friedman, "Why Some Prices Should Rise," *Newsweek*, Nov. 19, 1973; Milton Friedman, "FEO and the Gas Lines," *Newsweek*, March 4, 1974.

59. "Man of Energy; William Simon Works Hard, Decides Fast, and Expects Results," *Wall Street Journal*, Dec. 7, 1973, 1, 23; "Fourth Down for the 'Vince Lombardi of Energy,'" *New Times*, March 8, 1974, 9–10.

60. Simon, *Time for Truth*, 51.

61. Simon to I. W. Burnham II, Feb. 21, 1974, WSP, ser. I, drawer 1, folder 20.

62. "Simon Announces Stand-By System on 'Gas' Rationing," *New York Times*, Dec. 28, 1973, 1, 12; "37 Gallons Possible as Monthly Gas Ration," *New York Times*, Jan. 21, 1974, 14.

63. "Gas Rationing Coupons Found to Activate Dollar Bill Machine," *New York Times*, May 10, 1974, 39.

64. Shultz to Nixon, Jan. 10, 1974, RNL, WHSF, SMOF, HAIG, box 15; news summary, Feb. 5, 1974.

65. Urich to Simon, Dec. 28, 1973; David C. Hoopes to Simon, Jan. 5, 1974, both in RNL, WHSF, SMOF, HAIG, box 24.

66. Cotton to Bush, Nov. 13, 1973; Bush to Love, Nov. 19, 1973, both in RNL, WHCF, SF, UT, box 10.

67. Simon, *Time for Truth*, 60.

68. William E. Simon, "Big Government of Freedom: The Line of Economic Freedom Leads to Slavery" (speech delivered at Kansas State University, March 18, 1975), WSP, ser. VIII, drawer 48, folder 34; "Growing an Energetic Monster," *St. Louis Globe-Democrat*, March 12, 1976, 16.

69. Jamieson to Simon, Jan. 21, 1974, WSP, ser. IIIA, drawer 13, folder 1.

70. Ash to Nixon, Feb. 11 and 15, 1974, RNL, WHSF, SMOF, POF, box 26; Ash, memorandum for the president, Feb. 12, 1974, WSP, ser. IIIA, drawer 13, folder 29.

71. "First Emergency Energy Bill Vetoed," in *CQ Almanac 1974*, 30th ed. (Washington, D.C.: Congressional Quarterly, 1975), 727–32.

72. William F. Buckley Jr., "On Filling One's Gas Tank with Dignity," *Los Angeles Times*, March 13, 1974, C7; Friedman, "FEO and the Gas Lines."

73. Cabinet meeting, Feb. 21, 1974, RNL, WHSC, SMOF, POF, box 93.

74. "Ford Doubts That Nation Will Need 'Gas' Rationing," *New York Times*, Feb. 14, 1974, 29.

75. "Why the GOP's Bush Is Hopeful," *Chicago Tribune*, Jan. 16, 1974, 12.

76. Cabinet meeting, Feb. 21, 1974.

77. "'Dear Senator: This Has Gone Far Enough,'" *U.S. News & World Report*, March 11, 1974, 31.

78. "Hays Lashes Out at Simple Simon," *Washington Post*, Feb. 5, 1974, 17.

79. U.S. Congress, Senate, *Current Energy Shortages*, 117.

80. News summaries, Feb. 18 and 23–26, 1974, RNL, WHSF, SMOF, POF, box 71; "Long Lines, Short Tempers," *Newsweek*, March 4, 1974, 65–66.

328 Notes to pages 110–116

81. News summary, Feb. 26, 1974.

82. Leonard Woodcock to Nixon, Feb. 1, 1974, RNL, WHCF, SF, UT, box 6.

83. Maraziti to Nixon, Feb. 14, 1974, WSP, ser. IIIA, drawer 13, folder 17.

84. Susan Parker et al. (Hopatcong, N.J.) to Nixon, Jan. 31, 1974; Kathy Burnett and Sandra Bellomo (Somerville, N.J.) to Nixon, Feb. 1, 1974; Joyce Porter et al. (New Brunswick, N.J.) to Nixon, Feb. 5, 1974, all in RNL, WHCF, SF, CM, box 22.

85. Concerned Citizens of Maryland (Baltimore County) to Nixon, Feb. 21, 1974, RNL, WHCF, SF, CM, box 22.

86. Ottens to Simon, Feb. 17, 1974, WSP, ser. IIIA, drawer 13, folder 31.

87. "Washington Wire," *Wall Street Journal*, Feb. 8, 1974, 1.

88. Docking to Nixon, Feb. 15, 1974, RNL, WHCF, SF, UT, box 6.

89. News summaries, Feb. 25–26, 1974.

90. Bob's Texaco to Nixon, Feb. 11, 1974, RNL, WHCF, SF, CM, box 22.

91. John Sawhill, Internal Revenue Agents Investigating Fuel Oil Price Gouging, Jan. 18, 1974, RNL, WHCF, SF, FG 6-26, (FEO), box 1.

92. "Oil-Price Rollback Voted by Senate on About 25% of U.S. Crude Output," *Wall Street Journal*, Feb. 20, 1974, 3.

93. Arthur Hadley, "The Agony and the Energy Bill," *New Times*, Feb. 22, 1974, 21–24.

94. Cabinet meeting, Feb. 21, 1974.

95. Simon, *Time for Truth*, 54–55; William E. Simon, *A Time for Reflection: An Autobiography*, with John M. Caher (Washington, D.C.: Regency, 2004), 96–97.

96. News summaries, Feb. 25–26, 1974; "President Says Crisis in Energy Is Over for Nation," *New York Times*, Feb. 26, 1974, 1.

97. "Nixon Tells G.O.P. Parley He Will Veto Energy Bill," *New York Times*, March 1, 1974, 1.

98. Cabinet meeting notes, March 8, 1974, RNL, WHSF, SMOF, POF, box 93.

99. Herbert Stein, speech to the National Economists Club, Feb. 27, 1974, RNL, WHSF, SMOF, POF, box 26; Clawson to Haig, Feb. 28, 1974, RNL, WHSF, SMOF, HAIG, box 17.

100. News summaries, March 10 and 23, 1974, RNL, WHSF, SMOF, POF, box 72.

101. News summary, Feb. 27, 1974, RNL, WHSF, SMOF, POF, box 71.

102. News summaries, Feb. 25–26, 1974; "Top Democrats Say U.S. Energy Crisis Has Not Subsided," *New York Times*, Feb. 27, 1974, 1, 46; "President Says Crisis in Energy Is Over for Nation."

103. "Nixon Vetoes Energy Bill and Is Upheld," *New York Times*, March 7, 1974, 1, 28.

104. News summary, March 22, 1973, RNL, WHSF, SMOF, POF, box 72.

105. "Nixon Vetoes Energy Bill and Is Upheld."

106. Ken Cole to Haig, May 3, 1974; Rees Lloyd to Bill Hill, April 10, 1974; Memo: Nationwide Trucker Shutdown, May 13, 1974, all in RNL, WHCF, SMOF, MRD, box 33.

107. Raoul-Duval to Cole, April 10, 1974, RNL, WHCF, SMOF, MRD, box 33.

108. *Wall Street Journal* as quoted in news summary, Feb. 20, 1974, RNL, WHSF, SMOF, POF, box 71.

109. "'Gas' Rationing Opposed," *New York Times*, Feb. 14, 1974, 44.
110. News summary, Feb. 5, 1974.
111. Shultz to Nixon, March 25, 1974, WSP, ser. IIIA, drawer 17, folder 3.
112. "White House Challenged by Environmental Chief," *New York Times*, March 11, 1974, 58.
113. "Nixon-Train Clash Averted," *Christian Science Monitor*, March 21, 1974, 2.
114. "Energy Shortage Both Favoring and Hampering Improvements in Nation's Environment," *New York Times*, March 29, 1974, 12.
115. "Tax Reform: No Final Action in 1974," in *CQ Almanac 1974*, 181–93.
116. Rachel Bronson, *Thicker Than Oil: America's Uneasy Partnership with Saudi Arabia* (New York: Oxford University Press, 2006), 107.
117. James Allen Smith, *Strategic Calling: The Center for Strategic and International Studies, 1962–1992* (Washington, D.C.: CSIS, 1993), 80.
118. Walter Laqueur, "Détente: What Is Left of It?," *New York Times Magazine*, Dec. 16, 1973, 293.
119. "Zumwalt Defends Indian Ocean Base," *Washington Post*, March 21, 1974, 3.
120. "The Debate over Diego Garcia," *Wall Street Journal*, April 4, 1974, 18.
121. "Plan for Indian Ocean Base Opposed," *Boston Globe*, June 9, 1974, 33.
122. "Retiring Navy Chief Says U.S. Has Lost Control of Sea Lanes to Russians," *New York Times*, May 14, 1974, 24.
123. James Reston, "Kissinger and the Joint Chiefs," *New York Times*, June 23, 1974, 201.
124. "Dealing with Moscow," *New York Times*, Aug. 7, 1974, 74.
125. "Warns of Weakness," *Los Angeles Times*, June 30, 1974, 7.
126. "Republican Right Preparing for a Comeback," *New York Times*, July 23, 1974, 29.
127. "Severe Economic Problems Are Being Left by Nixon," *New York Times*, Aug. 9, 1974, 45.

4: Finding a Way Out
1. Andrew Scott Cooper, *The Oil Kings: How the U.S., Iran, and Saudi Arabia Changed the Balance of Power in the Middle East* (New York: Simon & Schuster, 2011), 188–89.
2. Memorandum of Conversation, Dec. 15, 1974, *Foreign Relations of the United States, Volume 37: Energy Crisis, 1974–1980* (Washington, D.C.: Government Printing Office, 2012), 95.
3. "Europe's Summit," *New York Times*, Sept. 29, 1974, 38.
4. Walter Laqueur, "The Gathering Storm," *Commentary*, Aug. 1974, 23.
5. Kissinger quoted in Jeffrey A. Engel, ed., *The China Diary of George H. W. Bush: The Making of a Global President* (Princeton, N.J.: Princeton University Press, 2008), 39.
6. Cole to Haig, Aug. 23, 1974, GFL, PHF, box 50.
7. Yanek Mieczkowski, *Gerald Ford and the Challenges of the 1970s* (Lexington: University Press of Kentucky, 2005), 111.
8. "Looking Toward Summit," *New York Times*, Sept. 4, 1974, 57; William Walker to Donald Rumsfeld, Oct. 25, 1974, GFL, CHY, box 5.
9. Remarks of the president to the Ninth World Energy Conference, Sept. 23, 1974, GFL, TIM, box 23.

10. Memorandum of Conversation, Aug. 17, 1974, *Foreign Relations of the United States,* volume 37, 12.

11. "Ford Summit Doubleheader to Air Inflation Ills," *Boston Globe,* Sept. 22, 1974, 2.

12. Cooper, *Oil Kings,* 208.

13. "Ford Warns of Possible Retaliation If Oil Nations Threaten Economy," *Wall Street Journal,* Sept. 24, 1974, 3.

14. "Ford, Kissinger Warn Arabs to Cut Back High Oil Prices," *Los Angeles Times,* Sept. 23, 1974, 2.

15. Richard Cheney interview, May 20, 1977, GFL, REI, box 1.

16. Bill Bradford, "Alan Greenspan and Ayn Rand," *American Enterprise Magazine,* Sept./Oct. 1997; Ralph Nader, "Greenspan Shrugged: The Reserve Chair's Philosophy Differs Little from His Ayn Rand Days," *San Francisco Bay Guardian,* April 18, 2000. In 1987, President Reagan would appoint Greenspan as chairman of the Federal Reserve Board, where he remained for eighteen years.

17. "Young, Agile, Pragmatic, Rumsfeld 'Supports the Dickens out of' Nixon," *New York Times,* Dec. 13, 1970, 241; "Nation's New Defense Chief," *New York Times,* Nov. 4, 1975, 25; "Serving More Than Once Has Several Precedents," *New York Times,* Dec. 29, 2000, 18.

18. "A Congressman Views Washington from a New Vantage," *Wall Street Journal,* Dec. 21, 1979, 12.

19. Biography, Frank G. Zarb, Federal Energy Administration, GFL, SEI, box 64.

20. "Simon Asks Curb on Consumer Spending," *Wall Street Journal,* June 27, 1974, 3.

21. "Ford's Advisers Oppose Keynesians," *New York Times,* Sept. 2, 1974, 21.

22. "Why the G.O.P.'s Bush Is Hopeful."

23. Richard Cheney interview.

24. "50% Cut Proposed in Energy Growth," *New York Times,* Oct. 18, 1974, 1.

25. Greenspan, memorandum for the vice president, Jan. 22, 1975, GFL, GRN, box 19.

26. Zarb to Ford, Re: National Energy Policy and Energy Policy Briefing Book, Dec. 18, 1974; Cole, briefing on energy policy, Dec. 19, 1974, both in GFL, PHF, box 50.

27. Telegram from the Department of State to the Embassy in France, Nov. 12, 1974, *Foreign Relations of the United States,* volume 37, 71.

28. Zarb to Ford, Re: National Energy Policy and Energy Policy Briefing Book; Cole, briefing on energy policy; Zarb to executive committee of the Energy Resources Council, Dec. 31, 1974, GFL, GRN, box 43; Rumsfeld to Ford, Jan. 14, 1975, GFL, SEI, box 174; Richard Cheney interview, May 20, 1977, GFL, HWI, box 1.

29. "Message Gloomy," *New York Times,* Jan. 16, 1975, 1.

30. The president's economic and energy proposals, Jan. 31, 1975, GFL, CHY, box 4.

31. For a study that sees decontrol as an alternative to foreign diplomacy, see G. John Ikenberry, *Reason of State: Oil, Politics, and Capacities of American Government* (Ithaca, N.Y.: Cornell University Press, 1986).

32. Cooper, *Oil Kings,* 233.

33. I. F. Stone, "War for Oil," *New York Review of Books,* Feb. 6, 1975.

34. "White House Declines to Add to Kissinger Remark on Use of Force," *New York Times,* Jan. 4, 1975, 3.

35. Irving Kristol, "The Politics of Appeasement," *Wall Street Journal*, Feb. 12, 1975, 10; Ford to Rumsfeld, n.d., GFL, PHF, box 50.

36. Robert W. Tucker, "Oil: The Issue of American Intervention," *Commentary*, Jan. 1975, 21.

37. Miles Ignotus, "Seizing Arab Oil: A Blueprint for Fast and Effective Action," *Harper's*, March 1975, 45–62.

38. James Akins to Senator Charles Percy, Sept. 4, 1975, WSP, ser. IIIB, drawer 24, folder 54.

39. "Military Men Challenge Mideast 'Force' Strategy," *New York Times*, Jan. 10, 1975, 3.

40. Rumsfeld to Zarb and Jack Marsh, Jan. 3, 1975, GFL, FRD, box 12.

41. Mieczkowski, *Gerald Ford and the Challenges of the 1970s*, 231.

42. Ibid., 226, 231.

43. "Reaction Is Mixed to Ford Message," *New York Times*, Jan. 16, 1975, 1.

44. Quoted in Ikenberry, *Reasons of State*, 176.

45. "'Czar Zarb': Federal Energy Chief Goes All Out to Sell President's Program," *Wall Street Journal*, March 3, 1975, 1, 17.

46. "Ford Wins Praise for His Energy Efforts, but Not His Policy," *New York Times*, Feb. 13, 1975, 19.

47. Jules Witcover, *Marathon: The Pursuit of the Presidency, 1972–1976* (New York: Viking, 1977), 45.

48. Mieczkowski, *Gerald Ford and the Challenges of the 1970s*, 155.

49. "Congress Likely to Pursue Its Own Plan on Taxes and Energy," *Wall Street Journal*, Jan. 15, 1975, 3.

50. Press release, Senator Henry M. Jackson and Senator Edward M. Kennedy, Jan. 20, 1975, GFL, FRD, box 12.

51. Memorandum of Conversation, Jan. 30, 1975, *Foreign Relations of the United States*, volume 37, 124.

52. "Keynoter Hits at Reactionaries, Extremists," *Los Angeles Times*, Aug. 25, 1964, 1.

53. "Oil Import Quota, Gasoline Tax Seen Included in Democrats' Energy Program," *Wall Street Journal*, Feb. 19, 1975, 4.

54. "The Economy and Energy: A Congressional Program of Action," Feb. 1974, GFL, PHF, box 50.

55. John A. Hill, memorandum for Jim Lynn, March 1975, GFL, DUV, box 9.

56. Raoul-Duval to Jim Cannon, March 10, 1975, GFL, DUV, box 9.

57. Resolution before the Young Republican Leadership Conference, March 1, 1975, GFL, CHY, box 19.

58. "8 in Senate Oil Tax Study Linked to Industry's Gifts," *Los Angeles Times*, March 11, 1975, 5.

59. "House Panel, 22–14, Refuses to Tie Repeal of Oil Depletion Allowance to Tax Cut," *New York Times*, Feb. 5, 1975, 17; "Tax Cut Bill Gets Panel's Approval," *New York Times*, Feb. 20, 1975, 15; "Democrats Press for a Showdown on Oil Depletion," *New York Times*, Feb. 26, 1975, 1; "House Votes to Cut Taxes $21.3 Billion and Also End Oil Depletion Allowance," *New York Times*, Feb. 28, 1975, 1; "Compromise Weighed on Oil Depletion Bill," *Washington Post*, March 11, 1975, 2.

60. Raoul-Duval, memorandum for the president, Re: Energy Policy, March 4, 1975, GFL, DUV, box 6.

61. "Retailers and Refiners Urge Price Control Revival," *New York Times*, Sept. 5, 1975, 27.

62. "Federal Oil Controls End," *New York Times*, Sept. 1, 1975, 1.

63. Thomson to Cheney, n.d.; Ed Wren to Cheney, May 30, 1975, both in GFL, CHY, box 19.

64. *The Right Report*, July 2, 1976, GFL, CHY, box 16.

65. Glenn Schleede interview, May 1, 1976, GFL, HWI, box 1.

66. Cheney to Rumsfeld, May 24, 1975, GFL, CHY, box 5.

67. "Simon's Rejection of City Aid Plan Scored by Beame," *New York Times*, May 12, 1975, 44.

68. "Simon Leaves Little Hope of U.S. Aid to N.Y. Now," *Los Angeles Times*, July 26, 1975, 1.

69. "New Lead Actor in Détente Cast," *Chicago Tribune*, Nov. 24, 1975, 10.

70. Greenspan, memorandum for Rumsfeld, Cheney, and Bob Goldwin, Sept. 25, 1975, GFL, GRN, box 19.

71. "Reviving Auto Industry Signals Cheer in Detroit," *New York Times*, Nov. 14, 1975, 1.

72. GOP leadership meeting, Nov. 13, 1975, GFL, PHF, box 51.

73. Young to Ford, Nov. 26, 1975, GFL, PCR, box B79.

74. Republican Policy Committee, "S. 622—Energy Bill: Bad Policy," Dec. 11, 1975, GFL, PCR, box H40.

75. Greenspan, memorandum for Zarb, "The CEA View on the Energy Policy Decision," Dec. 13, 1975, GFL, GRN, box 19.

76. Greenspan, memorandum for Cheney, "Energy Bill: Political Considerations," Dec. 5, 1975, GFL, GRN, box 19.

77. Simon, memorandum for the president, Energy Policy and Conservation Act of 1975, Dec. 8, 1975, GFL, PHF, box 51; Simon, *Time for Truth*; David Gergen interview, Feb. 21, 1978, GFL, REI, box 1.

78. George Gallup, "Reagan Wrests Lead from Ford as '76 Choice of GOP Voters," Gallup Poll, Dec. 12, 1975, GFL, PCR, box H48.

79. Zarb, memorandum for the president, Recommendations on Energy Bill, Nov. 7, 1975, GFL, PHF, box 51; Zarb, memorandum for the president, Analysis of the Conference Energy Bill, Dec. 4, 1975, GFL, ZRB, box 2.

80. Zarb, memorandum for Jack Marsh, Meetings with Various Congressional Leaders Concerning the Energy Bill, Dec. 9, 1975, GFL, ZRB, box 2; Hartmann, memorandum for the president, The Energy Policy and Conservation Act, Dec. 18, 1975, GFL, HRT, box 39.

81. Press conference of Frank G. Zarb and Alan Greenspan, Dec. 22, 1975, GFL, DUV, box 6.

82. Mieczkowski, *Gerald Ford and the Challenges of the 1970s*, 255, 257.

83. Jack Donahue, *Wildcatter: The Story of Michel T. Halbouty and the Search for Oil* (New York: McGraw Hill, 1979), 223.

84. Dan Wright to Max Ulrich, May 10, 1976, GFL, CAN, box 12; Bo Callaway to Cheney, Jan. 5, 1976, GFL, PCR, box A1; "Texas and Energy," *Wall Street Journal*, April 30, 1976, 8.

85. "Reagan and Ford," *Los Angeles Times*, Nov. 23, 1975, 12.
86. Burton I. Kaufman, *The Presidency of James Earl Carter* (Lawrence: University Press of Kansas, 1993), 11.
87. Simon to James Connor, July 19, 1976, GFL, DUV, box 27.
88. Memo, An Explanation of the Reagan Victories in Texas and the Caucus States, May 1976, GFL, JON, box 25.
89. Raoul-Duval, Campaign Strategy for the Ford Campaign, Aug. 1976, GFL, DOW, box 1; Raoul-Duval interview, post–Nov. 2, 1976, GFL, HWI, box 1.
90. "Poll Shows Ford Gains on Carter," *Boston Globe*, Aug. 26, 1976, 8; Louis Harris, Harris Survey, Oct. 25, 1976, GFL, HRTP, box 163.
91. Jack Marsh, memorandum for the president, Oct. 27, 1976, GFL, CHY, box 16.
92. Transcript, *Meet the Press*, interview with Milton Friedman, Oct. 24, 1976, GFL, NES, box 71.
93. Mieczkowski, *Gerald Ford and the Challenges of the 1970s*, 340.
94. Simon, *Time for Truth*, 76.
95. Mieczkowski, *Gerald Ford and the Challenges of the 1970s*, 265.

5: Freeze a Yankee

1. "Carter, Security Aides Meet," *Boston Globe*, Jan. 23, 1977, 16.
2. "1.5 Million Left Jobless, 45 or More Dead in Freeze," *Baltimore Sun*, Jan. 31, 1977, 8.
3. "Congress Clears Emergency Gas Bill Quickly," *CQ Almanac 1977*, 648.
4. M. Elizabeth Sanders, *The Regulation of Natural Gas: Policy and Politics, 1938–1978* (Philadelphia: Temple University Press, 1981), 125–64.
5. Opening statement by D. K. Davis (independent oil and gas producer) to Jimmy Carter for President, Energy Conference, Plains, Ga., Aug. 17, 1976, JCL, OCL, MRE, box 4.
6. Rowland Evans and Robert Novak, "A Carter Promise on Natural Gas," *Washington Post*, Feb. 18, 1977, 19.
7. David S. Broder, "Carter and O'Neill, an Unlikely Alliance," *Washington Post*, April 27, 1977, 19.
8. Kaufman, *Presidency of James Earl Carter*, 24.
9. Mary McGrory, "A Fox for the Chicken Coop?," *Chicago Tribune*, Dec. 22, 1976, C4.
10. Louis A. Beecherl Jr. to Carlton Neville, Sept. 17, 1976, JCL, OCL, MRE, box 4.
11. Amory B. Lovins, "Energy Strategy: The Road Not Taken?," *Foreign Affairs*, Oct. 1976, 65–96.
12. "New Tenants at the White House Move In," *New York Times*, Jan. 21, 1977, 3.
13. "States Warn FPC of Natural Gas Shortage Dangers," *Washington Post*, Jan. 14, 1977, D7.
14. "Friedman Blames Energy Mess on Federal 'Helpers,'" *Los Angeles Times*, Feb. 10, 1977, 12.
15. William Safire, "Making Consumers Burn," *New York Times*, Feb. 24, 1977, 34.
16. Patrick Buchanan, "Energy for the Winters Ahead," *Chicago Tribune*, Feb. 6, 1977, 6.
17. "Home Gas Cutoff Looms," *Chicago Tribune*, Jan. 29, 1977, 1.

18. "Oil from Alaska Might Go to Japan," *Washington Post,* Jan. 19, 1977, 2.
19. "FPC Authorizes Transfer to East of Natural Gas," *Wall Street Journal,* Feb. 4, 1977, 2.
20. Rowland Evans and Robert Novak, "The Natural Gas Fight: 'Politics of Winter,'" *Washington Post,* Feb. 2, 1977, 15.
21. "Congress Clears Emergency Gas Bill Quickly," *CQ Almanac 1977,* 649.
22. Milton Friedman, "Gas Crisis: Weather or Washington?," *Newsweek,* Feb. 27, 1977, 69.
23. "200 Faces for the Future," *Time,* July 15, 1974.
24. Sanders, *Regulation of Natural Gas,* 132.
25. Kennedy and Muskie to Frank Moore, Jan. 28, 1977, JCL, OCL, MRE, box 29.
26. "Gas Controls Offer Cold Comfort," *Wall Street Journal,* Feb. 3, 1977, 12.
27. "Why the Big Shortage?," *Newsweek,* Feb. 7, 1977, 20.
28. Gary D. Allison, "Natural Gas Pricing: The Eternal Debate," *Baylor Law Review* 37 (1985): 21.
29. "Nader Asks U.S. Inquiry of Natural Gas Industry," *Wall Street Journal,* Feb. 10, 1977, 25; "New Yorkers Believe Gas Crisis Was Artificial," *Chicago Tribune,* Feb. 28, 1977, 2.
30. "Fuel Cost Increase of $139 Per Home Seen This Winter," *Washington Post,* Feb. 3, 1977, 1; "Bill Seeks Oil-Giant Breakup," *New York Times,* Feb. 9, 1977, D9.
31. Martha Derthick and Paul J. Quirk, *The Politics of Deregulation* (Washington, D.C.: Brookings Institution Press, 1985).
32. Sanders, *Regulation of Natural Gas,* 148–49.
33. Eizenstat to Carter, Feb. 10, 1977, JCL, OCL, MRE, box 28.
34. "Demos Energy Solution: High Taxes, More Controls," *Human Events,* Feb. 26, 1977, 152.
35. "How the Energy Shortage Will Change America," *U.S. News & World Report,* Feb. 14, 1977, 22.
36. Interview with Stuart Eizenstat, Jan. 29–30, 1982, Carter Oral History Project, Miller Center, University of Virginia.
37. *The Cambridge Report, Second Quarter, 1977* (Cambridge Survey Research, 1977), 179, JCL, COM, SND, box 24.
38. Schlesinger to Carter, April 7, 1977, JCL, OCL, MRE, box 28.
39. "What Price Energy?," *Newsweek,* May 2, 1977, 14.
40. "Carter's First Big Test," *Time,* April 25, 1977, 8.
41. "Gasoline: Pay More, Buy Less," *Boston Globe,* April 26, 1977, 23.
42. "What Price Energy?"
43. "Carter's First Big Test." See also R. Douglas Arnold, *The Logic of Congressional Action* (New Haven, Conn.: Yale University Press, 1990), 248–59.
44. Russell Baker, "A Meow in Search of an Enemy," *New York Times,* April 23, 1977, 19.
45. Tip O'Neill, *Man of the House* (New York: Random House, 1987), 320–21.
46. "Carter Energy Bill Fails to Clear," *CQ Almanac 1977,* 708.
47. O'Neill, *Man of the House,* 320.
48. Ibid., 321.
49. Representative Henry Waxman, April 26, 1977, *Congressional Record,* H3583, JCL, OCL, BRD, box 99.

50. "The Energy War," *Time*, May 2, 1977, 11.
51. Summary of congressional mail to the president, May 9, 1977, JCL, OCL, BRD, box 99.
52. Bob Thomson to Moore, Re: Hill Reaction to Energy Message, April 20, 1977, JCL, OCL, MRE, box 28. "Carter Energy Program Draws Praise, Criticism," *Washington Post*, April 21, 1977, 18.
53. Yankelovich to Carter, June 7, 1977, JCL, OCL, BRD, box 100.
54. "The Uphill Road," *Nation*, May 7, 1977, 546.
55. "Senate GOP Energy Initiative," *Congressional Quarterly*, May 21, 1977, 957–58.
56. Representative Jack Kemp, speech on the House floor, April 22, 1977, *Congressional Record*, H3465-57, JCL, OCL, BRD, box 99.
57. Edward J. Mitchell, "Energy Politics: The Irrelevant Debate," in *Options for U.S. Energy Policy* (San Francisco: Institute for Contemporary Studies, 1977), 275–87.
58. Melvin R. Laird, *Energy: A Crisis in Public Policy, a Report from the Chairman of the American Enterprise Institute National Energy Project* (Washington, D.C.: American Enterprise Institute for Public Policy Research, 1977), 1–2, 4.
59. William E. Simon, "The Energy Policy Calamity," *Wall Street Journal*, June 10, 1977, 8.
60. "Simon Speaks of Returning to Public Arena," *New York Times*, June 14, 1977, 53.
61. "How on Gasoline?," *Wall Street Journal*, April 4, 1977, 18.
62. "The 'Energy Crisis' Explained," *Wall Street Journal*, May 27, 1977, 19.
63. "Tinker, Tinker, Tinker," *Wall Street Journal*, April 14, 1977, 26.
64. M. Stanton Evans, "Carter's Energy Package: Controls and More Controls," *Human Events*, May 7, 1977, 7.
65. Alice Widener, "How Liberals Caused the Energy Crisis," *Human Events*, May 14, 1977, 8–9.
66. "Carter's Anti-energy Package," *Human Events*, April 30, 1977, 1.
67. Milton Friedman, "A Department of Energy?," *Newsweek*, May 23, 1977, 62.
68. "Creating a Monster," *Wall Street Journal*, May 24, 1977, 22.
69. Milton Friedman, "Energy Rhetoric," *Newsweek*, June 13, 1977, 82.
70. "3 in Congress Cite Study on Ending Gas Price Curb," *New York Times*, July 12, 1977, 43.
71. "A $48 Billion Presidential Error," *Wall Street Journal*, July 13, 1977, 22.
72. "Energy Bill Is Assailed by Petroleum Institute," *New York Times*, Aug. 17, 1977, 79.
73. Milton Copulos, "Carter's Energy Program: An Update," Heritage Foundation newsletter, July 15, 1977.
74. Milton Copulos, "Economic Impact of Carter's Energy Program," Heritage Foundation newsletter, July 22, 1977.
75. "Of, by, and for the Regulators," *National Review*, Aug. 19, 1977, 929–30.
76. "Taxing Energy," *Wall Street Journal*, April 13, 1977, 1.
77. "Energy Legislation Coordinator," *New York Times*, May 4, 1977, 32.
78. "Putting Energy Pieces Together Will Be a Complicated Task," *Boston Globe*, July 17, 1977, 49.
79. Amory Lovins, "Resilience in Energy Strategy," *New York Times*, July 24, 1977, E17.
80. Sanders, *Regulation of Natural Gas*, 171.

81. Jeffrey Denny, "Whatever Happened to Toby Moffett?," *Common Cause Magazine* (Winter 1992); "Carter Energy Bill Fails to Clear," 723.

82. "Do Pro-divestiture Ads Violate Fairness Doctrine?," *Human Events*, Aug. 6, 1977, 594.

83. "Barbour Meeting Opponents of Fuel-Adjustment Fee," *New York Times*, Sept. 20, 1977, 87.

84. Summary of issue concerns of the American people, DNC Field Survey, Aug. 31–Sept. 12, 1977, JCL, OCS, JOR, box 33.

85. Jordan to Carter, "Political Strategy for Passage of the Energy Bill," n.d., JCL, OCS, JOR, box 34A.

86. Melvin R. Laird, "The Energy Crisis: Made in the U.S.A.," *Reader's Digest*, Sept. 1977, 56–60.

87. Hedrick Smith, "The Big White House Error on Energy Was Overconfidence," *New York Times*, Oct. 2, 1977, E1.

88. "Carter Energy Bill Fails to Clear," 710.

89. "Gas Filibuster Continuing as Compromise Is Sought," *New York Times*, Sept. 28, 1977, 78; "Mondale Wins a Fight, and Much Rancor," *Los Angeles Times*, Oct. 10, 1977, D5.

90. "The Energy Talkathon," *Newsweek*, Oct. 10, 1977, 30.

91. "Gas Filibuster Ends as Byrd Overrides Customs of Senate," *New York Times*, Oct. 4, 1977, 1, 57.

92. "Launching the Energy Blitz," *Time*, Oct. 31, 1977, 13.

93. Jordan to Carter, Oct. 20, 1977, JCL, COM, RAF, box 2.

94. Meeting with the president and Senator Edward M. Kennedy, Oct. 20, 1977, JCL, OCL, MRE, box 28.

95. "Carter's Oil War," *Newsweek*, Oct. 24, 1977, 40.

96. Frederick P. Hitz, memo on meeting of the House Democratic liberals, Dec. 1, 1977, JCL, OCL, MRE, box 28.

97. "Schlesinger Oil Muddies the Water," *Chicago Tribune*, Dec. 4, 1977, 6.

98. Daniel Yergin, "Why the Energy Crisis Won't Go Away," *Newsday*, Oct. 8, 1978, D1.

99. "Launching the Energy Blitz."

100. "Gas-Price Bill Faces Renewed Resistance," *New York Times*, Aug. 2, 1978, D3.

101. Eizenstat, memo, Meeting with Consumer Groups, April 13, 1978, JCL, DPS, EIZ, box 198.

102. "Bill to End Natural-Gas Price Curbs, Key Part of Energy Plan, in New Peril," *New York Times*, Aug. 4, 1978, D2.

103. "How Carter Can Win Big in 1980," *Washington Post*, Sept. 10, 1978, C1–2.

104. "Kennedy Instead?," *Detroit Free Press*, Sept. 3, 1978.

105. Eizenstat to Carter, May 1, 1978, JCL, COM, SND, box 44.

106. Bob Arnold and Bill Sturgeon, "Freeze a Yankee," *Folksee Records*, 1978.

107. "Freeze a Yankee," *Wall Street Journal*, June 30, 1978, 10.

108. "Regulations Ire Connally," *Dallas Times Herald*, Oct. 21, 1977, 6.

109. Bush to Ashley, Nov. 28, 1977, TAP, box 114.

110. Jimmy Carter, *Keeping Faith: Memoirs of a President* (New York: Bantam Books, 1982), 108.

111. Senators Howard Metzenbaum and Clifford Hansen to the Senate, Aug. 23, 1978, JCL, OCS, BUT, box 117.

112. Moffett and Brown to the House, Sept. 6, 1978, JCL, OCL, MRE, box 29.

113. Carter, *Keeping Faith*, 104.

114. Scott Kaufman, *Plans Unraveled: The Foreign Policy of the Carter Administration* (DeKalb: Northern Illinois University Press, 2008), 84.

115. "Confident Carter: A New Suit, Image," *Philadelphia Evening Bulletin*, Sept. 29, 1978, 2.

116. Houghton to Robert Strauss, Sept. 8, 1978, JCL, OCS, BUT, box 117.

117. Sanders, *Regulation of Natural Gas*, 186–88.

118. "Launching the Energy Blitz."

119. Rafshoon to Carter, Subject: Style, n.d., JCL, COM, SND, box 28.

120. Ben Sargent, 1978 cartoon, *Austin American-Statesman*, in JCL, COM, SND, box 45.

121. Rafshoon to Carter, Sept. 1, 1978, JCL, COM, SND, box 28.

122. Bruce Bartlett, "Kemp-Roth: Revolution of 1978," *National Review*, Oct. 27, 1978, 1333–36.

123. Caddell to Carter, Dec. 14, 1978, JCL, COM, SND, box 32.

124. Roscoe Drummond, "Why Carter Moves Right," *New York Herald Tribune*, n.d., 1978, JCL, COM, SND, box 45.

125. "Budget Fights Loom in Congress with Few New Initiatives Likely," *New York Times*, Nov. 12, 1978, 1.

126. Matthews to Greg Schneiders, Dec. 15, 1978, JCL, COM, SND, box 33.

6: Hot Summer Mad

1. "The Fallout of Iranian Crisis on Oil Importers Around World," *Boston Globe*, Jan. 8, 1979, 2; "Carter Says U.S. Could Stand Loss of Iranian Oil," *Wall Street Journal*, Jan. 18, 1979, 2.

2. "Death of Infant Brings a Gas Shut-Off Protest," *New York Times*, Feb. 9, 1979, 32.

3. Caddell to Carter, Jan. 17, 1979, JCL, COM, SND, box 32.

4. Eizenstat to Rafshoon and Greg Schneiders, Jan. 13, 1979, JCL, COM, SND, box 33.

5. Hedrick Smith, "Economic Platform for 1980," *New York Times*, Jan. 23, 1979, 1.

6. Schlesinger to Carter, draft memo, Jan. 1979, JCL, KHN, box 16.

7. "Gas Will Cost More—If You Can Get It," *U.S. News & World Report*, Feb. 12, 1979, 11.

8. "Big Oil's Pinch at the Pump," *Time*, Dec. 18, 1978, 64–65.

9. Kahn to Carter, March 26, 1979, JCL, KHN, box 16.

10. "Lines at the Pumps Again?," *Time*, Feb. 12, 1979, 83–84.

11. "GAO Study Predicts Oil Prices May Rise," *Wall Street Journal*, March 8, 1979, 2.

12. "Representative Moffett Elected as Chairman of Panel After Quiet Campaign," *New York Times*, Feb. 1, 1979, 20.

13. Gerald L. Parsky, "Lifting the Lid on Our Domestic Oil Prices," *Los Angeles Times*, March 25, 1979, E1.

14. Milton R. Copulos, "The Price of Power," *National Review*, Feb. 2, 1979, 156–59.
15. "Blocking Alaskan Oil," *Human Events*, April 7, 1979, 1.
16. "The Energy Tangle," *Newsweek*, April 16, 1979, 22–23.
17. Richard Burt, "How U.S. Strategy Toward Persian Gulf Region Evolved," *New York Times*, Jan. 25, 1980, 6.
18. Olav Njolstad, "Shifting Priorities: The Persian Gulf in U.S. Strategic Planning in the Carter Years," *Cold War History* 4, no. 3 (April 2004): 26.
19. Ibid., 23, 29.
20. "Crescent of Crisis: Iran and a Region of Rising Instability," *Time*, Jan. 15, 1979, 18.
21. William Safire, "Checkmate," *New York Times*, Jan. 4, 1979, 19.
22. "Foreign Policy: End of an Era," *Wall Street Journal*, Jan. 18, 1979, 16.
23. William E. Odom, "The Cold War Origins of the U.S. Central Command," *Journal of Cold War Studies* 8, no. 2 (Spring 2006): 52–82.
24. Leonardo Maugeri, *The Age of Oil: What They Don't Want You to Know About the World's Most Controversial Resource* (Guilford, Conn.: Lyons Press, 2007), 122–23.
25. "Carter Draws the Line?," *Wall Street Journal*, March 8, 1979, 18.
26. "Gas Ration Plan Barred," *New York Times*, April 26, 1979, D1, 4.
27. "Jackson Bill Would Block Carter Oil Decontrol Plan," *Washington Post*, April 11, 1979, 9.
28. "Carter's Energy Plan," *U.S. News & World Report*, April 16, 1979, 19–20.
29. "Decontrol of Oil Narrowly Clears Hurdle on Hill," *Washington Post*, May 3, 1979, 1.
30. Rafshoon to Carter, Subject: Style, n.d.
31. "The First Gasoline Panic," *Newsweek*, May 14, 1979, 89.
32. "Odd-Even Gas Rationing," *Los Angeles Times*, May 4, 1979, 1.
33. "First Gasoline Panic."
34. "Gas Lines Expected to Shorten," *Los Angeles Times*, May 9, 1979, B3.
35. White House news summary, June 29, 1979, JCL, BAU, NWS, box 10.
36. "Hundreds Join Gas Vigil at All-Night L.A. Station," *Los Angeles Times*, May 13, 1979, 1.
37. "On the 7th Day, Resignation Comes over Those Who Wait," *Los Angeles Times*, May 16, 1979, B3, 23.
38. "Carter Urged to Hike Gas Production," *Los Angeles Times*, May 7, 1979, B6.
39. Metzenbaum and Moffett to Elmer Staats, May 7, 1979, JCL, DPS, EIZ, box 211.
40. "Carter's Oil Plan Hurts the Poor, Kennedy Warns," *Washington Post*, May 13, 1979, 1, 8.
41. Eizenstat to Carter, May 2, 1979, JCL, OCL, MRE, box 29; "65,000 Demonstrate at Capitol to Halt Atomic Power Units," *New York Times*, May 7, 1979, 1.
42. "Democrats in House Split with Carter and Back Oil Curbs," *New York Times*, May 23, 1979, 1.
43. Moffett and Maguire to Carter, May 24, 1979, JCL, OCL, MRE, box 29.
44. Myra MacPherson, "The Moffett Show—Brought to You by the Gas Crisis," *Washington Post*, June 26, 1979, B1, 2.
45. "Rep. Moffett Presses Energy Issues in Campaign Trip," *New York Times*, May 21, 1979, D10.

46. Cambridge Survey Research to the Democratic National Committee, Re: The Political Situation and President Carter, May 25, 1979, JCL, OCS, JOR, box 33.

47. Francis to Frank Moore, May 29, 1979, JCL, OCS, MRE, box 29.

48. Eizenstat to Hertzberg, energy address, draft 2, May 22, 1979, JCL, DPS, EIZ, box 210.

49. Ibid.

50. Warren to Carter, May 26, 1979, JCL, DPS, EIZ, box 210.

51. "Who's to Blame?," *U.S. News & World Report*, May 28, 1979, 20.

52. Rafshoon to Carter, May 29, 1979, JCL, COM, RAF, box 18.

53. Hugh Carter to White House department heads, June 6, 1979, JCL, OCS, BUT, box 98.

54. "Rep. Moffett Presses Energy Issues in Campaign Trip."

55. "President Asks Oil Leaders to Join Common Effort to Close Fuel Gap," *New York Times*, June 1, 1979, 1.

56. Frank Moore, memo on Republican Congressional Leadership Breakfast, June 7, 1979, JCL, OCL, CPD, box 178.

57. Moore to Carter, June 5, 1979, JCL, OCL, CPD, box 178.

58. Francis to Moore, June 5, 1979, JCL, OCL, CPD, box 178.

59. "The Politics of Gas," *Newsweek*, July 9, 1979, 29.

60. Eizenstat to Carter, June 5, 1979, JCL, DPS, EIZ, box 278.

61. "Politics of Gas."

62. Eizenstat to Carter, June 5, 1979; Caddell to Carter, June 11, 1979, JCL, OCS, JOR, box 33.

63. "Politics of Gas."

64. Eizenstat to Carter, June 5, 1979.

65. Eizenstat to Katherine Schirmer, May 17, 1979, JCL, DPS, EIZ, box 202.

66. Eizenstat to Carter, June 5, 1979.

67. Eizenstat and Schirmer to Carter, June 5, 1979, JCL, DPS, EIZ, box 278.

68. Eizenstat to Carter, June 5, 1979; Cutler to Eizenstat, June 12, 1979, JCL, OCL, MRE, box 29.

69. White House solar system, June 20, 1979, JCL, DPS, EIZ, box 278.

70. Solar Energy Ceremony, June 6, 1979, JCL, DPS, EIZ, box 278.

71. "One Hellacious Uproar," *Time*, July 2, 1979, 22.

72. "Strike by Truckers over Fuel Expands," *New York Times*, June 14, 1979, 16.

73. Alan Butchman, memo for the president, June 1, 1979, JCL, DPS, EIZ, box 161.

74. "Truckers in Revolt," *Newsweek*, June 25, 1979, 45.

75. "Independent Truckers Calling National Work Stoppage," *New York Times*, June 19, 1979, 18.

76. "Truckers Easing Strike in Places; Others Push On," *New York Times*, June 26, 1979, B8.

77. "40% of Trucks Idle for Major Haulers as Stoppage Widens," *New York Times*, June 22, 1979, 1.

78. "One Hellacious Uproar."

79. "Truckers' Fury Seems Unfocused on Eve of Strike," *New York Times*, June 21, 1979, 18.

80. Oberg to Carter, June 21, 1979, JCL, DPS, EIZ, box 108.

81. Kennedy to Carter, June 22, 1979, JCL, DPS, EIZ, box 108.

82. California congressmen to Carter, June 21, 1979, JCL, DPS, EIZ, box 113.

83. White House news summary, June 26, 1979, JCL, BAU, NWS, box 10.

84. "Truckers Abduct and Rob Driver, Then Lecture Him on Their Strike," *New York Times*, June 24, 1979, 20.

85. "Truckers' Strike Intensifies in Violence and Disruptions," *Washington Post*, June 22, 1979, 12.

86. "Truckers, Motorists in Pa. Protest Gasoline Shortage," *Washington Post*, June 25, 1979, 9.

87. Tom Morganthau, "The Energy Plague," *Newsweek*, July 2, 1979, 24.

88. "Tension at Hartsdale Gas Station Eases as Odd-Even Plan Begins," *New York Times*, June 21, 1979, 17.

89. "Notes from the Gas Line," *New York Times*, June 22, 1979, B6.

90. "Gas Prices and Lines Are the Worst Ever on 'Driest' Weekend," *New York Times*, June 24, 1979, 1, 21.

91. "Man Shot in Gas Demonstration," *New York Times*, June 25, 1979, D9.

92. "Rioting Follows Protests by Truckers in Levittown, Pa.," *New York Times*, June 26, 1979, B8.

93. George F. Will, "Levittown Revisited," *Newsweek*, July 9, 1979, 84.

94. "Mondale Offers Protection to Haulers Who Return," *New York Times*, June 28, 1979, 1.

95. "White House in Final Offer to Truckers," *New York Times*, June 30, 1979, 15.

96. "Truckers Choose 'Direct Action,'" *New York Times*, July 1, 1979, E4.

97. "Hours of Waiting to Fill the Tank," *Time*, July 2, 1979, 19.

98. "Gas Crisis: Experts Find Mixture of Causes," *New York Times*, June 24, 1979, 1.

99. "Motorist, 29, Is Killed in Brooklyn Stabbing at a Gas Station," *New York Times*, June 10, 1979, 30; "Man Killed on Gas Line," *Newsday*, June 10, 1973, 3; "Much of U.S. Feeling Impact of Gas Crisis," *New York Times*, June 26, 1979, 1.

100. "Metropolitan Area Faces Tightest Time for Supply of Gas," *New York Times*, June 23, 1979, 1, 8.

101. "Bloc in Congress from New York Angry over Gas," *New York Times*, June 28, 1979, 1.

102. "Intimates Fearful for Re-election If Carter Fails to Tame the Gas Crisis," *New York Times*, June 29, 1979, 1, 13.

103. "Long Gas Lines? Not for a Chosen Few," *U.S. News & World Report*, June 25, 1979, 44.

104. "Long Angry Lines and Meetings of Ministers," *New York Times*, June 24, 1979, F15.

105. "The Big Villain in Gas Crunch? Try Washington," *U.S. News & World Report*, July 2, 1979, 47.

106. "The Great Energy Mess," *Time*, July 2, 1979, 16, 19.

107. White House news summary, June 26, 1979.

108. "Gas Prices of up to $1.50 a Gallon Fail to Daunt Desperate Motorists," *New York Times*, June 22, 1979, B5.

109. "Politics of Gas."

110. White House news summary, June 26, 1979.

111. Morganthau, "Energy Plague," 22.
112. David Pauly, "The Next Blow from OPEC," *Newsweek*, June 25, 1979, 65.
113. White House news summary, June 29, 1979, JCL, BAU, NWS, box 10; "OPEC's Painful Squeeze," *Time*, July 9, 1979, 12.
114. White House news summary, June 29, 1979.
115. White House news summary, June 30, 1979, JCL, BAU, NWS, box 10.
116. "Intimates Fearful for Re-election If Carter Fails to Tame the Gas Crisis."
117. Eizenstat to Carter, June 28, 1979, Subject: Energy, JCL, OCS, BUT, box 98.
118. Ibid.
119. Tom Morganthau, "The Crunch Continues," *Newsweek*, July 9, 1979, 25.
120. Marshall Loeb, "How to Counter OPEC," *Time*, July 9, 1979.
121. "Red Tape and More Red Tape," *Time*, July 9, 1979, 20.
122. Eizenstat to Carter, June 28, 1979.
123. Ibid.
124. Morganthau, "Crunch Continues."
125. Calandra to Carter, May 22, 1979, JCL, GOV, box 39.
126. "A Mood of Resignation Comes over Those Who Wait in Lines," *Los Angeles Times*, May 16, 1979, 23.
127. "If U.S. Decided to Hit Back at OPEC," *U.S. News & World Report*, May 28, 1979, 29.
128. "'Crude' Effort Pays Off in Protest on Oil Prices," *New York Times*, June 22, 1979, B4.
129. Gagliano to Carter, June 25, 1979, JCL, GOV, box 39.
130. "U.S. Wary of Way to Foil OPEC," *New York Times*, July 4, 1979, D3.
131. LaPorte to Carter, July 5, 1979, JCL, GOV, box 39.
132. White House news summary, June 30, 1979.
133. Odom, "Cold War Origins of the U.S. Central Command," 60; Njolstad, "Shifting Priorities," 33.
134. White House news summary, June 26, July 1, and July 3, 1979, JCL, BAU, NWS, box 10; "Gas Crisis: Color the White House Blue," *Washington Post*, July 1, 1979, 1.
135. White House news summary, July 2, 1979, JCL, BAU, NWS, box 10.
136. White House news summary, July 3, 1979.
137. Eizenstat, Rafshoon, and Hertzberg to Carter, July 3, 1979, JCL, COM, SND, box 46.
138. "Energy Speech," draft, July 3, 1979, JCL, COM, SND, box 46.
139. Ibid.
140. Schlesinger to Carter, July 5, 1979, JCL, KHN, box 15.
141. Moore to Carter, July 8, 1979, JCL, DPS, EIZ, box 162.
142. "Carter Castigates House on Rejection of Gas-Ration Plan," *New York Times*, May 12, 1979, 1, 10.
143. Moore to Carter, July 8, 1979.
144. "The Regional Gas Supply Game," *Washington Post*, July 4, 1979, 24.
145. "Aides Lay Delay on Energy Plan to Uncertainties," *New York Times*, July 6, 1979, 1.
146. Kahn to Carter, July 11, 1979, JCL, KHN, box 33.
147. Arthur M. Schlesinger Jr., "The Challenge Facing Liberals," *Chicago Tribune*, July 5, 1979, B4.

148. Mark Green and Harvey Rosenfield, "Carter's Bad Energy Bargain," *Chicago Tribune*, July 8, 1979, 6.
149. White House news summary, July 6, 1979, JCL, BAU, NWS, box 10.
150. "What the Polls Say," *U.S. News & World Report*, July 16, 1979, 21.
151. Mondale to Carter, memorandum, "Energy Speech," July 4, 1979, quoted in Daniel Horowitz, *Jimmy Carter and the Energy Crisis of the 1970s* (Boston: Bedford, 2005), 95.
152. Kahn to Carter, July 7, 1979, JCL, DPS, EIZ, box 162.
153. Schneiders to Rafshoon, July 10, 1979, JCL, COM, SND, box 28.
154. Ibid.
155. Kahn to Carter, July 11, 1979, JCL, KHN, box 33.
156. John M. Berry, "Carter's Energy Policy: The Vital Ingredient Is Still Missing," *Fortune*, Aug. 13, 1979, 109.
157. White House news summary, July 6, 1979.
158. Matthews to Schneiders, July 13, 1979, JCL, COM, SND, box 24.
159. Rafshoon to Carter, Subject: Style, n.d.
160. "Wide Criticism Is Aimed at Energy Department," *New York Times*, July 16, 1979, 1.
161. "Behind the White House Purge," *U.S. News & World Report*, July 30, 1979, 14.
162. White House news summary, July 21, 1979, JCL, BAU, NWS, box 10.
163. "Behind the White House Purge."
164. White House news summary, July 21, 1979.
165. Louis Harris, "A Slight Gain for Carter," *Chicago Tribune*, July 27, 1979; Adam Clymer, "Speech Lifts Carter to 37%," *New York Times*, July 18, 1979, 1.
166. For an alternative interpretation that sees the speech as a potential turning point for Carter, see Kevin Mattson, *"What the Heck Are You Up To, Mr. President?": Jimmy Carter, America's "Malaise," and the Speech That Should Have Changed the Country* (New York: Bloomsbury, 2009).
167. Clymer, "Speech Lifts Carter Rating to 37%."
168. Elmer B. Staats, "Iranian Oil Cutoff: Reduced Petroleum Supplies and Inadequate U.S. Government Response," report to the Congress of the United States, Sept. 13, 1979.
169. "Reagan and Bush Blame Carter for His Own Woes," *Los Angeles Times*, July 17, 1979, 3.

7: Running on Empty
1. Francis to Jordan, July 30, 1979, JCL, OCS, JOR, box 44.
2. Moore, memorandum for the president, Republican Congressional Leadership Breakfast, July 31, 1979, JCL, OCL, MRE, box 40.
3. Fact sheet on the president's Import Reduction Program, July 16, 1979, JCL, OCS, BUT, box 78.
4. "House Votes to Let Congress Veto Plan for Gas Rationing," *New York Times*, July 26, 1979, 1.
5. "Energy War Helps Coal Firms Dig In Against Stripmine Law," *Washington Post*, Aug. 20, 1979, 2.
6. "Carter's Energy Plan," *Newsweek*, July 30, 1979, 54.

7. White House news summary, July 31, 1979, JCL, BAU, NWS, box 10.

8. Iwan Morgan, "Liberalism and Inflation in the 1970s," paper delivered at the Policy History Conference, Richmond, VA, June 2012, 7.

9. Harris, "Slight Gain for Carter."

10. "The Auto Workers' Windmill," *New York Times*, Aug. 26, 1979, 160.

11. "Senate Panel Seeks to Cut Carter Plan for Synthetic Fuel," *New York Times*, Aug. 2, 1979, 1.

12. "Summertime Slowdown," *Time*, Aug. 13, 1979, 17.

13. Frank Moore, meeting with Senator Alan Simpson, Nov. 5, 1979, JCL, OCL, MRE, box 40.

14. Stockman, Dear Colleague letter, Aug. 1, 1979, JCL, OCS, SLG, box 173.

15. Gene Godley, Memorandum of Conversation with Senator Gravel, July 25, 1979, JCL, OCL, MRE, box 55.

16. Milton Friedman, "The Energy Boondoggle," *Newsweek*, July 30, 1979, 56.

17. "The Real Jimmy Carter," *Wall Street Journal*, July 17, 1979, 18.

18. Talking points for Charles Duncan, Sept. 1979, JCL, OCS, SLG, box 173.

19. Rafshoon to Carter, Aug. 2, 1979, JCL, COM, SND, box 28.

20. "The Energy Program's Not-So-Fast Track," *Business Week*, Aug. 6, 1979, 21.

21. Frank Moore, meeting with Energy Committee leadership, Nov. 5, 1979, JCL, OCL, MRE, box 40.

22. "Powerful Hill Foes Flattened by Synfuels Bandwagon," *Washington Post*, Nov. 16, 1979, 2.

23. "Go Slow Plan Recommended for Synfuels," *Washington Post*, Sept. 6, 1979, D10.

24. "Synthetic Fuels Not Likely to Become Alternative to Foreign Oil, Congressional Report Holds," *Washington Post*, Sept. 29, 1979, 13.

25. White House news summary, July 7, 1979, JCL, BAU, NWS, box 10; "Oil Price Rise Stirs Review of U.S. War Moves in Crisis," *New York Times*, July 5, 1979, 3.

26. Ben J. Wattenberg, "It's Time to Stop America's Retreat," *New York Times Magazine*, July 22, 1979, 16.

27. "Schlesinger Says Survival of U.S. Rests on Arab Oil," *Los Angeles Times*, Aug. 17, 1979, 1; "Schlesinger, in Farewell, Demands Balance with Russians in Mideast," *New York Times*, Aug. 17, 1979, 8.

28. "Oil Industry Target of Demonstrations," *New York Times*, Oct. 18, 1979, D3.

29. "House Votes to End Gasoline Price Controls," *Los Angeles Times*, Oct. 13, 1979, 1; "House, in Reversal, Continues Controls on Gasoline Prices," *New York Times*, Oct. 25, 1979, 1.

30. "Democrats and Decontrol: A Losing Battle," *CQ Almanac 1979*, 610.

31. Moore to Carter, congressional telephone call, Nov. 6, 1979, JCL, OCL, MRE, box 40.

32. "Senate Begins Fight on Rival Energy Bills," *Washington Post*, Nov. 6, 1979, 4.

33. "Powerful Hill Foes Flattened by Synfuels Bandwagon."

34. "How Much Should You Pay for Gas?," *Newsweek*, Sept. 3, 1979, 53.

35. Janette Quimby (Attleboro, Mass.) to Kahn, Nov. 11, 1979, JCL, KHN, box 15.

36. Judith Smyser (Rockaway, N.J.) to Kahn, Nov. 13, 1979, JCL, KHN, box 15.

37. Alice Kensey (Williamstown, N.J.) to Kahn, Nov. 10, 1979, JCL, KHN, box 15.

38. Edward Ciampa (Brighton, Mass.) to Kahn, Nov. 10, 1979, JCL, KHN, box 15.

39. "Kennedy Attacks President's Policy on Oil Price Controls," *Washington Post*, Nov. 4, 1979, 8; "Eizenstat Bars Kahn Proposal for Oil Parley," *Washington Post*, Nov. 7, 1979, E1.

40. "Marine Spirit: We Can 'Get 'Em Out,'" *Washington Post*, Nov. 11, 1979, 1, 11.

41. "Protesters Jeer and Burn Flags in Oregon, Texas, California as U.S. Backlash Flares," *Los Angeles Times*, Nov. 9, 1979, B7.

42. Ibid.

43. "Crisis Alters Attitude in U.S.," *New York Times*, Dec. 2, 1979, 1, 16.

44. "More Clout Seen for U.S. Military," *Washington Post*, Dec. 8, 1979, 14.

45. "Crisis Alters Attitude in U.S."

46. Aaron to Brzezinski, Dec. 27, 1979, JCL, BRZ, box 32.

47. Melvyn P. Leffler, "From the Truman Doctrine to the Carter Doctrine: Lessons and Dilemmas of the Cold War," *Diplomatic History* 7, no. 4 (1983): 245–66.

48. Odom to Brzezinski, Jan. 11, 1980, JCL, NSA, ODM, box 43.

49. Odom to Brzezinski, Jan. 7, 1980, JCL, BRZ, box 32.

50. Roy Reed, "George Bush on the Move," *New York Times Magazine*, Feb. 10, 1980, 23.

51. "Bush Urges Overhaul of Carter Policy," *Washington Post*, Sept. 6, 1979, 2.

52. "The World," *Los Angeles Times*, Sept. 6, 1979, B2.

53. "Bush Talks of Oil Flow," *New York Times*, Oct. 26, 1979, 18.

54. "Rumsfeld: U.S. Is Vulnerable," *Chicago Tribune*, Nov. 22, 1979, 8.

55. "Republicans Assail Policies of Carter," *New York Times*, Jan. 20, 1980, 19.

56. Edward N. Luttwak, "A 'Hands-Off' U.S. Policy on Afghanistan? No," *New York Times*, Jan. 6, 1980, E19.

57. Emile Nakhleh, "Securing the Gulf," *New York Times*, Jan. 8, 1980, 19.

58. Rowland Evans and Robert Novak, "Unease in Oman," *Washington Post*, Jan. 2, 1980, 21.

59. "Lost Opportunity," *Wall Street Journal*, Jan. 7, 1980, 12.

60. Moore, memo: Congressional Leadership Breakfast, Jan. 23, 1980, JCL, OCL, CPD, box 178.

61. "Reaction to Speech Is Sharply Partisan," *New York Times*, Jan. 24, 1980, 14.

62. Moore, memo: Republican Congressional Leadership Breakfast, Jan. 31, 1980, JCL, OCL, CPD, box 178.

63. "Reagan Blames Carter 'Failure' for Soviet Move," *New York Times*, Jan. 25, 1980, 12.

64. "Kennedy Criticizes New Carter Policy on the Persian Gulf," *New York Times*, Jan. 29, 1980, 1, 13.

65. "Transcript of Kennedy's Speech at Georgetown University," *New York Times*, Jan. 29, 1980, 12.

66. "'New' Kennedy Begins Push in New England," *Sun*, Feb. 1, 1980, 8.

67. "Call for Gas Rationing Revs Up Kennedy Crowds," *Washington Post*, Feb. 3, 1980, 4.

68. "Carter Budget Seeks More Military Funds," *Los Angeles Times*, Jan. 29, 1980, B1.

69. "Carter Budget Hikes Funds for Energy Conservation and Research," Associated Press, Jan. 29, 1980.

70. Louis Harris, "Carter Begins to Falter in Popularity Polls," *Chicago Tribune*, Feb. 14, 1980, B4.

71. Quoted in David Farber, *Taken Hostage: The Iran Hostage Crisis and America's First Encounter with Radical Islam* (Princeton, N.J.: Princeton University Press, 2005), 169.
72. "Paris-Bonn Summit Seeks Joint Position," *Washington Post*, Feb. 4, 1980, 20.
73. NSC memorandum, "Foreign Policy: Coherence and Sense of Direction," March 25, 1980, JCL, BRZ, box 32.
74. Ibid.
75. Ibid.
76. Ibid.
77. "Numbers Can Be Numbing but Attitudes Are Revealing," *New York Times*, Feb. 24, 1980, E2.
78. "Iran's Shadow on Primary," *New York Times*, April 2, 1980, 1, 10.
79. "Campaigns Shun Foreign Issues," *Los Angeles Times*, May 17, 1980, 1, 25.
80. "Advice for the New Man," *Time*, May 12, 1980, 29–30.
81. "More Clout for the Fed," *New York Times*, March 17, 1980, D2.
82. "Balancing Act: Carter Tries Synchronizing Economic and Political Aims," *New York Times*, March 16, 1980, E1.
83. "House Panel Clears a Budget," *New York Times*, March 21, 1980, 1.
84. "Shotgun Wedding," *New York Times*, March 23, 1980, E1.
85. Edward Kennedy, 1980 campaign brochure; Morgan, "Liberals and Inflation in the 1970s."
86. E. J. Dionne Jr., "The People Want Controls," *New York Times*, Feb. 3, 1980, F18.
87. "Carter Signs Oil Tax Bill into Law," *New York Times*, April 3, 1980, 67.
88. "'Windfall' Levy on Oil Revenue Passed by Senate," *Wall Street Journal*, March 28, 1980, 4.
89. "Tax on Windfall Profits Is Passed in the House," *New York Times*, March 14, 1980, D1.
90. "Oil Focus Shifts to State Bills," *New York Times*, April 24, 1980, D4.
91. "Taxing Away Our Power," *National Review*, May 2, 1980, 516; "The Close-the-Wells Tax," *Wall Street Journal*, Jan. 22, 1980, 20.
92. "Reagan Resisting Pleas to Clarify His Positions," *New York Times*, April 19, 1980, 11.
93. "Ronald Reagan's Economic Policy," *New York Times*, April 13, 1980, 13.
94. "Bush Accuses Reagan of 'Economic Madness,'" *Los Angeles Times*, April 11, 1980, B20.
95. Hobart Rowen, "Reagan Economics: Adam Smith Redoux," *Washington Post*, May 4, 1980, G1.
96. Sidney Blumenthal, "Defining 'Reaganomics,'" *Boston Globe*, Nov. 2, 1980, H10.
97. "Reagan Resisting Pleas to Clarify His Positions."
98. Blumenthal, "Defining 'Reaganomics,'" 49.
99. Nicholas Lemann, "The Republicans: A Government Waits in Wings," *Washington Post*, May 27, 1980, 1, 4.
100. Blumenthal, "Defining 'Reaganomics,'" 52.
101. Kaufman, *Henry M. Jackson*, 400, 403.
102. "Synfuels: Answer to the Energy Crisis?," *U.S. News & World Report*, July 14, 1980, 25.

103. William Rasberry, "Our Own Energy Enemy," *Washington Post*, June 20, 1980, 13.

104. "Carter Savors a Bittersweet Energy Victory," Associated Press, June 29, 1980.

105. "House, by 232–131, Kills Carter Plan for Energy Board," *New York Times*, June 28, 1980, 1.

106. Ibid.

107. "Synthetic Fuels Bill Ready for Signing," *New York Times*, June 27, 1980, D1.

108. "Energy Mobilization Board Proposal Killed," *CQ Almanac 1980*, 483.

109. "Oh, Those Decadent Days of 'Dallas,'" *Philadelphia Inquirer*, April 6, 1991.

110. "Reagan Wants a Different Energy Policy," *New York Times*, July 27, 1980, E3.

111. "President Says Reagan Distorts Administration's Energy Record," *New York Times*, Sept. 11, 1980, D17.

112. "Reagan Criticizes Clean Air Laws and EPA as Obstacles to Growth," *Washington Post*, Oct. 9, 1980, 2.

113. "Out of the Game," *Wall Street Journal*, Sept. 24, 1980, 30.

114. Walter J. Levy, "Oil and the Decline of the West," *Foreign Affairs* (Summer 1980): 999–1015.

115. "Fears Feeding Hostage Issue," *New York Times*, Oct. 23, 1980, 1.

116. "The National Security Issue," *Wall Street Journal*, Oct. 16, 1980, 28.

117. "Transcript of the Presidential Debate Between Carter and Reagan in Cleveland," *New York Times*, Oct. 29, 1980, 28.

118. E. J. Dionne Jr., "A Shifting Wind Alters Energy and Environment as Political Issues in Presidential Race," *New York Times*, Oct. 28, 1980, 25.

119. "Conservationists Bite Bullet, Accept Senate Bill," Associated Press, Nov. 13, 1980.

8: I Can't Drive Fifty-Five

1. Charles J. DiBona, "Will We Emerge in the 80's from the Dark Ages of Energy Policy?," *New York Times*, Feb. 22, 1981, NJ20.

2. Gregory A. Fossedal, "Failure Unlimited," *Dallas Morning News*, Feb. 24, 1982, RRL, BOG, box OA 11471.

3. Peter Behr, "Decontrol Shows Reagan Won't Try to Even Out Oil Shock," *Washington Post*, Jan. 30, 1981, E1.

4. "Reagan Decontrols Gasoline, Crude in Deregulation Debut," *Washington Post*, Jan. 29, 1981, 1.

5. "Industry Welcomes Decontrol," *New York Times*, Jan. 29, 1981, D6.

6. "Beating the 'Oil Shock,'" *Wall Street Journal*, Dec. 30, 1980, 14.

7. Kevin Hopkins to Martin Anderson, Jan. 26, 1981, RRL, BOG, box OA 11471.

8. "Reagan Advisers Favor Opening Lands, Boosting Incentives to Spur Drilling," *Wall Street Journal*, Nov. 10, 1980, 8.

9. "Reagan Group Seeks Shift in Pollution Law," *New York Times*, Nov. 14, 1980, 18; "Regulatory 'Balance' May Shift to Dismantlers," *Washington Post*, Jan. 11, 1981, L5.

10. "1-Year Moratorium Recommended on New Regulations," *Washington Post*, Nov. 9, 1980, G1.

11. Richard Brookhiser, "What Do Conservatives Want?," *National Review*, Feb. 6, 1981, 82.

12. Richard A. Harris and Sidney M. Milkis, *The Politics of Regulatory Change: A Tale of Two Agencies* (New York: Oxford University Press, 1996), 256.

13. James A. Baker III, *Work Hard, Study . . . and Keep Out of Politics* (New York: Putnam, 2006), 126.

14. "Oil Price Decontrol and the Poor: A Social Policy Failure" (a staff study prepared for the Subcommittee on Investment, Jobs, and Prices of the Joint Economic Committee, Feb. 1981), RRL, BOG, box OA 11471.

15. Joel Jacobson, "Government and the Oil Industry: The Myth and the Reality," *New York Times*, Jan. 11, 1981, 28.

16. "Reagan Decontrols Gasoline, Crude in Deregulation Debut."

17. "U.S. to Cut Funds for Rationing," *New York Times*, Feb. 23, 1981, D3.

18. "A Willing Dismantler If Called On to Be One," *Washington Post*, Dec. 23, 1980, 4.

19. "James Watt vs. the 'Extremists,'" *Washington Post*, Jan. 4, 1981, K2.

20. "Reagan Nominates Key Officials for Interior," *Washington Post*, Jan. 28, 1981, 2.

21. "Anne Gorsuch Burford, 62, Dies; Reagan EPA Director," *Washington Post*, July 22, 2004, B6.

22. Hays, *Beauty, Health, and Permanence*, 495.

23. Harris and Milkis, *Politics of Regulatory Change*, 254–55.

24. "Deregulating Deregulation," *Wall Street Journal*, Feb. 19, 1981, 30.

25. Judith A. Layzer, "Environmental Policy from 1980 to 2008: The Politics of Prevention," in *Conservatism and American Political Development*, eds. Brian J. Glenn and Steven M. Teles (New York: Oxford University Press, 2009), 232; Harris and Milkis, *Politics of Regulatory Change*, 256.

26. "In the Pipeline: The Fight over Faster Natural Gas Price Decontrol," *Washington Post*, Jan. 19, 1982, 4.

27. "The New Battle over Natural Gas," *New York Times*, Sept. 6, 1981, F1.

28. "In the Pipeline."

29. "Gas Price Decontrol Hopes Dim," *New York Times*, Feb. 8, 1982, D1.

30. "Emergency Oil Allocation," *CQ Almanac 1981*, 451–53.

31. "Reagan Energy Policy Seeking Return to Past," *Los Angeles Times*, Oct. 19, 1981, 1.

32. Boggs to Anderson, June 15, 1981, RRL, BOG, box OA 11471.

33. Boggs to Cabinet Council on Natural Resources and Environment, Dec. 4, 1981, RRL, DPC, BLD, box OA 17016.

34. Watt, memorandum for the president, July 16, 1981, RRL, BOG, box OA 11471.

35. Corcoran to John Block, March 9, 1982, RRL, BOG, box OA 11473.

36. "Broyhill Quiet Power of State GOP," *News and Observer*, June 5, 1983, in RRL, BOG, box OA 11473.

37. *NBC Nightly News*, March 20, 1982, Radio TV Reports for the Department of Energy, RRL, BOG, box OA 11473.

38. "Dogma Unleashed," *Los Angeles Times*, March 23, 1982, C4.

39. Joseph Wright, "The Proper Context for U.S. Energy Policy," *New York Times*, July 23, 1972, 22.

40. Danny Boggs, draft, "The U.S. Energy Situation," July 15, 1982, RRL, BOG, box OA 11474.

41. Boggs to secretariat members, Synthetic Fuels Corporation Options, July 15, 1982, RRL, BOG, box OA 11474.
42. Danny Boggs, "U.S. Energy Strategy," Nov. 15, 1982, RRL, BOG, box OA 11471.
43. "Economic Gains Tied to Ending Oil Price Curbs," *New York Times*, Sept. 8, 1981, 1.
44. Boggs to Anderson, June 15, 1981, RRL, BOG, box OA 11474.
45. "After Full Year of Oil Price Decontrol, Gasoline Costs Stable, Imports Down," *Houston Post*, RRL, BOG, box OA 11471.
46. "The Energy Non-crisis," *National Review*, Feb. 19, 1981, 156.
47. Douglas J. Feith, "The Oil Weapon De-mystified," *Policy Review* (Winter 1981): 39.
48. Feith to Allen, June 4, 1981, Subject: Wm. Safire's Column on OPEC, RRL, NSCF, box 81.
49. Dennis Ross, "Considering Soviet Threats to the Persian Gulf," *International Security* (Fall 1981): 168.
50. Albert Wohlstetter, "Half-Wars and Half-Policies in the Persian Gulf," in W. Scott Thompson, *National Security in the 1980s: From Weakness to Strength* (San Francisco: Institute for Contemporary Studies, 1980).
51. "Weinberger Hints U.S. Seeks Bases in Mideast," *Los Angeles Times*, March 9, 1981, B1.
52. "Haig: Confronting the Foreign Policy Vacuum," *Los Angeles Times*, Oct. 4, 1981, G1.
53. Craig Unger, *House of Bush, House of Saud: The Secret Relationship Between the World's Two Most Powerful Dynasties* (New York: Scribner, 2004), 60.
54. Yergin, *Prize*, 717–18.
55. Ibid., 722.
56. "Oil Industry Finds Footing Is Slippery as World Prices Plunge," *Chicago Tribune*, March 21, 1983, 4.
57. Boggs to Harper, April 12, 1982, RRL, BOG, box OA 11471.
58. Boggs to Harper, April 16, 1982, RRL, BOG, box OA 11471.
59. "Kissinger Blames U.S. for Gulf War," Associated Press, Sept. 29, 1980.
60. Department of State, "Iran-Iraq: Elements of U.S. Diplomatic Strategy and Plans," March 7, 1984, RRL, MAR, box RAC 4.
61. Department of Defense, Crisis Planning Notice: Persian Gulf Situation, Feb. 27, 1984, RRL, MAR, box RAC 4.
62. Reagan to Thatcher, March 16, 1984, RRL, MAR, box RAC 4.
63. Donald Hodel to Robert McFarlane, Feb. 8, 1984, RRL, MAR, box RAC 4.
64. Maugeri, *Age of Oil*, 139.
65. Walter Levy and Milton Lipton, "The Dark Side of Oil-Price Reductions," *New York Times*, Jan. 31, 1986, 31.
66. "6 Governors Ask for a Federal Tax on Imported Oil," *New York Times*, April 16, 1986, D24.
67. "Congress Splits over Remarks by Bush on Oil," *New York Times*, April 9, 1986, 1.
68. "U.S. Reiterates Oil Policy Based on Free Market," *New York Times*, April 3, 1986, 3.
69. "Shultz Says U.S. Is Helpful," *New York Times*, Feb. 10, 1986, D23.
70. Hobart Rowen, "Voodoo Oil Pricing," *Washington Post*, April 3, 1986, 21.

71. "U.S. Reiterates Oil Policy Based on Free Market."

72. "Goodbye to All That," *Wall Street Journal*, Aug. 25, 1986, 20.

73. L. J. Davis, "William Simon's Pacific Overtures," *New York Times Magazine*, Dec. 27, 1987, 15.

74. Greta R. Krippner, *Capitalizing on Crisis: The Political Origins of the Rise of Finance* (Cambridge, Mass.: Harvard University Press, 2011), 94–95.

75. Department of Energy, "Strategic Petroleum Reserve: Energy Security for America," Dec. 1988, GBL, CEA, SHM, OA/ID 03685.

76. Recent polling data, May 19, 1987, GBL, COS, FUL, OA/ID 14283.

77. David Broder, "Dukakis Goes for Votes, Not Groups," *Chicago Tribune*, July 15, 1988, 19.

78. "With Bentsen, the Democrats Look West, Not South," *New York Times*, July 19, 1988, 31.

79. "Bentsen Sees His Role as Wrestling the Depressed 'Oil Patch' from the GOP," *Los Angeles Times*, July 20, 1988, 4.

80. "In Lone Star State, 'Bubba' May Hold Key," *Chicago Tribune*, Sept. 14, 1988, 1.

81. Frank Zarb, "Ignoring the Energy Issue," *Washington Post*, Oct. 19, 1988, 23.

82. James J. MacKenzie, "Why We Need a National Energy Policy," World Resources Institute, Aug. 1990, GBL, COS, SUN, OA/ID CF00472.

83. "Calm Waters, Troubled Oil," *U.S. News & World Report*, July 9, 1990, 35.

84. Vito Stagliano, *A Policy of Discontent: The Making of a National Energy Strategy* (Tulsa, Okla.: PennWell, 2001), 189.

85. "Iraq President Hussein Sees New Mideast War Unless America Acts," *Wall Street Journal*, June 28, 1990, 1.

86. James Schlesinger, "Innocence Shattered," *Washington Post*, Aug. 5, 1990, D7.

87. "Iraqi Leader Shakes OPEC with Threats Against Overproducers," *Los Angeles Times*, July 20, 1990, 13.

88. Moore, NSC meeting, Aug. 3, 1990, cited in Stagliano, *Policy of Discontent*, 211–12.

89. Les Aspin, "Define Our Goals in the Gulf," *Washington Post*, Aug. 10, 1990, 15.

90. Schmalensee to Michael Boskin, memo, Oil Regulation in the 1970s, Aug. 6, 1990, GBL, CEA, BOS, OA/ID 08073.

91. "U.S. Says Oil Is Plentiful, Rejects Panic," *Los Angeles Times*, Aug. 7, 1990, 12.

92. "Office Seekers Revive 1970s Campaign Strategy of Bashing Oil Companies Over Spike in Prices," *Wall Street Journal*, Aug. 9, 1990, 12.

93. "Energy Lesson 1," *Wall Street Journal*, Aug. 8, 1990, 10.

94. "Two Oil Companies Cut, Freeze Prices," *Washington Post*, Aug. 9, 1990, E10.

95. "Office Seekers Revive 1970s Campaign Strategy of Bashing Oil Companies over Spike in Prices."

96. "U.S. Says Oil Is Plentiful, Rejects Panic."

97. "The Emergency's Here: Use the Oil," *New York Times*, Aug. 8, 1990, 20.

98. "Justice Department Plans to Investigate Sudden Increases in Prices of Gasoline," *Wall Street Journal*, Aug. 7, 1990, 8.

99. Reynolds to Boskin, memo, Thoughts on Oil, War, Inflation, and Bonds, Aug. 8, 1990, GBL, CEA, BOS, OA/ID 08073.

100. Moore to Ede Holiday, Aug. 17, 1990, GBL, CAB, KOR, OA/ID 03779.

101. "Energy Policy Trade-Off," *New York Times*, Aug. 18, 1990, 1.

102. Glenn Schleede, memo, Energy Markets—1973 to 1989, Sept. 4, 1990, GBL, COS, SUN, OA/ID CF00154.

103. George Bush, National Security Directive 45, Aug. 20, 1990.

104. Remarks by president on Gulf crisis to cabinet, Sept. 4, 1990, GBL, NSC, HAS, OA/ID CF01478.

105. Burns to Baker, Sept. 12, 1990, GBL, NSC, OA/ID CF01584.

106. Stagliano, *Policy of Discontent*, 251–52.

107. "Oil Prices Rise; Officials Discount Supply Threat," *Washington Post*, Aug. 8, 1990, 1.

108. R. Patrick Thompson to Bush, Sept. 27, 1990, GBL, SMZ, OA/ID CF01986.

109. Holiday to Card, Nov. 21, 1990, GBL, CAB, KOR, OA/ID 03779.

110. Holiday to Jack Houston and Richard Marshall, Dec. 3, 1990, GBL, CAB, KOR, OA/ID 03779.

111. "Oil and the Middle East Crisis," Public Affairs, Chevron, Jan. 1991, GBL, COS, SUN, OA/ID CF00472.

112. Stagliano, *Policy of Discontent*, 320.

113. Ibid., 292, 313.

114. George Bush, "Why We Are in the Gulf," *Newsweek*, Nov. 26, 1990, 28.

115. Wellstone to Bush, Nov. 28, 1990, GBL, COS, SUN, OA/ID CF00472.

116. Bush to Dole, n.d., GBL, COS, SUN, OA/ID CF00472.

117. "Capitol Hill Urges Patience in Gulf," *Christian Science Monitor*, Nov. 3, 1990, 1.

118. U.S. Congress, Senate, Committee on Armed Services, *Crisis in the Persian Gulf Region*, 101st Cong., 2nd sess., Nov. 27, 1990, 114.

119. Excerpts from Secretary Cheney's Statement to the Senate Armed Services Committee, Dec. 4, 1990, GBL, COS, SUN, OA/ID CF00472.

120. Prepared text of remarks by the vice president, Pinehurst, N.C., Dec. 10, 1990, GBL, PAW, GEA, OA/ID 03417.

121. Bush to Nixon, n.d., GBL, COS, SUN, OA/ID CF00472.

122. Excerpts from Chairman Powell's statement before the Senate Armed Services Committee, Dec. 4, 1990, GBL, COS, SUN, OA/ID CF00472.

123. PA/Opinion Analysis, Dec. 12, 1990, GBL, PAW, GEA, OA/ID 03418.

124. Thomas L. Friedman, "U.S. Jobs at Stake in Gulf, Baker Says," *New York Times*, Nov. 14, 1990, 14.

125. News from Senator Bob Dole, Jan. 4, 1991, GBL, COS, SUN, OA/ID CF00472.

126. Freedom Task Force, "Stop Saddam," Jan. 8, 1991, GBL, PAW, GEA, OA/ID 03417.

127. National Security Directive 54.

128. Statement by Helga Steeg, executive director, International Energy Agency, Jan. 17, 1991, GBL, NSC, MEL, OA/ID CF01434.

129. Gary Bennethum to Bob Grady, Jan. 14, 1991, GBL, NSC, MEL, OA/ID CF01434.

130. Wald, "Why America Still Hates the Words 'Energy Policy.'"

131. Mary McGrory, "Bush Avoids the Obvious," *Washington Post*, Dec. 4, 1990, 2.

132. "Americans Are Loath to Curb Energy Use Despite War Concerns," *Wall Street Journal*, Jan. 30, 1991, 1.

133. Fischer to Bush, Feb. 4, 1991, GBL, COS, SUN, OA/ID CF00470.

134. Peter A. A. Berle, president, National Audubon Society, Jan. 1991, GBL, COS, SUN, OA/ID CF00470.

135. Environmental leaders to Bush, Feb. 8, 1991, GBL, COS, SUN, OA/ID CF00470.
136. Office of the Press Secretary, "Fact Sheet: The National Energy Strategy," Feb. 20, 1991, GBL, COS, SUN, OA/ID CF00472.
137. William Appleman Williams, *The Tragedy of American Diplomacy* (New York: Norton, 1959), 38; Walter LaFeber, *The New Empire: An Interpretation of American Expansion, 1860–1898* (Ithaca, N.Y.: Cornell University Press, 1963), 400.
138. "Americans Are Loath to Curb Energy Use Despite War Concerns."
139. Wald, "Why America Still Hates the Words 'Energy Policy.'"
140. "Will War Yield Oil Security?," interview with James Schlesinger, *Challenge*, March–April 1991, 32.
141. Carter and Ford to Brock Adams, Sept. 30, 1991, GBL, COS, SUN, OA/ID CF00472.
142. "U.S. Finds War 'More Fun' than Saving Energy," *Milwaukee Sentinel*, Oct. 29, 1991, 9.

Conclusion: A New Project Independence?

1. Lay to Bush, Nov. 4, 1991, and Bush to Lay, Nov. 26, 1991, GBL, WHO, LAY.
2. Robert L. Bradley, *Capitalism at Work: Business, Government, and Energy* (Salem, Mass.: M & M Scrivener, 2009), 223.
3. Michael J. Graetz, *The End of Energy: The Unmaking of America's Environment, Security, and Independence* (Cambridge, Mass.: MIT Press, 2011), 57.
4. Jackson, "The Danger of Doing Nothing."
5. "Carter Energy Bill Fails to Clear," 710.
6. "Energy War."

Acknowledgments

In the process of writing this book, I came to understand something about my childhood: why my father got so many speeding tickets. He commuted on the LIE into New York City every day, and from my recollection he seemed to get pulled over quite a bit. What I realize now is that it wasn't his fault—or at least not entirely, or at least he could be forgiven for not adjusting to the new fifty-five-mile-per-hour speed limit imposed by Richard Nixon. The energy crisis and the need to cut back must have also explained my mother's trading in her station wagon for a green Hornet, a bug-like compact car that is an otherwise-hard-to-understand purchase, especially when considering it had to fit me and my three older sisters. Growing up in the 1970s on Long Island, I remember the gas lines. But if I grew up in an age of limits, my parents, Arthur and Eleanore Jacobs, never told me to slow down, and for that I am deeply grateful.

On the journey of writing this book, I have incurred many debts. First is to Nelson Lichtenstein, a stalwart friend and ally whom I can always count on. Nelson has read almost every word and version since the first talk I gave on the energy crisis in a seminar at Harvard. Along the way, many others have helped me, offering advice, critiques, and support. Thanks to Sven Beckert and the Harvard Political Economy Seminar, where I began this project, to the Radcliffe Institute, where I spent a fabulous year, and to generous funding from MIT, my professional home for many years. In Cambridge, Bruce Schulman, Dan and Helen Horowitz, David Engerman, Chris Capozzola, Brooke Blower, and Walter Friedman read early chapters. I am grateful, too, to Pauline Maier, a wonderful mentor during my time at MIT. More recently, I have had the benefit of a new scholarly community, and I thank Princeton University's Woodrow Wilson School and History Department. I extend a special thanks to Peter Conti-Brown and Jeremi Suri for going over the book closely in the final stages. Others have graciously given their time, wisdom, and the opportunity to present my work, including Bruce Schulman, Robert Brenner, Matt Lassiter, Steve Pincus, Tony Badger, Nolan McCarty, Chuck Cameron, Kevin Kruse, Robert Self, Dirk Hartog, and Ira Katznelson.

I am appreciative of the team at FSG who helped guide this book to completion. Alex Star inherited the book as a new editor and gave me invaluable insights and a careful read. Thanks, too, to Thomas LeBien, who saw the potential in the beginning, and to my agent Jill Kneerim for finding the project a good home. Jake Blumgart provided top-notch assistance as the book went into production.

To get me where I was going, I have relied on friends and family. Debbie, Lynne, and Katie, my three sisters, have been there since the station wagon days. Katie, you inspire me and serve as a role model in so many ways. My in-laws, Viviana and Jerry Zelizer, are as good as they come, supplying endless support and much warmth. Our Monday night family dinners are a weekly highlight. I am so very grateful to the Martha's Vineyard crew, Anna Aizer, Melinda Abrams, Liza Landsman, and their amazing families, all always there for me, especially when I have hit bumps in the road. Thanks to Jenny Eisenpresser, my oldest friend, and to Eric Alterman, my newest.

My trip through life would not be worth taking without my four children, riding along in the backseat and lots of times leading the way. Abigail, Sophia, Claire, and Nathan, you bring me daily joy. Every moment that goes by, I feel lucky for the way you enrich our lives.

No one has traveled with me, through all of life's twists and turns, more than my husband, Julian Zelizer, to whom I dedicate this book. He has accompanied me on every leg of this journey, giving encouragement, guidance, and above all love. He has shown me how to strive for a destination, keep my eyes focused on the road straight ahead, and yet enjoy life along the way. Thank you, my love, for putting a smile on my face, filling me with happiness, and joining me on this incredible ride.

Index

gasoline (*cont.*)
  price rollbacks and freezes, 84–85,
    92–93, 96, 98–101, 108, 112–15,
    148–52; rationing, 44, 49, 61, 62–85,
    89–101, 106, 116, 141, 253, 273, 297,
    300; shortages and lines, 5, 9, 44, 49,
    61, 62–85, 89–122, 199, 206–32, 236;
    station closings, 64, 80, 95, 111–12,
    216–19; taxes, 78, 173, 175, 176, 182,
    190, 224–25, 243–44; truckers' strikes,
    74–79, 84, 89–101, 131, 214–17;
    unleaded, 29
General Accounting Office (GAO), 200,
  208, 231–32
General Motors, 66, 99, 102, 109, 189
Georgia, 59, 66, 80, 165, 183, 192
Gergen, David, 47, 60
Germany, 29, 127, 248; Nazi, 52, 106,
  248; reunification, 294
Get Oil Out (GOO), 24
Gilder, George, 261
Gilligan, John, 74
Gingrich, Newt, 192, 261
global warming, 294, 305, 311–13
Golan Heights, 49, 50
gold, 33
Golden Gimmick, 19
Goldwater, Barry, 20, 103, 104, 108,
  114, 121, 141, 150, 188
Goodlett, Carlton, 67
Gorbachev, Mikhail, 294
Gorsuch, Anne, 275–76, 284
government, 6–10, 16; Bush agenda,
  71–92; Carter agenda, 161–95,
  196–232, 235–50; Eisenhower agenda,
  17–20, 39; Ford agenda, 123–57;
  interventionist policies, 7–10, 16–20,
  62, 71, 99, 102, 105–6, 155; Johnson
  agenda, 20–21; limits on, 35–36; New
  Deal policies, 6, 16, 17, 23, 31–33, 62,
  99, 105–8, 129, 145; Nixon agenda,
  6–10, 23–48, 49–85, 89–122; of 1960s,
  20–26; 1973–74 energy crisis and,
  49–85, 89–122, 123–34; 1975–76
  energy crisis and, 134–57; 1977–78
  energy crisis and, 161–95; 1979 energy
  crisis and, 196–232, 235–50; of 1980s,
  250–70, 271–307; Reagan agenda,
  271–92; twenty-first-century, 309–14
Gravel, Mike, 239
Great Britain, 29, 41, 98, 118, 127, 140, 286

Great Society, 20, 23, 32, 103, 130, 194,
  229, 260
Greece, 124
Green, Mark, 226
Greenspan, Alan, 128–34, 143, 147, 149,
  151, 155, 156, 261, 290, 330n16
Greider, William, 186
gross national product, 125
Gulf Oil, 4, 15, 20, 81, 82
Gulf War (1991), 10, 296–307, 310

Haig, Alexander, 47, 59, 68–69, 73, 97, 100
Halbouty, Michel, 152, 272–73
Haldeman, H. R., 43
Halleck, Charles, 21
Hamilton, Lee, 120
Hansen, Clifford, 148
hard-hat riots, 100
Harper, Edwin, 284
Harper's Magazine, 137
Harrison, Benjamin, 213
Hart, Gary, 185, 202, 238–41, 246, 287
Hartley, Fred, 24, 47
Hartmann, Robert, 150–51
Hatfield, Mark, 237
Hathaway, Stanley, 147
Hawkins, Augustus, 153
Hayek, Friedrich von, 129; *The Road to
  Serfdom*, 102–3
Hayes, Denis, 27, 214
Hays, Wayne, 110
health care, 253, 258
Heath, Edward, 98
Heinz, John III, 99–100
Heller, Walter, 67, 237
Heritage Foundation, 103, 104, 179, 200,
  263, 273, 281
Hertzberg, Hendrik, 209–10, 223
highways, 15; truckers' strikes, 74–79,
  84, 89–101, 131, 214–17
Hill, John, 139, 141
Hill, William, 75, 217
Hitler, Adolf, 106
Hodel, Donald, 275
Hoffa, Jimmy, 96
Holtzman, Elizabeth, 67
home heating oil, 36, 38, 54, 64, 71, 77,
  82, 157, 190; deregulation of, 157
Hooks, Benjamin, 219
Hoover, Herbert, 262
House Commerce Committee, 180, 205

A Note About the Author

Meg Jacobs teaches history and public affairs at Princeton University. Her first book, *Pocketbook Politics: Economic Citizenship in Twentieth-Century America* (2005), won the Organization of American Historians' Ellis W. Hawley Prize, as well as the New England Historical Association's James P. Hanlan Book Award. She is also the coauthor of *Conservatives in Power: The Reagan Years, 1981–1989* (2010).